THE
HITLER
LEGACY

THE
HITLER
LEGACY

The Nazi Cult in Diaspora

*How it was Organized, How it was
Funded, and Why it Remains a
Threat to Global Security in
the Age of Terrorism*

PETER LEVENDA

IBIS PRESS
Lake Worth, FL

Published in 2014 by Ibis Press
A division of Nicolas-Hays, Inc.
P. O. Box 540206
Lake Worth, FL 33454-0206
www.ibispress.net

Distributed to the trade by
Red Wheel/Weiser, LLC
65 Parker St. • Ste. 7
Newburyport, MA 01950
www.redwheelweiser.com

ISBN 978-0-89254-210-9

Library of Congress Cataloging-in-Publication Data

Levenda, Peter.
  The Hitler legacy : the Nazi cult in diaspora : how it was organized, how it was
funded, and why it remains a threat to global security in the age of terrorism / Peter
Levenda.
     pages cm
  Includes bibliographical references and index.
  ISBN 978-0-89254-210-9 (hardback)
  1. Terrorism--History--21st century. 2. Political violence--History--21st century.
3. National socialism and occultism. 4. War criminals--Germany--History--20th
century. 5. Nazis--Middle East--History. 6. Nazis--South America--History. 7.
Secret societies. 8. Occultism. I. Title.
  HV6431.L486 2014
  320.53'3--dc23   2014035585

Disclaimer

The opinions expressed and conclusions reached in this book are those of the
Author and do not necessarily represent those of the Publisher.

Please note that every attempt has been made to determine the proper
copyright holder of the images presented here. We apologize for any
inadvertent errors and request you contact us with corrections.

Book design and production by Studio 31
www.studio31.com

Printed in the United States of America [MV]

Contents

To Julian

Primus inter pares

Pro meliorum mundi

Any man who sees Europe now must realize that victory in a great war is not something you win once and for all, like victory in a ball game. Victory in a great war is something that must be won and kept won. It can be lost after you have won it—if you are careless or negligent or indifferent.

—President Harry Truman, Radio Address, August 9, 1945

It is not mere chance that millions in Germany are of the holy conviction that National Socialism is more than politics, that in it the word and the will of God proclaim itself, that the bulwark it has created against Bolshevism was conceived on higher inspiration as the last salvation of Occidental culture before the threat of Asiatic atheism.

—Joseph Goebbels, *From Kaiserhof to Reich Chancellery*, 1934.

INTRODUCTION

In the early morning hours of Saturday, October 11, 2008, the government-issued Volkswagen Phaeton V6 luxury sedan sped along the slick road outside of Klagenfurt, Austria. There was little traffic at that hour, and the driver was confident of the road having driven it for much of his life, and having been in an accident previously, was especially cautious. But, after all, the Phaeton was a top-of-the-line automobile with an excellent safety record and numerous fail-safe features such as anti-lock brakes, a traction control system, and an electronic differential lock that transfers power from one wheel to another when the first one is going faster than the second.

The posted speed limit was 42 miles per hour.

The driver was doing 88.

He had had a few drinks that evening and was feeling no pain. It was a time to celebrate, after all. His party had won another resounding victory and it meant that the *Bruderschaft* was even more firmly entrenched in the Austrian government. Their position on immigration was one major factor in their success. Of course, his deputy had made the mistake of using the word in public that everyone used in private—*Umvolkung*—a word from the past that was used to refer to ethnic cleansing, and was criticized for it immediately. But it was there, out in the open, and anyway it was ten years ago and didn't seem to harm his party's position.

There was a car in front of him, going painfully slow, so he swerved around it and continued on his way. The steering control of the Phaeton was excellent. One felt truly in command of the car, as it responded to every touch.

He had segregated the Austrians from the Slovenes, and removed public signs written in Slovene. What was the point of coddling Slavs who happened to live in Austria? If they wanted to be Austrians, let them speak German. Until they did, they were to be as isolated as possible from Austrian public life. It was another victory for his party, and another reason he won the last election easily.

For a moment he thought of Huber. Poor old "Ahmed" Huber, the Swiss patriot who died a few months before. Another of the old guard, a man who represented right-thinking, right-acting men of Aryan ancestry. His "conversion" to Islam didn't fool anyone, of course. Huber was much more "out there" than *he* could afford to be. No pictures of Hitler or the Ayatollah in *his* house! No point in exercising all the lumpen proletariat with their survivor guilt and liberal ideas of atonement. Huber was visible and vocal, and he got shut down. They closed his banks and his financial networks ... or thought they did, anyway.

He smiled.

It was pleasant to drive a little drunk, he thought to himself. The speed, the motion, the scene outside the windshield, the control of the five thousand pound vehicle on the polished black macadam in the early morning ...

His parents. His parents had been Nazis when it was illegal, back in the days before the Anschluss. And they paid for it after the war, his father reduced to manual labor, digging graves, and his mother reviled and forbidden to remain a teacher. Why was he thinking of his parents now? Would they have been proud of the way he validated their sacrifice by bringing the old ways back to Austria?

He thought briefly of Stefan, and tried to block the thought from his head. They had quarreled, as usual. That's why he was a little drunk right now. Had to drown his anger and his sadness somehow. His wife would never understand. What did women know or understand about men, really?

His mother, now, was a real woman. He was on his way to her birthday party this very day. She will be ninety years old, he thought with something like pride. A true nationalist, like her husband. A smart woman. Accomplished. Faithful to her convictions. She was born just as Germany was losing the First World War, and then had to watch the Third Reich defeated in the Second World War. But still she hung on.

Lights in front of him. Another car. Damned slow, too.

He swung the wheel too sharply to the left to pass, and something went wrong. All those safety features. Air bags. Anti-lock brakes.

Suddenly he was in the air, rolling over and over, and then it was finished.

The newspapers and electronic media reported that Jörg Haider, the Governor of the Province of Carinthia, in Austria, far-right demagogue and apologist for the Nazi regime, had hit a lamp pole going 88 miles per hour in a 42 mile per hour zone. His blood alcohol level was three times the legal limit, but there were those who were certain he had been assassinated. That someone knew of his penchant for speed, and tampered with his state-of-the-art braking system.

Soon thereafter news of Haider's financial relationships with Saddam Hussein and Muammar Gaddafi became public knowledge. Millions of dollars had passed through Haider's hands to a series of blind accounts in Lichtenstein. Handwritten notebooks were discovered. Files accessed. Suspects questioned. The darling of the New Right in Austria, the man some called the "Yuppie Fascist," had been dealing with Arab dictators and providing some kind of service for them which has yet to be identified.

That same year I returned to the United States after an extended stay in Southeast Asia where I was researching the material that became *Ratline*. While I greeted the news of Haider's death with mild interest, it was the revelation concerning his longtime relationship with Saddam and Gaddafi that attracted my attention. That was because the object of my research was an Austrian, too: an Austrian doctor who fled to Indonesia after the war, converted to Islam, and never set foot in Europe again. In Indonesia, they say the old doctor was none other than Adolf Hitler. While I understandably was far from convinced as to the accuracy of that claim, what the research proved to me was that there had been an extensive Nazi network in Southeast Asia before, during, and after the war. Further, that Nazi funds had made their way from Europe to Indonesia and might have been used to overthrow the government of left-leaning

Sukarno in favor of the more right-wing, anti-Communist leader General Soeharto, as the involvement of former Reichs Finance Minister Hjalmar Schacht would imply.

Since then I have seen documentation that proves beyond any doubt that networks existed after the war to assist Nazi war criminals in their escape and survival, and that these networks were far more pervasive than even the fantasies of Frederick Forsyth and Ira Levin would have us believe. More to the point, the evidence that there existed (and still exists) a strong relationship between underground Nazi organizations and underground "Islamist" organizations is strong, incontrovertible, and deeply troubling.

In addition, documentation has become available—some of it recently declassified—to show that these networks were relegated not only to Latin American dictatorships and "banana republics" but to nations in the Middle East, Asia, and North America. The number of Nazis who "converted" to Islam after the war is astounding. The number of Americans who participated in the Nazi underground is even more astounding.

When we discuss the rise of what the press calls "jihadism" or "Islamist fundamentalism" or "Islamist terror cells," we have to put these terms and what they represent into context.

This is the Hitler Legacy. From terror bombings in Europe in the 1960s and 1970s, to assassinations of political leaders around the world, to drug-running and arms smuggling, to Operation Condor, and all the way to the events of September 11, 2001 what we have to confront is the possibility that our governments and our intelligence agencies have become Sorcerer's Apprentices. Like the Disney movie, our Mickey Mouse savants and spies have clumsily summoned forces beyond their control. What began as an effort to contain the Soviet Union and the Peoples Republic of China has become the template for a campaign of global terrorism directed at *us*.

This is that story.

A Personal Note

Historians often write about events that transpired long before they were born, or at least events that had taken place without their involvement. The New Journalism school has not had much of an impact on academic historians who prefer the purely objective recitation of facts and the sober, impersonal analysis of same. Subjectivity is the domain of the blogger, the journalist, the novelist. Ernest Hemingway and Norman Mailer could be in the middle of important political events and write about them eloquently but it's not "history". You can have a Michael Taussig in anthropology, with a chatty and sometimes confessional style, and he is still an anthropologist because this is, after all, a post-modern (or a post-post-modern) era, except when it comes to the writing of history. There can be no subjectivity in history for history, after all, is the recitation and analysis of facts. As the saying goes, "you're entitled to your own opinion, but not your own facts."

There are those of us, however, who realize that history books are as fictional as novels. That is why Mailer and Truman Capote were comfortable with the "non-fiction novel" as a genre. One may pose as an objective observer and recorder of historical fact, but the selection process itself—which facts to include, which to exclude—reveals the potential for all sorts of novelistic foreplay. Add to that the truism that the victors write the history books, and one realizes that much of what we think we know is wrong or at best woefully incomplete and biased: like a criminal case in which everyone knows the defendant is guilty but the jury returns a different verdict, either based on a technicality or due to solidarity with the accused. The fact of the case is the "not guilty" verdict, regardless of who actually pulled the trigger.

So it is with history.

I have had the fortune to become involved in some seminal historical events, either through accident or because I was bold enough or stupid enough to become involved. My connections were largely indirect, but they were there. For instance, my youthful obsession with Arabia.

I had been interested in the Middle East since I was in primary school. The impetus was an event that I will never forget: going with my sixth grade class to see *Lawrence of Arabia* when it was released. It was considered an educational film, and there was a great deal of promotional material available at the school, including maps, posters and the like. I paid attention to none of it at the time, but sitting in the huge theater (in those days movie theaters were large, single-screen affairs with excellent sound systems) and having that film wash over me in all its exotica and with that rousing score by Maurice Jarre caused an emotional and psychological resetting of my entire being.

Here was an outsider, an Englishman, leading Arab tribes in battle against a mechanized enemy, blowing stuff up. He wore Arab robes, and understood Arab language and culture. As I found out later, he was also quite short. I was diminutive as well, especially during primary school when I was the shortest kid in the class every year. (I grew twelve inches the year I reached puberty.) I was also an outsider. I had tested in the genius range that year, and was largely understood to be teacher's pet – or I should say "teachers's pet" since teachers from other classrooms came to gawk at me when the test results were released. Nonetheless I had poor social skills, and was daily the target of bullies.

But here was an actual person, an historical figure, who had the same shortcomings (no pun intended) as I did and who found a way to overcome them by simply … going somewhere else. He used his intellect, his creativity, and his determination where others might have been gifted as more physically imposing and socially-comfortable. He had a problem with authority, and so of course did I, beginning with the nuns in Catholic school and extending to virtually anyone who tried to tell me how to behave or what to do, or who criticized my stutter or my poor posture or my silence in social gatherings. I found I did not really occupy my physical space; I did not own it. I was not really in my body, at least not until I had emergency surgery for a collapsed lung when I was in my early twenties and for the first time in my life felt like a human being with physical substance. Corporeality.

As I grew older, I realized that my salvation lay outside the country. I had to travel, to see the world, to find the place where I could fit in and be accepted as who I am and not have to adapt to the expectations of others. I studied foreign languages and realized I had a knack for them. I copied foreign words and phrases I came across in my reading—and I read a great deal—and memorized them. I was a failure at Latin with all of its rules and tables, but somehow found French easy. And later, Spanish. And eventually Mandarin after a brief foray into Church Slavonic. I couldn't find anyone to teach me Arabic in those days (pre-Internet, pre-personal computer, pre-Rosetta Stone) so I did the best I could with what I could find, and prepared myself for a possible future.

Now here I was, forty years later, walking through the Javanese rainforest in search of Nazis and temples. I already had decades of foreign travel under my belt. Had risked my life in South America. Had been a business executive in Europe and China. Had lived in Malaysia, awakening each morning to the cry of the muezzin from a dozen mosques. In China, I had worked with the People's Liberation Army. A military limousine with a uniformed driver would pick me up each day from the Beijing Hotel and drive me down the rainswept streets to another meeting, another discussion. In Malaysia, I drove myself (on the other side of the road, Malaysia being a former British colony) and visited government agencies, high-tech centers, computer network device distributors. It was always different, and I was exposed to such a variety of cultures one would think it was enough for any one life. But my worldly trajectory was somewhat different.

In 1968, I met with Dr. Izzat Tannous who at that time was running the office of the Palestine Liberation Organization (PLO) in New York City, close to the United Nations. I had been startled by the Six Day War between Israel and Egypt that had taken place in 1967 and was still in the throes of reading all I could about T.E. Lawrence and the Arab Revolt. I began researching the Six Day War, writing letters to foreign governments, to the chambers of commerce of Middle Eastern countries including even the Trucial States (I had read and been captivated by *The Doomed Oasis* by Hammond Innes) and always asking for more information. When other teenagers were cramming for tests or looking for ways to get lucky with girls, my interests were clearly elsewhere. I received a reply from the PLO and an invitation to come down and see them at their office.

The headquarters of the PLO Mission to the UN (they had observer status since Palestine was not officially a country) was in a non-descript office building on Second Avenue in midtown. The door was reinforced steel (alone of all the other doors in the same corridor) and locked. I had to knock quite loudly, which was a bit disconcerting, and a woman's heavily-accented voice called out from behind the door asking who I was, which was worse since I had to identify myself in an equally-loud voice believing there were FBI agents hiding behind the opposite door recording every word. I said I had a meeting with Dr Tannous, and the German-speaking assistant finally let me in.

Dr. Tannous was a dapper man, thin and elegant. He had authored a book on the occupation of Palestine by the Israelis, based on British reports of the time (the 1940s) during which Menachem Begin was said to have described the British army as Nazis. His son also happened to be there, and we had a lively discussion on the situation in the Middle East and especially that of Palestine and Jordan. The purpose of the PLO in the United States, he said, was not to recruit fighters against Israel but to educate Americans as to the reality of the situation in Palestine so that they would withdraw their unconditional support of Israel. The PLO had printed pamphlets condemning the alleged use of napalm by Israel against Palestinians, among other issues, and they were almost timidly trying to convince Americans that their cause was just. I never saw Dr. Tannous after that meeting.

A little while later, he was replaced by Sadat Hassan, an altogether different administrator. Where Dr. Tannous was slender and charming, Hassan was solidly-built and aggressive. I met him perhaps two or three times in the late 1960s-early 1970s and maintained a basic sort of correspondence, including receiving in the mail one day a letter signed by Yassir Arafat himself. My last meeting with Sadat Hassan was instructive, or at least it now seems instructive from the remove of decades: he had arranged for me to join the Syrian Orthodox Church as a clergyman if I so desired, my having left the rather more poisonous embrace of another Eastern Orthodox church which served as a front for American intelligence, about which more later. It was his ability to coordinate a network that was composed of Muslims and Christians (both of which were pro-Palestinian and anti-Israel) that interested me and made me realize that the political issue was a bit more complex than I had thought, or that had been discussed in the popular media.

Of course, meeting with the PLO in New York did cause me some problems. One day coming out of my parents' home in the Bronx my photograph was taken with a wide-angle lens from a car parked across the street. This same incident would be replayed years later, during the first Gulf War when I was photographed once again; but by that time it was anyone's guess what had triggered that particular episode for by then I had met Nazis, Klansmen, Satanists of various disciplines, strange churchmen, Black Panthers, the Weather Underground, met Irish radical Bernadine Devlin, as well as an ex-CIA officer, and had traveled to South America to stumble into an interrogation center in the Andes.

I got my first full-time job in the garment district of New York City in 1970, and held a variety of other jobs until I finally joined the Bendix Corporation in 1973, at their International Marketing Operations on Broadway. While there, I was exposed to the military-industrial complex in a very real way as our operation was staffed by personnel from all over the world, representing every kind of political ideology and ethnicity, united in the desire to make millions in the defense business. We supplied guidance systems to Asian customers, sophisticated radar equipment (to Pakistan, as an example), and almost everything we made to the Shah's Iran. I worked with Muslims from Guyana, Germans with questionable pedigrees, a Dutch submarine commander, and a sales rep from Venezuela who showed up at our offices wearing sidearms and cowboy boots.

It was during Watergate, and it was reported in the New York

Times that Bendix was used as a cover for intelligence and military training operations around the world. I witnessed reams of computer printouts being shredded at our offices at that time, as some of the financial arrangements we made with our far-flung network of sales representatives and agents would have revealed some darker truths. The Yom Kippur War broke out in 1973, the first year I began working for Bendix, and tensions were strained between some of our personnel. A month earlier, the administration of Salvador Allende in Chile was overthrown in a military coup supported by the Nixon administration. It was also the year of an Israeli invasion of Beirut, at which time our sales office there was in the middle of the free fire zone, our only link a sputtering telex machine. We were engaged in monitoring all of this activity worldwide and in some cases actively supporting one side or another with emergency shipments of spare parts, avionics equipment, and the like. In 1976, the head of Bendix—W. Michael Blumenthal—became the Secretary of the Treasury under President Jimmy Carter. Blumenthal was a German Jew who had been raised in Shanghai during the war and who spoke fluent Mandarin and Shanghainese.

It was that kind of time.

Then, in 1980, I began working for an Israeli bank. Headquartered at Rockefeller Center, it had been the site of the original Tonight Show studio. I worked there for four years, before my entry into China trade in 1984.[1]

I am telling you all this because as I report on the events that follow it is important to understand that I have a context for this information, and to know what that context is. Naturally, most of what I relate is carefully sourced and footnoted where possible; but it was due only to my own proximity to the individuals and the groups in question that I was able to piece together the various, seemingly disparate, elements that make up the larger narrative.

Maybe what I am writing will annoy more mainstream historians. Maybe this is something different, a kind of anthropology of

---

1 Some of which was described in my *The Mao of Business*, New York, 2007.

political and religious extremism. No matter what, the facts remain as facts. This is not conspiracy theory, commonly understood. I don't have a *theory* about any of this; it doesn't really need one. The facts as they stand are damning enough.

We have to stop being drunks. We have to stop looking for our keys under the streetlamp because the light is better there. We have to look where we lost our keys in the first place: in the darkness and the shadows. It's harder, sure, but we have a much greater chance of success even though what we blindly touch and feel in the stygian night might make us squirm in revulsion. Regardless, our keys are there.

Part One

Origins of 21st Century Conflict

CHAPTER ONE

AMERICAN REICH

Between 1933 and 1941, at least 120 anti-semitic groups were
founded in the United States, and that figure excludes most of
the ethnic fascist movements.
    —Philip Jenkins, *Hoods and Shirts*, 1997

The story of Jörg Haider is not an isolated one. Austria has been
struggling with Nazi and pro-Nazi groups since long before
Anschluss made the land of Mozart and *kaffe klatsches* a part of the
Third Reich. Hitler, after all, had been born and raised in Austria.
Many of the Reich's most notorious and violent Nazis were Austrians, such as Ernst Kaltenbrunner. Haider's parents had been Nazis
in Austria when it was still an illegal political party, risking their
liberty and reputations in support of Hitler's ideology. Revelations
in the 1980s concerning Kurt Waldheim's Nazi past made headlines all over the world, calling into question his role both as the
head of the Austrian government as well as his tenure at the United
Nations.

And it was in Austria—in the salt mines and underground cav-
erns in and around Salzburg—that the Nazis had planned to make
their last stand. And it was from this same region—and specifically the offices of the Counter Intelligence Corps (CIC) of the US
Army—that men like Klaus Barbie, the "Butcher of Lyons," were
hired to work for American intelligence—before they were aided
in their escape to Latin America. Kaltenbrunner, Skorzeny, Hanna
Reitsch: these and many other celebrities of the Reich were either
captured in Austria, or worked for a time for the CIC in Austria, or
both. Travel through the Tyrol to the Italian border was relatively
easy and many refugees made it to the Italian town of Bolzano
(Bolzen), where they awaited papers and funds to make it the rest
of the way to Rome or to Genoa, and from there to the ships that
would take them to safety.

One of the most famous Nazis to have survived the war relatively intact was General Otto Remer, the man in charge of the clean-up campaign after the failure of Operation Valkyrie: the plot to assassinate Hitler. Remer rounded up the conspirators and had them shot, and for that earned a special place in Hitler's estimation as a man who could be trusted when all others were suspect. Remer went on to become involved in post-war Austrian politics for various extreme right-wing parties and was suspected of being involved in a plot to resurrect the Nazi apparatus during the Naumann Affair. He became a sought-after speaker at various ODESSA-like events in Europe, and was even an invited guest at a conference held by Wilis Carto's Liberty Lobby in the United States. (an event at which former Nixon speechwriter Pat Buchanan was in attendance).

Otto Remer is one of the links in the chain that connects the Nazis of the Second World War to the right-wing underground in Europe, the United States, the Middle East, and Latin America after the war. He, along with Otto Skorzeny and Hans-Ulrich Rudel, was one of the most visible and unapologetic members of the Reich in the post-war period. His role—and that of his colleagues—is one of the reasons I resist calling this movement "neo-Nazi." So many actual Nazis who held rank and privilege during the war were involved in helping the Party apparatus survive after the war; there is nothing "neo" about "neo-Nazism."

The ODESSA File

The term ODESSA was popularized by the novelist Frederick Forsyth in his bestseller *The ODESSA File* and by the movie inspired by the book, starring a young Jon Voight as a German journalist on the trail of the post-war Nazi underground. Aside from an opening sequence that takes place in the Middle East as Israel becomes aware that former Nazi scientists are in Egypt working on missile technology, the action takes place completely in Germany and Austria.

ODESSA thus entered the mainstream consciousness as a catch-all term for any one of several groups of former SS officers and other assorted Nazi war criminals engaged in a kind of secret society of murder and world domination. In fact, as Argentine journalist and investigator Uki Goñi has shown,[2] ODESSA did, in fact, exist and was one of the names given to the extensive escape routes taken by the war criminals out of Germany, through Austria and Italy, to South America: escape routes that were also known as the *ratlines*.

What many investigators have missed, however, is the true extent of this network in the United States. While we have all heard of former concentration camp guards being arrested in America and deported to stand trial abroad, we have not learned of the underground support systems that existed in the United States before the war, and how many individuals offered covert support to war criminals after the war. Some of this has been revealed in declassified files of American intelligence agencies, who were complicit in the escape of at least one well-known war criminal—and that of course was Klaus Barbie, the infamous "Butcher of Lyon," who was eventually discovered in Bolivia and extradited to France to stand trial in the 1980s. We have also heard of Operation Paperclip: the US government's program of bringing Nazi rocket scientists to America to jump-start the space program (a *military* program, it should be remembered, at that time and still under the aegis of the Department of the Army).

But there were other, lesser known, individuals in America who were part of a quiet ODESSA of their own, men and women who believed in the Nazi ideal and who idolized its heroes. Some of these were revealed when an address book belonging to one of the leaders of the real ODESSA was recently declassified (possibly in error, since some of the names in that book are of individuals still alive as this is being written). What is important to understand is that this was not a new, perverse sort of hero-worship that only began when Germany was defeated. Rather it had roots in America long before the war began.

It is easier to understand the post-war Nazi underground if we realize the extent to which there was a *pre-war* Nazi underground:

---

2 Uki Goñi, *The Real ODESSA.*

not only in Europe (principally Germany and Austria) but also in North America, South America, the Middle East and Asia. Many individuals, groups, corporations and politicians were sympathetic not only to Germany's situation in the aftermath of World War One and the punitive Treaty of Versailles, but also to Germany's intellectual contribution to discussions (and policy positions) on race, eugenics, and Social Darwinism. The Russian Revolution took place a year before the end of World War One, and the perceived threat of a global Communist movement mobilized right-wing elements across the globe even as it inspired many others.

Secret Politics, Secret Religion

Germany at the end of World War One was in shambles. The Treaty of Versailles had restricted the size of its military to a token force, while placing all the guilt for the war squarely on Germany and demanding huge reparations in return. Valuable territory was lost, and to add to its burden, there was a growing Communist presence in the country that threatened to turn it into the next Soviet Union.

When World War One began, Russia was ruled by the Czar. By 1917, however, the Bolshevik Revolution had begun and the Czar and his entire family were arrested and eventually executed. A new political and economic regime was installed under Vladimir Lenin, and the Russians stopped fighting on the side of Great Britain and France (the three countries had formed what was called the Triple Entente). Instead, Russia signed a peace treaty with Germany. The Allies had thus lost Russia as an ally against the Kaiser.

At the same time, returning German soldiers were bringing the Communist message back to their homeland. Various German *lander* were in danger of having Socialist or Communist governments. The German Navy raised the red flag of Communism over its ships in the port city of Kiel; Berlin had a Socialist leader; and in Munich the Bavarian Soviet Republic was proclaimed. The German Revolution had begun.

As an example, a battle took place in the streets of Munich in May of 1919 between the swastika-helmeted Freikorps brigades (a kind of militia or paramilitary force made up of former German soldiers) and the Reds. The Freikorps eventually won and saved Munich for the anti-Communist—or "White"—forces. A provisional Communist government had tried to take power in Bavaria, but suffered from factionalism within its ranks. The right-wing Freikorps took advantage of this weakness and reclaimed the territory after the Reds had made the fatal error of arresting—and then executing—seven members of a bizarre secret society that nevertheless numbered important German nobility among its ranks.

This Order was the *Thule Gesellschaft*, or Thule Society. Nominally under the charge of one Baron von Sebottendorf—a mystic and astrologer who had spent time in Egypt and who fought for the Ottoman Empire in its Balkan War—it combined Nordic runes, Theosophy, occultism, yoga, and other esoteric disciplines with a heavy dose of racial ideology imbibed from the font of such race-mystics as Guido von List and Lanz von Liebenfels. It met at the Four Seasons Hotel in Munich, the same locus for meetings of the German Workers Party, the organization that would become the National Socialist German Workers Party: the NSDAP or Nazi Party. The memberships of these two organizations—the Thule Society with its milky gaze fixed on the legendary origin of the Nordic race, Thule (a kind of Teutonic Atlantis), and the Nazi Party (a collection of thugs, unemployed laborers, and bitter ex-soldiers)—often overlapped. The young Adolf Hitler, a corporal in the defeated German army, was sent to infiltrate the suspiciously-nomenclatured German Workers Party and report back on what he found. Instead, he took it over and made it the vehicle for his own mission: trendy socialist-sounding sentiments masking an anti-internationalist, racist, and hegemonic platform to restore Germany's greatness and wreak vengeance on those whom he felt betrayed the nation: the Jews, the Communists, and the liberal elite.

At the same time, the Middle East was reeling from various European decisions that had been made, either without consulting its leaders or through ignoring promises that were made and then summarily broken. The Balfour Declaration of 1917—which made Palestine a Jewish homeland—was one of these, entered into without a thought to discussing it with the Arab leaders who had thrown in their lot with the Allies against the Ottoman Turks (thereby defying the Caliph's *fatwa* that called all Muslims to jihad against the Triple Entente). There was also the Sykes-Picot Agreement (which essentially carved up the former Ottoman Empire in the Middle East between France and Great Britain, redrawing the map of the region completely—again without consulting the indigenous populations). Declassified correspondence reveals the extent of the British and French double-cross where the Arab Revolt was concerned. It is a trail of deception worthy of comparison to the hundreds of peace treaties signed by the US government with the Native American populations—only to be matched perhaps by the notorious Hitler-Stalin Pact, or the sadly optimistic Munich Pact signed by Neville Chamberlain and Adolf Hitler.

Revolts against British and French rule in the Middle East in the decades after the end of the First World War were numerous and were put down with brutal efficiency. This was the cauldron in which the witches' brew of Arab nationalism, Islamism, and anti-Western activism were mixed and fermented, becoming the intoxicating (in both senses of the word) beverage that we loosely call "terrorism" or more insistently "Islamist terrorism." The French became a colonial power in Syria and Lebanon due to the Sykes Picot Agreement and, in 1920, ousted King Faisal from Damascus by force. The French general who led the campaign to retake the city at the Battle of Maysalun is reported to have insulted the tomb of the great twelfth century Muslim commander Saladin, bragging that he had raised the Cross over the Crescent. This cavalier appropriation of historical and religious icons is a hallmark of Western-Eastern and especially Christian-Muslim relations of the 20th century and its aftermath affects the world we live in today.

Thus, the experience of Germans in the 1920s ran oddly parallel to that of the average Arab citizen in the Middle East at the same time. Rightly or wrongly, both felt victimized and betrayed by the Allied powers, especially Great Britain and France and to some extent Russia. Both began to see the Jews as symbolic of the sinister forces at work in the world: Germany, because it believed that Communism was a Jewish invention to enslave the world, and the Middle East, because suddenly there would be a Jewish home-land—administered by England—in the middle of its territory, thus proving there was, indeed, a conspiracy of Jews and European Christians against Islam.

In both cases religion and race were made to be seen at the heart of the problem, rather than the more intellectually demanding and complex forces of politics and economics.

This was as true in America as it was in Europe. While groups such as the National Socialist German Workers Party were being formed—largely underground in Germany and later in Austria—in response to the very real threat of a Communist takeover in Germany, organizations sympathetic to the plight of the Germans began forming in the United States.

This phenomenon took on tremendous energy with the 1929 stock market crash. The resulting anxiety and financial ruin only contributed to the paranoia of those who suspected a worldwide conspiracy of bankers and industrialists to impoverish and enslave the masses while enriching themselves. This paranoia took two forms, a leftist interpretation and a rightist one.

The leftist view said that the global conspiracy was one of the bosses against the workers, and the bosses were fat-cat capitalists. The leftist viewpoint was devoid of racist rhetoric for it had been influenced by Marxist thought which described the inevitable development of socialism and communism from the ashes of capitalism in the aftermath of the industrial revolution. Marx's famous dictum—Workers of the World, Unite!—was meant to be an international call to all working people to throw off the yoke of capitalism. This was the sentiment that eventually won the day in Russia and resulted in the overthrow of the Czarist superstructure and the elevation of the worker and the peasant to positions of control over the means of production (at least theoretically).

The rightist view agreed in part that the global conspiracy was one of the bosses against the workers, but added a racial and spiritual component to the conflict. While the left blamed Capitalism and touted Communism as the solution, the racist right blamed Communism and furthermore identified Communism with the Jews.

The early Nazi Party was a battleground between these two points of view. There was a "left wing" of the Nazi Party—represented most notably by Otto Strasser (1897–1974)—that believed in an international workers party that would support the right of workers to strike, an idea that was not welcome to the industrialists who were backing Hitler.[3] Strasser also called for closer ties with the Soviet Union and an end to the anti-Semitic policies of the Nazi Party. He and his group were eventually expelled from the Nazi Party and Strasser himself was forced into exile. He remained a committed Nazi to the end of his days. Although Strasser had participated in the early post-World War One *Freikorps* movement that opposed Communism, his form of Nazism became completely out of synch with the right wing of the Party, represented by Hitler, which became the dominant force. There were those Nazis after the war who entertained Strasser-ist ideas by urging alliances with the Soviets; however, this was less the result of ideological conversion to Strasser's point of view than it was a pragmatic decision to pit the Soviets and the Americans against each other in an effort to weaken both.

As the struggle between the warring viewpoints of Hitler and Strasser was taking place in Germany, in America a number of pro-Nazi parties and groups found their voice among the disaffected and disenfranchised whites who feared that their way of life was being threatened by Jews, African-Americans, and Communists—who, they believed, had engineered not only the Russian Revolution but also the election of Franklin D. Roosevelt. Thus it was that the Hitler racist right position on National Socialism became the dominant one in America, leaving little room for a leftist, Strasser interpretation.

Many anti-Roosevelt broadsides of the time—from the 1930s to the early 1940s—are vitriolic attacks on the Democratic President for being a Communist, a Jew, a dictator, and every combination of these. The White House was seen as a hotbed of Commu-

---

3 As we will see in a later chapter, both American industrialists such as Henry Ford, and German industrialists were strong supporters of Hitler and the Nazi Party, in part due to their rejection of Communism and the denial of workers' rights.

nist agents bent on destroying America from within. This radical point of view found fertile ground among working-class men and women in the cities where rumors spread that Jewish firms were firing Gentile workers in order to hire recent Jewish immigrants. These and other variations of the "blood libel"—in this case sacrificing the income of Gentiles rather than their infant children—were common currency at the time among the newly-formed extreme right-wing parties.

While the German-American Bund is probably the most famous of these parties, there were other "patriotic" American societies that claimed similar pedigrees, as we shall see; and these favored a spiritual component in addition to the rather more mechanistic one of the German intellectual establishment.

Spiritual Darwinism

There have been many opinions advanced in popular and academic circles as to how a country as cultured and sophisticated as Germany could have provided fertile ground for something as heinous and savage as the Third Reich and the Holocaust. It is probably easier to understand what happened if we realize that Germany was, indeed, at the forefront of science and philosophy in the early twentieth century—a time when the work of Charles Darwin was having its greatest effect on both religious and scientific thinking. Darwin's Theory of Evolution shook the Church to its core, in much the same way as Galileo had done hundreds of years previously when he averred that the earth revolved around the Sun (and was imprisoned by the Church for his audacity in insisting on the facts). The Theory of Evolution was another blow to Christianity for it challenged the Biblical story of how humans were created, and instead demonstrated that human beings were only the latest in a chain of creatures that had evolved from single cell organic structures, through an amphibious, lizard-like stage, and finally—via the apes—to present-day homo sapiens. While this idea was originally rejected by the Church (and remains controversial within Evangelical and Christian Fundamentalist circles today that insist the universe is less than seven thousand years old), it was embraced by

Western esotericists and occultists. Darwin's theory mirrored long-held beliefs concerning spiritual evolution, as evidenced in everything from the ascent literature of Jewish mysticism to the initiatory rituals of Freemasonry, all of which presumed that human beings were in an imperfect state and were progressing along a path to ultimate perfection. This was perhaps no better represented than in the writings of Madame Helena Blavatsky, the nineteenth century author, occultist, and political adventurer, who gave Social Darwinism a mystical interpretation that we may call Spiritual Darwinism.

It was Blavatsky (1831–1891) who popularized the idea of an advanced "Aryan" race and who promoted the swastika as an esoteric symbol representing the highest spiritual state. While the swastika is an Asian symbol with associations of auspiciousness, Blavatsky managed to Europeanize the sign so that it accrued other meanings and implications. It became, indeed, the official symbol of the Aryan Theosophical Society—a Theosophical sect that broke off from the original Theosophical Society founded by Blavatsky—and was led by William Q. Judge and later by Katherine Tingley from a base in California. The Aryan race—according to Blavatsky—was the fifth in a series of seven "root races." While Blavatsky did not consider these "races" to be ethnicities in the traditional sense, the terminology of "Aryan race" became identified with German ideas about eugenics and anti-Semitism. (That Blavatsky was herself anti-Semitic can be discerned from a careful reading of her published works.) Thus, while it can be argued that Blavatsky did not consider the Nordic "race" to be superior to all others and exclusively identifiable with the fifth root race of her system, it is nonetheless obvious that the concept of an Aryan "race" was adopted by German racial theorists (via Blavatsky admirers such as proto-Nazis Guido von List and Lanz von Liebenfels) and eventually became synonymous with Nazism.

At the same time, there was an understanding by German scientists that if Darwin's theory was true—accepted as a scientific fact—then it stood to reason that, once conscious of the process of evolution, human beings could involve themselves in it: i.e., they could take direct action to accelerate evolution and take measures intended to facilitate the "survival of the fittest"—weeding out those human specimens that would have been eliminated anyway over the course of thousands, if not millions, of years. It was Darwinism taken to its logical conclusion: if human beings are the latest result of the process of evolution, and if we have evolved certain traits and characteristics that enabled us to survive all those millions of years, then those among us with less desirable characteristics should be eliminated in order to allow the fittest to thrive. What Darwin saw as a natural process of selection became, for the German eugenecists and for those who were on the same page, a system that could be deliberately and consciously controlled and manipulated. In fact, one could say that—once Darwinian theories became understood—it was incumbent upon scientists and political leaders to take immediate steps to encourage a rationally-administered evolutionary process.

In a sense, the Nazis saw themselves as servants of Nature in much the same way European alchemists saw themselves as facilitating what they believed was the natural evolution of base metals into the spiritual perfection of gold. Inasmuch as the alchemist saw the chemical process of transmutation as mirroring an interior process of spiritual illumination, so the Nazis understood the Darwinian "process" as reflective of a path of spiritual initiation that was accessible only to those of pure blood: a genetic aspect that is impossible to fake, resistant to any form of "conversion" or artifice. Purification of physical substances is an essential component of European alchemical literature, as it is of religious and spiritual texts in many cultures (such as that of the Qumran sect made famous by the discovery of the Dead Sea Scrolls). Purification in the Nazi sense meant "unmixed" with other elements, as it was essential to protect the genetic heritage of the *Völk*: a nearly untranslatable term that has come to mean "the people," not in a nationalistic sense (i.e., "Americans" would not be considered a *Völk* because of the multiethnic and multi-racial component of the American population) but in the sense of a homogenous gene pool with common origins, beliefs, culture, and aspirations that are reflective of that homogeneity. The German *Völk* had a parallel in Japanese political and military thought according to at least one observer, a Gestapo chief in Tokyo during the war, who became one of the West's most influential Zen philosophers of the post-war period.[4] The well-known ethnophobia of the Japanese of that era—illustrated by their hatred of the Chinese and their enslavement of the Koreans—indicated to the Nazis that they had similar if not identical beliefs about race, and that they identified themselves in terms of racial (and cultural) purity, albeit not the same race or culture as the Aryan but one that was just as worthy of admiration if not emulation.

I submit that it was this level of perceived responsibility that caused the collective nervous breakdown of an entire society that we know under the rubric of the Holocaust. While there were many other reasons for the growth of Nazism in post-World War One Germany (economic, political, military and cultural), the racial theories that led to the Nuremberg Laws, and eventually to the death camps, were the result of German thinkers, scientists, and academics who saw that it was their duty to humanity to protect the gene pool and to accelerate the evolutionary process, a process that was at once spiritual as it was biological. This is evident in the Nazi pronouncements of the New Man: the next step in evolution, courtesy of the Nazi Party and the SS. If only the fittest survive then one had to demonstrate that one was, indeed, the fittest through a process of selection where cruelty and the willingness to participate in savagery were considered emblematic of the necessary new warrior caste. War, eugenics, and genocide demonstrated the iron will of the New Man to do whatever was needed to ensure the survival and eventual triumph of the *Völk*. It was this assumption, that the Aryan "race" was the highest-existing form of human evolution, and the identification of that "race" with pure German or Nordic blood, that allowed the Nazi race scientists to create the labyrinth of laws that would dispossess entire ethnicities and subject them to the worst forms of slavery and extermination. Needless to say, this was not what Darwin had in mind.[5]

---

4 We will get into more detail on this enigmatic figure—Graf Karl von Dürckheim—in a later chapter.

5 My reading of Darwin's Theory indicates that it was based on the understanding of a natural process taking place over millions of years and not amenable to human intervention or tinkering. However, humans are presumably the only creatures who are aware of this process, so perhaps it is inevitable—even

While these theories were being discussed and debated in Germany during the period between the two World Wars, they were also being debated—and put into practice—in the United States. Racism was largely a factor in this phenomenon—from such infamous projects as the Tuskegee Syphilis program that targeted African-Americans as unwitting guinea pigs in medical tests, to the laws against "miscegenation" in many states, laws that forbade the "mixed" marriages of whites and blacks. Add to that the forced sterilization of those deemed mentally unfit to have children, and you have the parameters for what would become Nazi Germany's racial laws, euthanasia programs, and the experimentation on prisoners in the camps. When one considers the policies of the US government in the 19th century where the Native Americans were concerned, you have a precedent for Nazi Germany's policy of *lebensraum*: the idea that, since the German people needed more room to expand, it was necessary (and permissible) to invade the territories of neighboring countries and enslave or exterminate their inhabitants.

In addition to the race science that was taking the western world by storm, there was also the problem of Bolshevism.

"Godless Communism"

The Russian Revolution had taken place in 1917 at the height of the first World War. Bankers, corporate elites, and industrialists were thrown out of power in the ensuing chaos by people identifying themselves as Socialists, Bolsheviks, or Communists. Communism was seen as an enemy to everything the West considered the bedrock of its culture: religion, the free market, and a stratified class structure. Further, Communism was an international movement. Internationalism threatened the hegemony of nation states that had built their wealth on the colonization of other countries and the careful maintenance of zones of influence, such as that represented by the Monroe Doctrine in the Americas. By raising the working class above all other classes, Communism further threatened to

---

in a Darwinian sense—that humans would take steps to control or manipulate this process.

upset the balance between slave and master, between colonized and colonizer, between wage slave and boss.

Germany had been on the front lines of this conflict. There were dozens of Socialist parties in Germany, and in some cases they won elections and controlled individual cities, if only for short periods of time. Thus, it was acknowledged that Germany had first-hand experience of Bolshevism and had fought successfully to remove it from its borders. And, inasmuch as Bolshevism, Marxism, and Communism were seen as products of Jewish thought and personalities—Karl Marx, after all, famously was Jewish even though his writings show him as violently anti-Semitic—it was asserted that the Jew and the Communist were one and the same.

In the United States, these themes were taken up by a variety of celebrities and by a coven of bizarre, right-wing political organizations that claimed to be patriotic, but were at the same time taking money and support from German political parties and operatives and—after 1933—from the German government itself. This came at a time of the rapid growth of labor unions, which threatened the profit structures of industry. Inasmuch as these unions were being influenced by Socialist and Communist parties and "fellow travelers," the world was suddenly perceived to be in a state of tremendous danger from a secret global conspiracy designed to rob corporations of their power, the bankers of their money, and citizens of the traditions and values of Western civilization as they understood them.

The political atmosphere in the United States at the time was poisonous, reminiscent of the state of affairs that obtains at the time this book is being written. As mentioned above, President Franklin D. Roosevelt was being accused by the extreme right of being a Communist, and allegations were made that he was Jewish as well. A number of assassination plots against him had been foiled, and passions were running high in the wake of the Great Depression. Labor unions were seen as tools of international Communism, and corporate leaders and factory directors were cracking down hard against labor unrest. Roosevelt's New Deal—exemplified by the establishment of Social Security and various labor programs—was seen by some as evidence of the president's plan to install a Communist dictatorship in the United States, and charges were made that the White House was a hotbed of Communists and fellow-travelers.

In the midst of all of this, Nazism attracted the attention of many of America's most famous personalities. Men like Henry Ford and Charles A. Lindbergh openly admired Adolf Hitler and his nationalist, anti-Communist agenda. Ford actively contributed to the Nazi Party in its earliest days, using Hitler's close friend Dietrich Eckart as his "bag man" in the transference of funds to the Party in the years before Hitler's 1923 Beer Hall Putsch attempt to take control of the German government. Ford's collected writings on the evils of Jewish bankers and international Communism were published as a book entitled *The International Jew*, distributed widely in Germany as well as around the world. To this day, the book enjoys popularity in areas as diverse as the Middle East, Latin America and Southeast Asia and it has been translated into dozens of languages. In those areas, Ford is almost better known for his anti-Semitism than for the automobiles that bear his name. Charles Lindbergh became a featured spokesperson for a group calling itself "America First": an isolationist organization designed to keep America out of the European conflict being waged by Hitler against his neighbors.

More quietly, other corporate leaders and captains of American industry were in support of Nazi political agendas and racial programs. It is by now well-known that Prescott Bush (grandfather of George H. W. Bush) was an early supporter of Hitler, as were his fellow Brown Brothers Harriman & Co. executives George Herbert Walker (after whom the first President Bush was named) and W. Averell Harriman. The company was an investor in German industry at a time when the United States was gearing up for war against Hitler, and even after war had been declared. Due to the relationship between Brown Brothers Harriman and the German industrial giant Thyssen (through the Union Banking Corporation), as well as other German firms, Brown Brothers assets were seized under the Trading with the Enemy Act in 1942, and held for the duration of the war. Such other icons of American capitalism as Standard Oil, ITT, and IBM were all implicated in the deliberate support of Hitler's agenda and the smooth running of his war machine, as has been described and extensively documented in many other places. If such highly-regarded captains of American industry were supportive of the Nazi Party, then it became increasingly difficult to demonize the rank and file anti-Semites and America Firsters as ignorant, "low information" voters. In other words, the Nazi context in the United States was not simply one of the uneducated, the hateful and the paranoid. It was a network of associations and individuals with tremendous—albeit often clandestine—reach into every aspect of American life, from education and religion to the media and to the houses of Congress itself. Nazism attracted the highly-educated and the self-made millionaires as much as it did the sociopathic personalities who formed Storm Trooper clubs and armed militias that marched in American streets. In that sense, it was no different from the Nazi phenomenon in Germany itself.

In America, with its strong tradition of religious freedom—largely created in the seventeenth century by Christian sects that combined fundamentalist Biblical teachings with a healthy dose of mysticism and even Rosicrucianism—Nazi ideology took on a messianic and apocalyptic tinge.

Racism as Religion

Money is its own religion, especially in a country largely dominated by the Calvinist equivalency between financial success and divine favor; but other spiritualities were abroad in the land in the 1920s and 1930s. Such sentiments were easily manipulated by those who wished to see a fascist or pro-Nazi regime in the United States as a hedge against Communism, with its corollaries of labor unions, internationalism, and anti-colonialism. Even democracy was considered suspect, as Hitler believed it was just another obstacle created by International Jewry to accelerate the demise of national identities. Democracy, theoretically, is a great leveler: all citizens have equal rights before the law and an equal say in the running of the government. This concept is anathema to those who believe that equality contributes to the elevation of the weak and the diminution of the strong: in other words, to those who believe in the Nazi version of Social Darwinism, which requires the strong to rule the weak and the white race to rule all others. Internationalism is also proscribed by the Nazi viewpoint, for it implies that all nations are equal in some sense. Communism is an international movement of class against class rather than nation against nation, and as such it would be illogical to expect a German nationalist to embrace it.

It would also go against the grain of those who feel that the Indian caste system is an ideal way to run a society.

During the early days of the author's research involving the Nazi underground, he made the acquaintance of James Madole, the founder and leader of the National Renaissance Party: a Nazi organization with a pedigree going back to the immediate post-war era in the United States. Madole's group blended doctrinaire Nazism with esotericism and mysticism, influenced heavily by the writings of Blavatsky as well as by other "orientalist" authors like Savitri Devi, who saw in the Indian caste system a perfect template for organizing society along racial and class lines. Madole would constantly invoke this system in his talks with me, emphasizing that the world would be better off if there were strict divisions between the *kshatriya* or warrior caste and the *brahmin* or priestly caste, for instance. In fact, he seemed to favor elevating the warrior caste above the priestly caste, at least at the present time when warriors are more necessary—in his opinion—than priests. This idea is reflected in some of the lesser-known writings of Zen Buddhist scholar D.T. Suzuki, an issue we will pick up in our chapter on the Japanese element in the Nazi underground.

Madole and his National Renaissance Party came to the attention of the House Committee on Un-American Activities in 1954, and was the subject of a forty-page report on "Neo-Fascist and Hate Groups" published that year. In that report, Madole is linked with a variety of interlocking Nazi and fascist organizations as well as with H. Keith Thompson, a wealthy supporter of Nazi causes before, during, and after the war. In that report, Thompson's relationship to SS General Otto Remer and his Austrian Socialist Reich Party is mentioned, and this is an important connection. Remer had a role to play not only in the ODESSA-like Nazi underground after the war, but also with a variety of American political groups and personalities, from Wilis Carto and the Liberty Lobby to former Nixon speechwriter Pat Buchanan.[6]

But aside from the purely esoteric or mystical Nazism of groups like Madole's National Renaissance Party, much of the agitation by pro-Nazi organizations in the United States were informed by Christian ideas, especially those concerning the Jews as "Christ killers." Anti-Semitism alone was not the main thrust of pro-Nazi sentiment in the United States in the period before the war however, but the identification of Jews with Communists.

Thus, in an environment of passionate views concerning foreign policy, race, and religion—as much in 1934 as in 2014—it should come as no surprise that there were those who favored a violent solution to the problems they believed the country faced. The growth and spread of armed militias, for instance, was just as much a problem in the 1930s as it is in the America of today; the difference being that these militias were openly pro-Nazi, such as William Dudley Pelley's Silver Legion and the German-American Bund. While heroes such as Otto Skorzeny and Hans Ulrich Rudel would organize the networks and provide funding, jobs, and other options for the Nazis *after* the war, these home-grown American Nazis would provide the demographic stratum and the ideological motivation to attract new recruits to the cause and would modify the Nazi Party's platforms to accommodate the post-war reality

---

6   Pat Buchanan has a history of supporting extreme right individuals and groups, and the feeling has been mutual. H. Keith Thompson—an American member of the *Sicherheitsdienst* (the intelligence branch of the SS) and a man who swore a loyalty oath to Hitler—contributed generously to Buchanan's political campaigns. Buchanan himself revealed that it was he who convinced then-President Reagan to lay a wreathe at the SS cemetery in Bitburg, Germany "because they were victims, too." Buchanan has appeared as a guest on syndicated radio programs hosted by the extreme right, such as Stormfront, and has blamed the Holocaust on Winston Churchill, saying that England's entry into the war somehow forced Hitler to begin slaughtering Jews, Gypsies and other "undesirables." The meeting at which SS General Otto Remer spoke (as a guest of H. Keith Thompson) was held under the auspices of the Liberty Lobby which has been an outspoken supporter of Holocaust denial. Thompson, it should be noted, was a registered US agent of Remer's Socialist Reich Party.

while not abandoning the Party's core issues: race (particularly white supremacy), anti-Semitism, and an anti-Western "third position" that was neither capitalism nor Communism, but German-style fascism. At the same time these groups—led by individuals with varying degrees of charisma—would incorporate blatantly spiritual, esoteric, occult, or even UFO-related themes into the overall Nazi *weltanschauung*.

Often these people and their groups are not taken seriously, either by academia or by government security agencies, and certainly not by the population at large. In the first place, the Nazis lost the war so why pay attention to a bunch of crackpots who can't accept that the war is over and their side lost? In the second place, they seem odd, neurotic, paranoid, or whatever other psychological term you wish to apply because of their anachronistic political positions and their fascination with fringe spirituality and eccentric interpretations of mainstream religion, science, and culture. Thus, they do not demand careful examination or investigation, any more than one might give to a schizophrenic wandering the streets and talking to the voices in his head. In the third place, they represent such a minority view (in the United States) and command the allegiance of only a relative handful of members, so why be bothered writing or talking about them?

It was just this constellation of factors that allowed the Nazi underground in America to flourish after the war; they were able to fly under the radar, so to speak, precisely because of their very odd characteristics. In addition, in the post-war period, the enemy was international Communism; we had no time to waste on watching, following or infiltrating movements that claimed a Nazi pedigree when the Nazis no longer had a country of their own.

However, while the Nazis were either ignored or even at times tolerated by western intelligence agencies, they succeeded in committing assassinations and terror bombings throughout the post-war period and on virtually every continent in a series of campaigns using multinational terror cells and charismatic personalities that would later provide the template for future, Al-Qaeda-type, terrorist operations. Al-Qaeda, after all, didn't have a country of its own, either.

I submit that the laissez-faire attitude of western intelligence towards the Nazi underground leads us directly to the events of September 11, 2001 and thereafter, and that our lack of interest in this underground—both in the United States and abroad—made us vulnerable to international terrorism and the rise of what has been called Islamist movements. These are anti-Western and anti-Semitic and wish (like their Nazi predecessors) the demise of the United States and the installation of a global government based on ideological principles involving the superiority of one group over another (again, like their Nazi predecessors). Everything from the clandestine movement of funds around the world to the establishment of individual cells and "lone wolf" operators in dozens of countries to assassinations and bombings targeting civilian populations—phenomena that today we associate with Islamist terrorism—were all prefigured in the Nazi underground that survived the Second World War and which continues to exist to the present day. And this underground could not have survived the Second World War without a pre-existing infrastructure and the quiet cooperation of governments: in Europe, the Middle East, Asia, Latin America … and the United States.

Thus, readers will be forgiven if they always had believed that the Nazi phenomenon was strictly a German affair. Events that were taking place in America at the same time as Hitler's rise in Germany have largely been ignored, even as they illustrate in alarming detail that a similar political movement was forming in the United States. This movement would connect and even collaborate with the German movement and lend credibility to some of the planks of Nazism's ideological platform—such as anti-Semitism, racism, and anti-Communism—while at the same time providing a network of logistical, military and intelligence support in North and South America that would long survive the end of hostilities in 1945.

The United States in the 1920s and 1930s was in the midst of a great sociological upheaval, exacerbated by the Great Depression which officially began in 1929 with the stock market crash on October 29: Black Tuesday. Waves of Irish and Italian immigrants threatened the comfortable homogeneity of white, Protestant America by bringing in Roman Catholic minorities. Jewish immigration from

Eastern Europe made the "melting pot" boil over in violence, ethnophobia, and anti-Semitic prejudice. The Russian Revolution had taken place a decade earlier and threatened the European status quo in ways more profound and far-reaching than the First World War, because it introduced concepts like Communism and atheism into a wider audience, far beyond the Russian borders. The Comintern—or Communist International—was at once a political movement as well as a kind of missionary effort targeting the working class of all nations in an existential conflict against religion, capitalism, and slave labor. Many Americans were so shocked by the barbarity of the First World War that they adopted an isolationist position when it came to foreign policy and especially foreign wars. They did not want to entertain hordes of foreign immigrants who did not share their values, their religion, their language, or their race within America's borders for it could lead to America being pushed into involvement in another global war. The Great Depression merely underlined that attitude, for now America could no longer afford to feed, clothe and house the destitute visitors who filled the ships docking at Ellis Island; nor could it afford another foreign military adventure.

Roosevelt was inaugurated President of the United States on March 4, 1933, little over a month after Adolf Hitler was named Chancellor of Germany on January 30, 1933. Both leaders would survive a number of assassination attempts and would, of course, square off against each other during World War II. Roosevelt would die in office on April 12, 1945, and Hitler is believed to have committed suicide on April 30, 1945. The War in Europe would end the following month, in May of 1945 (with the Pacific War ending only with the Japanese surrender four months later).

During the twelve-year period of Roosevelt and Hitler's concurrent leadership, enormous changes took place in the world economy and in the global political situation. A massive Depression, a World War, the rise of tyrants and dictators, the Holocaust, the first use of atomic weapons, and the collapse of empires all took place within that short period of time. The fates and agendas of both Roosevelt and Hitler (and therefore of America and Germany) were inextricably linked.

In America, the situation was not identical to Germany but it was grim. The Depression had taken its toll on the lives of millions of its citizens and strong leadership was needed to keep the nation from plunging even deeper into despair. The leader they elected (an unprecedented four times) was Franklin D. Roosevelt.

Where Hitler would govern by fiat, Roosevelt had to govern with a certain amount of finesse if not subterfuge. Both had to rescue their respective nations from economic chaos. Roosevelt did so by creating various programs that would put Americans to work building infrastructure, and by setting up social welfare programs that would keep the neediest from starvation, and which would guarantee a certain level of security once they attained retirement age, part of an overall philosophy he called the "New Deal." To some Americans this smacked of socialism and communism— people were never quite sure what the difference was between the two—and they began to call for Roosevelt's impeachment, or worse.

The ugliness of the political rhetoric of the 1930s was a precursor to that of today, including hate radio, yellow journalism, and conspiracy theories. In fact, some of the broadsides that were printed attacking Roosevelt for being Jewish (he wasn't), are reminiscent of accusations against Obama as being a "Muslim." In both cases there is the tacit understanding that these religious affiliations, real or imagined, are evidence of anti-Americanism or even of treason.

As mentioned, there were several attempts on Roosevelt's life. One of these, by Italian immigrant and naturalized American citizen Giuseppe Zangara on February 15, 1933 in Miami, targeted president-elect Roosevelt as a dictator. The claim that Roosevelt was a dictator was common currency in the anti-Roosevelt diatribes of the time, ignoring the fact that he eventually was elected four times and that his 1936 re-election victory in particular was a landslide.

Emblematic of the tenor of extreme anti-Roosevelt rhetoric is the rant of prominent anti-Semitic South Philadelphia schoolteacher Bessie R. "Two Gun" Burchett. She was the founder of the Anti-Communist Society (ACS), and a critic of what she called the "Jew Deal." She had this to say about Roosevelt in a pamphlet she distributed in 1939:

"The president is a traitor. We must do all we can to break down the president, and have the people know what kind of man he really is, and then proceed to impeach him. If Hitler does come here, he should drop a bomb on the right place in New York. You all know where I mean. ... a skyscraper full of Jews."[7]

That this would anticipate the events of September 11, 2001 when New York City skyscrapers were indeed "bombed" by anti-Semitic Arabs, has gone unnoticed by most. But Burchett's odd presentiment of events that would take place sixty-two years in the future was not the only one.

Another influential right-wing movement that became progressively more pro-Nazi was William Dudley Pelley's Silver Legion, usually referred to as the Silver Shirts.

William Dudley Pelley (1890–1965) was a journalist and foreign correspondent for the *Saturday Evening Post* who became a Hollywood screenwriter in the 1920s, writing scripts for Lon Chaney. In 1929 he left Hollywood and moved to Asheville, North Carolina. Here he began building a movement around a near-death experience he had in 1925 in which God instructed him to begin the spiritual transformation of America, an experience that he detailed in an article he wrote for *American Magazine* in 1928 entitled "Seven Minutes in Eternity." He combined apocalyptic ideas about the Second Coming of Jesus with anti-Semitism, and conspiracy theories about secret cabals of Jews, the Illuminati, and Communists running the world. Becoming active in politics during the Great Depression, Pelley was a vocal critic of President Roosevelt and the New Deal, seeing the Roosevelt administration as another manifestation of the Soviet system that Pelley had seen first-hand during his days as a foreign correspondent in Russian Siberia during World War I. Pelley defined Communism as part of a worldwide Jewish conspiracy to control the world, and the Depression as part of a master plan by this same conspiracy to destroy America and bring

---

7 From Philip Jenkins, *Hoods and Shirts: The Extreme Right in Pennsylvania 1925-1950*, University of North Carolina Press, Chapel Hill, 1997, p. 130–131.

it under the aegis of the Comintern. In this, he was similar—if not identical—in thinking with Bessie Burchett (indeed he had close ties to the ACS), both of whom opposed the presence of Jews in America and who accused new Jewish immigrants of taking jobs away from "white Americans."

When Hitler came to power in 1933, Pelley was inspired to form a paramilitary organization of his own that he called the Silver Legion. Their uniform consisted of silver shirts emblazoned with the scarlet letter "L" for Legion, and they subsequently became known as the Silver Shirts (in emulation of Mussolini's black-shirted fascists and Hitler's brown-shirted Nazis). Pelley was unabashedly pro-Nazi and as such came to the attention of the House Committee on Un-American Activities. Pelley's Nazism was mixed with millennialism, occultism and esoteric teachings. While this combination might seem strange, it is of a piece with the origins of the Nazi Party itself which had its roots in the mystical Aryan theologies of the Thule Society—as well as of such groups as Lanz von Liebenfels's Order of the New Templars, as promoted in the magazine *Ostara* which the young Hitler read avidly while struggling as a postcard artist in Vienna.[8]

Pelley was also inspired by the works of David Davidson, a British-Israelite (a movement founded around the belief that the English and not the Jews are the true Israelites) and member of the Silver Shirts, who wrote that the Great Pyramid of Giza was a kind of cosmic calendar that could be used to foretell future events. The most important of these events was the Second Coming when Jesus would return to rid the world of the Jews and bring about Paradise on earth (with the assistance of the Silver Shirts, of course). According to the calculations of Pelley based on those of Davidson, the exact date when the Jews would be destroyed was given as September 17, 2001.[9]

---

8   This story is told in more detail in my *Unholy Alliance*, as well as in Nicholas Goodrick-Clarke's *The Occult Roots of Nazism*.
9   See Michael Barkun, *Religion and the Racist Right: The Origins of the Christian Identity Movement*, University of North Carolina Press, Chapel Hill, 1997, p. 52–54.

Six days off from the day "the world was changed" on September 11, 2001; we might say "close enough for government work." Both Burchett's and Pelley's statements were published about the same time, in 1939 and before America entered the Second World War. This eerie prediction of Pelley's—when combined with the plea of Bessie Burchett that Hitler come to New York City and bomb a skyscraper full of Jews—seems to indicate more than just a coincidence of history but a deeper preoccupation of the radical Right that will persist to the present day.

Pelley would eventually be arrested by the US government and indicted for a variety of offences including sedition, and he would spend some years in prison, getting out only in 1952. Although the political involvement of his Silver Shirt militia would wane once the war started, its ideological influence would be felt for decades. Pelley's Silver Legion was the inspiration for the Christian Identity movement and the Posse Comitatus, another extreme-right, conspiratorialist movement founded by a former member of the Silver Shirts, Henry Beach. Both Christian Identity and Posse Comitatus exist today, Christian Identity philosophy and teachings having a major influence on white supremacist groups like the Aryan Nations, while Posse Comitatus has claimed that the US government is in the hands of the international Jewish conspiracy—the "Zionist Occupation Government" or ZOG—and as such refuses to recognize any government authority above that of the local county level. Both groups have been involved—through their individual members—in political terrorism and assassinations in the United States. The Order is one such group that was composed of both Christian Identity members and those who joined a neo-pagan Nordic or Odinist denominaton. The Order committed a series of armed robberies and engaged in shoot-outs with the police until it was wiped out in 1984. Another Christian Identity-affiliated group has been implicated in the Soweto bombings in South Africa in October and November, 2002.

It may seem that an ideology that looks forward to the Second Coming of Jesus and the End of Days would not have much in common with Nazism. Except that it was just those teachings— that Jesus was not Jewish, that true Christianity is Aryan, and that

Jews are the spawn of Satan—that informed one of the strangest religious movements in Nazi Germany, that of the *Deutsche Christen*, or the German Christian sect.

Formed in 1931 to rid Christianity of "Jewish influences," the Deutsche Christen aimed to de-emphasize (or excise or rewrite entirely) those portions of the Old Testament that were concerned primarily with Jewish ideas, and to promote the concept of an "Aryan" Christ. By 1933, after Hitler's rise to power as Chancellor, the Deutsche Christen was instrumental in the formation of the German Evangelical Church, used by the Nazis to centralize Protestant Christianity in Germany under a state-sponsored aegis. Openly anti-Semitic and supportive of Nazi racial ideas, the German Christian movement flourished until the end of the war, after which it diminished considerably in numbers and influence. But its central themes of the Aryan Christ, the Jews as sons of Satan, and the race-consciousness and ethnophobic platforms would find themselves renewed in the Christian Identity movement and its fellow-travelers: in the Aryan Nations; the Order; The Covenant, Sword, and Arm of the Lord; and many others. The role of Christian Identity as a political movement has been abbreviated in the past few years and indeed it was never very well-organized or centralized to begin. But its ideology has had many admirers in organizations that can be considered white supremacist, anti-Semitic, and anti-Communist: some of its adherents have called for the overthrow of the US government, which is seen as a tool of the international Jewish conspiracy as detailed in the famous hoax document, *The Protocols of the Learned Elders of Zion.*

Pelley's pro-Nazi, Hitlerite, Christian, and anti-Semitic views were largely in harmony with those of the Deutsche Christen. Pelley's contribution to the discussion was a heavy dose of mysticism and esoteric ideas—such as pyramidology, spiritualism, and the like—combined with conspiracy theories (in those days such theories were always focused on a purported global Jewish cabal) all wrapped in the American flag. At its height, the Silver Legion numbered about 15,000 members in the United States, and that does not count the numerous other individuals and groups that were sympathetic to its aims and comfortable with its rhetoric of armed resistance to the perceived Communist takeover of the country represented by the hated President Roosevelt.

One should not believe that Pelley was strictly a crazed occultist and conspiracy theorist with wild ideas about the Apocalypse and "pyramid power." He was a skilled activist as well. His ties to the German-American Bund—the pro-Nazi society led by Fritz Kuhn that was eventually banned as the war started—are well-established, as are Pelley's Silver Legion connections with other right-wing groups that advocated close cooperation with the Nazis and their secret service—the *Geheimstaatspolizei* or Gestapo. Pelley was also well-acquainted with Nazi ideologue Francis Parker Yockey and with Father Charles Coughlin (1891–1979), the infamous Roman Catholic priest and radio personality whose pro-Nazi sentiments became more pronounced as the music of the 1930s progressed from Depression blues to the drums of war.

> One thing is sure. Democracy is doomed. This is our last election. It is fascism or communism. We are at the crossroads—I take the road to fascism.
> —Father Coughlin, 1936[10]

Coughlin was representative of the ideology embraced by Hitler of a "third way": a political and economic system that was neither capitalism nor communism. Coughlin attacked the greed inherent in the capitalist system but feared communism more because its atheist philosophy denied the possibility of God and an afterlife. Coughlin had successfully helped to create a third political party to challenge Roosevelt in the 1936 presidential election, but when that election was lost he removed himself from the limelight for a short time, returning to the stage a year later even more anti-Semitic and anti-Communist. His radio broadcast was finally silenced by the Roosevelt administration in 1940 as the country prepared for war with Germany. Coughlin himself came dangerously close to being

---

10　Dale Kramer, *Coughlin, Lemke and the Union Party*, Minneapolis, Farmers Book Store, 1936. Also see Norman Thomas, "What's Behind the Christian Front?" New York, Workers Defense League 1939, p. 15.

arrested for sedition. It was Coughlin, for example, who defended the Nazi atrocity known as *Kristallnacht*—the Night of Broken Glass in 1938 when hundreds of Jewish shops and synagogues in Germany had their windows smashed and defaced with swastikas and signs like *Juden Raus!* ("Jews Out!"). He said, essentially, that the Jews had called it on themselves for their persecution of Christians—a snide reference to the Russian Revolution for which the alleged global Jewish conspiracy was considered responsible, and its assassinations of the Czar and his family as well as the murders of thousands of Russian Christians.[11]

Like Pelley's influence on current forms of New Age Christianity, spirituality, and fascism, Coughlin was the American model for a generation of pro-Nazi Catholic priests and hierarchs in Europe who would aid directly in the escape of German, Croatian and other war criminals in the immediate post-war period. It has also been reliably reported that Coughlin was the beneficiary of funding from Nazi Germany itself.[12] It was only his popularity as a radio personality that kept Father Coughlin from being arrested and indicted for sedition, especially as he was in the middle of an important Nazi espionage ring (see below) that included everyone from Fritz Kuhn's German-American Bund to pro-Nazi Ukrainian emigre groups and German agents throughout the United States and Mexico. It was Coughlin who repeatedly referred to President Roosevelt as "President Rosenfeld" in an attempt to stigmatize him as Jewish and Roosevelt's opposition to Hitler as indicative of the former's support of Communism.

Father Coughlin's support for Germany extended considerably deeper than even his radio program would indicate. From his base in Royal Oak, Michigan—a suburb of Detroit—Coughlin enter-

---

11 See Donald Warren, *Radio Priest: Father Coughlin the Father of Hate Radio*, The Free Press, New York, 1996 for a study of this controversial priest and the way he can be considered a prototype for the current wave of emotive, politically-motivated talk radio shows.

12 Warren, pp. 235–244. See also Charles Higham, *American Swastika*, for a detailed description of Coughlin's subversive activities in the 1930s and his relationship with Eastern Orthodox emigre groups from Russia and Ukraine, as well as his work with Nazi agents in the United States and Mexico.

tained fascists and Nazi spies and facilitated their operations in North America. These included William Pelley's Silver Legion and the German-American Bund, but also involved a group of White Russian emigres who were agitating for a Nazi invasion of Russia in order to remove the Communist regime. Coughlin's support extended as well to members of the Christian Front: a short-lived anti-Semitic organization that went on rampages in Jewish neighborhoods in American cities, notably in New York City, until it was disbanded after the start of America's entry into the war.

The White Russian community is an insular group that, in the decades before the fall of the Soviet Union, revolved around the Russian Orthodox Church Outside Russia (ROCOR). Its US headquarters were in New York City on Park Avenue, in a beautiful building that had been home to an American railroad magnate before it was purchased by emigre members of the Romanov family. For conspiracy aficionadoes, this was the same Church that is mentioned—usually fleetingly—in accounts of Lee Harvey Oswald's relationship to the mysterious George de Mohrenschildt and the Russian emigre community in Dallas. ROCOR was violently anti-Communist, as was the Ukrainian Orthodox Church. These religious groups would provide political, monetary, and even logistical support to American intelligence activities against the Soviet Union and its allies both in the United States and abroad, and their full story has yet to be told. However, there are many similarities in the way in which the Eastern European churches aided and abetted fascist and Nazi organizations, espionage rings, and escape networks, and the activities of the Roman Catholic Church during the same period, and to the same ends. Pope Pius XII—who has often been criticized for his role during the War—refused to censure Father Coughlin, even when some (but by no means all) American bishops begged him to do so.

American sympathies with the Nazis were not limited to a handful of cranks, crazed clergymen, and sociopathic personalities dressed up as storm troopers, marching at the Bund's infamous Camp Siegfried however. As mentioned earlier, many American politicians and industrialists were unashamed supporters of Hitler and the Third Reich and actively sought to prevent Roosevelt from antagonizing the Führer, whom they considered a bulwark against Communism. Ideologues like Coughlin and Pelley—among many others—merely gave a theoretical framework for what actually was taking place behind the scenes as prominent members of Congress, allied with financiers and industrial giants, threw their weight (both covertly and overtly) behind a movement to depose Roosevelt and establish a fascist-friendly administration in the United States before Roosevelt could end American isolationism and go to war against Hitler.

One can drill as deep as one likes into these complex relationships (and the especially disturbing participation of leaders mentioned earlier such as Ford, Lindbergh, Bush, Harriman, Walker, et al) and never run out of material for despair at the callous disregard for anything remotely suggestive of human values that these individuals and companies displayed. Banking and industrial relationships between American and German companies during the war never really ended and, on the contrary, were often expanded considerably. Allen Dulles—who would eventually become Director of the Central Intelligence Agency (until fired by President Kennedy over the Bay of Pigs fiasco)—played both sides of the fence during the war. Dulles is on record for his disinterest in the Holocaust and his desire to work with Nazi leaders and insiders, such as former Reich Finance Minister Hjalmar Schacht, to bring hostilities in Europe to an end so that Germany could re-arm for the eventual conflict with the Soviet Union. When the war ended, these sympathies did not die with the signing of peace treaties and unconditional surrenders. The end of the war was merely one stage in a long-term strategy that involved support for fascist and Nazi ideas, individuals, and organizations in order to combat the forces of Communism around the world. The military defeat of the German armed forces was, in a sense, misdirection. The signing of the unconditional surrender in Europe was a bit of theater that lulled the world into a false sense of security by implying that the *ideals* of the Third Reich had been defeated along with its armies.

With a long history of pro-Nazi organizations and their underground activities in the United States in the 1930s, nothing could be further from the truth. The American ODESSA had been established early on and the defeat of the Third Reich was not accepted as the death of the Nazi program, but as a bump in the road, a setback to be sure, but not the end of the struggle. The Soviet Union was still there, rattling its own sabres against Eastern Europe and threatening the West. Fear of Hitler was transferred to fear of Stalin and the "Red Menace." Mao was taking over in China, bringing Communism and the "Yellow Peril" to the Asian mainland. Ho Chi Minh was fighting the French in Vietnam. A band of revolutionaries led by Sukarno was removing Dutch influence from Indonesia. Korea was about to fall to Communists from the north. Great Britain was about to lose its colonies in India and Malaya.

There was much work to be done still, and who better to oversee the global project of resistance to Communism than the very people who had started it as long ago as 1919? The Germans felt that they had been the first to recognize the dangers of the Soviet system and had fought—city by city—to eradicate it from their borders. They had a kind of proprietary interest in the subject. When the Second World War was over and the West geared up for a confrontation with Russia, it would be the Germans who would say "I told you so."

While the more flamboyant members of the radical right got most of the attention due to the same tactics that enabled Hitler and the Nazi Party to rise to power in Germany—notably the ability to use patriotic slogans and iconography, in combination with a strong appeal to paranoia and fear-mongering by means of conspiracy theories that targeted minority groups—there were more sober individuals within the radical movement who were just as committed as their flashier colleagues but who were able to keep a lower profile and thus work behind the scenes. This category included spies and saboteurs, of course—and America had its share of Nazi fifth columnists in the years leading up to the war—but it also included ideologues and specialists in psychological warfare and public relations campaigns who would go on to form the backbone of the Nazi Underground after the war due to their more pragmatic approach. These were intelligent men and women who remained devoted to the Nazi cause, but who were clever enough to understand that an overtly pro-Nazi movement would not play well in Peoria.

The American psyche already had enough elements that were

in line with Nazi ideology that a subtle approach was more likely to win converts than a platoon of goose-steppers in home-made SS uniforms. These elements included a certain degree of ethnophobia, racism, and anti-Semitism (i.e., fear of the unknown and the different) combined with an overall distrust of a foreign policy concerned with the defense of democracy abroad, or the rescue of captive peoples of other races, or in countries with—to American ears—unpronounceable names. Both America and Germany were suffering from economic setbacks that crippled their respective economies (at least insofar as the average workers were concerned) and someone had to take the blame. Jewish bankers and Communists were the scapegoats in both countries, and some of the American rhetoric against Jews was just as vociferous as anything found in Germany at the time.

Before the two World Wars, isolationism was very popular in America. In the 1930s, as noted, there were both Republican and Democrat isolationists who wanted to keep America out of foreign wars. This sentiment—with a patriotic, pro-American veneer overlaying a covert hostility to cultural change and Jewish and Asian immigration—became enshrined in the America First Committee (AFC). America First was a clearing house for those with pro-fascist or pro-Nazi points of view who wished to enjoy a certain patriotic prestige to go along with their avowed aim of keeping America focused on Americans and away from the gradually deteriorating situation in Europe and Asia. A focus on Americans was an easy sell; but the sub-text was quite different.

The America First movement wanted to ensure that the United States would not enter a war in Europe on the side of England against Germany. Isolationism, in this context, was equivalent to aiding and abetting the Third Reich in all of its policies. The idea was to allow Hitler free reign in Europe by turning American sentiment against another conflict abroad. Supporters of America First included Father Coughlin—who was himself implicated in a Nazi spy ring, as mentioned above—and a somewhat more enigmatic H. Keith Thompson as we shall see. Other high-placed isolationists included the heir to the Quaker Oats fortune, the owner of Morton Salt, the chairman of Sears, Roebuck, Walt Disney, and the publishers of the New York *Daily News* and the Chicago *Tribune*. These were names with which every American was familiar, names that added a comfort factor to the message the AFC was promoting. That message was couched in the homely and familiar, the *gemutlichkeit* of the American middle class, making it appear as if the AFC was a bottom-up organization, a grass-roots movement of right-thinking (no pun intended) and hard-working people, when in reality it was a top-down political action committee being manipulated by Old Money.

There were politicians who were supporters of AFC as well, such as future president and Warren Commission member Gerald Ford when he was still a college student, some Democrat senators from Montana and Massachusetts, and even the head of the Socialist Party of America. AFC had successfully branded itself as a patriotic organization that put the interests of the American people ahead of all other considerations, and many found it a convenient vehicle for promoting their own political platforms. Gradually, however, the true nature of the movement was revealed as speech after speech by movement leaders identified the problems facing America as those of international communism, the Jewish lobby, and the threat of American intervention in the war about to rip Europe apart. "America First" became synonymous with allowing Hitler to rampage unimpeded throughout Austria, Czechoslovakia, Poland and the rest of Europe, keeping American troops out of the conflict, and letting Great Britain fend for itself. It was vitally important to Hitler that America stay out of the conflict because he was already stretched too thin across two fronts and didn't need the country who helped defeat Germany in the First World War to come back to Europe and do it a second time. Roosevelt knew the danger of permitting Hitler free reign, but he could not convince the American people of this. He ran on a platform of keeping America out of war, and as time went by it was becoming increasingly difficult to honor that commitment.

On September 11, 1941 Charles Lindbergh gave an important speech before his followers in Des Moines, Iowa (today a state whose primary elections are looked upon as bellweathers for the success or failure of presidential candidates). In this speech he railed against the Jews as being in control of the media and agitating for war against Germany. (Of course, the hugely influential New York *Daily News* and the Chicago *Tribune*, supporters of America First, were exempt from this characterization which leads one to wonder to which media specifically Lindbergh was referring.) He blamed the British for trying to drag America into the conflict, and the Roosevelt administration for collaborating with both the Jews and the British in this regard. While he expressed sympathy for the Jewish plight in Germany, he also warned American Jews that things could get a lot worse for them if they persisted in dragging America into the conflict.

Precisely three months later, to the day, America First was disbanded as the United States was attacked by Japanese forces at Pearl Harbor on December 7, 1941. The position of the America First Committee became untenable. However, while the organization as such disappeared, the individual members did not abandon their faith. Some wholeheartedly joined the fight for victory over Hitler, but others waited for events to turn in their direction. (Even H. Keith Thompson—who bragged of being a member of the Nazi *Sicherheitsdienst* or Security Service (SD)—enlisted in the US Navy.) Many interpreted the war as a Jewish war, a Communist war, part of an overall struggle that was essentially racial and spiritual in nature and that would not end with the signing of a peace treaty or defeat on the battlefield.

After all, Christianity itself survived underground for more than three centuries before Constantine made it a state religion.

CHAPTER TWO

ORIGINS OF GLOBAL JIHAD

An antisemitism based on the notion of a conspiracy of World Jewry is not rooted in Islamic tradition, but is based rather on European ideological models. The decisive transfer of this ideology took place between 1937 and 1945 under the impact of Nazi propaganda.

—"European Roots of Antisemitism in Current Islamic Thinking," Matthias Küntzel

I thank God that the interests of Islam are entirely identical with those of Germany.

—Prince Faisal to Max von Oppenheim, 1915[13]

Before we go much further into our story, it would be well to examine the situation in the Middle East at the end of the First World War because the seeds of our present conflict were sown there at that time. As I have stated before in several places, we are still fighting the First World War and it is possible that future generations will refer to the period 1914-present as the "Second Hundred Years War."

It is astonishing how greatly events in the Middle East affect the peace and security of the entire world, yet at the same time how little most of us know about the origins of those events. When we speak today of the Muslim Brotherhood, of the Israeli-Palestinian conflict, the situation in Iraq or Afghanistan or Iran, of the "Arab Spring," we are not really speaking about recent events but about circumstances that were set in motion a century ago; and when we throw around the term *jihad* as if we know what it means and what it represents, what we do not realize is that the *current*, contempo-

---

13 As referenced in Sean McMeekin, *The Berlin-Baghdad Express*, Harvard University Press, Cambridge, 2010, p. 195.

rary phenomenon we call "global jihad" or what some journalists and academics call *jihadism* has its origins not in the Middle East but in Europe, not from Muslims but from Christians, and not in the seventh century but in the twentieth: long after the death of the Prophet.

While the concept of jihad as religious struggle is enshrined in Islam, the political application of global jihad is relatively recent and dates to the First World War. At that time, Germany and Turkey (the "Axis Powers") were allies against the British, the French, and the Russians (the "Triple Entente"). As we will see, in the period October–November, 1914, the Kaiser's representative in Turkey urged the Ottoman Caliph, Sultan Mehmed V, to declare a holy war, a *jihad*, against the Entente. This he did, on November 12, 1914, which was followed by a *fatwa* issued by the Sheikh-ul-Islam (the leading spiritual authority of the Empire) a few days later on November 14. This jihad was to encompass the entire world and the call went out to Muslims everywhere on the planet to rise up against the European colonizers and destroy them.

That this was motivated by purely political motives is obvious from the context. Germany was at war with the European powers of Great Britain, France and Czarist Russia. The proclamation of jihad and the accompanying fatwa specified these nations as "enemies of Islam." Germany was just as Christian as the countries named in the fatwa, but that was clearly not the issue. Cynically, religious sentiment was used by both political and religious leaders to incite revolt. Jihad was a stratagem, a means to an end, and that end was the elimination of the colonial powers from the Middle East. It was a stratagem devised by the Germans and implemented by the Turks in order to control access to the oil fields of the Middle East and, of course, the Suez Canal, wresting access away from the colonial powers and replacing one set of masters with another.

This was a carefully-conceived attempt to unite the otherwise woefully disunited "Arabs" in a military campaign designed to stretch from Tunisia to Mesopotamia, Persia, and Afghanistan, encompassing all of what is now Saudi Arabia and the Levant: the countries of Lebanon, Palestine, Syria and what is today the

Hashemite Kingdom of Jordan. Anyone familiar with the facts on the ground in this region at the time understands that it was not a monolithic ethnic entity, just as Islam is not a monolithic faith with a central cathedral and a pope. Instead, the region was—and to a large extent still is—populated by factions and rivalries and cultural differences that are just as vast as those between (for instance) Hungarians and Italians, only more so. The 18th century fundamentalist Islamic revival of Wahhabism found its supporters in the Arab tribes under Ibn Saud—for instance—while this same doctrine was considered heresy by the Hashemite rulers of the Hejaz (the area where the holy cities of Mecca and Medina are located). The peoples of what is today Saudi Arabia are almost exclusively Sunni Muslims, who view the Shi'ite Muslims of what is today Iran and most of Iraq as heretics and infidels. Throw into the mix the Kurds, the various Christian sects, and antinomian groups like the Yezidis, and you begin to realize that there is no such thing as the "Arabs" except as a kind of convention for referring to people whose primary language is Arabic. Of course, that would not include Persia/Iran (who speak a different language and who are ethnically distinct from the Semitic Arabs), or the Urdu-speaking populations of Central Asia, the Turks, and many others.

A call to the common faith of the majority of the population in the region, however, could sidestep these obvious difficulties and unite these fractious, warring clans into a common cause against the British, the French, and the Russians if it was claimed that the Caliphate itself was in danger from them.

That, anyway, was the idea.

The Ottoman Empire had suffered a string of humiliating defeats at the hands of the colonial powers in the decades prior to the outbreak of the First World War. The Caliphate had lost territories in North Africa (Libya to the Italians, and Egypt to the British) and the Balkans (the First and Second Balkan Wars of 1912 and 1913, respectively, which contributed directly to the assassination of Archduke Ferdinand by a Serbian nationalist that ignited the First World War). A military alliance with Germany would give the Empire an opportunity to regain some semblance of national pride, as well as unite the various warring factions in its domain by identifying the foe with a kind of cosmic evil: "enemies of Islam."

While the war proved disastrous for the Ottoman Empire and led to its collapse, the idea of jihad as a weapon that could be wielded by the non-Muslim Western powers did not lose its luster. As Czarist Russia fell to the Bolsheviks during the war, a new enemy was found to unite the Western powers and Islam in a new common cause. This time it was atheistic, "godless" Communism which, conveniently, was considered an invention of the Jews. This, coupled with the news that England and France were betraying the Arab revolt against Turkey by dividing up the Middle East between them (the Sykes-Picot Agreement, to which there were no Arab signatories), while providing a homeland for European Jews in Palestine (as set forth in the Balfour Declaration, to which there also were no Arab signatories) meant that the European powers were once again intent on colonizing the Middle East—and the nefarious Jews were behind it all. The cosmic struggle against the "enemies of Islam" was thus refined to the extent that it was now a struggle between Islam and the Jews (and their allies, the Christian "crusaders"). What began as a holy war against European colonialism and the effort to remove the European powers from the lands of the Levant, Central Asia, and the Maghreb gradually was being transformed into a religious conflict *per se*. Or, at least that was the way it was being presented.

And once again it would be Germany that would come to the rescue of the Faithful.

Max Freiherr von Oppenheim, Abu Jihad

Invoking jihad was the idea of Max von Oppenheim, the German "Abu Jihad." In late October 1914, before the Ottomans had entered the war (siding with the Central Powers) he designed a master plan "fomenting rebellion in the Islamic territories of our enemies."

—Wolfgang G. Schwanitz, "German Middle East Early Years."

The man most often credited with having single-handedly created the idea of global (as opposed to localized) jihad was an amateur archaeologist. Max von Oppenheim (1860–1946) was one of that breed of late-nineteenth and early-twentieth century adventurers who longed after exotic locales, ancient ruins, and international intrigue. Coming from the famous Oppenheim banking dynasty, Max's mother was Catholic but his father was a Jewish convert to Catholicism, thus making Max what the Nazis would call *Mischlinge*, a "hybrid" or "mixed race." Early on, Max decided he did not want to be a banker but wanted instead to travel abroad, and this he did first in the military and later as an archaeologist and adventurer in the decades before the outbreak of the First World War.

He considered himself an expert on Middle Eastern affairs, although he had no academic credentials at all in the fields in which he felt most comfortable: archaeology, ancient civilizations, and most importantly Islam. He lived in Cairo for years, in an apartment near Al-Azhar University where he literally kept a small harem; he actually "bought" slave girls from the market on an annual basis. His exploits in that area became so well-known that a liaison with another man's wife led to her being murdered by a jealous husband, who drowned her in the Nile.

Oppenheim became something of a celebrity in his native Germany, and was known to entertain all sorts of famous people, German and foreign, both in the Middle East and back home. Most people took it for granted that "the Baron" (as he was known) was a spy for the Kaiser's government. He was on close terms with the Sultan of the Ottoman Empire, and later with the Grand Mufti of Jerusalem—and therein hangs a tale.

Oppenheim was twenty-three when he first visited Greece and Turkey, and two years later—in 1886—found himself in North Africa, where he began to engage in the type of serial monogamy that is practiced in some Islamic cultures wherein one marries a woman for a short period of time and then divorces her, only to seek another to replace the first.

This fascination with the "Orient" fueled Oppenheim's travels and intrigues for the rest of his life. In 1892, Oppenheim began his first serious investigation of the Levant, traveling to Beirut,

Damascus, and then eventually to Cairo where he put down stakes. Ostensibly he was there as an archaeologist, interested in digging for buried civilizations and ruined cities. Of course, he also spent some time as a kind of government agent, building relationships with Bedouin tribes in Arabia, and cultivating friendships among the influential denizens of the mysterious East.

Oppenheim's archaeological expeditions took him far afield. While he is better known for his excavations in Syria at Tell Halaf, he also spent considerable time in North Africa—from Algeria and Tunisia to Libya and of course Egypt. His contacts among the indigenous peoples across the region convinced him that a summons to an unprecedented global jihad against the Kaiser's enemies would be fruitful and would unite the entire Muslim world against the Entente. Key to this strategy was the cooperation of the Ottoman government and its spiritual leader, the Sheikh ul-Islam, whose fatwa was considered an important element of the strategy for fomenting a region-wide revolt against the British, French and Russians. As the intrigues between Germany and Turkey began to take form, Oppenheim's idea of global jihad developed as a tool of German military policy. Oppenheim had the Kaiser's ear; he was named an official adviser to the Kaiser and supplied him with hundreds of reports every year on the situation in North Africa (the Maghreb) and the Middle East. So it was with the Kaiser's approval that the Sultan of the Ottoman Empire was approached in October of 1914 with the proposal that he declare a jihad against the Kaiser's enemies, thus sealing the relationship between Germany and the Ottomans during the First World War.

It should be remarked that even though Germany had foreign colonies, these were largely in Africa. While these colonial territories numbered upwards of two million Muslim inhabitants, oddly they were not considered "Muslim territories." Thus the Kaiser could get away with pointing the Ottomans at the other European powers who did have colonies in lands whose populations were largely Muslim. Germany also had territories in East Papua and in some South Pacific islands but their populations were not Muslim. Italy—ostensibly Germany's ally for at least part of the war—was nervous about the call to jihad against the "enemies of Islam," for they had occupied Libya, and were afraid that those living in this predominantly Muslim country would heed the call to arms and turn on them. This, of course, was always the possibility and something very like this would come to pass in the years to come. The intelligence community has a word for it: blowback.

This ploy may not have worked at all save for the fact that the Kaiser himself was a fan of the Middle East and particularly of Islam, so much so that he was given the honorific of "Hajji Wilhelm," a title normally only conferred on someone who had made the pilgrimage—the *hajj*—to Mecca. The Kaiser and the Baron were drunk on the same Orientalist fantasy of whirling dervishes, sensuous concubines, gorgeous architecture, flowing robes, flashing scimitars, and vast, lonely desert spaces that was the stuff of European dreams of the "Orient." The Kaiser had received a hero's welcome on a pre-war visit to Jerusalem and had stood in awe before the tomb of the famous Muslim commander Saladin: the man who put an end to the Christian Crusader dreams of conquest for a thousand years. Thus, the Kaiser not only saw the idea of global jihad as a practical political asset, but he also dreamed of an alliance with the Caliph and the emirs, the sheikhs and the Bedouins of the exotic lands of *Arabia Deserta* and the fabled cities of Baghdad, Damascus, Jerusalem, Mecca, and Cairo.

Both he and his trusted advisor—Max von Oppenheim—saw what they wanted to see. Oppenheim was convinced that the entire region would rise up in support of the Turkish-German alliance in response to the call of holy war; and that the Kaiser would thus have an easy time of controlling the Suez Canal; and, in the process, develop lucrative trade routes and business relations with Constantinople and the East. They saw their own reflections in the shimmering desert sands and the glow of a thousand minarets.

The fatwa was translated into Arabic, Farsi, and Urdu, as well as French, thus targeting not only the Arabs of the Levant and the Maghreb, but also those Muslims living in Persia (Iran) who were Shi'ites, and those living in India and Afghanistan. This was intended to be a truly global jihad, designed to summon warriors from the entire region that had been colonized by the French and the British, from North Africa all the way to India. It was to be an uprising encompassing millions of the faithful—Sunni and Shi'a, Arab and Persian, Afghani, Turk, and Central Asians—in a call to arms against the European "enemies of Islam." As such, it could be considered the first of its kind.

There were other elements in the fatwa that bear repeating here. For instance, Oppenheim suggested that the jihad not be limited to pitched battles and armies in the field (that would be the responsibility of the Ottoman Army), but that the struggle could be carried out by individuals, using assassination and other terror tactics against the infidels. It also suggested that "bands" of jihadists be created in various countries to wage war against the occupiers.[14] Thus, the "lone wolf" and "terror cell" concepts were enshrined in the idea of global jihad as early as 1914 ... and by a German of mixed Catholic and Jewish ancestry who was neither Arab nor Muslim.

Unfortunately for both, the call to jihad was not embraced by all Muslims. The Saudi princes in particular were not comfortable with the arrangement and—as is well known—they rose up in revolt *against* the Ottoman Caliphate, aided and abetted by the British government with promises of gold and independence. This is the revolt that made another archaeologist—T.E. Lawrence (1888–1935)—famous throughout the world, thanks partly to the public relation efforts of American journalist Lowell Thomas. Lawrence was a British intelligence officer with experience in the region and with some Arabic language capability, who saw in the putative Arab Revolt a possibility to remove Ottoman rule from the Saudi peninsula and from there to the region generally. While the Ottomans were fighting pitched battles in the nineteenth century tradition, Lawrence understood that guerrilla war against them would be more efficient and successful. His approach was a type of "asymmetrical warfare" that we will examine later, as it comes up in the context of not only "global jihad" but also in terms of the Nazi underground.

---

14 See Sean McMeekin, *The Berlin-Baghdad Express*, Cambridge, Harvard U. Press, 2010, pp. 136–137.

Thus, we had the English archaeologist Lawrence on one side of the conflict, and the German archaeologist Oppenheim on the other: each trying to convince his side of the righteousness of his respective cause, and each manipulating the situation (and the trust) of the Arabs in service to European masters, and a post-war strategy that would have benefited no one but the Europeans.

While the jihad strategy did not work as it was intended (the German-Ottoman alliance was defeated in World War One, and the Ottoman Empire fell a few years later) it did sow the seeds of what would become a grander and more articulated tool of Western foreign policy—one that the Germans would revisit less than twenty years later when the war drums again were beating in Europe and vibrating beneath the sands of Arabia. The Oppenheim concept of global jihad was nothing less than the weaponization of religion in the service of German territorial ambitions; and it was a weapon that could be wielded with cold efficiency only by those who had no religious sensitivity themselves. (Oppenheim had repudiated his Jewish origins and only identified himself as Catholic in order to avoid the opprobrium attached to his Semitic background. As far as we know, he was not a convert to Islam, which made his urging of jihad particularly hypocritical.) In sum, global jihad was originally conceived as a tool for Western, European colonialists to (ironically) manipulate anti-colonial sentiments by elevating them to the status of divine ordinance, taking what was a political and economic situation—colonialism—and interpreting it within a purely religious context. The struggle of the colonized against the colonizers (an ancient construct going back to at least the time of the Roman Empire) was recast as the cosmic, Manichaean conflict between the forces of good and the forces of evil. (A precedent might be seen in the revolt of the Jews against the Romans in the first century CE, which produced the Book of Revelation.)

This approach required a level of cynicism and a degree of *sang froid* that still is astonishing, even when examined from the remove of one hundred years. The willingness of the Sultan to go along with this strategy is evidence of just how morally bankrupt the Ottoman Empire was at the time. It goes a long way toward explaining why the Saudis in particular—infused with the fundamentalist doctrines of Wahhabism, which center on a complete rejection of modernism and foreign influence—did not accept it, and instead raised their swords against the Sultan's armies in defiance of the fatwa. They had indeed opposed the Ottoman Empire since the early nineteenth century, but again and again were defeated militarily. It was only with the end of World War One and the collapse of the Empire that the Kingdom of Saudi Arabia—founded on Wahhabi principles—was created.

But that was not the end of Oppenheim or of the idea of global jihad at the service of non-Muslims. By the time Hitler had become Chancellor of Germany, the idea of global jihad had been combined with another European invention: anti-Semitism.

And thus the die was cast for the great global terrorism epidemic of the twentieth and the twenty-first centuries.[15]

The Grand Mufti

The armistice that was signed in November, 1918 formally ending the First World War was not the seal of enduring peace that everyone desired. If anything, it set the pieces on the chessboard for even greater conflict to come. The Treaty of Versailles was one problem, for it was seen by many as unnecessarily punitive to Germany. This is not the place to go into a discussion of all the factors that led to the outbreak of war and its devastating aftermath; suffice it to say that this era is still being discussed and debated; and that there is no consensus among scholars and historians as to who (if anyone)

---

15 Ironically, Oppenheim was related to two individuals who have their own places in history, albeit for slightly different reasons. The first was the man who assassinated Kurt Eisner (the organizer of the Bavarian Socialist Revolution of 1918), Anton Graf von Arco-Valley (1897–1945); and the other was Karlfried Graf Dürckheim (1896–1988), who was the Gestapo chief in Tokyo during the war and who became a renowned expert on Zen Buddhism after the war. Both Arco-Valley and Dürckheim were related to the Oppenheim banking dynasty and, interestingly enough, the name Oppenheim crops up again in our research via a connection with the Escape Organization that was being run out of the German Archaeological Institute in Rome (as mentioned in *Ratline*).

should bear the sole culpability for what was seen as the most horrendous war in modern times. At the same time as the war was coming to a close, Czarist Russia had become the Soviet Union; and on the other side of the Mediterranean from Europe, North Africa and the Middle East were still in flames.

The Arab Revolt clearly had been betrayed. That was the idea all along. The despised colonizers of Great Britain and France had lived up to their reputation and carved up the region between themselves, deciding who should be their regents on the ground and where. In Arabia, there was a struggle between the House of Saud and the Hashemite Kingdom for control over the region, with the Hashemites eventually losing Arabia to the Saudis (who were heavily influenced by the Wahhabi sect). Faisal—the Hashemite leader immortalized by the English actor Alec Guinness in the film *Lawrence of Arabia*—became briefly King of Syria until ousted by the French, and then King of Iraq (a region where no one knew who he was). It was Faisal who wanted to create a pan-Arab state uniting Sunnis and Shi'ites and who even considered helping the Jews find a homeland in Palestine (if it were under Arab control).

Thus the early post-World War One history of the Middle East is one of Arab leaders jockeying for position among themselves and currying favor with their new landlords—the British and French rulers who had replaced the Ottomans as the force to be reckoned with in the region. There was also the thorny issue of Israel and the British Mandate of Palestine, which seemed to indicate that the European powers were planning on establishing a state within the Arab world that would be answerable to (and controlled by) them. Faisal and Chaim Weizmann—the famous Zionist leader, and eventually the first President of Israel—came to terms on the plan for a Jewish homeland. Faisal hoped that an alliance with the Zionists would assure him of continued British support, especially against the French. Add to this the fact that the boundaries of the new Arab nations of Iraq, Kuwait, Saudi Arabia, Syria, Transjordan, etc. were being drawn by two English archaeologists—T.E. Lawrence and Gertrude Bell—and you have a cauldron in which future conflicts and unbelievable tragedies would begin to boil.

In other words, it was political chaos.

In Palestine itself, there was growing resentment against the presence of the European powers and the perceived intentions of the Jews to take over the Al-Aqsa Mosque in Jerusalem. This idea was spread by the spiritual leader of Palestine's Muslims, Haj Amin al-Husseini, the Grand Mufti of Jerusalem and friend of the aforementioned Max von Oppenheim. It led to the outbreak of real violence during the 1929 Palestine riots.

Al-Husseini (1897–1974), a native of Jerusalem, had served with the Ottoman army during World War One, but after the war shifted his allegiance to Faisal and the notion of a pan-Arab Empire. However, Faisal would be defeated in his aims in Syria by the French army, leaving al-Husseini disillusioned with Arab internationalism. He left Damascus for Jerusalem and decided to explore a more nationalist agenda in Palestine. A riot that broke out between Muslims and Jews during the Nabi Musa procession in Jerusalem in 1920 gave form to al-Husseini's developing ideology.

The Nabi Musa ("Prophet Moses") procession had been an annual event for a thousand years, since the time of Saladin (according to tradition). It always took place during the Easter festival, beginning on the Friday before Great Friday (the Catholic Good Friday) in the Eastern Orthodox Calendar, and involved a procession from Jerusalem to Jericho, to a site where it is believed Moses is buried.

By the time the Ottoman Turks had renovated the buildings along the route of the procession in 1820, the date of the festival was changed to Easter Sunday itself, thus allowing both Christians and Muslims to celebrate on the same day in honor of the prophets of both religions: an ecumenical tradition that it would be difficult to conceive taking place today.

In 1920, however, political tensions in Palestine were already running high. Al-Husseini was in the middle of the controversy, instigating what would become a full-fledged riot between Arabs and Jews that would last for days—with nine killed (both Arabs and Jews) and hundreds more injured. This was al-Husseini's public "coming out" as an anti-Zionist, and he made speeches to that effect accompanied by his uncle, the mayor of Jerusalem. Al-Husseini reiterated that the Balfour Declaration made it impossible for the indigenous populations of Palestine to have the right to self-determination which had already been granted to other populations in the Ottoman Empire. By declaring a National Home for the Jews in Palestine, the British had effectively told the Palestinians that they had no rights over their own territory. In addition, there were Socialist elements among the Zionists in Palestine, and this increased the paranoia being felt by the local population at this perceived Jewish-Communist conspiracy.

The Nabi Musa riots of 1920 introduced the concept of a global plot—aided and abetted by the European powers—to invade and conquer Palestine, to put native Palestinians under first British and then Jewish rule, and eventually to take over the al-Aqsa Mosque: one of the three most important Islamic sites after Mecca and Medina. A few weeks previously, Faisal had been proclaimed King of Syria and claimed Palestine as part of his Kingdom, a step that proved disastrous for Syria was French territory, and the British were still in control of Palestine. In addition, this declaration alarmed the Jewish population for it implied that they would be living under an Arab—and a Muslim—ruler and would lose the protection of the British Mandate. In fact, there was division over this issue even among the Arabs over whether or not they wanted to be under the rule of a Hashemite king. As noted previously, Faisal's ill-timed coronation led to the French-Syrian "war" of 1920 in which he lost his crown, only to reappear a few years later as the King of Iraq.

Haj Amir al-Husseini was blamed by some British diplomats in the region for having fanned the flames of Muslim outrage against the British and the Jews; but they also cited similar inflammatory rhetoric coming from the Zionist leadership, who were nervous that the British were cooperating much more closely with the Arabs than with them. Chaim Weizmann characterized the Nabi Musa riots as a "pogrom" because he felt that some British military officers and diplomats were behind the manipulation of the Arabs, inciting them to riot in order to show the world that the idea of a Jewish homeland in Palestine was hopeless. In the end, the British Palin Commission blamed both sides for the riots, and even cited Bolshevism as having an influence over the Zionist activists (not a charge that could be levelled against the Muslims).

As for al-Husseini, he was convicted *in absentia* for his role in the riot but was pardoned by the British the following year. In March of 1921, he was appointed Mufti of Jerusalem (the title used for high-ranking Islamic scholars) even though he had no academic qualifications for the post; and in 1922, he won the election to the position of Grand Mufti—which means the highest authority on Islamic law in a given country, able to issue fatwas (decrees or edicts) and to issue judgments on particulars of Islamic jurisprudence. He was disqualified for this role in initial balloting, but some Byzantine, behind-the-scenes maneuvering managed to place him ahead of the more moderate Islamic scholars, and he held the title for life.

Al-Husseini's academic career was a major sore point with the *ulama*, the Islamic scholars, of Palestine. He did indeed attend the prestigious Al-Azhar University in Cairo and studied under the controversial Rashid Rida—a Salafi scholar who argued for a return to the fundamental principles of Islam, while at the same time embracing science including the Theory of Evolution—but he never finished his studies or received a degree. Instead, he enlisted in the Ottoman army during the First World War and when that war was over flirted with the idea of pan-Arabism under Faisal until that experiment failed at the Battle of Maysalun.

By all accounts, al-Husseini was a charismatic speaker and orator who identified the enemies of Islam as modernization and Westernization. The Jews were carriers of modern thinking and ideas—including, of course, Bolshevism—and their very presence in Palestine was the cause of moral decay and decadence.

By the middle of the 1920s, al-Husseini's political platform was becoming more concretized, even as England's was descending into confusion. Although the Balfour Declaration, which provided the framework for a Jewish National Home in Palestine, was a British creation, many Britons were hostile to the idea including many military men and diplomats on the ground. As the Jews began creating a self-defence force in Palestine known as the Haganah the British were understandably unsympathetic, even though the Nabi Musa riots had shown that the British were either incapable of defending Jewish life and property, or were more or less completely disinterested in doing so. After the riots had ended, a community of local sheikhs actually issued a proclamation repudiating the violence against the Jews, but the die had been cast. A new narrative was about to be born, and it became the Grand Unified Theory of Islamist terrorism: anti-Zionism became equivalent to anti-Semitism; the Jews had created Bolshevism as a mechanism for dividing and conquering all other races; they were aided and abetted in this program by the European powers—the "Crusaders"—who cooperated with the Jews in order to enslave the Muslims; and that the only way to defend Arab, i.e. Muslim, territories against the invaders was to proclaim a jihad. Since the Arabs did not have the same access to money and military equipment as the Crusaders and the Jews, the jihad would have to be waged "by any means necessary." This included the regimen suggested by Oppenheim[16] of individual assassinations, independent bands of jihadists, and guerrilla warfare that included targeting civilian populations. Once Jews were identified as the enemy of Islam, the designation of enemy combatant could be extended to include not only able-bodied men who carried arms and fought in pitched battles, but anyone who was Jewish: women, children, and all those previously considered non-combatants.

This was not a war of armies against armies; that paradigm had lost the Axis Powers the First World War. This would be instead a war of civilians against civilians, of religion against religion, of ethnicity against ethnicity. This new paradigm would become enshrined in the concept of "total war," a phrase coined by former German General Erich Ludendorf (1865–1937) to designate a state in which all the resources of a nation had to be mobilized in the war effort. When two such states are at war, then it is inevitable that civilian populations on both sides would be slaughtered in an effort of each side to deprive the other of the raw material of conflict—to destroy logistical support, industry, agriculture and most of all every human being who could grow food, make ammunition, or fire a weapon. To Ludendorf, war was the actual, permanent state of human activity:

---

16 Indeed, Oppenheim and al-Husseini were friends and colleagues. See, for instance, McMeekin (2010), p. 360. This was a relationship that lasted throughout the Second World War and is a link in the chain of the Kaiser's "global jihad" in 1914 and al-Husseini's revolt against the British beginning ten years later.

intervals of peace only served to replenish the human and material stocks of nations in preparation for the next war.

Ludendorf had taken part in Hitler's failed Beer Hall Putsch in 1923, and once Hitler had come to power in Germany he openly courted Ludendorf's approval and support; but by this time, the old general had become something of a mystic who believed the world's problems had been created by Jews, Christians, and Freemasons (in other words, a veritable template for al-Husseini's political theory as well as for the Nazi Party itself). Nevertheless, Ludendorf's "total war" had become the jihadist's "holy war."

As the decade of the 1920s progressed, the situation in Palestine became worse. Tensions between the Palestinians and the new Jewish immigrants were transformed into open hostility resulting in several massacres and pitched battles. The British appeared increasingly helpless to manage the territory, and with every new conflict al-Husseini's reputation grew. He became the face of Palestinian resistance against the British mandate and against Jewish immigration. In his position as Grand Mufti, he was also the supreme religious authority among the Muslims of Palestine. Like his idol, Hitler, al-Husseini would combine political goals and anti-Western ideology with a call to religious conviction and spiritual necessity. It would prove to be an irresistible combination.

The situation in Europe was growing more dangerous for Jews by the hour. Hitler's Beer Hall Putsch had taken place in Germany in 1923, and his anti-Semitic newspaper *Der Stürmer* began publication that year. Arrested by the authorities, but given only a slap on the wrist for what was, after all, high treason Hitler spent 1923–1925 in prison writing the memoir that would become *Mein Kampf*. During that time a wave of pogroms in Poland in 1924 resulted in an overwhelming number of refugees seeking sanctuary in Palestine, to the tune of more than 65,000, and a violent reaction by Palestinians to this new influx. That same year Arabs attacked Jewish communities and confronted not the British army but the Haganah. When the dust cleared more than 100 each of Jews and Arabs were dead and many others wounded.

Things only got worse as the global economic crisis deepened. The Jewish Agency decided to include non-Zionists in its ranks in order to raise more funds for the ongoing settlement project. This development deepened Palestinian fears that a European-Jewish cabal was being created to disenfranchise the considerably poorer Arabs in the region. The combination of tens of thousands of new European Jewish immigrants, plus an undisclosed amount of money to back them up, indicated to Arab leaders like al-Husseini that the Jews had a long-range plan that would inevitably include seizure of the holy places of Islam and the forced evacuation of all Arabs from Palestine.

In 1929 violence erupted as Arab gangs attacked Jewish settlements near Jerusalem in a wildfire campaign which expanded to include Hebron, Safed, and the Gaza Strip. The riots went on for six long days and saw the death once again of more than one hundred Jews and many wounded. It should be noted that the British Army did not intervene until nearly a full week of violence had taken place.

A commission that was named to discover the reasons for this outbreak of violence in the Holy Land came to the conclusion that ambiguous promises by the British Government to both Arabs and Jews had contributed to the current state of affairs. The Shaw Commission, as it was known, recommended that some clarity be interjected into the situation and issues like land tenure and immigration be reviewed in order to forestall further violence.

However, by 1930, the release of yet another British document on Palestine—the Passfield White Paper—insisted that England's promises to the Arab leaders were sufficiently important that to ignore them in favor of Jewish settlement and the National Home project would be inadvisable. It seemed as if the government was about ready to overturn the Balfour Declaration, and the British Prime Minister found himself forced to write a letter to Chaim Weizmann saying, essentially, that the Declaration still stood and Britain's commitment to the establishment of a National Home for the Jews was unswerving.

The seesaw effect of all these mixed signals was demoralizing to both Jews and Arabs. There was no clear-cut and unequivocal position being taken on the plan for a Jewish homeland in Palestine, but by the 1930s it seemed to many like a fait accompli. More than 160,000 Jews had already settled in Palestine by this time, and although the Arab population was greater (more than eighty percent of the total population of 1,035,000), the Jewish presence was more powerful and determined. They had the backing of European governments and European funds.

But in 1933, Adolf Hitler was proclaimed Chancellor of Germany.

And by 1935, the Nuremberg Laws were passed which denied Germany's Jews the rights of citizenship.

No matter who was considered right or legally or morally justified in their position concerning Palestine and the putative Jewish Homeland, by 1935 the stakes had risen to an astonishing degree. The Jews now were on the verge of losing everything they had in Europe, including even their lives.

CHAPTER THREE

ZEITGEIST

The forces of life and blood exist and will be effective. The very state that today charges us with crimes against humanity, the United States of America, ought to listen with particular attentiveness to the theories of race and heredity if it wishes to preserve its power. Fourteen million Negroes and mulattos, four to five million Jews, the Japanese in the west, and the rest, are more than America can carry without endangering the heritage of her pioneers. But if the present generation fails to do something to elude the fate of some day having twenty-five million Negroes and mulattos, ten million Jews and half-Jews in America, then a later generation will certainly be harsh in its judgement. The Americans will have to decide whether they want a white America or whether they want to make the choice of their President ever more a question of additional concessions toward mulattoisation. In the latter case, the United States of America, in a few centuries, will go the way of Greece and Rome; and the Catholic Church, which even today has black bishops, will be the pacemaker. The day will come when the grandchildren of the present generation will be ashamed of the fact that we have been accused as criminals for having harboured a most noble thought, simply because of its deterioration in times of war through unworthy orders.
—Alfred Rosenberg[17]

It would be wrong to believe that the events of the 1930s in Germany and Palestine went somehow unnoticed by the rest of the world; it would be equally wrong to believe that they were anomalies, that they represented some kind of idiosyncratic ideologies and

---

17 Alfred Rosenberg, *Memoirs*, written in prison in 1946 before being sentenced to death in the Nuremberg Trials for crimes against humanity. On https://archive.org/details/NoneRosenbergMemoirs, accessed on June 6, 2014.

cultural phenomena that were native to other peoples in strange lands.

In fact, many Americans were on intimate terms with what was happening overseas and they took sides according to their own beliefs, many of which were religious as well as political, cultural as well as ideological. The same was true of individuals and groups in Hungary, Romania, Ukraine, France, Spain, Portugal, the Netherlands, and other countries in Europe, as well as in Latin America, South Africa, and Asia. Nazism became a global phenomenon even as it resisted any attempts at being "internationalized" like Communism or Socialism. It was, first and foremost, a "white" ideology and those in foreign countries who self-identified as coming from white European stock—even if they were living in Latin America, South Africa or Asia—were part of the Nazi "demographic." The mistake some historians make in categorizing Nazism as a purely German (or German-Austrian) affair are missing a vital aspect of why and how it was able to survive the war as an ideology and as a political action network in regions as remote from Germany as Argentina and Paraguay, South Africa and Indonesia.

Chicago and New York.

As we saw in Chapter One, there was a vocal minority of Americans on the extreme right who supported Hitler's goals and who harbored a deep suspicion and hatred of Jews and a pronounced antipathy towards Russia and Communism. With the outbreak of World War Two, many of these individuals and groups either went underground or affirmed their allegiance to the United States of America and enlisted in the war effort, patriotism thus outweighing ideology, at least in the short term. Before December 7, 1941 however, the presence in the United States of a cohesive network of Nazi agents aided and abetted by German government officials was attracting considerable attention from the FBI as well as the media. As in the rest of the world—especially Europe but also including Latin America—many people believed that anyone who had a strong opinion against Nazism or Fascism had to be a Communist or a Communist sympathizer, what was known as a "fellow traveler." Books and articles that attacked Nazism often bore imprints of publishing companies that were known fronts for socialist groups in the United States. Outspoken opponents of the Nazis were labeled "Jews" or "Communists" and often both. As we have seen, even President Franklin D. Roosevelt was not immune from these charges, and he was elected four times.

In addition, antipathy towards Roman Catholicism was also at an all-time high. It is perhaps not as well known, but the Nazis had passed laws discriminating against Catholics as well as Jews, forbidding Catholics to hold political office or to function as professors in universities, etc. The Nazis had lumped Jews and Catholics together, for some of the same reasons: Catholics represented a religion whose members had allegiance to the Pope in Rome and this was a challenge to Nazi supremacy, just as the perceived unassimilatability of the Jews was a challenge. Both the Jews and the Church were believed to have hidden assets of considerable wealth. And the Church's origins were, of course, in the same books of the Bible as the Jews: the Tanach.

To some, this should have meant that the Church would form an allegiance with European Jewry since they had a common enemy. In actuality, although the Church hierarchy understood that Nazism represented a religious threat—as it was not a political party per se but a well-organized and well-armed cult that sought to replace all religion in the Reich with Party ritual and ideology—the Church knew that if it formed too close an association with the Jews it was in danger of inviting the same consequences: isolation leading to internment and eventual extermination.

Thus, while the Church objected most strongly to Nazism on theological grounds (and to Communism in Russia and Fascism in Italy) it did little on a practical level to oppose the Reich. Some apologists have said that this was a pragmatic decision designed to preserve the Church and especially those Catholics living in Germany, Austria, and the countries subsumed under the Reich. However, in light of the considerable assistance given to the Nazis after the war by the Church, it becomes increasingly difficult to accept this argument at face value.

Eugenio Pacelli (the future Pope Pius XII) was a Papal nuncio in Germany at the end of the First World War and remained in Germany for a decade after. He witnessed first-hand what had happened when Communists tried to take over the country and had sympathies with the Germans who wanted to oppose Communism in any form. At the same time, he was uncomfortable with the anti-Semitism being openly and aggressively promoted in Germany long before the Nazis came to power, and increasingly so once Hitler became Chancellor. He tried to formulate a Church policy that involved invoking "charity" (*caritas*) as a universal principle: i.e., that all people (regardless of race and religion) deserved the benefit of Catholic charity, that God's peace was not reserved for one race or one nation alone but for all human beings. This was an affront to German nationalism, of course, and to the entire philosophical edifice (if such it might be called) of Nazism.

Ironically, it would be this principle of universal charity that the Church would invoke again when it came time to rescue Nazi fugitives after the war. *Caritas* was the name of the umbrella organization run by Pacelli and supervised by Cardinal Montini (the future Pope Paul VI) to help the Nazis escape.

In the United States, the Church was in a difficult position as well. While many bishops and other clergy were opposed to Nazism, there were those—like Father Coughlin—who supported Nazism and who promoted such flagrant political hoaxes as *The Protocols of the Learned Elders of Zion* as if it were a real blueprint for global domination by the Jews.

This was the spirit of the times, the *zeitgeist* that haunted not only America but the world at large. Once Hitler was installed as Chancellor of Germany in January 1933, and later proclaimed the Third Reich, German embassies and consulates around the world had their ambassadors and consuls replaced by those loyal to the Nazi Party. That meant that Hitler's *ideology* (not only his government) now had a global presence; and the Party went to great lengths to ensure that its message was being promoted aggressively around the world even as its agents—both overt and covert—began making contacts and issuing orders to operatives in the media, in political office, in the military, and in every aspect of daily life. Key figures in industry, politics and culture were identified as being sympathetic to Hitler's aims and cultivated accordingly. The goal was not only to promote the Nazi ideology abroad and win converts. There were other missions and they were often more sinister: such as identifying and protecting sources of much-needed war materiel; or developing intelligence networks in foreign countries targeting the United States (from Mexico, for instance, which was a hotbed of Nazi intrigues) and Latin America (from bases in Chile and Argentina); and for developing resources for refueling and resupplying U-boats (in Colombia and in Southeast Asia).

The Reich's relationship with Franco's Spain and Salazar's *Estado Novo* regime in Portugal might have been problematic at times but they were all essentially on the same page. Nationalist and Catholic, both Franco and Salazar were not only sympathetic to Hitler's aims but—especially in Franco's case—willing to lend quiet logistical support to the Reich. Franco supplied refueling bases for the German Navy's submarines, and when the war was in its final year, allowed the shipment and transshipment of Nazi gold and artwork to and through Spain to get them out of the hands of the Allies. Portugal provided safe haven for Nazi gold, and when the war was over more than forty tons of it was reported to have made its way by U-boat to the Portuguese colony of Macau—from which half made its way to China and the other half to Indonesia.

Thus the Nazi movement clearly was not restricted to the Greater German Reich but extended in one form or another around the world. This is an important factor to address, for it means that Nazism was not simply another political party or ideological movement that would—sooner or later—be consigned to the dustbin of history. Nazism was—and still is—a living ideology that manages to subsume so many different groups, economies, and even spiritualities for the very reason that it remains non-specific and often vague in an intellectual sense, but clearly recognizable in an emotional and psychological context. We know what the Nazis were against: Jews, Communism, Freemasonry, miscegenation, "mongrel races," "useless eaters," and Christianity (among other things). What the Nazis were *for* is rather more difficult to define. The information is certainly there, but it has been overshadowed so completely by the war and by its program of genocide, that it has become convenient to characterize Nazism simply as an ideology of hate. There is more to Nazism—and we ignore the other dimensions of the Party, its leadership, its organizing principles, and its agenda at our peril.

Race and Politics

By the time the Nuremberg Laws were enacted in 1935, Germany already knew that world opinion would not have a negative impact on its domestic policy or impair its ability to wage war. The voyage of the *MS St Louis* from Hamburg to Havana, Cuba in 1939 illustrates the confidence given to Hitler and the Party by the rest of the world: first Cuba and then the United States itself refused entry to the more than nine hundred Jews aboard the ship, forcing it back to Germany and certain death for more than two hundred of its Jewish passengers in the concentration camps.[18] This highly-publicized event seemed to give an American seal of approval to what would become known as the Holocaust.

One of the academic sponsors of this racial program was a well-known and well-respected anthropologist and chairperson of the Vienna Anthropological Society, Dr. Helen Pöch. Documents have come into the author's possession demonstrating just how influential Dr. Helen Pöch's views were on deciding who was, and who was not, a Jew. Working for the Orwellian-nomenclatured Race and Resettlement Office of the Reich, Helen Pöch interviewed subjects and performed questionable tests to determine the degree of "Jewishness" in an individual, and whether or not they qualified as Jews or as German citizens: a decision that had, of course, enormous implications. It was this same Helen Pöch who, it is believed, eventually emigrated from her native Austria in 1952 to Sukarno's Indonesia along with her husband, Dr. Georg Anton Pöch, the chief medical officer of the Reich's Salzburg Gau.

With the stereotypical German passion for legality and precision, the Reich's various programs involving citizenship, property, and eventually genocide required a sound academic and scientific basis. Institutes and agencies sprang up throughout the Reich's bureaucracy to satisfy this need to prove to the world (and to them-

---

18 Thomas, Gordon and Witts, Max Morgan (1974). *Voyage of the Damned.* Konecky & Konecky.

selves) that the measures they were taking were decided upon using the same critical and rational approach for which Germany had always been famous. Yet, this desire to find justification for their actions—in effect, putting the cart before the horse—resulted in a caricature of science and law. It would have made a rousing plot for a comic opera had the consequences not been so horrendous, leading to a loss of life and destruction of cultures that is still, at this remove, almost impossible to contemplate.

The same ideology was at work abroad. While many countries looked to Germany as a role model for their eugenics programs, their incorporation of bad science into government procedures and laws, the United States had its own version to offer. While many American eugenicists admired what Germany was doing to rid their country of the incurably ill and the mentally- and physically-handicapped, and in the forced segregation and sterilization of their people, the United States itself was suffering a collective schizophrenic breakdown over the same issues.

The Invisible Reich

The 1920s saw a tremendous rise in popularity of the Ku Klux Klan, that quintessential racist movement characterized by white-robed night riders, burning crosses, and lynchings. While the Klan is usually identified with anti-Black racism, they were equally anti-Semitic—and a series of bombings of synagogues in the 1960s was evidence of this—as well as being anti-Catholic, anti-Asian, etc. They ran candidates for public office even as they were terrorizing the countryside.

The first Ku Klux Klan came of age in the Reconstruction Era after the end of the Civil War. It was another of the political movements based upon nostalgia for a former age, and its members wanted to turn back the clock to the antebellum period when African-Americans were slaves and knew their place. As Hitler did in Germany when it came to the Jews, so did the Klan when it came to Blacks: they were the scapegoat for the loss of a war, a race that first had to be segregated from "white" people and then deported or, barring that, eliminated entirely from the planet.

The second incarnation of the Klan took place around 1921, with its nativist demands for a return to conservative, white American principles, and an attack on "Popism" (i.e., Roman Catholicism) and Jewry, as well as on Communism and immigration. Italians, Irish, and Eastern European immigrants were targets of Klan opprobrium in the 1920s. Klansmen sought to return America to its prelapsarian age when only white, Anglo-Saxon Protestants were considered Americans. In 1920, an estimated four million Americans had joined the Klan. By 1924, that number had jumped to six million, or about five percent of the total population of 114 million. Coincidentally, 1924 was the year the Immigration Act was signed which severely limited immigration to the United States and especially barred Asian immigrants. New immigrants were permitted from Western Europe and Great Britain, but immigrants from Southern and Eastern Europe were restricted. According to the Office of the Historian of the United States, when it came to what was known as the Gentlemen's Agreement[19] between Japan and the United States concerning immigration, an Agreement that was now abrogated:

> ... it appeared that the U.S. Congress had decided that preserving the racial composition of the country was more important than promoting good ties with the Japanese empire.[20]

It seemed that at least part of the program of the Ku Klux Klan had been achieved: by denying entry to Southern and Eastern European immigrants there was an effective ban on Catholics and Jews. A decline in Klan membership by 1930—due to scandals and internal disagreements—did not alter the general mood of anti-Semitism and racism in the country. Instead, other outlets were discovered

---

19 The Gentlemen's Agreement was an informal agreement between the United States and Japan that the United States would not restrict Japanese immigration, but that Japan would not permit further Japanese to emigrate to the United States. The Agreement was undertaken in 1907 but was never ratified by Congress.

20 https://history.state.gov/milestones/1921-1936/immigration-act (accessed on May 2, 2014)

that seemed more inclusive of new immigrants—Catholics, and Northern whites—and the Nazi phenomenon provided them.

At that time, Nazi movements began sprouting all over the country in response to the New Deal of the Roosevelt administration. Both the American Nazi and the Klan movements wanted America to go back to the way it was before the Great Depression, before the First World War, to a time that never really existed the way they thought it did: a time before the advent of Communist states like the Soviet Union; a time before blacks and Jews could be considered equal citizens of the nation. Like many of today's extreme right protestors, the Nazis and Klansmen of the 1920s and 1930s wanted to "take their country back," in this case—and possibly in the present case also—"back" meant "back in time."

In the nineteenth century the Ku Klux Klan was known as the Invisible Empire, the *Unsichtbare Reich* if you will, to Germany's later *Dritte Reich* or *Tausendjährige Reich*. It was a terror organization whose members met in disguise and who murdered people in the middle of the night, torching their homes or hanging family members from trees in very visible locations. Later, in the third manifestation of the Klan in post-World War Two America, groups in the loosely-organized Klan became responsible for bombings and assassinations, largely targeted at African-Americans, but extended to include Jews, synagogues, and those white Americans who were involved in the Freedom Rider movement and other Civil Rights groups.

While the violence and the weird torchlight meetings in the middle of the night of robed and masked Klansmen may have seemed almost comic, if nonetheless lethal, it was a manifestation of racism gone amok. There were, however, other, subtler forms of racism abroad in America at the same time that the Klan and the Nazi movements were gathering force. One was the grossly unethical Tuskegee Syphilis program.

Although word of its existence did not come to light until a whistleblower appeared on the scene in 1972, the Tuskegee Syphilis Experiment was one example of the type of endemic racism that could be found in scientific and academic circles in the United States (and which was openly practiced in Nazi Germany). It ran from1932 until it was exposed in 1972. For forty years, black men from poor, sharecropper backgrounds were used as guinea pigs in a pointless series of experiments, ostensibly designed to monitor the evolution of the disease. The men were not told they had syphilis, and they were not given treatment for it. (Penicillin did not become available until the 1940s and therefore could not have been used to treat the disease in the 1930s; however, its availability and its use to treat syphilis from about 1943 until the end of the experiment in 1972 did not affect the progress of the experiment. Penicillin has enjoyed widespread use in the treatment of the disease since 1947.) Men with syphilis were allowed to unwittingly infect their sexual partners, and babies were born with syphilis as a result of these unions.

The rationale behind the study was the idea that men of African-American origin were more promiscuous than men of other races and willingly engaged in risky sexual behavior. In other words, a value judgement was made by the American medical establishment (and in the absence of any kind of evidence) that the presumed risky behavior of African-Americans made it permissible to use them as laboratory material: petri dishes for the cultivation of syphilis.

The men were told that they were being treated for something called "bad blood," a generic term covering a wide range of symptoms. There were 399 men in the study, of which 28 had died of the disease by 1972. Another 100 died of complications due to the illness. These numbers do not include 40 wives who were infected by their husbands in the study, and nearly 20 children who contracted syphilis in the womb. Since the experiment focused only on African-American men, the others were ignored.

This is a single example of the type of race-based decision-making that was prevalent in America in the same period that Nazism was on the rise in Germany. Laws against the marriage of whites and blacks (and in some cases with other races, including Native Americans, Native Hawaiians, Asians, and in some states specifically against Filipinos) were on the books in forty-one states. Such laws were repealed in eleven states by 1887; but remained in many other states until the final Supreme Court decision finding miscegenation laws illegal in 1967. Add to this the academic fad of eugenics, which had attracted a wide audience among non-scientists including industrialists and politicians, and you had all of the elements necessary for a government-sponsored control of sexuality, reproductive rights, and other aspects of population control, including forbidding sexual reproduction involving those the medical or the legal profession declared "unfit," a mindset paralleling that of the Third Reich.

At the heart of the eugenics debate was the idea so dear to the bureaucrats and ideologues of the Third Reich—that humanity was on the path of evolution as described in the works of Darwin and others since then, and that human beings should do what they could to contribute to evolution in a positive way, thus hastening the next step in the evolutionary chain, the creation of the "New Man." It provided justification for the creation of euthanasia programs in the Reich, which was the first phase of what would become known as the Holocaust.

In this phase, those whom the Nazis determined were "useless eaters" were slated for death. First, they had to be sterilized to ensure that they would not reproduce. Various chemical agents were used in these programs, as well as radiation and castration, all involuntary. These "useless eaters" included the physically and mentally infirm, or those the Nazis deemed were infirm. The aged were also considered eligible for "processing." It is important to point out that these individuals were Germans, by and large. This was not a racial program, but one designed to ensure that future generations of Germans would not carry genetic material deemed weak or deleterious to German evolution. Thus, the first victims of Nazi medical and scientific policies were not Jews or Gypsies or Communists, but Germans themselves.

Once the "useless eaters" or "life unworthy of life" (*Lebensunwertes Lebens*) were purged from the system so that only healthy Germans remained, the force of the Reich was turned on other undesirables. Communists were arrested and sent to the camps created for political prisoners. Some religious denominations were singled out as well, such as the Jehova's Witnesses. Freemasons were on the list, and other members of secret societies or esoteric organizations were rounded up in the aftermath of Rudolf Hess's flight to England in 1940. Homosexuals were arrested and thrown into prison camps as well, and a project undertaken to exterminate the entire Roma ("Gypsy") population (which led to the decimation of the Roma and Sinti to the extent that the percentage of their people killed in the genocide can be considered even greater than that of the Jews).[21] The object was purification: purification of Germany's bloodlines, its spirituality, its sexuality, its politics, and its economics.

Lebensborn units were created to enable only the best and the brightest of the German military and political elite to father children on women especially selected for their racial purity and fertility. These were not marriages or actual romantic relationships; the Lebensborn units were basically stud farms to increase the German population through selective breeding. It was another iteration of the basic eugenics philosophy to weed out the bad seed and propagate the good or desirable seed. It was the other side of the genocide coin.

This focus on purity could be seen as a desire to return to a more primitive time—*in illo tempore*—when the world was pristine. That this time probably never existed did not occur (or was not acceptable) to those promoting this "return to nature" and "return to our roots" philosophy. Legends of ancient Greece and Rome were conflated with legends concerning Atlantis and Thule: the latter the presumed ancient homeland of the Aryans. With the coming of Western civilization—according to this theory—much of humanity's basic goodness and inherent physical and psychic powers were lost, a kind of Samson and Delilah moment when the virile and pure Samson is shorn of his hair and thus loses his potency and strength to the Levantine, Semitic seductress. Psychologically, this may be understood as the desire to return to childhood—to a pre-pubescent state before the onset of sexual awakening—when a child can still believe in magic and wonder, in invisible beings, in the

---

21 It should be noted that the Nazi puppet regime in Croatia—the Ustase— also willingly participated in the arrest and murder of the Gypsy populations in that country, with many Roma and Sinti facing their death at the Jasenovac Concentration Camp run by Franciscan clergy.

potential power to change the world—in short, a time when the child is the center of the universe and all things come into being through a child's wishes and dreams. A child is thought of as pure in this state—at least, until the time of Freud who fled Nazi Germany when the "Jewish" field of psychology was condemned by the Reich—and a return to purity is a return to childhood and its fantasies.

It is also an implicit acknowledgment of failure. This yearning for a return to some other state in the distant past indicates an incapability of dealing with present-day issues in any other way. It represents a desire to wipe the slate clean and start over, which may be attractive as a fantasy but not practicable in life. In Weimar Germany, the trauma of having lost the first World War and surrendering valuable territory, assets, and prestige to the victorious allies—coupled with the intensity of the economic collapse of 1929—made everyone yearn for a better time. There seemed to be no way to grapple with the severe problems facing the nation, and perhaps some of the attraction that Hitler and the Nazi Party had for the German people was the idea that they would fight that war all over again and this time be the victors. It was either that, or find a more positive—albeit more demanding and time-consuming—way to confront the various issues facing them, accepting responsibility for the war, finding ways to increase their economic status, negotiating better contracts and loans with other governments, and all the consequent maturity of a nation those measures would imply.

Germany had been arguably the most intellectually and culturally sophisticated Western country in the world at the time, having contributed immortal works of literature, music, philosophy, and science. It is a measure of the psychological trauma the country experienced that the only way this creative and energetic people could find to improve its state in the world was to murder or enslave as many of the world's inhabitants as possible. In the author's own conversations with prominent Nazis in the 1970s and 1980s, this point was raised again and again: if the Germans were the people who produced Bach, Beethoven, Brahms, Wagner, Goethe, Heine, Rilke, Hegel, and Kant, why was their only solution to their problems the "caveman" solution of war and mass murder? There was never an answer to this question, and often the person being interviewed would simply go silent, or in some cases begin extolling the virtues of a Spartan approach to life, of continuous war being the only way a race could survive and thrive. *In illo tempore.* This lack of imagination and incapability of Nazi theorists when it came to problem-solving has been one of the most astonishing aspects of the movement in general; and it is this lack of imagination, coupled with violent fantasies of revenge and purification wrapped in spiritual justifications, that informs what I have been calling the Hitler "legacy."

If Germany had been defeated in the First World War then it wasn't Germany's fault, according to the Nazi idea. They had been betrayed from within, by the Jews, the Freemasons, the bankers, and the Communists. Eradicate those elements from German society and the nation would inevitably improve. The German people would return to that golden age when there were only Germans within its borders: no Jews, no immigrants of any kind except perhaps as slave labor. No alien religions, or foreign—i.e., decadent—culture. It was the era of the Germanic tribes defeating the Roman legions at the Battle of Teutoburg Forest in the first century CE: pagan warriors successfully defending their territory against the global reach of the Caesars. This idea became a powerful meme during the Third Reich. Esoteric groups such as the *Armanenschaft* (named after Arminius, the commander of the German forces against the Romans) and the *Germanenorden* were founded before the First World War by such occult theorists and anti-Semites as Guido von List and his followers. They set the stage for wild theorizing about Germany's "origins" and helped to instigate a back-to-nature movement known as the *Wandervogel*, founded in 1901 and representing nationalist ideals and Teutonic romanticism. This movement received the enthusiastic support of German and Austrian youth in the years following Germany's defeat in World War One.

I have written elsewhere about the role occult ideas and organizations had in the formation of the Nazi Party, Nazi ideology, and specifically on the activities of the SS,[22] so I will not belabor

---

22 Levenda, *Unholy Alliance*, Continuum, New York, 2002.

the point here. What I have said about the Nazi Party not being a political party the way most of us would understand it, but a cult, still remains the best characterization of the Nazi phenomenon that I can find. It also goes a long way toward helping us to understand how it could have survived the way it did, and still influences the ideas and actions of peoples and political leaders around the world. It also helps us to realize that the growth of new Nazi movements in Europe is a validation of this basic premise. Nazism began as a cult, and survived as a cult. As an idea it is vague enough to attract a collection of philosophies and political movements around it, each seeing in the Nazi archetype a version of their own belief system; as a cult, it has the power to communicate viscerally to its followers through an elaborate symbol system, ranging from the omnipresent swastika to the death's head insignia and black uniforms of the SS. Nazism is about the will to power, merciless and proud in its extremism and cold-bloodedness; its success lies in its ability to take the superman concept found in the works of Nietzsche, and build an organizational and operational structure around it that includes: a political apparatus, race science, fringe archaeological and anthropological theories and practices, euthanasia, and a complete cultural identity composed of works of art, music, and literature that are acceptable and consistent with the Nazi *Weltanschauung*. The first use of the word "holocaust" in reference to Nazism did not refer to the crematoria and the death camps, but to the burning of prohibited books. Purity of ideas. Purity of art.

The difference between the overt excesses of Nazi Germany and the subtler, institutionalized racism in the United States was due to the fact that in Germany, the Nazi Party was in power. In the United States, there were Nazi groups, pro-Nazi groups, and Nazi sympathies, but the man at the top of the political pyramid was a president who was also a Democrat. Hitler came to power in Germany through a series of political machinations; Roosevelt came to power—and stayed in power for the rest of his life—through the ballot box. The racism and anti-Semitism of a large segment of the American population was no secret to Roosevelt, or to anyone else in America at the time.

After all, it was an age of new media.

Flowers of Evil

The extreme right had been ignoring a potential ally in the war against Jews and Communists, and it was the Catholic Church. While the white extremism of the Klan targeted Catholics as well as immigrants from predominantly Catholic countries such as Ireland and Italy, the Nazis had formed an uneasy alliance with the Vatican. Many ultra-nationalists of the time—such as Franco in Spain and, later, Peron in Argentina—were also observing Catholics who saw in the Church a powerful ally against the rising tide of Communism from the East. Hitler himself had been born a Catholic, as were many of the Party's leadership.

In Europe, clergymen such as Bishop Alois Hudal of Austria began as critics of Nazism as a rival cult. But as the world edged closer to war, such men became outspoken Nazis and figured prominently in the efforts to rescue as many Nazi war criminals as possible and get them safely to sanctuaries in Latin America and the Middle East. While the role of Pope Pius XII during the Holocaust has been hotly debated, what is not questioned is the fact that many Roman Catholic clergy were sympathetic to the vigorous anti-Communism of the Nazi Party and saw in its unequivocal opposition to the Soviet Union the best hope for the survival of Christianity. While some of these clergy were uncomfortable with the Party's anti-Semitism, the Jews could be considered collateral damage in the larger struggle against atheistic Communism.

One of these outspoken Catholic Nazis was Father Charles Coughlin (already mentioned) whose parish in the Royal Oaks suburb of Detroit was known as the Shrine of the Little Flower. It was Coughlin (and Catholic clergy like him) who bridged the gap between the Irish, Italian, and Eastern European Catholic immigrants, and the white supremacist extremists of the Ku Klux Klan. His political agenda was virtually identical to that of the Nazi Party and the pro-Nazi organizations in the United States, including their anti-Semitism. He was also on intimate terms with American industrialists and politicians who saw in his celebrity a way to validate their own pro-Nazi sentiments.

In November of 1933, in the first year of his presidency, Franklin D. Roosevelt decided it was finally time for America to recognize the government of the Soviet Union. The USA had been the last holdout among the leading nations of the world by refusing recognition of the regime that had taken power in Russia in 1917. His rapprochement with the Soviets infuriated many on the right who saw Roosevelt as a Communist-sympathizer or a closet Communist himself. One of the conditions of the recognition was that the Soviets would cease providing support for the American Communist Party, a promise they never kept.

That same year the Reichstag Fire gave Hitler the excuse he needed to demand dictatorial powers in order to protect Germany from what was believed to be the Communist terrorists who had set the blaze. In March of 1933 he was given extra-constitutional powers by the Reichstag, and upon the death of President Hindenburg in 1934, Hitler assumed full power over the German Reich. The following year, the Nuremberg Laws were enacted which robbed German Jews of citizenship in the Reich. With that, the road to the concentration camps was paved.

It was in this atmosphere that personalities like Father Coughlin, and organizations like the German-American Bund, William Pelley's Silver Legion, and others of similar ideological provenance could thrive. If it had only been a question of freedom of speech and freedom of assembly—rights guaranteed by the Bill of Rights to the American Constitution—then this episode might have been forgotten once the war began. As it was, however, these groups actively plotted the overthrow of the American government. It is doubtful that their plots would have proceeded very far, but violence had been used, intelligence networks created, and assassination plots advanced. Weapons caches were uncovered, and perpetrators were sent to prison for sedition. An environment had been created in the United States that was conducive to paranoia, suspicion, and conspiracy theory; combine this with racist scapegoating by the Klan and the Bund (and its fellow travelers) and you had a formula for rebellion that was analogous to—if not identical with—that obtained in the Reich.

In Father Coughlin's case, it was an organization he created called the Christian Front. Coughlin had long been promoting Nazi ideas—some of them cribbed from the newspaper owned by his friend, Henry Ford, the *Dearborn Independent*. It published a series of articles by Ford on the dangers of international Jewry—since collected and published as a book, *The International Jew*—and quoting from *The Protocols of the Learned Elders of Zion* as well as Nazi apologist Alfred Rosenberg's *The Myth of the Twentieth Century* (a book that was on the Catholic Church's *Index* of forbidden books). Coughlin's own newspaper, *Social Justice*, carried excerpts of both the *Protocols* and Rosenberg's writings. It was Rosenberg, after all, who brought the *Protocols* to the attention of Adolf Hitler in the early days of the Nazi Party. (In fact, Rosenberg joined the Party months before Hitler did.)

Rosenberg's magnum opus is considered by many to be virtually unreadable and Rosenberg himself, in his *Memoirs* written in prison awaiting the Nuremberg Trial verdict that would condemn him to death, admits that it could have used a rewrite. Basically, it's theme is that race determines culture determines religion, with its corollary that a religion that has no connection with a specific race is alien to it. In this way, Rosenberg felt that both Christianity and Judaism were alien religions to the German people: faiths that were grafted onto the Germans like monstrous hybrids, stunting their spiritual and political growth and making them vulnerable to the machinations of other races, other political agendas. Christianity and Judaism were "Oriental" faiths that had no place in the "Aryan" culture of northern Europe, and their influence had led to the catastrophe of the First World War and its aftermath. To Rosenberg, spirituality was the key to a German revival. This required a major overhaul of German culture to eradicate that which was alien, weak, and decadent in its spirituality, its art, music and literature, and its racial composition. As the quotation from his *Memoir* that is at the beginning of this chapter states, Rosenberg advised America that it faced the same dangers if it allowed its racial composition to become "mulatto-ized."

Hitler had placed such confidence in the young Nazi of Baltic origins that he designated Rosenberg as leader of the movement while the Führer was in Landsberg Prison due to his involvement in the Beer Hall Putsch of 1923. This acknowledgement of his contribution to Nazi ideology is important when we realize that Father Coughlin felt the same way, and made copies of Rosenberg's *Myth of the Twentieth Century* available at the bookstand at his Shrine of the Little Flower in Michigan—even though it had been banned by the Church itself.

Coughlin's Christian Front was founded to advertise and promote these ideas in a very practical way. It was a Nazi movement designed to be more American in character than the German-American Bund, and more traditionally Catholic than William Pelley's Silver Legion (which was an amalgam of racial politics, anti-Semitism, and esoteric lore). It would appeal to the large numbers of Irish Catholics who had come to America in the decades before the First World War, at a time when Irish nationalism was in full flower against the British Empire (thus making common cause with other anti-British movements such as al-Husseini's political action groups in Palestine, and anti-colonialist parties in India, to name a few). This "strange bedfellows" coalition of Catholics, Muslims, Arabs, and Indians with the goals of the Nazi Party would set the stage for events in the century that would follow.

It is important to emphasize from time to time that not all Catholics, or all Muslims, Arabs, Indians, etc. identified with the mission of the Nazi Party. In fact, it could be said that a minority of members of these groups felt that way. However, it was a very vocal and oftentimes violent minority, with whom some in the majority felt sympathy, or with whom they had ambiguous or only partially-conscious identification, and this is the point of this study. The type of threat the world faces today after the fall of the Soviet Union is less from established "state actors" than it is from independent, autonomous, non-state actors such as the terror cells usually identified as belonging to Al-Qaeda or Al-Qaeda affiliates. The type of terrorist activity we usually associate with this type of group is to be found in America in the 1920s and 1930s at the sharp edge of the nativist, racist, and anti-Semitic sword. It represents a "sub-cutaneous" layer of paranoia and ethnophobia just below the surface skin of American tolerance and desire for universal justice, often described or justified as an attempt to protect America and Americans from foreign influences that seek to harm the country from within.

One of these attempts was the result of Father Coughlin's unre-

lenting attack on the Roosevelt administration and on the measures adopted by Congress and the President during that period.
In November, 1938, Coughlin founded the Christian Front set up
in opposition to what he called the "Communist Front." It was a
vehicle for attacks on Jews, Communists and the perceived Red
infiltrators of the US government, and was heavily promoted and
propagandized in *Social Justice*. It received the overt support of
such high-profile clergymen as Bishop Fulton J. Sheen and Bishop
Thomas Molloy of Brooklyn, and was quietly tolerated by Arch-
bishop Spellman of New York.

The Front was most active in New York City, with its large
complement of Jewish immigrants. Through the Coudert Committee in 1940 it agitated for the removal of Jews from teaching positions at City College of New York, and thirty-five teachers were
suspended on charges that they had turned the college into a hotbed of Communism. The son of one of the suspended teachers was
attacked by Christian Fronters and his "forehead was branded with
a swastika."[23]

Christian Fronters attacked Jews on the streets of New York
City in actions reminiscent of *Krystallnacht*. Indeed, this show of
Nazi barbarity in Germany and Austria in November of 1938 was
discussed sympathetically by Father Coughlin himself in one of his
radio addresses at the time. It thus became impossible to differentiate the ideology and the tactics of Father Coughlin's Christian Front
from those of the Storm Troopers during Hitler's rise to power.

But behind all of this frenetic activity on the part of the Christian Front—including one alleged attempt to overthrow the government by a cabal of Christian Fronters in Brooklyn—there was
another layer of action that was known only to government investigators and intelligence operatives at the time. Coughlin was at the
center of a web of Nazi intrigue involving not only Catholic organizations like the Christian Front but also Pelley's Silver Legion,
the German-American Bund, and a whole menagerie of Eastern
European activists who represented immigrants from nations held

---

23   Charles Higham, *American Swastika*, New York, 1985, p.75.

captive by the Soviet Union. These included White Russians and Ukrainians.

In 1941, Coughlin's circle was penetrated by a Ukrainian Orthodox priest at the behest of Hoover's Federal Bureau of Investigation. This was the notorious Pelypenko affair.

Alexei Pelypenko was ordained in 1915 and in the 1930s he worked as a teacher in Munich during the time of the Third Reich. By 1937 he was in Argentina, working for the local Gestapo chief, and by 1940 was in Valparaiso, Chile, still working for the Nazis. As a Ukrainian, he was opposed to the occupation of his country by the Russians and as a priest he was opposed to Communist atheism. Many Ukrainians saw in Hitler a viable alternative to the regime in Moscow and were organizing themselves into a revolutionary force to support the Nazis at the time of their invasion of Russia. However, these same Ukrainians were disillusioned when the Hitler-Stalin pact was signed and it appeared that Russia and Germany would work together, thus robbing the Ukrainians of any hope of liberation. Hitler's invasion of the Soviet Union renewed the enthusiasm of some of the Ukrainians for Nazism and an entire Waffen-SS division, comprised of Ukrainian troops, was formed (and eventually many of these were resettled in the United States after the war). This historical episode has other ramifications for it led to the formation of several important lobby groups that agitated for political and military resistance against the Soviets under the general rubric of "captive nations" organizations such as the World Anti-Communist League (WACL). The Pelypenko affair reveals the extent of the American Nazi network and the intention of its perpetrators to overthrow the US government and install a military dictatorship that would remove Jewish and Communist influence at all levels of American life.

Pelypenko eventually decided that working for the Americans for a Communist-free bloc in Eastern Europe made more sense than waiting for Hitler to liberate his country. He contacted the FBI directly in 1940 and offered his support in infiltrating the Nazi networks he knew existed in the United States.

What he had to tell them was nothing short of astounding. Pelypenko knew the extent of Nazi and Japanese plans concerning the Panama Canal; the frustration of the Soviets with the United States in not cracking down more severely on White Russian activities in America; and that the Axis Powers were running agents in the United States using Ukrainian and other Eastern European groups, including the White Russians.

In addition, Pelypenko also knew the identity of a White Russian assassin who was being brought in by the Nazis to assassinate President Roosevelt. This latter fact might have seemed almost too much to believe, except that the assassin was located in Latin America as per Pelypenko's information, and terminated.[24]

Father Pelypenko became the FBI's golden boy from that point on. He had the impeccable Nazi credentials, a mastery of foreign languages, the Ukrainian pedigree, and long experience working for Nazi intelligence. They decided he would be useful as an infiltrator in American Nazi circles, and they prepared him for that mission.

The first step in Pelypenko's infiltration was the estate of Count Anastase Vonsiatsky, in Thompson, Connecticut.

Vonsiatsky (1898–1965) was of White Russian ancestry, born in Warsaw, whose family had a distinguished pedigree in the Czar's army, and who identified with the White Russian struggle against Communism. In the United States, he was an openly-avowed fascist who colluded with Nazi agents in the United States, and was a colleague of Father Coughlin, William Pelley, and the other American Nazis. His background was colorful and exotic, and he attracted a lot of interest from both the Nazi underground as well as from the US government. His estate in northeastern Connecticut was elaborate, filled with Russian and Nazi memorabilia, and served as the headquarters of his own political party organized for the liberation of Russia from Communism.

Vonsiatsky had married well. After making his way from Crimea in 1920 to Constantinople to recover from war wounds (he had been shot in his back, his arm, and his stomach), he later made his way to Paris where he met the American woman who would become his wife. She was an heiress to the Nabisco fortune and his wealth came largely through her. He sailed to America in the

---

24 Charles Higham (1985) p. 128.

summer of 1921, and by the following year he was married to the heiress, becoming a naturalized American citizen in 1927.

After a period of relative political inactivity, Vonsiatsky decided that it was time to form a party that would prepare for the day when the Soviet Union would fall and Russia would be free of Bolshevism. He admired the political philosophy represented by Benito Mussolini and Adolf Hitler, and in May of 1933 (four months after Hitler became Chancellor of Germany) Vonsiatsky formed the Russian National Revolutionary Labor and Workers Peasant Party of Fascists. The aim seemed to be to gather together all the Russian emigre groups that were proliferating throughout the United States, Latin America, and Europe under one umbrella with Vonsiatsky as its leader. The headquarters of the All Russian National Revolutionary Party, as it was known for short (!), was called The Center and was located at Vonsiatsky's estate.

The Count's involvement with other fascist organizations is well-known and documented. He claimed not to be anti-Semitic, and that his brand of fascism indicated only a desire to overthrow Soviet Communism and liberate Russia from the Bolsheviks. The problem with this type of platform is that it lends itself too easily to alliances with other anti-Communist groups, and in the extreme case, it leads to a partnership—if not identification—with Nazism. Of all the anti-Communist organizations that ever came into existence since the 1917 Russian Revolution, Nazism is the only one with an easily identifiable profile. Nazism became an unapologetic opponent of Communism, and the Nazis were determined opponents of Russia itself. If one wished to "liberate" Russia, the only country that seemed intent on doing so militarily was Nazi Germany. It therefore behooved the nationalist, anti-Communist forces of Eastern Europe to align themselves with the Reich, and to follow behind its invasion force, in order to set up provisional governments in Russia, Ukraine, and the other captive regions that comprised the Soviet Union and its satellites. To those tired of policies of appeasement, tolerance or acceptance—such as those proferred by the governments of the United Kingdom and the United States—where the Soviet Union was concerned, Hitler's approach seemed fresh and invigorating. Just as Hitler had successfully invaded Poland,

France, the Low Countries, etc., so (it was believed) he could invade Russia and turn it into another extension of the Reich.

By the time Father Pelypenko had walked through the iron gates of The Center, Vonsiatsky was already deeply embroiled in various fascist intrigues. The United States had not yet entered the war, and there was an energetic movement to keep America isolated from the conflict: an attitude that was exploited by the Nazis. Ukrainian fascist groups had been planning acts of sabotage in the United States since at least 1934, and it has been claimed that the OUN (*Organizace Ukrajinska Nacionalistov* or Ukrainian Nationalist Organization) was working with the Abwehr (German military intelligence), and the ODWU (Organization for the Rebirth of Ukraine, founded in the United States in 1931) was involved in a series of kidnappings and murders that took place at the Ukrainian National Home on East 6th Street in New York City. Ukrainian fascists even were believed to have been behind sabotage of the Cleveland-Pittsburgh express train in 1941, although it was never proved.

Vonsiatsky himself welcomed the Ukrainian Father Pelypenko to The Center and they talked for hours concerning the state of the world and the threat of world communism. Pelypenko's bona fides were established early on: he knew what names to drop and what references to make, as he had been, after all, a devoted Nazi for years until the demoralizing Hitler-Stalin pact. He had worked in South America for the Gestapo, and was considered loyal to the cause. Only the FBI knew otherwise.

The Count felt comfortable enough to reveal some sensitive information to the priest, including his connection with Dr. Wolfgang Ebell. Ebell was a German national (b. 1899) who served in the German army during World War One and who went to medical school in Freiburg. He became a naturalized American citizen in 1939 after first working for awhile in Mexico (1927–1930). He was then based in El Paso, Texas and while there was discovered to be running Nazi agents south of the border. Also involved in the Mexican operation was Gerhardt Wilhelm Kunze, who had taken over control of the German-American Bund. Kunze was in fact working for Nazi intelligence at the same time he was the Bund's figurehead. In that capacity he was in contact with Japanese agents in Mexico on behalf of the Reich, and to Pelypenko's surprise he was informed that Kunze was shortly to go to the Pacific coast of Mexico to make contact with Japanese submarines.

Vonsiatsky bragged that he was also in radio contact with the Nazi consul in San Francisco—Fritz Weidemann—who passed his messages on to Japan and from there to Germany in an effort to avoid the American censors.

The importance of this information cannot be overstated and, indeed, it formed an essential part of the US government's case against the espionage ring. In one conversation, the German-American Bund and Vonsiatsky's Russian Fascists were all revealed to be working together with the Third Reich and the Empire of Japan in the months and years leading up to America's entry into the war. A spy ring in Mexico being run out of El Paso, Texas was connected with the Nazi consul in San Francisco and Japanese submarines, White Russian émigrés, and American Nazis. While historians strive to study these various threads separately, history itself is rarely so neat and tidy. It is, in fact, quite messy as this particular case demonstrates. While the goals of the Russian Fascists and those of the Bund, the Japanese, and the Third Reich may have been different in particulars—representing different ethnicities, histories, ideologies—they had enough essentials in common that they would make a joint effort to undermine American national security and materially support the war efforts of the Axis Powers.

As it would later transpire, this group of conspirators would also extend to include Father Coughlin himself, as well as the Lutheran minister Kurt Molzahn of Philadelphia, and the head of the Chicago chapter of the Bund, Otto Willumeit. Pelypenko was urged to attend a clandestine meeting of the leading Nazis in Chicago at the Bismarck Hotel (where else?) in June, 1941. The meeting was bugged by the FBI.

At the meeting—attended by Vonsiatsky, Kunze, Ebell, Willumeit and Molzahn in addition to Pelypenko—it was learned that Kunze was to quit the leadership of the Bund so that he could disappear into Mexico and rendezvous with the Japanese. On June 20, 1941, Pelypenko met with Willumeit himself at Bund headquarters and was urged to go to Detroit and meet personally with Father Coughlin. Willumeit further informed the priest that Coughlin received regular messages from the Reich by way of the German embassy in Washington, DC. The German consul in Detroit—Fritz Hailer—confirmed to Pelypenko that Coughlin was one of their friends and intimated a degree of financial and other support for the radio priest.

Thus it was that Father Pelypenko finally would meet the infamous Father Coughlin and learn of the extent to which the seemingly comic-opera American Nazi underground—replete with storm troopers, swastika armbands, and weapons training in the national parks—was actually part of the extensive network of spies, saboteurs, agents provocateurs, propagandists, and financiers that existed before the war began, and which would be around (albeit in somewhat different form) once the war was over.

As Charles Higham writes, in *American Swastika*:

> Now Coughlin really opened up. He revealed to the astonished priest that he was a coordinating link with all subversive groups in the country; that he was connected to the whole White Russian Nazi groups under Vonsiatsky, that he was in direct touch with Ukrainian terrorist groups in Detroit, and that he was linked to John Koos, the Nazi Ukrainian working for Henry Ford.[25]

John Koos was the leader in America of the Ukrainian Hetman Organization (UHO). This was a Nazi group, based in Berlin, composed of ethnic anti-Communists and engaged in terrorist activities against the Soviets, as well as against pro-Communist or anti-Nazi individuals and groups everywhere else. Koos worked out of the Ford Motor Company factories in Detroit where he arranged for the hiring of thousands of Ukrainians to work the plants and to form a fifth column working directly for Henry Ford. The position of Koos was so secure in the eyes of the Reich that Hitler himself sent the message that Koos would be named Minister of Internal

25   Charles Higham (1985), p. 129.

Affairs in Ukraine once it had been liberated by the Nazis.[26] Koos received a medal awarded by Alfred Rosenberg, the Nazi ideologist mentioned above.

(It should be remembered that the most famous leader of the German-American Bund was Fritz Kuhn, who was himself a Ford Motor Company employee. And it was the son of a Ford Motor Company executive in Chile who masterminded the assassination of Orlando Letelier in Washington, DC: Michael Vernon Townley, currently in prison in the United States and in witness protection. Townley was involved with the Nazi Party in Chile which is where he was in regular contact with the Chilean secret police—DINA— under dictator General Augusto Pinochet. He was also the man who designed the interrogation cells at Colonia Dignidad.)[27]

Coughlin insisted that Pelypenko bring him as much anti-Semitic literature as possible, that he would be remunerated for any material brought to him, and gave him a letter of introduction to an agent working at the German Embassy in Washington. At that point things began to heat up.

In November, 1941—and only weeks before the attack on Pearl Harbor—Kunze was waiting in Texas for the false documents he would need to cross the border into Mexico. The man arranging for the fraudulent paperwork was the Lutheran minister, Molzahn, who used the Lutheran Church's printing office for this effort. This would not be the last time the Lutheran Church was involved in helping a Nazi escape by providing false papers. As evidenced in the Pöch address book and elsewhere, the Evangelical Lutheran Church was running Nazis out of Europe after the war in parallel with the Catholic Church's program.

Kunze had spent the previous few weeks touring America's west coast, identifying vulnerabilities in her defenses, and liaising with White Russians along the way. Once in Texas, he received the phoney documentation and made it across the border into Mexico. He was on his way to be picked up by a German U-boat when FBI

---

26 Max Wallace, *The American Axis: Henry Ford, Charles Lindbergh, and the Rise of the Third Reich*, New York, 2004, pp. 137–138.

27 The story of Townley, Colonia Dignidad and the Leterlier assassination is described in the author's own *Unholy Alliance*.

agents, posing as Mexican fishermen, arrested him just as the peri-scope breached the surface.

Kunze's arrest—coming as it did only months after the attack on Pearl Harbor—was part of a broader sweep of Nazi agents. Mol-zahn, Willumeit of the Chicago Bund, Wolfgang Ebell of El Paso, and Vonsiatsky himself were all arrested and charged with espio-nage.

Father Coughlin was named as a co-conspirator in all of Pelypenko's debriefings; Coughlin had obviously been the lynch-pin to the spy ring, and Pelypenko met him several times during the course of his espionage work. But Coughlin was never arrested, never made to answer for his role in the affair. He was too hot to arrest, too hot to try in open court, too popular with too many Americans. It was decided that it was safer to leave him alone.

And Pelypenko? Did he get the key to the city? The gratitude of grateful nation? A medal? US citizenship?

No. Pelypenko was arrested by the Immigration authorities because—due to his infiltration of one of the most dangerous Nazi espionage rings of the time—he had overstayed his visa! He was released but told he had to leave the country at once. Where could he go? It was the middle of World War Two, and he had been a double agent. His life was in danger no matter where he went.

So he was arrested again and interned for the rest of the war.

This, briefly, was the spirit of the times. Paranoia, suspicion, scapegoats, ethnic rivalries, religious bigotry, fear of new immi-grants, cynical clergymen, corrupt politicians, a polarized nation. A yearning for an America that used to be, or might have been. Toler-ance interpreted as weakness. Anger and hatred as strength.

The cover of Vonsiatsky's tabloid, *The Fascist*, had a photo of a battalion of German troops. Over it is the legend "The Army of the Holy Swastika."

War. And Faith. And Holy War. What is past truly is prologue.

PART TWO

THE POST-WAR NETWORKS

CHAPTER FOUR

THE SOURCE MATERIAL

*Each age of humanity has left its mark. We live on top of an enor-
mous palimpsest.*
        —Jean-Claude Carrière

Normally, one places information on sources at the end of a
book, but in this case the provenance of the source material is
important towards an understanding of the value and relevance of
the narrative as a whole. Primary sources on the Nazi underground
are few and far between and are usually the work of Allied governments and intelligence agencies and not that of the members of
the underground itself. That is not to suggest that the material in
these sources is suspect, but that it would inevitably be one-sided
and lacking many essentials that only the personal diaries and notebooks of the actual fugitives themselves could provide. My intention was to remedy that situation as much as possible, for only in
this way could original research be accomplished and new discover-
ies made. That meant I had to travel extensively, as well as revisit
old archival material and painstakingly decode hundreds of pages
of handwritten documents with an eye towards identifying what
appeared to be random bits of data.

There is not a lot of primary source material written in the hand
of the actual underground organizers themselves, for obvious reasons, but those that do exist throw a great deal of light on the otherwise shadowy networks of Nazi survivors around the world. They
also illuminate the extent to which non-military and non-political
actors were involved in the creation and the maintenance of Nazi
ideology and programs throughout the entire period under review
here. These include academics with backgrounds in anthropology,
archaeology, medicine, genetics, and the like as well as industrialists,
arms dealers, and those who operated safe houses along the ratlines.

The Address Books

There were several address books that were utilized in this research. The relevance of these documents will become obvious as this research progresses.

The first such document consists of various pages of the address book kept by Dr. Georg Anton Pöch, the Austrian doctor that I profiled in *Ratline*. I never had access to the entire document, even though it was contractually promised to me, but what I was able to view during several contentious months in Singapore was enough to assure me that the source is genuine. In these pages I will only refer to material that was already seen by others or published in books or other printed or electronic media, or seen by me before the mentioned contract became effective. I will not refer to any documents that were not seen previously either by me or by other investigators. The contribution I make is my ability to identify persons, places, and institutions in the previously exhibited documents that other investigators could not, probably due to their lack of the appropriate background in the subject.

The address book was small, the kind of thing you could keep in a jacket pocket, bound in green, and written in various colors of ink. It was not alphabetical in any way; in fact it seemed more chronological than alphabetical, as if names and addresses were added as soon as they were known. Thus, the earliest entries seemed to be those most concerned with the escape routes out of Germany and Austria, while the later entries were of those friends and colleagues of the Pöch couple who had survived the war. Some entries were of those who fled to Latin America and were easily identifiable; others were somewhat less so. I understand from previous accounts of the address book that there was at least one entry for South Africa, but I did not see that one (many pages were withheld from me); in another case, a reported entry for Tibet was clear and unambiguous. The address book also contained a brief account of the escape of Dr. Pöch, one that had been published in a small volume in the Indonesian language.

Along with the other Pöch memorabilia, there were passports, some photographs (again, I never saw all of these), and other *disjecta membra*. Taken altogether, these items may tell a more complete story of the Pöch escape, and may even go some way towards telling us who the Pöchs really were: the same Austrian medical doctor and his famous academic wife, or in reality two other persons who had taken the Pöch identity in order to get as far away from Europe, and the Middle East, and Latin America as possible: as far away, in other words, from their Nazi colleagues as geography would allow since they could not be trusted.

The second document consists of a volume of photocopied pages that were part of the CIA's file on Josef Mengele, the notorious "Angel of Death" at the Auschwitz extermination camp. While it was included in Mengele's file, and only recently declassified, it is most likely not the address book of Dr. Mengele himself, but that of Hans-Ulrich Rudel: Hitler's favorite Luftwaffe ace, who was instrumental in propping up the post-World War Two Nazi underground. The names and addresses in this document are an astonishing record of the global Nazi network, and even includes the pseudonym and address of Klaus Barbie in Bolivia in the years before he was extradited to France to stand trial for war crimes. To the best of my knowledge, I am the only researcher who took the pains to identify the names in this important text and while I did not succeed in identifying *all* the names (usually due to the illegibility of the handwritten text) what I did identify is an incredible amount of information, including some data on persons still alive in the United States.

The third document has already been exhaustively researched by generations of investigators but its relevance to our case remains important. This is the address book kept by the alleged assassin of President John F. Kennedy, Lee Harvey Oswald. There are several reasons why I decided to include this data here, in a book on the Hitler legacy, and they will become apparent as we go along.

In the Appendix, the entire contents of the Rudel address book are listed with as many of the entries identified as possible, including addresses and phone numbers (some of which are still valid today). I believe that since this document was released into the general public by the US Government that its publication here is justified. The Oswald address book appears in various places and collections and does not need to be reproduced completely here.

As for the infamous Pöch address book, publication of that in its entirety will have to wait for its present owner to come to his senses. What I do reproduce is data found on the pages that were available to me before I entered into contractual negotiations with its owner, plus information that was available to other investigators, journalists, and authors before me (albeit in different languages and countries and therefore not easily accessible by English-speakers).

Other Documentation

Other primary documentation that was used to support the research in this volume includes US Government reports on Nazi gold; declassified CIA and FBI files on various subjects and individuals, where noted; records of the Nuremberg and other trials; captured German documents, and other verifiable specimens. Secondary sources include scholarly and journalistic books and articles on the subjects covered here, and some selected videos including interviews with important individuals, and these are noted where relevant.

Photographs of World War II personalities are usually courtesy of the German archives, as noted. Some photographs were taken by me, and are so identified.

All sources are listed in the Bibliography at the end of this book.

Where sources are in languages other than English, the translations are mine except where specifically mentioned. Any errors in translation are therefore mine alone.

Interviews

In addition, many persons were interviewed by me over the course of more than forty years of investigating this story. I personally met with members of the Palestine Liberation Organization, the Ku Klux Klan, the National Renaissance Party, the leaders of Colonia Dignidad in Chile, members of the American intelligence community, the Chinese military, experts in Tibetan religion, high-ranking clergy of various Eastern Orthodox denominations, the leadership of the American Orthodox Catholic Church (a front for US intelligence operations), the leader and founder of Jemaah Islammiyah (the terror organization responsible for the Bali Bombings of 2002), and many, many others. Where relevant, these meetings and discussions are noted in the body of the text.

I also have traveled to many of the locations noted here. I have spent considerable time visiting and working in Latin America, Europe, and Asia. I have intimate knowledge of Muslim societies in Indonesia and Malaysia, and possibly for that reason was, for awhile, on a TSA list for "special screening." The story of my brief detainment at Colonia Dignidad in Chile in 1979 is told in my first book, *Unholy Alliance*, and will not be repeated here.

A certain degree of subjectivity is unavoidable, especially when one has spent decades doing this type of research, and often in close proximity to the individuals and groups most strongly associated with the Nazi underground, as well as with Arab and Islamist organizations some of which are on terror watch lists. When one winds up on a list oneself, the experience is a little uncanny. However, I have tried to present as coherent and balanced a study as possible under the circumstances. We are entitled to our own opinions, they say, but not our own facts. Keeping that maxim uppermost in my mind, I have tried to present as much as possible by way of facts. The opinions of mine that are expressed—hopefully they are few—are stated as such. The interpretation of the facts and their analysis is mine, of course, but I am open to other analyses, other ways of looking at this material, and drawing other conclusions.

CHAPTER FIVE

EXIT STRATEGY

We must preserve a sort of reserve off of which we can feed in the future.

> —Ratline organizer Msgr. Krunoslav Draganovic when asked by Klaus Barbie, the Butcher of Lyon, why the Church was helping him as the latter was boarding the ship for Argentina using papers created by the Catholic priest.

By the summer of 1944, it was obvious that the Third Reich was about to collapse. The D-Day invasion had put paid to any idea that Germany would be able to hold onto its occupied territories in Western Europe. France was being liberated and the Allies were soon to march into the Low Countries. The Russians were advancing inexorably from the east. North Africa had been lost. The Balkans were already in the grip of socialist partisans under Tito.

> —Father Pelypenko's Ukraine was lost.

Hitler might have been insane, or deluded, but that did not mean his subordinates were crazy. The men who had financed and supported the Reich from its salad days in the 1920s and 1930s now realized that other arrangements had to be made. Industrialists, bankers, engineers and scientists had to find a way to pool their resources and hide as much money, information, and technology as possible from the Allied forces so that Germany could be rebuilt quickly. At the same time, the SS knew that it had been declared a criminal organization by the Allies and that the days of its members were numbered. It had, however, an extensive network of spies, informants, and sympathizers all over the world, some of whom had begun to engage in anti-colonial movements against the British, the

French, and the Dutch. These would become useful in the months and years to come.

Imagine that the Sicilian Mafia had begun as the legitimate government of Sicily, but that Palermo was being overrun by another army; the Mafia would simply go underground and form a government-in-exile, waiting for the day its membership could quietly return to Palermo to retake power. That was the SS in 1944 and 1945: what had started as an official German government agency and paramilitary and military force was suddenly declared a kind of Mafia, an organized crime syndicate whose members would be hunted to the ends of the earth and prosecuted to the fullest extent of the (newly created) law: the Nazis would be charged with crimes against humanity and all SS-men would be declared criminals by virtue of their membership.

At the same time, as the Allies marched into Germany, other groups were making decisions that would have tremendous implications for global security in the decades after the war. While the Allies were fixated on the Germans as war criminals, many others of different ethnicities had committed some of the same war crimes. Cadres of pro-Nazi Ukrainians, Croats, Romanians, and others were running for the exits. The Ukrainians had fielded an entire Waffen-SS division; the Croats had a puppet Nazi government in the Ustase, now on the run to Argentina; and the Romanians had the Iron Guard, responsible for pogroms against the Jews as well as the torture of prisoners.

A new paradigm was taking place, something rare in world history. A defeated nation had been occupied by its enemies, but a defeated ideology survived the military defeat and reorganized and rebranded itself. What the Allies did not realize at the time was that Nazism could not be eradicated with guns and bombs. What the Nazis knew was that they could carry on their ideological struggle from anywhere on earth, and they did. The war was not over for them; they had simply moved the theater of operations: to the Middle East, the Americas, Central Asia, and to South and Southeast Asia. And they did all of that with assistance from the very governments that had defeated them. This would be absurd if it wasn't true.

The Red House Report

After the war, the existence of a highly-classified report from a French spy on a meeting held at the Maison Rouge ("Red House") Hotel in Strasbourg came to light. It had been buried in the National Archives since at least 1976 (which is the date on the stamp on the top of the document), but was little known until recently. It is referred to as the Red House Report, but it's official name is *US Military Intelligence report EW-Pa 128, Enclosure No. 1 to despatch No. 19,489 of Nov. 27, 1944, from the Embassy at London, England.* It was marked SECRET and addressed to: "SUPREME HEAD-QUARTERS ALLIED EXPEDITIONARY FORCE Office of Assistant Chief of Staff, G-2." The subject of the report was fascinating:

> SUBJECT: Plans of German industrialists to engage in underground activity after Germany's defeat; flow of capital to neutral countries.[28]

It detailed a discussion that was held at the Maison Rouge Hotel on August 10, 1944 to which the heads of German corporations such as Volkswagen, Messerschmitt, Krupp, Brown-Boverie, and others were in attendance. They were told by an SS General that it was imperative for as much German capital and other assets to be transferred out of the country and to neutral nations, away from the grasp of the Allies. This included all industrial material currently in France, and wherever else the Germans could reach.

In other words, as the rest of the SS was preparing escape routes for personnel and gold, the SS chief in Strasbourg was preparing for a different kind of escape route. The money, the industrial base, and the personnel would go together; it was nothing less than the recreation of the Reich somewhere else, out of the reach of the victors.

---

28 It also can be found in a US Government volume entitled *Elimination of German Resources for War*, dated June 22, 1945, pp. 44–49. There is another reference to the meeting on page 464 of this massive, 1215 page collection of testimony and documentation.

The plan was to arrange for the resurrection of the Reich and the reconstitution of the German economy as soon as the Allies gave them the opportunity.

According to the French agent's report:

> From now on also German industry must realize that the war cannot be won and that it must take steps in preparation for a post-war commercial campaign. Each industrialist must make contacts and alliances with foreign firms, but this must be done individually and without attracting any suspicion. Moreover, the ground would have to be laid on the financial level for borrowing considerable sums from foreign countries after the war. As examples of the kind of penetration which had been most useful in the past, Dr. Scheid cited the fact that patents for stainless steel belonged to the Chemical Foundation, Inc., New York, and the Krupp company of Germany jointly and that the U.S. Steel Corporation, Carnegie Illinois, American Steel and Wire, and National Tube, etc. were thereby under an obligation to work with the Krupp concern. He also cited the Zeiss Company, the Leica Company and the Hamburg-American Line as firms which had been especially effective in protecting German interests abroad and gave their New York addresses to the industrialists at this meeting.

The fact that many American firms had been supporting the Reich in the years before the war—and some during the war—was not new to American intelligence, of course. It was to be expected that German industrialists would do what they could to cement earlier relationships to ensure their own survival and that of the firms they represented. What is important to realize from the above paragraph is that the Germans were to be pro-active in these relationships. It then begs the question: what was the motivation of, for instance, the hundreds of Nazi rocket scientists the United States invited to work on the American space program? Was the dynamic simply one of the Americans salvaging as much of the Nazi program as possible, both to reap the rewards themselves and to keep them out of the hands of the Soviets? Or were the Nazi scientists being pro-active in their relationship with the Allies, cultivating the US military and promising the moon (literally) in pursuit of some other agenda?

The Red House Report goes on to state that there was a second, smaller meeting involving the German Armaments Ministry and representatives from Krupp, Hecho, and Rochling:

> At this second meeting it was stated that the Nazi Party had informed the industrialists that the war was practically lost but that it would continue until a guarantee of the unity of Germany could be obtained. German industrialists must, it was said, through their exports increase the strength of Germany. *They must also prepare themselves to finance the Nazi Party which would be forced to go underground as Maquis (in Gebirgaverteidigungastellen gehen).* From now on the government would allocate large sums to industrialists so that each could establish *a secure post-war foundation in foreign countries. Existing financial reserves in foreign countries must be placed at the disposal of the Party so that a strong German Empire can be created after the defeat.* It is also immediately required that the large factories in Germany create small technical offices or research bureaus which would be absolutely independent and have no known connection with the factory. These bureaus will receive *plans and drawings of new weapons* as well as documents which they need to continue their research and which must not be allowed to fall into the hands of the enemy. These offices are to be established in large cities where they can be most successfully hidden as well as in little villages near sources of hydro-electric power where they can pretend to be studying the development of water resources. The existence of these is to be known only by very few people in each industry and by chiefs of the Nazi Party. Each office will have a liaison agent with the Party. As soon as the Party becomes strong enough to re-establish its control over Germany the industrialists will be paid for their effort and cooperation by concessions and orders. (emphasis added)[29]

---

29 It should be noted that the veracity of the Red House Report has been

Thus, in August of 1944, the local SS commander in France was aware of detailed plans for the resurrection of the Third Reich which involved foreign assets, the financing of an underground terror organization, and the development of new weapons. He would have received this information from Berlin, presumably from Himmler himself, as no one else would have dared to utter such defeatist sentiments or to plan for a post-war Germany using wealth and technology that had been secreted abroad. As we now know, Himmler's second-in-command—SS General Ernst Kaltenbrunner— had been sent to oversee the resistance movement that was said to be headquartered in Austria, near Salzburg, in the last days of the war. Prior to that, he was in charge of the legal proceedings against the Hitler assassination plotters and demanded their execution. He was a trusted SS officer, an Austrian, and fanatically loyal to the Führer. Would Kaltenbrunner have been aware of the strategy to expatriate as much of the Reich's wealth and technology (and personnel) as possible, as early as August of 1944?

---

called into question, most recently by Heinz Schneppen (*Odessa und das Vierte Reich: Mythen der Zeitgeschichte*, Berlin, Metropol-Verlag, 2007) who, in the same work, questions the existence of ODESSA as well as the Nazi-Argentina nexus. Research by Argentine journalist Uki Goñi (*The Real ODESSA*) and others dispute Schneppen's findings where both ODESSA and Argentina are concerned, and the event described as the Red House meeting in Strasbourg was considered genuine enough by US Government intelligence and military analysts at the time. The fact that German industry had diversified its holdings to the extent that at the end of the war I.G. Farben alone had dozens of subsidiaries in foreign countries and German corporations in general had more than 750 foreign subsidiaries abroad in 1945, including in Turkey and Argentina, argues against Schneppen's analysis. Schneppen's point is that this was all "business as usual" and should not imply a nefarious Nazi underground network. However, the US Government report cited above also mentions a document in which Himmler "informed all gauleiters that certain party men in whom Hitler had confidence would be sent abroad for special missions; in February 1945, 345 party members received orders to prepare to leave Germany." (*Elimination of German Resources for War*, dated June 22, 1945, p. 646). This would seem to offer evidence that, far from being a fantasy, the threat of an underground Reich was a real and present danger.

Or would these orders have come from someone even higher up in the command bureaucracy? If not Kaltenbrunner or Hitler, then the only other name that seems plausible is Martin Bormann.

Bormann is often mentioned in the same breath as the Nazi gold reserves and post-war Nazi financing. There has been considerable controversy surrounding Bormann, with many researchers suggesting that he survived the war despire a somewhat questionable eye-witness account that says he died in Berlin in May, 1945. A distinguished CBS journalist and associate of Edward R. Murrow, Paul Manning, followed the Bormann story for years. Manning provided credible evidence pointing to Bormann's survival and to his management of Nazi finances around the world, evidence that was ignored or devalued by his colleagues in the media.

Whether or not Bormann himself survived the war is not the issue before us, however. What is relevant is the fact that a post-war strategy was already in place to protect the assets of the Reich (both monetary and otherwise), rescue the Nazi Party and insure its survival, develop new weapons, and use guerrilla tactics to enable the Reich to resist defeat as long as possible. Central to the success of this mission was the expedient of escape. None of this money or technology would do the Party any good unless its personnel were there to organize it, protect it, and invest it. These persons had to be true believers, otherwise the wealth of the Reich was in danger of being sold off to the highest bidders, piecemeal, as Germany lay devastated and hopeless.

The most trustworthy of all the Nazis—and the ones most sought after as war criminals—were the SS. Not the Wehrmacht, the Army whose generals had tried to assassinate Hitler—but the SS.

The Red House meeting took place two months after the D-Day invasion in June of 1944, and a month after the Generals' Plot to assassinate Hitler in July of 1944 (known as Operation Valkyrie). Secret cables from the OSS (the Office of Strategic Services, forerunner of the CIA) to Washington revealed that the ringleader of the plot—Colonel von Stauffenberg—was part of a cabal that was ready to sign a treaty with the Soviet Union, believing that it would be better for Germany to side with the Russians than with the British and the Americans.[30] Had the plot succeeded, German industrial and military assets would have been transferred (at least temporarily) to Soviet control. This would have been a disaster for American post-war policy (forgetting for a moment that the Soviets, who had lost twenty million of its own citizens fighting the Nazis, would never have honored such a commitment to the Nazis even if they made it). It would have been equally disadvantageous militarily, as it would have given the Soviets complete access to the secret Nazi weapons facilities that had developed the V-1 and V-2 super weapons, and which were in the process of creating even more advanced weaponry. It was vital that Stauffenberg be stopped; it was not as essential that Hitler be saved from assassination, but it was important that the Stauffenberg cabal not be permitted to take control of the country: important to the Nazis, and also important to the Allies.

Enter SS Major-General Otto Remer.

One of the original conspirators, at the last minute Remer decided to throw in his lot with the Nazi establishment and blow the whistle on the conspiracy, identifying von Stauffenberg as the chief conspirator.[31] Stauffenberg's network was rolled up, and he and other conspirators were executed (as mentioned, on orders from Ernst Kaltenbrunner).

After the war, Remer would be implicated in the Naumann Affair: an attempt to resurrect the Nazi Party in Austria that was foiled by British Intelligence. And it would be Remer who would find himself addressing a meeting of the Liberty Lobby thirty years

---

30 One of these, a Memorandum For The President, is dated 27 January 1945 on OSS stationery, and signed Charles S. Cheston, Acting Director, was declassified by the CIA in 1973. It reports that one of the conspirators in the assassination plot against Hitler escaped to Switzerland, and claimed to investigators that von Stauffenberg had planned to cut a peace deal with the Soviets.

31 As discussed in another declassified OSS memorandum, this one dated 1 February 1945, and signed by Acting Director Cheston. This memo also references the desire by the von Stauffenberg group to cut a deal with the Soviets who ensured that "Germany would receive a just peace from the Soviets and the Wehrmacht would not be wholly disarmed."

later, maintaining his anti-Communist (and Nazi) credentials to the very end of his life.

The D-Day invasion was the handwriting on the wall for the Third Reich, and the generals and the SS knew that whatever military action they performed now was only a stalling tactic. The Soviets were pouring through the east, and the British and Americans were pouring through the west. Those faithful Party members and SS men who were not completely insane understood that they had to do what they could to prepare for the defeat of Germany.

The Generals' Plot demonstrated that neither Hitler nor the SS could trust the army. The Wehrmacht dealt in the hard-core realities of the battlefield; they were led by career soldiers who were fighting Germany's wars long before there was a Nazi Party. Once they realized that the war was lost (after the D-Day invasion and the successes of the Soviet Army on the eastern front) they knew, as soldiers, that their only course of action was to surrender with as much dignity as they could muster, and to save as many lives as possible. This attitude was unacceptable to Hitler because it demonstrated a loss of faith in the eternals of the Party and all it stood for, no less than a loss of confidence in the Führer himself. The Nazi Party, however, was a cult and its most fervent members—the SS—were true believers, the priesthood of the cult. That does not mean they were not pragmatic or wise, however. They knew that their most prominent leaders would be arrested and probably imprisoned, if not executed. They had to be sacrificed for the greater good. The rest would perform a strategic withdrawal of their forces to areas around Europe and around the world, where they could manage the resources left to them from such planning sessions as the Red House meeting and others which doubtless took place all over Nazi-occupied Europe at the same time.

The Red House Report was only one indication that the Nazis were planning for their survival almost a year before the surrender in May of 1945. They had ample time to move gold and valuables out by truck and submarine to points all around the world, and the evidence shows that they did. They had a network of agents in the Americas, Europe, Asia, and the Middle East who would facilitate these transfers, as well as the transfer of personnel, and these networks were all in place before the end of 1944.

In the meantime, they would set up a rear-guard action designed to delay the Allies as much as possible while these other preparations were being made; thus the "myth" of the National Redoubt was born. As we will see in a later chapter, there was considerable evidence that such an underground fortress existed, and many prominent Nazis were found to be making their way to the Salzburg region of Austria where it was believed to have been established.[32] Top Nazis such as Foreign Minister Ribbentrop (hanged at Nuremberg) had summer homes in the region, and SS General Kaltenbrunner (hanged at Nuremberg) was captured there, disguised as a medical doctor.

Salzburg, however, was only a way-station on a much longer route. Established largely due to the tireless efforts of the Croatian Catholic priest—Krunoslav Draganovic—the ratline was first created solely to rescue the leaders of the puppet Nazi government of Croatia, the Ustase. Later, the same routes and methods were used to move other Nazis out of the reach of Allied justice. Monasteries, churches, and rectories from Austria through the Tyrol and northern Italy to Rome and Genoa were used as safe houses, and fraudulent identification papers were fabricated by the Catholic Church to enable the Nazis to obtain passports issued by the International Red Cross.

Much has already been discovered and reported about this episode in world history, no less in the author's own books on the subject. The flight of Nazis to South America, especially to Argentina, has become something of a cliche and the subject of novels, films, documentaries, and academic research and reportage. However, one aspect of the Nazi post-war strategy that often has been overlooked by popularizers and Hollywood screenwriters is the flight of capital.

---

32 Allen Dulles, from his position as OSS representative in Bern, Switzerland, was one of those who alerted Donovan—head of the OSS—that the Nazis had planned their last stand at the National Redoubt. See the declassified OSS Memorandum for the President dated 9 February 1945, and signed by William J. Donovan, Director.

This is an essential aspect of the Nazi exit strategy—as evidenced by the Red House Report—and the ready availability of cash meant that the Nazi underground could continue to function without worrying about how they would finance their operations. The amount of gold and other treasure that was taken out of Europe has yet to be adequately calculated, but it was enough to ensure—with careful planning and investments, legal and illegal—an operating fund that was the equal of the budgets of small countries.

Due to the complexity of international trade and finance and the obscurity of offshore accounts, encoded wire transfers, and foreign currency transactions—as well as the involvement in the trafficking of Nazi gold by other members of the Axis powers and sympathizers, including Argentina, Chile, Spain, Portugal, Switzerland and most notably Japan—this aspect of the ODESSA story resists all attempts at accurate accounting. What we can do is start with what is known, and that means with newspaper accounts of banking investigations taking place in Germany, Switzerland, Spain, Portugal, and elsewhere.

Government-sponsored research, such as the Eizenstat Report also makes clear the extent of the financial holdings that are known ... and the extent of the holdings that are unknown. Compiled in 1997 by Stuart E. Eizenstat, who was Under Secretary of Commerce for International Trade, and Special Envoy of the Department of State on Property Restitution in Central and Eastern Europe under the Clinton Administration. The report involved participation by the CIA, the FBI, and virtually the entire Cabinet. Entitled *U.S. and Allied Efforts To Recover and Restore Gold and Other Assets Stolen or Hidden by Germany During World War II*, it begins with a warning:

> ... this study is preliminary and therefore incomplete. Not every U.S. document related to looted Nazi assets could be located and analyzed in the very short time we had to conduct and complete the study. As we progressed, additional documents were constantly found. While we were compelled to rely mostly on U.S. documents, we are well aware that not until the documents of other countries are examined can a more complete picture be drawn.

This is the crux of the problem. While the Eizenstat committee was able to estimate the accummulated amount of wealth stolen by the Nazis as US $580 million (US $5.6 billion in 1997 dollars), it admitted there were "indeterminate amounts in other assets." Between 1939 and 1945, according to the Report, "Germany transferred gold worth around $400 million ($3.9 billion in today's[33] values) to the Swiss National Bank in Bern." It is to be emphasized that these amounts are the result of traditional bookkeeping and accounting methods and practices necessary for the Nazis to purchase raw materials from other countries for the prosecution of the war, as well as to provide nest eggs for high-ranking Party and SS members. In other words, there was much gold and other assets that did not pass through the formal channels of banks and federal institutions; there were also assets that were transferred not to Swiss banks but to banks in Spain, Portugal and elsewhere and these countries have been very slow to account for these assets. As more and more investigations are undertaken—usually by independent journalists and investigative reporters in other countries, from Europe to the Americas to Southeast Asia—the fiscal profile of the greatest theft in modern history keeps expanding.

Add to this hidden treasure the financial support of those regimes sympathetic to the Nazi cause, and there exists a slush fund of considerable size and power. As we have seen in the opening chapter, Jörg Haider and his pro-Nazi Alliance for Austrian Progress Party was the recipient of just this type of largesse, from Libya and Iraq. Ahmed Huber, his Nazi colleague, was another: he was on the board of directors of Al-Taqwa Bank, believed to have been a conduit of funds for Al-Qaeda.

Just how did this start, and why has this essential aspect of the Nazi underground not been shut down and rolled up?

The Freundeskreis Himmler

This meeting between Hitler and Papen on 4 January 1933 in my house in Cologne was arranged by me after Papen had

---

33 I.e,. 1997 dollars.

asked me for it on about 10 December 1932. Before I took this step I talked to a number of businessmen and informed myself generally on how the business world viewed a collaboration between the two men. The general desire of businessmen was to see a strong man come to power in Germany who would form a government that would stay in power for a long time.[34]

Historians as a rule do not focus on the minutiae of finance, especially when the larger issues of wars, treaties and revolutions are being considered. However, money is the fuel that powers governments and this is especially true in time of war. Books could probably be written on World War Two from a strictly financial viewpoint and they would be quite revealing. Instead, we are usually offered ideological explanations, analysis of strategy and tactics, even biographical and psycho-biographical studies of the main protagonists. This misses an essential point, and that is that these governments could not possibly wage war without a reliable source of income; just who provides this income and what may be their motivation to do so is usually ignored.

In the case of Germany after World War One, this need for a reliable source of funds was especially true. German assets were seized; valuable land and other resources were carved up by the Allies; and on top of that a Great Depression was looming over the horizon. The Nazi Party was just coming into its own in the years after Hitler was released from Landsberg Prison for his abortive putsch in Munich in 1923. It needed votes in the Reichstag in order to consolidate power in the federal government, and to get votes one needed cash to pay for advertising, staff, and travel. Every politician knows this, of course, and Hitler was no different. He could rely on donations from devoted Party members and supporters, but only to a point. More than anything else, he needed finan-

---

34 "Sworn Statement by Kurt Baron von Schroeder to the American Investigatory Committee of the International Military Tribunal in Nuremberg on the Negotiations with Hitler at Schroeder's House in Cologne on January 4, 1933" in Jeremy Noakes and Geoffrey Pridham, eds., *Nazism 1919–1945*, Vol. 1, *The Rise to Power 1919–1934*. Exeter: University of Exeter Press, 1998, pp. 115–16.

cial experts who could help him woo the bankers and industrialists who held the real power and the real financing. He needed to be able to convince them that his anti-capitalist rhetoric was just that: political expediency.

Hitler was not a communist by any stretch of the imagination, but he did see capitalism as representing the decadence of the city, and the curse of the industrial revolution which took people out of the countryside and enslaved them in unhealthy urban areas. One wing of the Nazi Party—the Strasser wing—flirted with socialist ideas and dreamed that the Party would be a "workers party" with solidarity among workers parties of other nations. Hitler, however, could not align himself or his Party with foreigners, communists, or leftists of any kind and the Strasserites were suppressed. Hitler was against class warfare, believing instead that the classes could be organized into an efficient structure in which each individual member of each class contributed to the overall success of the country, each organization having its own leader—it's *führer*—and each leader having another leader, up to the ultimate leader, the Führer himself. This was not the communist "dictatorship of the proletariat": it was simply a dictatorship by a single leader. While the communist theory held that the means of production in a communist state would be owned by the state, in Hitler's Reich the industrialists cooperated with the state and held onto control of the industrial apparatus, at least for the time being. The concept of total war would mobilize the entire country and be a more or less constant state, with every aspect of life, culture, and industrial production employed in the service of total war. Hitler wanted the cooperation of the industrialists; he did not want the state to become an industrial enterprise itself, for that went against his *völkisch* ideas of the beauty of nature and the superiority of a life lived outside the cities and away from the factories. Hitler, indeed, did not understand industry or care much for it, but he needed the power of industry and the capital of the bankers and financiers if Germany was to become great again. He had no time for a workers revolution that would see factory laborers try to run corporations and find a way to make them work. Hitler was about to declare war on most of Europe, and the industrial and financial strength he needed was already available. He wanted to build a strong and invulnerable Reich, and the ideologies of the Left and of communism held no appeal for him.

This encouraged German and foreign financiers to support the Nazi Party against its communist and leftist adversaries. As early as the days before the Beer Hall Putsch, American industrialist Henry Ford was a generous contributor to the Party coffers due to his hatred of labor unions, communism, and Jews. In Europe, the German and Austrian business magnates would throw in their lot with the Nazi Party and create a war machine under the noses of the Allies, in collaboration with their American counterparts.

To that end, a *Freundeskreis* was formed.

A *Freundeskreis* is a "Circle of Friends." A number of important German corporate leaders had gathered together to form a kind of lobby or political action committee to raise funds and organize influence for the Nazi Party, under the titular leadership of the head of the SS, Heinrich Himmler. The SS was the violent priesthood of the Nazi cult, composed of men who had taken an oath of allegiance to Adolf Hitler. They were men who could be trusted, unlike the Prussians in the Wehrmacht who looked down on the Austrian corporal and his ragtag bunch of followers. These members of the Circle of Friends were those who could see that Hitler had the answer to the malaise of Weimar Germany. They wanted to see Germany strong again, and to avenge what they saw as the injustices of the Versailles Treaty which had emasculated their country and blamed them for the war. Moreover, they wanted a leader who understood their values and who would stand by them: a leader who hated the communists as much as the corporate executives hated the unions.

Among these Friends were names famous in German business and industry. Begun by businessman Wilhelm Keppler (1882–1960) in 1931 as the *Freundeskreis der Wirtschaft* ("Circle of Friends of the Economy"), it was known familiarly as the Keppler Circle until, after Keppler's joining the SS in 1932, it became known as the *Freundeskreis Heinrich Himmler*, named after the head of the SS.

Keppler was the first Economics Minister of the Third Reich upon the accession of Hitler to power in 1933. He previously had been the chairman of a small I.G. Farben subsidiary, and also held a position at the Reichstag as the representative of Baden until the end of the war. His most important contribution, however, was in organizing the Freundeskreis on behalf of Himmler and the Reich. It brought together the real power brokers in Germany in an exclusive club that would exert tremendous influence over the re-arming of the country, and in ensuring preparedness for war, despite the restrictions placed upon it by the Versailles Treaty.

It was this Freundeskreis or Circle of Friends that would later meet in the Maison Rouge Hotel in Strasbourg in 1944 to decide what to do about Germany's assets in the face of almost certain defeat.

Members of the original Freundeskreis include:

Kurt Baron von Schröder of ITT, the Schröder Bank (which had Allen Dulles on the board of its American branch, Schrobanco, in 1937), and the J.H. Stein Bank (Himmler's bank, and the official bank of the Freundeskreis), as well as the Bank for International Settlements (BIS) as appointed by Hjalmar Schacht

Emil Heinrich Meyer of ITT

Hjalmar Schacht, President of the Reichsbank and architect of the Bank for International Settlements

Gottfried Graf von Bismarck-Schönhausen (grandson of Chancellor Bismarck and *Brigadeführer-SS*)

Friedrich Reinhardt, Chairman of the Board at Commerzbank

Otto Steinbrinck, Vice President of the Vereinigte Stahlwerke AG (United Steelworks, the largest steel manufacturer in Europe, manufacturing at least 50% of the Reich's total pig iron production)

August Rosterg, General Director of Wintershall, one of the largest oil companies in Europe

Ewald Hecker, chairman of Ilseder Hütte (major steel producer)

Carl Vincent Krogmann, Mayor of Hamburg and fanatical Nazi

Emil Helfferich, Director of the German-American Petroleum Company (i.e., the *Deutsche-Amerikanische Petroleum Gesellschaft*, better known by its English name as Standard Oil)

Of the above list, two personalities will stand out as being particularly important to this study. The first, of course, is Hjalmar Schacht, the talented and creative financier who made it possible for the Third Reich to re-arm even though it had little in the way of actual funds. Schacht would survive the war only to become deeply involved in the Nazi underground in Europe and in Southeast Asia.

The other name is Emil Helfferich, whose position with Standard Oil obviously was important to the Nazi war machine, but who also had a very different pedigree as a plantation owner in what was then the Dutch East Indies: what would become today's nation of Indonesia.

We will return to both of these individuals later on. For now, we will look at the Nazi funding mechanisms and how they survived the war years only to resurface in unexpected places.

BIS and OSS

> But the real significance of this flow of capital was not just financial. The bonds between the American bankers, businessmen, and industrialists, and their German counterparts, would prove far more durable than the doomed Weimar Republic, and even the Third Reich. With the BIS as the central point of contact, these links would endure during the SecondWorld War and reshape Europe after 1945.[35]

The Red House (Maison Rouge) meeting took place in August, 1944. However, the month previously reports were filed by the OSS under the signature of spy chief William J. Donovan that show the Allies were aware of capital flight taking place at that time. In one communique, Donovan reports that the Argentine Military Attache in Madrid was in contact with agents of the Nazi armament plants, Skoda and Bruenn, to obtain manufacturing rights for the Argentine military. The report goes on to state, "The money would

---

35   Adam LeBor, *The Tower of Basel*, (New York, 2013) p. 28.

be paid in free foreign exchange and a Spanish intermediary would be used for purposes of camouflage."[36]

A few days later, Donovan sent another communique to the President detailing plans for a Nazi exit strategy that involved "higher Nazi bosses" moving with their families to Austria. The report goes on to state:

> Diplomatic baggage is being sent to Spain every day. So far, diplomats are taking large packing cases, and countless valuables have already been shipped from the Reich to that country.[37]

(That report also contains information on a Hitler "double" as one possible reason why the assassination attempt known as Operation Valkyrie failed.)

Thus, the Red House meeting came at least a month after the OSS was already aware that the Nazis were moving assets to Spain. Further, the OSS was aware that deals were being struck with Spain and Argentina for the movement of funds and technology out of Germany shortly after the D-Day invasion.

In Switzerland, however, plans for salvaging Germany's wealth had been in motion long before the invasion and the subsequent assassination attempt on Hitler. This was at the offices of the Bank for International Settlements (BIS), a financial institution that was the brainchild of Hjalmar Schacht, ostensibly as a device for handling Germany's World War One reparations as required by the Treaty of Versailles.

BIS was created by Bank of England chairman Montagu Norman in collaboration with Schacht; the first, tumultuous meetings that finally gave the BIS its formal blessing involved American financier Charles G. Dawes and American industrialist Owen D. Young. Dawes was chairman of the board of City National Bank

---

36 Memorandum for the President, 17 July 1944, from William J. Donovan on OSS stationery.

37 Memorandum for the President, 26 July 1944, from William J. Donovan on OSS stationery.

and Trust of Chicago, and had been a Director of the US Bureau of the Budget, involved with German reparations arrangements after World War One. Young was the founder of the RCA Corporation and chairman of General Electric. The idea was to create a kind of clearinghouse for the funds that Germany would pay (to the tune of over 130 million gold marks per year, as per the Versailles Treaty, a sum that increaed to more than 500 million marks per year as the discussions evolved) as reparations to those countries that had lost blood and treasure in the war. BIS would be "the central bankers's central bank," a kind of super-bank, whose members included representatives from Germany, France, Belgium, Italy, Japan, and the United Kingdom. It would be immune from any country's laws and politics, the luggage of its members not subject to search by the police forces of any nation. The members of BIS were and are economic and financial diplomats, whose loyalty is not to the countries that sired them but to the Bank itself. Until 1977, in fact, the location of its headquarters in the Swiss town of Basel, hidden behind a chocolate shop, was a secret known only to a few. Outsiders were—and are—not permitted to observe meetings, or even to view the rooms where meetings were held. Its deliberations are secret, save for the annual reports, which presumably have been sanitized of any incriminating evidence.

Schacht, as president of the Reichsbank at the time of the founding of BIS (January 20, 1930), was deeply involved in its inspiration and creation. He saw BIS as a tool that could be used to move money around discretely, paying off Germany's war debts in the kind of sleight-of-hand for which Schacht was understandably famous. It was Schacht who stabilized the German mark in the years after the war, implementing what was known as the Hellferich Plan (named after Karl Hellferich, the brother of Emil who was a founding member of the Freundeskreis). The role of the Hellferich brothers cannot be overemphasized in this study, for they had tremendous influence not only in securing Germany's financial future and stability (and its ability to re-arm and wage war again), but also in supporting the rise of the Nazi Party and Adolf Hitler. Karl Hellferich was an important banker and an outspoken opponent of the Versailles Treaty. His financial acumen enabled Schacht and his colleagues to rescue Germany from the damaging reparations demands. Emil Hellferich was equally important as a high-profile supporter of the Third Reich, and in addition, had considerable experience in Indonesia, where a young Walter Hewel—confidant of Hitler since the days of the Beer Hall Putsch—would spend ten years developing the Nazi Party. After the war, as we shall see, twenty tons of Nazi gold would make its way to Indonesia, and so would Hjalmar Schacht.

For all intents and purposes, BIS was the Nazi bank during the war years—essentially the foreign branch of the Reichsbank, where deals could be cut in safety and secrecy with the heads of other central banks, including the consortium of American banks that were represented by Thomas H. McKittrick.

In 1944, meetings were being held at the highest level at the BIS headquarters in Basel to determine how to best allow the Nazi machine to survive what was seen as its inevitable defeat on the battlefield. It was a surreal composition, and if the documentation did not support it, we would have a difficult time believing it. The bankers present at these meetings included representatives from countries that were currently at war with each other, discussing how to hide and move Nazi gold to ensure continuity of the German economy in the post-war period. Indeed, according to US Treasury Secretary Morgenthau—a devoted anti-Nazi—at the 1944 Bretton Woods meeting that created the International Monetary Fund, there were a total of fourteen BIS directors, of which twelve were Nazis or members of regimes controlled by the Nazis (such as the Czechs who had to surrender all their gold to the Reich's accounts at BIS). Morgenthau's efforts to shut down the BIS were doomed to failure when the Swiss bankers threatened to walk out of the conference.

The head of the BIS at this time was an American, the said Thomas H. McKittrick, who was a friend of both Allen Dulles (at the time running the OSS office out of Bern, Switzerland) and his brother John Foster Dulles. McKittrick's policy was to ensure a smooth flow of currency into and out of BIS coffers as the Nazis provided gold that BIS could convert to other currencies to enable the Reich to purchase much-needed war materiel abroad. As late as 1943 McKittrick[38] was praising the Reich's internal stability, and stability is what the world's industrialists and bankers wanted to hear.[39] In fact, on May 1, 1943, Emil Puhl of the Reichsbank met Per Jacobssen, the Swedish BIS board member (and Nazi collaborator), to discuss Allied post-war plans.[40] Officials of the Nazi regime were perspicacious enough to realize that they might lose the war or, at the very least, be stopped before they could expand much further. There were reversals on the Russian front and supplies of much needed war materiel were being threatened on all sides.

BIS came into existence to facilitate the rise of the Third Reich by arranging reparations to be paid in such a way that Germany would not feel the pain. The Dawes Plan, and later the Young Plan, made it easier and easier for Germany to restore itself after World War One, even as the Allies were pressing for greater and greater reparations payments. Eventually, by 1932, the entire reparations plan was scrapped due to the worldwide economic crisis and the inability of Germany to pay down the debt. Even though the requirements of the Young Plan were now null and void, BIS still stood. It had been doing exactly what Nazi Germany's financial wizard Hjalmar Schacht had intended; and now he returned to the Reichsbank after a brief hiatus and took his seat on the board of BIS.

---

38 As an aside, it is worthwhile to note that McKittrick's eccentric reading habits included noted esotericist Lewis Spence's work, *The Occult Causes of the Present War* (London, Rider, 1940) which introduced the theme of Nazism as Satanism and "witchcraft." It does not seem to have convinced McKittrick, who worked diligently with Nazi bankers throughout the conflict. (LeBor, 2013, p. 69)

39 These brief characterizations of an almost impossibly complex situation are summarized from the work of Jason Weixelbaum (historian and PhD candidate at the American University in Washington, DC) as published on his excellent website, http://jasonweixelbaum.wordpress.com/2010/05/24/the-contradiction-of-neutrality-and-international-finance-the-presidency-of-thomas-h-mckittrick-at-the-bank-for-international-settlements-in-basle-switzerland-1940-46/ , last accessed July 06, 2014, and especially from Adam LeBor, *The Tower of Basel: The Shadowy History of the Secret Bank that Runs the World* (New York, PublicAffairs, 2013), perhaps the definitive text on the subject.

40 LeBor, p. 91.

The efforts of McKittrick to enable US firms such as IBM, ITT, Standard Oil, and others to do business with Nazi Germany were essential to the Reich's initial successes, both in the industrial arena and subsequently on the battlefield. The Dulles brothers also had a morally ambiguous relationship to Nazi Germany; even though Allen Dulles ran OSS intelligence operations against the Nazis, he also befriended many of them, including General Karl Wolff, whom he persuaded to surrender along with his forces in northern Italy. Both Allen Dulles and John Foster Dulles were members of the prestigious New York law firm of Sullivan & Cromwell, which itself was handling some of the legal matters for BIS—as well as for a list of American corporations who would remain friendly to the Reich for the duration of the war, such as Brown Brothers, Harriman and Co., Kuhn & Loeb, etc. The Dulles brothers had deep ties to Europe and especially to Germany, beginning in the days of the Paris Peace Conference after World War One. Their involvement in international business, finance, and espionage—and their easy accommodation with German nationalism—made them excellent contacts for the fledgling Nazi Party that they saw as the hope of a financially strong Germany.

As mentioned, McKittrick (OSS codename 644[41]) in 1943 was still encouraging investment in Nazi Germany due to its internal "stability." While this may make a great deal of sense to an investor or financier, it is just one of many indicators that the way war is perceived depends largely on who is doing the fighting. While ideologies and moral issues are important to the rank and file of every nation, and motivate young men and women to enlist and go to combat and die, to those who pay for the wars ideologies are simply fantasies with no real substance. What was different about the Third Reich was that an entire country was in the hands of ideologues and madmen who actually believed the ideologies, and who were planning on surviving long enough after the end of the war to resurrect the True Faith. In other words, the True Believers manipulated men like McKittrick, whose cynical pragmatism and moral imbecility worked well for them. Indeed, the Nazi goal of worldwide domi-

---

41 LeBor, p. 83.

nation was not so different from that of I.G. Farben or any other multinational corporation. The only difference is that the Nazis had all the guns and I.G. Farben had the camps.

I.G. Farben is the most notorious of the German corporations which were integral to the Nazi war machine, and I.G. Farben Auschwitz was one of their facilities designed for the use of slave labor. What may not be so widely known is the extent to which this company had tentacles reaching all the way into other parts of Europe and the Americas. The network of I.G. Farben subsidiaries is so vast, and the interlocking directorships of this company with American companies (and with BIS) is so intricate, that volumes have been written in an attempt to disentangle them. The company's immediate value to the Reich was in the production of oil and rubber, essential components in 20th century warfare. I.G. Farben , however, was tremendously diversified. After the war it was broken up into pieces with brand names that today are well-known, such as Bayer, Hoechst, GAF (the company's American subsidiary), and others. Indeed, the chairman of I.G. Farben —Hermann Schmitz—was a board member of BIS.

In addition, the company had an intelligence operation in the United States. Known as "Buro IG" it spied on American industry, and had agents under cover who had become American citizens and married American women to perfect their covers, as they worked to get as much technical, engineering and scientific knowledge as possible for onward transmission back to Germany.[42] This was taking place even as other German agents were infiltrating American society, managing propaganda campaigns, recruiting sympathizers, and plotting sabotage as well as espionage, as we saw earlier. Thus the Nazi war machine was functioning in virtually every arena of life, business, and culture, not only in Germany but everywhere abroad they had an interest. This was certainly unprecedented in modern history, and is reflective of an overarching worldview that is almost missionary-like in character. This was not a movement that would go quietly or surrender its faith easily, regardless of success or defeat

---

42 LeBor, 2013, p. 76.

on the battlefields. Indeed, they had taken all necessary measures to survive any eventuality.

As Allen Dulles would write in a memorandum concerning his meeting with Emil Puhl (a director of both the Reichsbank and BIS) in March of 1945:

> ... Nazism would not end with military defeat as Hitler and his fanatical followers would no more change their philosophy than would Socrates or Mohammed ... He emphasized that Nazism was like a religion and not merely a political regime.[43]

Thus, not only was Emil Puhl—tried and convicted at Nuremberg for war crimes stemming from his contribution to the Reich's financial machinery—stressing that Nazism was not going away no matter what happened in the war, but Allen Dulles, through this memorandum, was obviously aware of the conviction of this high-ranking Nazi of the durability of Nazism and of the implied threat of Nazi post-war survival. More importantly, the Allied intelligence agencies were being told, again and again, that Nazism was a cult, a religion, a faith: it was not a political party that had lost an election or a war. Religions don't die with battlefield reversals. Sometimes, defeat even enables them to thrive.

John Foster Dulles would become a Cold War Secretary of State. His brother, Allen Dulles, would become DCI: the head of the CIA, monstrous progeny of the OSS. It was Dulles who was CIA director when the Bay of Pigs operation failed against Cuba; it was Allen Dulles who was fired by President Kennedy who threatened to break the CIA into a thousand pieces; and it would be Allen Dulles who would find himself on the Warren Commission, charged with finding out what really happened that November afternoon in Dallas, 1963, when the president who fired him was shot and killed. It was Allen Dulles who ran interference at the Commission, derailing the interrogation of witness and friend of

---

43 As cited in LeBor, 2013, p. 108.

the Oswalds, Ruth Hyde Paine, when it became clear she might implicate his mistress and fellow spy, Mary Bancroft.[44]

It was also Allen Dulles who was in charge of the OSS end of Operation Safehaven, the Anglo-American plan to restrict the movement of Nazi gold and other assets out of the reach of the Allies, a plan that in the end proved to be not very successful.

Safehaven

The motivations behind Operation Safehaven were obvious: to prevent a resurgence of the Nazi Party after the war by cutting off their funds. Intercepted cables showed that the Nazis were moving large quantities of gold through neutral countries such as Spain, Portugal, Turkey, and, of course, Switzerland. Today, CIA believes that this represented the normal actions of a regime that was desperate to acquire as many foreign products as necessary (such as oil, wolfram, and other raw materials) to continue propagating the war, and was not designed to contribute to an underground Reich or a future Fourth Reich.[45] However, as other documentation (such as, but not limited to, the Red House Report) clearly demonstrates, the Reich did indeed plan for a reconstituted Germany after the war and was serious about providing a central role for the Nazi Party apparatus.

US Secretary of the Treasury Henry Morgenthau was adamant that Germany should not have an industrial base, and that the country should be reduced to the level of a basic, agrarian economy. Horrified at the obscene excesses of the Reich, and at what he saw as the willing cooperation of all its citizens, he was determined that Germany would no longer be able to wage war against its neighbors and wanted a scorched earth policy to flatten the country's indus-

---

44 As detailed in volume one of the author's *Sinister Forces* trilogy, Mary Bancroft was Dulles's mistress and the best friend of Ruth Young—Ruth Paine's mother-in-law and husband of Arthur Young, the famous inventor of the Bell Helicopter. Ruth Paine was the woman who befriended the Oswalds and who got Lee Harvey Oswald his job at the Texas Schoolbook Depository.

45 See CIA's own open source report on Safehaven at: https://www.cia.gov/library/center-for-the-study-of-intelligence/csi-publications/csi-studies/studies/summer00/art04.html, last accessed July 1, 2014.

tries. His Under Secretary, Harry Dexter White, was in total agreement with this. Both Morgenthau and White were determined to close down BIS and replace it with their own creation: the International Monetary Fund and the World Bank, which were announced at the Bretton Woods conference in 1944.

President Roosevelt also signed off on the proposal to curtail any future industrial growth of Germany after the war. This was essentially the position of the Allies in general, including Churchill. In this, they were to come up against Dulles and others—like McKittrick—who allegedly wanted a strong Germany to stand up to the Soviet Union and to be the lynchpin for Western Europe. Basically, what the pro-German lobby in the American government wanted was more or less what Nazi Germany had always wanted: a united Europe with Germany as the leader.

The strong anti-Nazi position of Morgenthau and White (as well as Roosevelt) was used against them, to paint them as leftists and Jews. Both Morgenthau and White were Jewish, and this was seen as one of the reasons behind their intractible stand against Germany. During the McCarthy period, White was accused of being a Communist agent, a charge he successfully defended. However, after his death, the publication of the so-called Venona transcripts—decoded Soviet traffic held in greatest security by the US government—seemed to prove that White was indeed spying for the Soviets. A careful examination of these transcripts in the context of the time tells a somewhat different story, and this has been described by various researchers in recent years and White's record defended.

By 1952 and the election of former Allied general Dwight D. Eisenhower to the American presidency, the position of the United States changed dramatically. The GOP establishment—and particularly those in the banking industry—were set on reversing as much of Roosevelt's New Deal as possible, and by painting anti-Nazis as "soft on Communism," they were able to characterize the accomplishments of the New Deal as virtual treason against the US government. The same strategy that had been used by Hitler to seize total control in Germany—fear of Communist plots—was used by a whole generation of right-wing zealots in the United

States to justify the witch hunts of the McCarthy era, as well as new measures undertaken to extend American hegemony around the world. One may agree or disagree with this strategy on ideological grounds, but the facts are incontrovertible. Even as the Truman administration ordered that no Nazis be accepted into the United States to work for the military or in any other capacity, Army officials ignored the wishes of their commander-in-chief and brought in hundreds of scientists, doctors, engineers, and technicians, who had known Nazi Party and even SS credentials under Operation Paperclip—sanitizing their war records to expunge any evidence of atrocities committed by them during their tenure with the Reich.

In the end, the Nazis stayed; BIS was left to do what it does best; the anti-Nazis in the US government were isolated from power; men with impeccable Nazi credentials from a number of countries (Germany, Austria, Romania, Hungary, Slovakia, Ukraine, etc.) became involved with various political lobby groups in Washington to press their interests; and the Cold War made every moral and ethical transgression not merely possible but justified in the name of anti-Communism. There was no middle way or, it should be clarified, no alternative to either Nazism or Communism. It was this political atmosphere that made it possible, for instance, for the 1950 Richard Nixon senatorial campaign in California to paint his opponent—Helen Gahagan Douglas—as a Communist and married to a Jew, and therefore unworthy of the office. In other words, the American political climate of the 1950s was little different from that of the 1930s, even after years of the bloodiest conflict in human history and the obscene spectacle of the death camps.

So while the British and American governments instituted Safehaven as a means for identifying and seizing Nazi assets abroad, men like Allen Dulles took a half-hearted approach to the problem, citing other, more pressing, intelligence issues in an effort to avoid responsibility for it entirely—even though Dulles, as a friend of McKittrick at BIS, was in the perfect position to glean economic and financial intelligence that might have helped advance Safehaven's goals considerably. While some data was obtained—famously not by Dulles, who was based in Switzerland—it was not the complete picture of Nazi asset movements that the Allies hoped for. Either

Dulles did not believe (in spite of all available intelligence reports) that the Nazis would survive the conflict and return stronger than before, or he simply did not care. Worse, he may have been hoping for just such a survival of the philosophy that had succeeded in the slaughter of forty million people, albeit with some slight modifications and adjustments. The anti-Communist hysteria of the 1930s had made it seem wiser to throw in with the Nazis than to oppose them, and Dulles was not immune to this point of view. Communism was the stated enemy of Capitalism, and Dulles was nothing if not a dedicated Capitalist. Due to the adversarial relationship between the two philosophies, it was always easier to point to the excesses of Communist regimes—the harsh and murderous rule of Joseph Stalin, for instance—than to acknowledge the brutality of many Capitalist regimes, such as the concentration camps under the Nazis, or the iron dictatorships of Franco in Spain and Salazar in Portugal (the latter two, supposedly neutral countries during the war, aided and abetted the Third Reich in covert ways and especially where moving Nazi assets was concerned). What the rest of the world saw as the hideous nature of the Third Reich and the necessity of exterminating every vestige of it on the planet, the insiders saw as an ally against a greater enemy: the Soviet Union.

It was as if Satan had appeared to Dulles (and to McKittrick, and to so many others) in the uniform of an SS officer standing on the peak of Mount Brocken, gesturing to Europe and saying "All this you shall have, if you but bow down and worship me." While Jesus famously rejected the offer,[46] Dulles accepted it with both hands.

Dulles was only part of a larger cabal of pro-Nazi American diplomats and spies that flourished in the post-war years, doing their best to control Allied response to the atrocities perpetrated by the Reich. One of those who was impatient with the liberals in the American government was William D. Pawley (1896–1977), a career diplomat with extensive ties to Latin America as well as to the famous Flying Tigers: the ersatz American-Chinese air force that fought the Japanese in China before Pearl Harbor. Pawley

---

46 Matthew 4:9–11.

fought tooth-and-nail with another US diplomat, Spruille Braden (1894–1978), who was just as involved with the corporations that would become synonymous with American involvement with Nazism (such as Standard Oil and W. A. Harriman & Co.), and with the US political and economic domination in Latin America (United Fruit).[47] Braden had created a copper mining operation in Chile, and was instrumental in getting Somoza on the presidential throne in Nicaragua. His anti-Communist credentials were impeccable if not a little tawdry, but his anti-Nazi credentials were just as strong, and this is what bothered Pawley.

Braden was outraged that the Peron regime in Argentina was harboring Nazi war criminals and was covertly assisting the remnants of the Axis powers by providing its own version of "Safehaven" by making Argentina a virtual sanctuary for Nazis on the run. Of course, this extended not only to personnel but to the valuable assets that the Nazis were using to pay their way around the world. In 1946, Braden published his infamous *Blue Book* which was a description of Argentina's collaboration with the Nazis both during and after the war.[48] In response, William Pawley (a staunch supporter of Peron, who had no patience with the breast-beating over the concentration camps or the other horrors perpetrated by the Reich) did his best to get Braden fired (unsuccessfully) and even accused him of harboring Communist sentiments: a charge which was ridiculous on its face. This case is illustrative of the way that a kind of polarity had set in where American politics was concerned after the war—a polarity with which we must contend even to the present day: to be anti-Nazi was to be pro-Communist. There was (and is) no middle way.

That was the leitmotif of the more than forty years that have passed from the end of World War II to the fall of the Soviet Union and the destruction of the Berlin Wall, and it remains the backbeat of the American political experience to this day. It is this type of simplistic template of political consciousness (or *unconsciousness*)

---

47 For a more detailed account, see my *Ratline* pp. 186–190.
48 It's official title was *Consultation Among the American Republics with Respect to the Argentine Situation.*

that is cleverly manipulated by politicians on both sides of every aisle, just as it was in Weimar Germany by men like Hitler and his propaganda chief, Goebbels.

As Germany became divided into West and East after the war as the Soviets claimed half of its territory—leaving only Berlin as an international city in the midst of the Red zone—the West German government became ground zero in the struggle against Soviet-style Communism. As German industrialists returned to resurrect the corporations and the factories that had fueled the Nazi war machine with slave labor, so too did many officials of the Nazi regime find new positions in the West German government. In addition, CIA created an anti-Soviet intelligence operation there composed of mostly former Nazis and SS-men with experience in espionage and counter-espionage against the Russians. This was run by former Nazi intelligence chief on the Eastern Front, General Reinhard Gehlen, and his operation became known as the Gehlen Organization or the Gehlen Org. In 1956, the Gehlen Org became the West German intelligence service, the BND (*Bundesnachrichtendienst* or Federal Intelligence Service)—and thus were many Nazis, including SS and Gestapo agents, incorporated into the German military and intelligence establishment as if nothing had ever happened.

Due to the deep involvement of the Dulles brothers with Nazi personalities and organizations and their pragmatic, *realpolitik* view of the world—as well as their associations with many of the firms that had been doing business with the Nazis right through the war— there would have been no real desire to focus on the post-war threat of Nazism lest it shine a light into uncomfortable corners of global finance and other *liaisons dangereuses*. It was more important to the bankers, financiers, and corporate executives that a strong Germany be rebuilt against the threat of Soviet-style communism than it was to worry about a resurgence of the Nazi Party, the SS, or its ideology. In fact, a vigorous German nationalism might well be the best fortress against the Soviet Union, as long as such nationalism could be directed in the right channels.

The exit strategy of the Reich was therefore twofold. In the first place, as many as possible of the trustworthy true believers had to be rescued, especially those whose intelligence and contribution to the war effort and to the success of Nazism had already been proven. This included the SS, of course, but also those Nazis who had demonstrated not only their loyalty but also their acumen. In the second place, as much of German technology, tangible assets, patents, engineering capability, and manufacturing capability as possible had to be expatriated. These assets would be employed in a variety of ways in countries that were sympathetic to Nazi aims or were, at least, not hostile to them. The Third Reich would be reconstituted abroad: not in a single country or region where it could be contained once again, but spread over the globe like a multinational corporation. Like I.G. Farben , in fact. The Nazis learned an important lesson from their involvement with the Bank for International Settlements, and that is that a nation need not be restricted to an idea of national borders, but that it could exist in a kind of virtual space, everywhere and nowhere all at once, like a bank account. The movement of currencies through the BIS coffers in Basel worked like a kind of magic. There were no teller windows at BIS. No adding machines. The physical plant of the bank consisted of some meeting rooms and some filing cabinets. The place had once been a hotel, and the hotel rooms had simply been refurnished with desks and chairs. There were telephones, enabling the bank's directors to conduct business worldwide. That was about it. These were men united in their desire to ensure the continuity of power and industry in Germany, regardless of the moral or ethical dimensions of their hidden agenda. The facilitation of the bank transfers, the movement of the gold (there was no illusion as to how the gold was obtained, and under what dire circumstances), the survival of the Nazi corporations were all accomplished with a wink and a nod, and a small commission.[49]

This nebulous construct was what enabled the Nazi corporations and their American and European subsidiaries and counterparts to keep the machinery of war running at full speed. Money has no national boundaries and neither, as the war wound down

---

49 The similarity of this to the *hawala* system used in the Middle East and Central and South Asia and as described later in this book, is revealing.

and the Reich lay devastated, did the Nazi Party. It had established branches throughout the world and attracted sympathizers in regions as remote from Germany as Latin America, the Middle East, India, Japan, and Southeast Asia. It had become a transnational cult, capable of eliciting the admiration of the colonized and the colonizer alike, depending on their own need for justification and empowerment. It was a doctrine of strength and will, of the worship of nature, and contempt for mercy, compassion, and the Judeo-Christian tradition, which was seen as servile and weak, a belief system for victims and not for champions, a True Faith for the collaterally damaged.

The Islamic tradition, however, was much more interesting to the Cold Warriors.

CHAPTER SIX

FASCISTS AND FEDAYEEN

Mohammed knew that most people are terribly cowardly and stupid. That is why he promised two beautiful women to every courageous warrior who dies in battle. This is the kind of language a soldier understands. When he believes that he will be welcomed in this manner in the afterlife, he will be willing to give his life, he will be enthusiastic about going to battle and not fear death. You may call this primitive and you may laugh about it, but it is based on deeper wisdom. A religion must speak a man's language.

—Reichsführer-SS Heinrich Himmler[50]

To accuse one's political adversaries of being Nazis is to engage in relatively meaningless polemic, since the term Nazi has been used by just about everyone to characterize just about everyone else. To equate Islamist terror groups with Nazis seems equally pointless, an appeal to emotion rather than logic: a shorthand for everything evil or sinister. However, as we shall see, the identification of Nazism with some of the more virulent ideological positions of Islamist groups is not all hyperbole.

Recent publications in the relatively new academic field of fascism studies have identified several characteristics that may be considered emblematic of fascism.[51] These include utopianism, or a desire to create the perfect society: often a nostalgic longing for what is referred to as *in illo tempore*, or "in that time," i.e., a golden age. This is a belief (in the face of all empirical evidence) that such

---

50   As quoted in the memoir of Himmler's masseur, Felix Kersten, *Totenkopf und Treue. Heinrich Himmler ohne Uniform* (Hamburg: Robert Mölich Verlag, 1952), p. 203.

51   See Tamir Bar-On, "The French New Right's Quest for Alternative Modernity" in *The Journal of Comparative Fascist Studies*, Vol. 1 (2012) pp. 18-52 for an introduction to the basic elements of this discussion.

a society was ever possible or ever existed. Nazi visions of a perfect state reflect this longing, especially when combined with its neo-pagan, pre-Christian trappings. Muslim longing for the return of the *khalifah*, or caliphate, is evidence of a similar vision of a perfect state.

This characteristic often appears paired with anti-modernity. The modern world is seen as sick and decadent, the product of the industrial revolution and the move to the cities, in which human beings are herded together in housing units of ever-decreasing size, working at meaningless jobs for which they receive only subsistence pay or benefits. Anti-modernity also includes attacks on modern art, literature, music, and other cultural expressions. Sayid Qutb, the founder of the modern Salafist movement that had such an influence on contemporary Islamism, attacked modernity as spiritually bankrupt and evidence of the decadence of the West. At the same time he criticized jazz and modern music as "savage" and the apparent freedom of women in America as revealing the decline of morality, a poison that he feared would infect the Arab (i.e., Muslim) world as well. Thus, anti-modernity has a spiritual component. To be modern is to be Western, is to be spiritually empty.

Islamism became the outgrowth of this moral position, a blending of conservative Islamic thought with an activist political agenda, a liberation movement targeting the colonial powers under the guise of attacking decadent Western culture. It was a reaction to the unacceptable status of Arabs as serfs in their own lands, perceived as the result of a loss of true faith. In this it was similar to the Nazi viewpoint that the defeat of Germany in the First World War was the result of the cultural, racial, and moral weakness of its leaders. Both Nazism (and fascism) and Islamism are revolutionary movements; but Nazism and Islamism, in particular, are revolutionary movements with a spiritual dimension, a desire to create a new spiritual state in combination with a new political reality. Both Nazism and Islamism see that there is no point in dividing church and state: that church and state, religion and political government, are indivisible. This is the Islamist as well as the Nazi point of view.

There are differences, of course, between Nazism and Islamism. In the first place, Islamism is international in scope, an appeal to all

Muslims anywhere in the world, whereas Nazism and fascism are by definition nationalisms. Islamism is not (overtly) racist, even though a subtle preference is given to Arabs over other Muslims, and the blood descendants of the Prophet are held in high esteem above all others, thus linking Islamist ideas of the blood to Nazi ideals of racial purity. Even then, however, Islamism cannot be considered racism, though accusations of anti-Semitism are legitimate enough. This may be due to the fact that at this time—the early decades of the 20th century—the Arabs in general were an oppressed people and not in a position to oppress anyone else. Further, they were hopelessly divided amongst themselves: tribe versus tribe, Bedouin versus city-dwellers, region versus region, even Shi'a versus Sunni. By declaring all non-Muslims as "other," there was the possibility of uniting these various factions into a pan-Arab movement, but all such efforts so far have failed.

By substituting religion for racism, the Islamist movement became international in scope. This was encouraged by the ruse of the Western powers who attempted to use the newly-minted concept of "global" jihad to unite Muslims against their (the Westerners') enemies—as discussed in chapter two. Thus, the Muslims became proxies of the West, and jihad was the tool used by the West to manipulate Muslim (primarily Arab and Central Asian) sentiments and arouse a religiously-infused militancy directed against Western targets.

Due to its internationalist character, global jihadists could potentially transcend their ultra-nationalist brothers on the extreme right (Nazis, fascists), but this is also their inherent weakness. Can the jihadists rely on a rudimentary religious bond and a superficial identity as "Muslim" to supersede centuries of mutual distrust and antagonism? As we have seen with the rise of groups like the Islamic State (formerly known as the Islamic State of Iraq and Syria (ISIS) or the Islamic State of Iraq and the Levant (ISIL)) and other militant or terror groups, there is no consensus among the jihadists as to who can rule, command, and inspire them. They will still fall victim to charismatic leaders (like Osama bin Laden) regardless of fine theological distinctions, and in this they are little different from the populist leaders like Hitler, Mussolini, Pavelic,

Franco, Peron, etc. who defined themselves much better than they could define an over-arching political philosophy. Of all the fascisms of the 20th century, Nazism survives due to its symbol set, its book, its charismatic leader, its adoration of violence, its worship of the masculine principles embedded in the heroic ideal, and its exclusionary positions. Italian fascism never had all of these to the extent that Nazism did. For jihadism to survive it must adopt more of these characteristics. While it can be argued that they have a book—the Qur'an—it is interpreted freely by all Muslims and in different ways by various theological factions. *Mein Kampf* is more powerful (in this sense) in that it is not studied, so much as held up as a kind of totem. Islamism requires a symbol set that transcends language (like the swastika), for its symbols to this date are largely Arabic verses and relate specifically to Arab language and culture; it needs a swastika equivalent.

It also needs a charismatic leader who is strong enough to unite the warring factions and so far this has not happened. Jihadism is still sectarian and subject to pressures from both within and without.

An Islamist-Nazi combination would be virtually unstoppable: a genuine, living spiritual tradition mixed with an inclusive internationalism; anti-modernity; anti-Semitism; a Manichaean worldview; hero worship; and a potent symbol system with a charismatic leader, the latter of which have yet to be discovered.

There have been a few attempts, however, and they can only provide us with a foretaste of what will come.

We have already shown how the concept of "global jihad" was invented, not by the Muslims, but by a German, an amateur archaeologist—who thought he had discovered the key to uniting the Arabs of the Middle East, as well as the Muslims of Central, South, and Southeast Asia into an uprising against the colonial powers of England, France, and Russia on behalf of the Kaiser's Germany. This militarization and politicization of the religious concept of sacred struggle was embraced by the Arab world's foremost proponent of anti-colonialism and avowed enemy of the English, the Hajj Amin al-Husseini, Grand Mufti of Jerusalem.

Al-Husseini had not been silent during the greatest conflict of
the twentieth century. He saw in the Nazis an important ally against
the British occupation of Palestine, especially so as the Nazis were
also aggressively anti-Semitic. It was a throwback to al-Husseini's
own history as a soldier with the Ottoman Turks, who had formed
an alliance with Germany during the First World War, declaring a
jihad against the enemies of Islam. Now, during the Second World
War, al-Husseini would revive the idea of global jihad in forming a
division of Bosnian Muslims for the Third Reich.

Known as the Handschar Division (the *handschar* was a type of
knife unique to the Turks who had control over the Balkans until
the early 20th century),[52] the 13th Waffen Mountain Division of
the SS was composed of mostly Balkan Muslims and some Croatian Catholics who would fight alongside the Nazis for the duration
of the conflict. These troops fought in Europe, not the Middle East,
but it was central to the Mufti's idea of global jihad that Muslims
should fight against the British, French, and Russians wherever the
"colonialists" and "Zionists" could be found. In fact, much of the
action seen by the Handschar Division was against the socialist
partisans under Josep Tito, who was attempting to form his own
Yugoslav Republic. This was analogous to the motivation behind
the Ukrainian SS unit, composed of men who wanted to fight on
the side of the Nazis in order to liberate their homeland from Soviet
rule. "The enemy of my enemy is my friend," so goes the Arab prov-
erb, and the truth of this dictum was nowhere more apparent than it
was during the Second World War. It was this polarization of ideology against ideology—rather than country against country—that
formed the template from which future conflicts, both global and
local, would be spawned.

Initially, the Muslims balked at serving with the Nazis, but it
was al-Husseini who assured the *ulama* that it was the right thing
to do. From the Nazi point of view, it was Himmler who stated that
he admired the Muslim fighters for their excess of valor and even

---

52 The definitive text on this bizarre SS division, with its full complement of
imams, is George Lepre, *Himmler's Bosnian Division: the Waffen-SS Handschar
Division 1943-1945*, Atglen (PA), Schiffer Military History, 1997.

brutality on the battlefield, and their willingness to die for a holy cause, a jihad. He even considered as plausible the arguments that were put forward by the Croatians and the Bosnians that they were, in reality, Aryans and not Slavs. Certainly, al-Husseini himself, with his fair hair and blue eyes, fit the Nordic stereotype.

Let loose upon the Balkan countryside, these troops proved to be as vicious as any other in the SS armory, committing atrocities against local Jewish and Serbian populations as well as fighting the socialist partisans. Their mission supposedly was to perform counter-insurgency operations against the partisans under Tito, and keep order for the Nazi puppet regime, the Ustase under Ante Pavelic. The Muslims, however, did not trust the Croatians, even after Pavelic built them a mosque in Zagreb. Pavelic's wooing of the Muslims was part of his overall plan to ensure that Bosnia (which had a large Muslim population) would remain an integral part of the country he was trying to form out of Croatia, Bosnia, Herzegovina, and parts of Serbia. Although a Catholic, Pavelic had no difficulty in exploiting Muslim sensitivities in his efforts to create a Nazi regime in the Balkans that would, at times, exceed even Nazi brutality in the concentration camps he created and left under the control of Catholic priests, such as the notorious Jasenovac Concentration Camp.

Eventually the tide of war turned against the Ustase and against the SS Handschar Division. The leaders of the Ustase regime found it necessary to flee abroad, to avoid capture and prosecution by the Allies. This also extended to some of the Handschar officers—those who managed to avoid being extradited to Yugoslavia to stand trial for war crimes, such as Major General Sauberzweig (who committed suicide), and SS Obersturmführer Imam Halim Malkoč who was executed in 1947.

When it came time to arrange for the escape of the Ustase leaders (and the Ustase treasure, much of it in gold), it was a Croatian Catholic priest—Monsignor Krunoslav Draganovic—who organized the itinerary and who provided the false papers necessary to permit Pavelic and virtually the entire Ustase government to flee to Argentina. Draganovic's name and contact information also appear in an address book kept by the Chief Medical Officer of the Salzburg Gau, Dr. Med. Georg Anton Pöch. As detailed in *Ratline*, Dr. Pöch provides the key to examining the extent of the Nazi escape routes to Southeast Asia, a fact heretofore never examined by other researchers in this field. It is also Dr. Pöch who introduces us to the bizarre phenomenon of Nazis who converted to Islam.

Towards the end of his life in exile on the Indonesian island of Sumbawa, the enigmatic Austrian doctor became a Muslim. A dedicated Nazi since before the Anschluss, Pöch had the impeccable credentials of a loyal Party member and capable (and well-connected) functionary of the Nazi regime. While I have had the opportunity to examine some of the documents left behind by Pöch during an extended research trip in Singapore, I cannot definitively say whether the individual who escaped to Indonesia after the war—after a lengthy sojourn in the Bolzano (Bozen) region of the Italian Tyrol—was in reality Dr. Pöch himself, or someone else who had appropriated his documentation for purposes of concealing his true identity, much as Ernst Kaltenbrunner had taken the identity of another medical doctor in his attempt to flee the authorities in the region outside Salzburg. What his papers do suggest, however, is that the doctor was a devoted Nazi, who had ample opportunity to make good use of the contacts he had to get out of Europe and to South America. Yet, rather than follow his colleagues across the Atlantic to certain safety in Argentina, Bolivia, Brazil, Chile, Uruguay, or any of the other countries that welcomed Nazi fugitives—countries that were at least Christian and Westernized to some extent, and where he could find European food and culture—he chose the largest Muslim country on earth, on the other side of the world, and on the most remote island he could find.

This decision seemed counter-intuitive at the time I encountered the story of Georg Anton Pöch, but since then enough information has come to light to suggest that his story is by no means anomalous. Rather, we can now show that *hundreds* of Nazi war criminals and SS members converted to Islam after the war, and many of these found themselves working for Arab regimes in North Africa and the Levant. This element of the Nazi exit strategy is one that bears close inspection, for it reveals the extent that Nazi ideology and Nazi personalities were able to influence political directions in the Middle East long after the end of hostilities in Europe—political directions that have taken an increasingly dangerous turn since the fall of the Soviet Union when one of Nazism's archetypal enemies was destroyed, leaving only Israel and the United States left with which to settle scores.

An appendix to this book will give a list of some of the known Nazis who converted to Islam. For now, it is enough to describe a few of the more prominent in order to demonstrate not only that they escaped justice, but that they continued their work for the Party and, in many cases, for the SS for decades after May of 1945. The relevance of this information cannot be overstated: Nazism continued to thrive after the war because it is not a political party per se but—as even Josef Goebbels admitted—a religion. It is a religion that made common cause with the anti-colonialist element of Islamic nationalism that was born in the Middle East as a result of British and French power politics in the region. Both Nazism and what is often referred to as Islamism are opponents of what they perceive to be decadent Western culture and rampant capitalism; they are opponents of what they perceive to be a global Jewish conspiracy to control the world; and they both idolize romantic notions of male dominance, the warrior ethos, and a return to the simplicity of a bygone age (ideas that are familiar to those who study *bushido*, the Japanese cult of the warrior, and indeed there were more than just ideological similarities, as we will see). Islamists wish to reconstitute the Caliphate in a region that some identify as stretching from the Middle East and North Africa to Southeast Asia. Nazis wish to reconstitute the Third Reich. Old empires, ancient dreams.

The stuff of religion and spiritual aspiration.

One of the first to realize that there could be an ally in Middle East Arabism was SS-Obersturmbannführer (Lieutenant Colonel) Adolf Eichmann (1906–1962). What is not generally known is that Eichmann visited Palestine in 1937 while already in the SS, and that he spoke some Hebrew and Yiddish. Eichmann's purpose in Palestine was to determine whether German Jews would be able to emigrate there. However, a larger Jewish presence in Palestine would ultimately have led to the Jews having a state from which they could organize themselves into a regional if not a global power, and that idea was scrapped as it ran counter to Nazi policy concerning the Jews. During that visit, however, Eichmann visited both Palestine and Cairo, meeting at one point with a representative of the Haganah who argued for a larger number of Jewish emigres. Germany and Italy had already been offering military and other assistance to the Palestinians in a somewhat sporadic manner, all arranged by the Mufti, so he was not an unknown entity to the Reich.

This was during the Arab Revolt in Palestine (1936–1939), and the position of the Jews at that time during the British Mandate was problematic. They saw their enemies as both the Arabs and the British, just as the Arabs saw their enemies as the Jews and the British. It is not known whether Eichmann met with leaders of the Arab resistance—such as the Grand Mufti[53]—or with elements of the Muslim Brotherhood (*Ikhwan*) in Cairo which was similarly anti-British (Egypt was under British control at the time as well) and anti-Semitic. It is known that Eichmann attempted to enter Palestine after his meetings in Cairo, but was turned away by the British. That same year, the Grand Mufti had to escape Palestine due to a British arrest warrant that had been issued for him due to his role in the Arab Revolt. Al-Husseini lived for awhile in Lebanon and Iraq before finally making his way to Rome and then Berlin in 1941.

Eichmann's interests also included Freemasonry, and his first job with the SS was to curate the Freemasonry material that had been seized from German lodges and, later, from lodges in the occupied territories. In other words, Eichmann's brief could be identified with that twin bugaboo of Nazi—and, later, Islamist—paranoia: the Jewish-Masonic conspiracy.

Eichmann traveled along the same ratline after the war that was taken by so many others. He wound up in Argentina, working as a clerk for other Nazi fugitives who had held much lower rank

---

53 There has been some controversy over an allegation that Eichmann and al-Husseini met at this time (1937) in Palestine, and that they had reached some sort of mutual understanding. Eichmann admitted meeting the Grand Mufti, but only after the latter's arrival in Berlin at a state function.

than he during the war, a situation that must have bothered him greatly. He found other servile employment in various companies in Argentina. He was often ostracized by his own people, possibly due to his notoriety as one of the architects of the Final Solution—a participant in the infamous Wannsee Conference, during which the details of the *Endlösung* were hammered out. His later kidnapping by the Mossad and subsequent trial in Jerusalem actually might have boosted his ego somewhat, even as it sealed his doom.

As exposed as he had been to Freemasonry, Jews, and Arab nationalism, however, he did not convert to Islam. His religion had always been Nazism and it remained that way until his execution. Others, however, were more pragmatic.

One of the pre-eminent Arabists within the Reich was Sturm-banführer-SS Dr. Johann von Leers (1902–1965). An early participant in the Freikorps brigades that fought communist groups in Weimar Germany after World War One, he was also a relatively early member of the Nazi Party (1929) and became an SS officer in 1936. Von Leers had studied law and was fluent in several languages, including Japanese. He was briefly a professor at the University of Jena, and had even worked for awhile at the Foreign Office. Tapped by Goebbels to work in the Propaganda Ministry, von Leers was a prolific writer of anti-Semitic tracts. He compared Islam favorably with Judaism, preferring the heroic warrior mystique of the Arabs to what he saw as the decadent condition of the Jews—who, he believed, measured success in purely financial (i.e., capitalist) terms and were thus essentially criminals. Like other Nazis, including Himmler, von Leers believed that the Prophet Muhammad had taken care of the "Jewish problem" in the Middle East. He believed that what he saw as the relatively lax position taken by Christian Europe towards the Jews was what led to the growth of Jewish cabals and to the empowerment of European Jewry.

When the war ended, von Leers escaped to northern Italy, where he remained for five years (roughly the same amount of time, and in the same region, as Dr. Georg Anton Pöch), before leaving for Argentina in 1950. In Argentina, he continued his pro-Nazi, anti-Semitic propaganda activities by publishing the National Socialist *Der Weg,* a German-language periodical that featured articles by von Leers and also by Otto Skorzeny, Hans-Ulrich Rudel, and Otto Remer—further evidence that the SS was composed of true believers who would not willingly abandon their faith, even years after the defeat of the Third Reich. An American, H. Keith Thompson, was their United Nations correspondent in New York, a personality to which we will return.

Von Leers was eventually convinced to come to Egypt by Hajj Amin al-Husseini himself. In Egypt, von Leers worked first for Egyptian President Naguib, and then for Naguib's replacement, General Gamal Abdel Nasser, working in Egypt's version of Goebbels's Propaganda Ministry, the Department for Jewish Questions in the Egyptian Information Ministry. It was about this time that he converted to Islam and took the name Omar Amin, a name that could be interpreted to mean "eloquent speaker" (Omar) of Amin, i.e., Amin al-Husseini, his mentor: in other words, the Grand Mufti's mouthpiece. Such an homage would not be out of the question for von Leers, for he remained a fanatic to the end of his life.

We would not need to dwell too much on von Leers except for the fact that he had tremendous reach, even into the United States, and was an associate of Ahmed Huber (1927–2008). Huber was the Swiss Nazi, and Muslim convert, who formed one of the contemporary links between Islamist terror groups and Nazi organizations and individuals. Von Leers is also known to have flown to France in the wake of the Eichmann kidnapping in 1960 to meet with the Belgian Nazi SS-Standartenführer (Colonel) Leon Degrelle, then at the hub of a global network of Nazi fugitives and their supporters in the United States, Latin America, and Europe, as well as the Middle East.[54] The idea was to come up with a way to manage the news fallout from the trial in order to spin the testimony in such a way that it would be beneficial to the Nazis (obviously, as late as 1960, this was still a concern that merited international consultations). Von Leers' relationship with SS General Otto Remer was also well-known—as it was Remer who became a kind of poster-

---

54   In fact, Degrelle's name and address appear in the Rudel address book.

boy for everything from Holocaust denial to ODESSA and its various manifestations.

Otto Ernst Remer (1912–1997) was a career Wehrmacht officer who left the service in 1945 with the rank of Brigadier General (*Generalmajor*). It was Remer whose role in stopping Operation Valkyrie—the assassination attempt on Hitler's life and the resulting military coup—made him one of Hitler's most trusted generals. Working alongside Remer in the aftermath of the assassination attempt, and the ensuing roundup and execution of its participants, was Ernst Kaltenbrunner and Otto Skorzeny.

Kaltenbrunner would be apprehended by the Allies near Salzburg at the end of the war and was eventually executed at Nuremberg. Skorzeny, also apprehended in the same area, managed to escape (or was allowed to escape) in 1948, and carried on his Nazi activities to the end of his life.

Remer, on the other hand, also was captured by the Allies but only remained a prisoner until 1947, at a time when the attitudes of the Allies had shifted to a more anti-Communist position. Remer, not content to remain in the background during the Cold War, cofounded the Socialist Reich Party on October 2, 1949, an openly pro-Nazi party that was eventually banned by the West German government about two years later. Regardless of this setback, Remer remained a profound influence on the underground Nazi movement for the rest of his life, and helped to formulate a "third way" philosophy for the generation of Nazis who would come after him, a philosophy that involved support for a variety of pro-Arab and pro-Islamist movements. While rejecting both communism and capitalism, the "third way" Nazi philosophy could appeal to a wide variety of groups that felt victimized or oppressed by the superpowers that were largely perceived as new colonialist regimes. It was a "plague on both your houses" ideology that garnered support from Islamist activists, who rejected what they saw as the crass materialism of capitalism as well as the militant atheism of communism. And as the decades moved from the 1940s to the 1950s and 1960s, colonialism began to take on different forms, including cultural and economic strategies that disempowered the former Ottoman territories even further. What began as colonies in the centuries prior to the Second World War, became "spheres of influence" in the post-war era, divided up between the Soviet Union on the one side and the United States on the other.

Before it was banned, Remer's Socialist Reich Party offered him a very public platform for the rejection of West German dependence on the United States. He even made overtures to the Soviet Union, in an attempt to create an imbalance within the West German government that would topple its leadership and create a vacuum for the Socialist Reich Party to fill. The party platform included Holocaust denial, and went so far as to accuse the United States of having fabricated film footage of the death camps and having created the crematoria for propaganda purposes. The Soviet Union saw the Socialist Reich Party as a useful tool for destabilizing the West German government, and went so far as to provide some financial assistance towards that end. Needless to say, by 1952, when the party was banned, Remer had to find other avenues for his political philosophy. Accused by the West German government of trying to revive the Nazi Party, a warrant was issued for his arrest. He fled to Egypt, where he developed a close working relationship with General Nasser, as well as with Johann von Leers, and became involved in the arms trade. His customers included mainly other Arab nations.

By 1956, Remer was involved in gun running in Syria and in providing arms to the Algerian National Liberation Front (and similar groups), through his own import-export house, the Orient Trading Company based in Damascus. There is evidence to support the claim that Remer had a close working relationship in Damascus with Alois Brunner—one of the most wanted Nazis in the world and Adolf Eichmann's deputy—a war criminal with tens of thousands of victims to his name. Brunner survived not only the war, but at least two assassination attempts by the Israeli secret service, the Mossad, who mailed him letter bombs that took an eye and some of the fingers of his left hand. There is no evidence that he has died. As late as 2001, there were Brunner sightings in Damascus. Indeed, he gave interviews to various reporters in the late 1980s, in which he voiced his satisfaction at the Holocaust and with his role in it (a situation that, in itself, gives the lie to Holocaust deniers who claim it never happened).

The various North African liberation movements were heavily supported by Nazis at various levels of the supply chain: from operational experts like Remer, Brunner and Skorzeny; to propagandists like von Leers and Rudel; to financial wizards like Hjalmar Schacht and the irrepressible François Genoud (see below). The groundwork for what would become the third attempt at global jihad, after the failed attempts of World Wars One and Two, was laid in the 1950s, and it would enjoy the financial and operational expertise of hundreds, if not thousands, of dedicated Nazis in the Middle East, North Africa, and around the world. They were assisted in this endeavor by new converts to Nazism as well as by Arab nationalists, and a growing demographic of Islamist jihadists culled from the meeting rooms of the Muslim Brotherhood. Groups like al-Qaeda and Jemaah Islamiyyah would not rise to pose a serious threat to the West until the breakup of the Soviet Union, when Islamists became emboldened by the retreat of Soviet forces from Aghanistan, the fall of the Berlin Wall, and the resulting power vacuum in the Middle East and elsewhere. The failure of Soviet Communism was only Phase One of the Nazi-Islamist "third way" strategy, however. The second phase would involve the elimination of the second major super-power from the world stage: that bastion of capitalism, the United States of America.

In the 1960s the Soviet Union and the United States were locked in a Cold War. This war had two levels of experience: on the one hand it was an ideological conflict between two mutually-exclusive points of view on how humanity should be organized. It was capitalism versus communism, and religion versus atheism. On the other hand, this was a power struggle between two military behemoths. Both sides courted the Arab nations due to their proximity to the oil fields, the Suez Canal, and the land bridge between Europe and Asia.

The third factor in the Cold War was the presence of large numbers of Nazi military, espionage, and scientific experts in Europe and the Middle East. These were professional anti-Semites who were only too happy to assist Egypt, Syria, and other Arab nations in their intrigues against Israel. Many had been recruited through the Gehlen Organization in West Germany, ostensibly under direction of the CIA. Others made their way to the Middle East through the ratlines. In the case of von Leers, he had already escaped to Argentina before setting his sights on Egypt. Others took a more direct route, such as Alois Brunner, who went directly from Rome to Cairo and then to Damascus.

And then there was Aribert Heim (1914–1992?), or "Doctor Death" as he was known at the Mauthausen Concentration Camp.

An SS doctor very much in the mold of Dr. Mengele, the "Angel of Death" of Auschwitz, Dr. Heim experimented on live prisoners by injecting their organs with toxic chemicals. An Austrian by birth, Aribert Ferdinand Heim received his doctorate in Vienna after studying in Graz (the cities where we also will find fellow Austrian physician Dr. Georg Anton Pöch during the same period, although Pöch was a generation older). Heim joined the SS only after Austria had become part of the Greater German Reich, and rose to the rank of captain by the end of the war. As numerous reports confirm, Dr. Heim, in at least one instance, hideously mutilated an 18-year old Jewish man, after which he made a paperweight of the victim's skull.

He was captured by the Allies in May of 1945, but was released and permitted to continue his medical practice as a gynecologist undisturbed; the authorities were unaware of the atrocities he had committed. However, by 1962 he had been identified as the Butcher of Mauthausen and a warrant was issued for his arrest. One step ahead of the authorities, and painfully aware of the arrest and conviction of Adolf Eichmann who was executed that year, Heim drove relentlessly through Europe to Gibraltar and caught a ferry across the Mediterranean to Morocco. From there, he wound up in Libya and then Egypt, where he converted to Islam, took the name Tarek Hussein Farid, and continued to function as a doctor until his alleged death in 1992 in Cairo. Heim was one of the most wanted Nazi fugitives in the world at the time, and rumors of his existence—everywhere from Spain to Latin America—were rife. But it was the discovery in Cairo of a battered suitcase with his documents that proved his flight to Egypt, and which satisfied the authorities that Doctor Death was indeed, himself, very much dead. It was rumored that he had assistance from Skorzeny in Spain on his flight to North Africa and, indeed, it seems almost impossible to believe that Heim would have made it very far without the connivance of ODESSA. From the false identification papers he would have needed to avoid capture by the police who had been alerted to the arrest warrant issued against him, to the funds necessary to survive until he could establish himself (he had left his medical office in the middle of the day without warning when he learned of the warrant by a phone call to his wife), the Brotherhood would have been there to help.

Otto Skorzeny was very much part of this network. He ran guns into North Africa and the Middle East through his arms dealership in Spain. For Skorzeny, the allure of the arms trade was not purely economics; he remained a true believer, and assisted those with whom he felt he shared a common ideology. Anti-Communism was a primary motivating factor; anti-Semitism ran a close second. Eventually, Skorzeny, Remer, Brunner, von Leers, and so many other wanted criminals wound up working for the Egyptian government of Gamal Abdel Nasser. By 1961 they were overseeing the creation of the Egyptian rocket industry, developing surface-to-surface missiles that were used to target Israel. In much the same way as Operation Paperclip scientists—made up of former Nazis and many SS men, such as Wehrner von Braun—were recruited by the US Army to develop offensive weaponry, the Egyptian program was designed to jump-start military technology. It resulted in the development of at least two missile systems by this time: the Al Zafir and the Al Kahir. Believed to have a range of 350 kilometers, the Al Zafir was a liquid-fueled rocket capable of delivering a modest 60 kilogram warhead; the Al Kahir was somewhat larger and modeled after the V-2 rockets developed at Peenemunde by Nazi scientists during the war, having a greater range and greater payload capability. Their only obstacle at the time was the guidance system, and there was some debate over using a wire-guidance system versus the traditional V-2 type, which was more accurate but considerably more difficult to design.

In the United States, NASA was using Nazi scientists to develop the technology that would put a man on the moon. In Egypt, Nazi rocket scientists, with essentially the same background as their counterparts working for the US, were developing strategic weapons to be used against Israel. In the middle of all this frenetic activity—the fascists supporting the fedayeen—were Remer, Skorzeny, Schacht, and Genoud. Given greater impetus by the 1960 kidnapping of Adolf Eichmann from Argentina by Israeli commandos, his subsequent trial in Jerusalem, and inevitable execution in 1962, the Nazis in Egypt felt tremendous pressure to ramp up their operations—not only against Israel, which had just demonstrated the kind of threat they posed, but against the wide range of their enemies worldwide. These included Nazi hunters like Simon Wiesenthal to liberal politicians, communist insurgents in Latin America and Asia, and their traditional foes such as the French, who were trying to hold onto what colonies they could in North Africa. Eichmann's defense had been arranged by von Leers, who obtained the financing from his colleague François Genoud. Just where that financing originated forms an integral part of the story of the Hitler Legacy, and for that we have to begin with the Skorzeny Hunting Society.

CHAPTER SEVEN

THE SKORZENY HUNTING SOCIETY

1949—Former members of SA, SS, Wehrmacht, and Hitler Youth reportedly were joining together to form groups, at first local, then gradually attempting to form statewide organizations. Some of these groups are reportedly anti-American while others are anti-Communist. Confusion existed, and negotiations were reportedly going on for the purpose of agreeing on a policy and selecting a leader. SKORZENY and Lt. RADEL [sic] were listed as representing the Armed SS (Waffen SS?).

> —(Source: FBI ltr 6 April 1949 to Department of State, subject, "Communist Party Plans in Germany," classified CONFIDENTIAL)

The above quotation is from a "Summary of Information" report dated 29 March 1951 from the Assistant Chief of Staff, G-2 (US Army intelligence) with the subject "Otto SKORZENY" and stamped "TOP SECRET CONTROL." The "Lt. RADEL" is actually a reference to Luftwaffe Ace Hans-Ulrich Rudel, and the two men—Skorzeny and Rudel—can be said to represent the face of what subsequent investigators and authors have identified as ODESSA. They are the "face" of ODESSA in that they were the two men most publically identified as belonging to, or running, the Nazi underground network in the decades after World War II, and they both were authors of popular books on their wartime experiences. Whereas Rudel's role seems more in line with that of a sales and marketing executive for the post-war Nazi Party, Skorzeny was actively involved in the operational aspect: running guns, arranging financing, and building bridges between fascist and Nazi sympathizers world-wide to assist in the smooth functioning of the underground.

Rudel was de-nazified at the end of the war, and according to my phone interview with one of the people listed in his address book—aviation engineer Pierre Sprey—who knew Rudel personally, the ace Luftwaffe pilot had never been a die-hard Nazi until the denazification process itself. It was the insistence of his Allied interrogators that Nazism represented all that was evil in the world, and their implication that Rudel himself shared in the culpability for all the atrocities committed in the name of the Reich, that soured Rudel completely on the Allies and made him a kind of "born again" Nazi determined to be what the Allies most despised. Since Rudel had not been indicted for war crimes, he was free to roam about the world promoting Nazism and becoming a kind of one-man clearinghouse for communications between Nazis in various parts of the world, many of whom were not as free to travel due to their need for security and the complex paper trails they had created to disguise their identities. In this capacity, Rudel could carry messages between fugitives, help arrange financial support, and keep the spirit alive among the members of the *Bruderschaft*, the "brotherhood." His address book is ample evidence of the connections Rudel had around the world with both prominent Nazis and sympathizers, and with those less well-known or living under pseudonyms. It also reveals the extent of Rudel's connections with influential and powerful members of various governments and multi-national orporations. In fact, his relationship with Pierre Sprey was based on just that kind of government contact, for it was due to Rudel's proficiency as a wartime ace pilot that his knowledge and experience was valued by the US Defense Department, for which Sprey worked in developing the F-16 and A-10 aircraft in the 1960s and 1970s. Sprey was encouraged to talk about aviation with Rudel if it would help aircraft engineers design a better plane. In other words, one could say that for awhile at least Hans-Ulrich Rudel worked for the Pentagon.

In this way, Rudel's address book is a blueprint of ODESSA.

In fact, as the above extract from the G-2 document shows, it was believed that both Rudel and Skorzeny held leadership positions within the Nazi movement as early as 1949, a movement comprising former SA and SS men as well as members in the regular army, the Wehrmacht. In Skorzeny's case especially this is not difficult to believe.

In another memo, this one dated 16 October 1949, with the subject heading "SKORZENY Movement," it is revealed that something called the Skorzeny Hunting Society[55] had been created as an anti-Communist organization in Munich composed of former SS men. It was claimed (in another CIC memo dated 16 November 1949) that this movement was formed subsequent to Skorzeny's escape to Latin America and specifically to Sao Paulo, Brazil. In other words, it was a "stay behind" organization being run by Skorzeny *in absentia*.

In 1949, Skorzeny was a fugitive having escaped from Allied custody in 1948 (or was allowed to escape, as rumors abound that he was working for Reinhard Gehlen's anti-Soviet spy organization under the auspices of the newly-formed CIA), and US military documents record various rumors concerning his whereabouts at this time. Argentina and Brazil were among the most popular destinations, but there was also substantial evidence that Skorzeny had been in Madrid, organizing a paramilitary force there with Franco's blessing.

In a CIA memo dated May 1, 1955, from the Assistant Director of the CIA to the FBI, it was reported that Skorzeny had made contact with former Nazi generals in Germany, "arranging for the removal of up to 200,000 men to Spain in the event of war. He is reported to have claimed to have United States approval and support for this project." In other words, as the Cold War began to heat up and it appeared as if there would be a shooting war over the fate of Berlin and West Germany with the Soviets, Skorzeny was arranging to salvage a small army of 200,000 German soldiers under command of Nazi officers, and claimed he had the blessing of the United States to do so.

Where would these 200,000 men have come from? Is this figure in any way related to the "Skorzeny Hunting Society" or what-

---

55 *Skorzeny Jagdverein*, possibly a reference to the *SS Jagdverbände 502*, the Waffen SS unit that Skorzeny commanded during the war which was involved in an attempt to recruit mountain tribes in Iran to sabotage Soviet supply lines, yet another example of Nazi intrigue with Islamic forces.

ever other name you wish to call the extensive stay-behind network in place in Germany and Austria (and parts of Eastern Europe) as early as the winter of 1944 and the spring of 1945? And would this organization really have the support of the US government? It is certainly a possibility, especially when one considers that the Gehlen Organization comprised of former Nazi spies was now working for CIA. Would it be so hard to believe that ODESSA—or whatever name you wish to call it—was (at least at times) working on behalf of US interests in Europe, especially when those interests dove-tailed so perfectly with Nazi interests? An ODESSA network of trained, blooded, anti-Communist fighters spread out around the world—and in political danger spots like Southern and Eastern Europe, Latin America, and Africa (and, as we will see, Asia)—would be an ideal, and ultimately deniable, resource for the Cold Warriors in Washington, DC.

Recent academic scholarship[56] on the subject of ODESSA has tended to downplay its existence as well as its significance. There is no doubt that discussions of ODESSA in the 1950s and 1960s tended to dramatize if not romanticize the concept, ascribing to it the status of a kind of James Bond villain: well-organized, struc-tured, centrally-controlled. It was this same characterization that was used to describe Al-Qaeda in the early years of its existence—as a kind of super-underground network of robot terrorists taking their orders directly from the mysterious Osama bin Laden in his well-fortified underground bunker.

However, we have come to understand that the strength of Al-Qaeda is to be found mostly in its moral leadership rather than in its day-to-day operations. There are a number of what are known as "Al-Qaeda affiliates" scattered around the world, such as Al-Qaeda in the Maghreb, Al-Qaeda in Yemen, and sister organizations such as Jemaah Islamiyyah in Indonesia and Malaysia, Lashkar-e-Taiba

---

56 For instance, Gerald Steinacher, *Nazis on the Run: How Hitler's Henchmen Fled Justice*, Oxford University Press, 2011. Steinacher also calls into doubt the entire Maison Rouge episode (p. xvii) although Allied intelligence considered it credible at the time, and events that have transpired since then tend to support its basic premise, if not the details of the meeting itself.

in Pakistan, etc. This lack of centrality has not altered the West's determination to subdue if not eradicate these groups; and while specialists understand there are operational and strategic differences between them—as well as cultural and linguistic differences—they are essentially working from the same set of readily-identifiable ideas that attract the identical type of recruit worldwide.

The same is true of what we have been calling ODESSA. The strength of this network is in its ability to morph into different manifestations in different countries and at different levels of society without losing sight of its central mission, which is the survival of Nazi philosophy as well as the survival of the Nazis themselves. As mentioned previously, there is nothing "neo" about so-called "neo-Nazism" if the leaders of the movement are all members of the original Nazi Party and held various ranks in the Nazi government, the military, the SS, and the espionage services such as the Abwehr, the Gestapo and the SD. There is a continuity of personnel, financing, and ideology that enabled these men to shift their theater of operations from western Europe to eastern Europe, the Middle East, Latin America, and Asia. Further, there existed—and still exists—a support structure of sympathizers and political operatives that enables the survival of these individuals and their philosophy, transferring their ideals to a younger generation capable of promoting the Nazi message in new media with subtle alterations of "spin" and, in addition, willing to commit the violent acts necessary to demonstrate their dedication to the cause. In this they are no different from the support systems and methods enjoyed by the Islamist jihadists.

The Nazi underground is, and was, composed of various seemingly disparate elements. No discussion of what we have been calling ODESSA is complete without also mentioning *Stille Hilfe*, HIAG, *Die Spinne*, the Amsterdam Group, the *Bruderschaft*, and other groups with varying individual missions but with a unified dream of protecting and resurrecting the Reich.

Stille Hilfe (or "Silent Help") was the name given to an aid organization begun about 1946 in Germany to aid SS prisoners of war. In 1951 it was officially organized around the personality of Helene

Elizabeth, Princess von Isenburg, an aristocrat with extensive connections among the financial and military elite of Germany who would be inclined to assist convicted Nazis by monetary and other means. One of the founding members was an assistant to convicted and executed war criminal Ernst Kaltenbrunner, SS-Obersturmmbannführer Heinrich Malz, as well as a chief of the RSHA (Reich Security Main Office) SS-Standartenführer Wilhelm Spengler. The full name of the organization was *Die Stille Hilfe für Kriegsgefangene und Internierte* or "Silent Help for Prisoners of War and the Interned," which seemed innocuous enough until it was realized that the prisoners and interned were almost all, without exception, former SS.

That there was a political agenda behind Stille Hilfe became more obvious in their association with Holocaust deniers, and eventually with the Naumann Circle. Dr. Werner Naumann was briefly Josef Goebbels's successor as head of the Propaganda Ministry after the suicide of Goebbels and his wife and the murder of their six children at the Berlin Bunker. He had sought to create a Nazi Party in Austria after the end of the war and intrigued with various underground groups in order to infiltrate the Austrian government with his *Gauleiterkreis*, or Circle of Gauleiters. This circle was broken up by British intelligence in 1953, and its failure to take over the Austrian government may be one of the reasons our Dr. Georg Anton Pöch, himself an Austrian Nazi who had served with the Salzburg Gau, decided to finally leave Europe in 1954.

Stille Hilfe went on to form alliances with important members of the Nazi underground, including Leon Degrelle and Manfred Roeder, as well as with the slightly insane Florentine Rost van Tonningen, the widow of a Nazi official accused of stealing a fortune in Dutch gold and valuables, and who was subsequently "suicided" while in Allied custody. Stille Hilfe was also involved in movements to free Klaus Barbie and Erich Priebke, among others, but by far its most famous member is Gudrun Burwitz.

Burwitz is the daughter of SS chief Heinrich Himmler, and is sometimes referred to as the "Nazi princess." Her efforts run the gamut from arranging legal representation for war criminals, to providing homes for them when they have become too old to care for themselves. For instance, she has been prominent in the attempt to keep Dutch war criminal Klaas Faber from being extradited to the Netherlands to stand trial.

Stille Hilfe may seem almost benign when compared to the other manifestations of the underground. HIAG or *Hilfsgemein-schaft auf Gegenseitigkeit der Angehörigen der ehemaligen Waffen-SS* ("Mutual Help Association of Former Waffen-SS Members") was founded about the same time as Stille Hilfe, but in this case by SS-Brigadeführer Otto Kumm (1909–2004) who led the SS Division Liebstandarte Adolf Hitler during the war. Denazified after the war, Kumm became a businessman and organizer of HIAG. HIAG was created in order to provide financial assistance to SS members who, because of the fact that they had been declared a criminal organization, were not able to collect their pensions. Ostensibly, HIAG was only there to provide economic relief for its members, but its ranks included men who had been convicted of war crimes and it was perceived by the West German government as a Nazi organization. It was eventually disbanded in 1992.

Die Spinne is another case entirely.

This was the creation of Otto Skorzeny (he of the Hunting Society) and it leads us into the deeper, darker world of ODESSA. More than any other single individual, Skorzeny is the entry-point to the world of the Nazi underground and the links between resurgent Nazism and what we are calling Islamist jihadism, with the connective tissue of the dictatorships of Latin America: first stop for most of the fleeing Nazi fugitives. Die Spinne and its offshoots provides us with a glimpse into the interface between Western intelligence agencies and their ideological conflict with Communism on the one hand, and with experienced and dedicated anti-Communists on the other. I have written elsewhere that the deal America made with Nazi scientists under the rubric of Operation Paperclip, and with Nazi spies under the rubric of the Gehlen Organization, was a Faustian pact with the Devil: the point at which America bartered its soul in exchange for a short-lived sense of security. The deal that American and other Western intelligence agencies and political leaderships made with the brutal presidents of Latin American and Asian nations in the 1950s, 1960s and through the 1980s is a codicil to that pact. What the American government could not effectively promote within its own borders—wholesale suppression of any opposition on a massive and unapologetic scale—it succeeded in accomplishing throughout Latin America, and by extension into Southeast Asia with the support of Marcos in the Philippines and Soeharto in Indonesia, among others. The breakup of the Soviet Union has been revealing—little by little—the extent of this complicity—as extreme right dictatorships have fallen through lack of purpose, and extremist religious groups have risen in response.

Otto Skorzeny was Hitler's favorite commando and a person upon whom the Führer came to rely increasingly in the days after the attempted assassination of July 1944. Skorzeny was a can-do commander, the famous rescuer of Hitler comrade and Italian Fascist leader Benito Mussolini in a daring mountain-top glider attack that made headlines around the world. Skorzeny's dedication to the Reich and his willingness to undertake the most dangerous missions on behalf of his Führer made him an indispensable servant of Nazism and he remained that way to the end of his days. The organization he founded after the war—*Die Spinne,* or The Spider—spread its web from Franco's Spain to Peron's Argentina, from Adenauer's Germany to Nasser's Egypt. Originally designed to help more than 600 SS and other war criminals to flee Europe after the war for the relative safety of right-wing dictatorships around the world, Die Spinne became the foundation upon which Skorzeny was able to create an arms-smuggling empire. Arms dealers are an essential aspect of this story, and we will come across another such businessman—the Indonesian prince Soeryo Goeritno—later on, in a similar capacity. Skorzeny and his colleague François Genoud were able to run guns throughout Europe and to the Middle East and North Africa with impunity. In Latin America, they were assisted by other members of Skorzeny's brotherhood, men like the "Butcher of Lyon" Klaus Barbie (operating under the pseudonym Klaus Altmann) in Bolivia, Freddy Schwend (who developed Operation Bernhard during the war, an attempt by the Nazis to mass-produce counterfeit British pounds to destabilize the global currency) in Peru, and the cooperative pedophile Paul Schäfer of

Colonia Dignidad and Operation Condor, in Chile: a direct beneficiary of the Skorzeny arms trade.

By 1950 Skorzeny was residing in Franco's Spain, operating Die
Spinne long-distance (the headquarters of its Austrian mission was
in Gmunden, Austria while Skorzeny remained in Madrid). By
1960, he was actively involved in the global arms trade, working with
groups that eventually were revealed to be supplying Arab nationalists in North Africa and the Levant, as well as fascist governments
in Latin America and South Africa. He was an agent of ALFA (the
Spanish arms company), and eventually joined (or co-founded, the
history is a little murky) the German armaments company Merex
along with former Wehrmacht officer Major Gerhard Mertins. In
that capacity Skorzeny would become involved with such infamous
right-wing terrorists as the Italian Stefano della Chiaie, who carried out bombings and assassinations on behalf of European and
Latin American dictatorships and underground terror cells long
before there was an al-Qaeda or a Taliban. As the Rudel address
book reveals, this network included everyone from notorious Swiss
financier François Genoud (who bankrolled many Arabist and
Nazi plots), to Klaus Barbie (who was running the secret police in
Bolivia and was a major player in the Operation Condor network of
spies, assassins and gun-runners, whose Chilean node was Colonia
Dignidad), to President Stroessner in Paraguay and the Peronists
in Argentina, as well as with Leon Degrelle—the Belgian Nazi
who maintained a circle of supporters long after the war and was
another node in the underground network—and North American
Nazis such as Ernst Zundel in Canada, a Holocaust denier and
publisher of pro-Nazi tracts. The far flung Rudel/Skorzeny network
included Savitri Devi, whom Rudel admired and befriended. Devi
was a fanatic Nazi ideologue, the bridge between the Hindu-style
Nazism (with Hitler as Kalki Avatar) of former Chilean ambassador to Austria and India, Miguel Serrano, and the more mainstream
Nazism of Degrelle, Skorzeny, and Barbie.

    In addition, Skorzeny was on intimate terms with Hitler's
financial guru, Hjalmar Schacht, who plays an important role in the

survival of Nazism, and in the inspiration for a new, global, jihad against the West. The Skorzeny-Schacht relationship cannot be over-emphasized, since Schacht had always been at pains to present himself as an anti-Nazi—pointing to his brief imprisonment for alleged involvement in the Hitler assassination plot as evidence of his bona fides. However, this episode has been criticized extensively by investigators who see it as a deliberate attempt to "de-nazify" Schacht in anticipation of the fall of the Reich, so that he would be free to carry on his mission of resurrecting the German economy after the war.

When Skorzeny was on the run from Allied forces after his escape from custody in 1948, he hid at the farm of one Ilse Luthje, or the Countess Finck von Finckenstein to give her noble designation. Ilse Luthje (1919–2002) was a niece[57] of Hjalmar Schacht. She and Skorzeny eventually developed a relationship that led to marriage, with Ilse moving to Skorzeny's villa in Spain. The two dedicated Nazis—Skorzeny and Schacht—were now related by marriage, as well as united by the desire to rebuild Germany, defeat Communism, and restore the Nazi Party to its former glory. While Schacht worked to create a global financial network that would enable sympathetic regimes to collaborate in this vision, Skorzeny worked to create a global military and espionage network that would ensure the original Hitlerian mission would not be abandoned. His partner, Hans-Ulrich Rudel, would move among the faithful worldwide, raising their spirits, making speeches, keeping the flame alive, acting as a fixer when necessary, passing information between the comrades, and doing what he could to protect them from the security forces of those nations still interested—due to political or public pressure—in apprehending war criminals and bringing them to trial.

---

57 That she was his neice is contested by Schacht biographer John Weitz who says she was related to the Schacht family doctor and had known the Schachts since she was a child. She adopted the sobriquet "neice" when the Schachts wound up in Madrid, according to Weitz, as a way of explaining her relationship to them in front of the Nazi entourage around Schacht. John Weitz, *Hitler's Banker: Hjalmar Horace Greeley Schacht,* Little Brown & Co., Boston, 1997.

With Merex, it would seem Skorzeny found the perfect vehicle for his mission. Merex was selling weapons worldwide, with Gerhard Mertins cutting deals with regimes in Pakistan, Egypt, and elsewhere with reckless abandon. Skorzeny's contacts with Latin American dictators and generals provided Merex with a larger market, and Hans Ulrich-Rudel (who lived in South America from 1948–1953) was an essential piece of the puzzle. He had excellent relations with President Stroessner of Paraguay, among others. In fact, it was Rudel who convinced Stroessner to give Dr. Josef Mengele—the "Angel of Death" of Auschwitz—Paraguayan citizenship, thus permitting the fugitive to live free from discovery and extradition until his death in Brazil in 1979. As Rudel's address book indicates, he was on excellent terms with many Paraguayan notables including politicians and military men.

As for Mengele, the "Angel of Death" once paid a visit to Colonia Dignidad in Chile as more recent investigation has revealed. A few months before Mengele's death in 1979, the author himself was in Chile attempting to get information on the Colony when he was detained by men acting under orders from Colony founder Schäfer. What the author did not know at the time was that Gerhard Mertins of Merex had formed a *Freundeskreis* or "Circle of Friends" of his own, this one based in Germany to help support Colonia Dignidad. That same year, Mertins made a deposition in a German court in which he denied that there had been any wrongdoing at Colonia Dignidad.

Ten years later, the Colony was raided by the Chilean security forces under newly-elected President Patricio Aylwin. The hideous truth was allowed to emerge of torture, sexual abuse, physical abuse, and the utilization of the Colony as a safe house for fleeing Nazis, including Mengele. It was also revealed that Colonia Dignidad was an important node in the communications network of Operation Condor: the multinational effort by Chile, Argentina, and other South American dictatorships to run guns, launder money, assassinate political opponents in the Americas and elsewhere in the world, and to develop weapons of mass destruction such as chemical and biological weapons.

This remote Andes mountain estate—with its barbed wire

fences and guard towers, designed after the ones at the concentration camps was just another element of ODESSA, albeit one of its most elaborate. It had hosted Skorzeny, Rudel, Mengele, and many other notables—both before the author had inadvisably paid it a visit and long after. Its utilization as a laboratory for the manufacture of WMDs is proven: there is photographic, video, and eyewitness testimony to the fact.[58] Yet there has never been any outcry by Western intelligence or military experts over this; never any condemnation from the White House or 10 Downing Street; no slide presentations before the UN Security Council.

How much of this information and lethal capability was shared with Skorzeny's and Rudel's jihadist counterparts (and clients) in Afghanistan, the Middle East, or Pakistan?

We know, for instance, that Mertins tried to sell Saddam Hussein Chinese-made weaponry during the Iran-Iraq War in the 1980s. He had been selling weapons to Egypt since the 1950s, when he was working with Skorzeny to prop up first the Naguib and then the Nasser regime, hiring Nazis as mercenaries and instructors of the Egyptian secret police in the humiliating aftermath of the 1948 war against Israel. By the 1960s, he was already heavily involved with such notorious American arms dealers as Interarms—selling Luftwaffe aircraft to Venezuela, and selling weapons to both sides in the India-Pakistan conflict in 1966. Eventually he became more deeply involved in South America, and in particular Chile under the dictatorship of President Pinochet. The story of Merex is also the story of Skorzeny and Rudel—the Hunting Society—and of the ways and means by which a Nazi ideology found new life in the right-wing dictatorships of the Middle East and Latin America. And Gerhard Mertins—close friend of SS General Otto Remer and true believer in the Nazi cause—continued the war against communism, liberalism, and the Jews in a business suit instead of a uniform, ensuring that his friends had all the weapons and ammunition they needed to continue the fight on a dozen different fronts.

58 See for instance the excellent documentary film on the Colony, *Colonia Dignidad: A Nazi Sect in the Land of Pinochet*, by Jose Maldavsky, and available on YouTube with English language subtitles: http://www.youtube.com/watch?v=5oObdFq78_s accessed on August 16, 2014.

Skorzeny wasn't satisfied with just Merex, however. As entrepreneurial as ever, he founded a series of other companies with dubious pedigrees: such as the Paladin Group. Based in Alicante, Spain it was designed to provide paramilitary training and support to a variety of causes around the world. Foremost among these tasks was tutoring security personnel in Egypt and Argentina, and for this he hired as manager one Dr. Gerhard Harmut von Schubert, who formerly worked for Goebbels's Propaganda Ministry (like Johann von Leers and Werner Naumann). Paladin Group also provided logistical support for the Palestine Liberation movement. In addition, Skorzeny worked with the H. S. Lucht Corporation, another of the ubiquitous "import-export" firms used to provide cover for unsavory trade, headquartered in Dusseldorf and directed by Werner Naumann himself.

One should not think for a moment, however, that Skorzeny—like Mertins—put on a business suit and eschewed the life of violence and terror he had known during the war. There were still enemies to be fought, and traitors to be discovered and dealt-with. One such case involved the hapless pair of Prof. Werner Heyde and Friedrich Tillmann.

Heyde was the chief of a neurological clinic at Würzberg during the war. In 1941, he transferred more than 200 Jews from Dachau to a mental institute at Bernberg so he could give them lethal injections. He was one of only four psychiatrists selected by the Nazis to go to the camps and choose Jewish prisoners to be sent to these "nursing homes," where they would be murdered. Tillmann, on the other hand, provided the ambulances that would transport these "patients" to their final destination.

Due to their vulnerability as a result of their crimes, they were suspected by Skorzeny of talking to Dr. Fritz Bauer, the famous prosecutor of Nazi war criminals, about the inner workings of ODESSA.

They were both found murdered on the same day, February 13, 1964, before they could give their testimony to Bauer.

In Egypt, however, it was a different story.

As information was revealed in the 1950s about the presence of large numbers of Nazi scientists (estimates range up to 450) in

Egypt for the rocket program, and equally large numbers of Nazi military and security personnel, individual Nazis were identified as part of this program and attacked (presumably by Mossad agents). One of these was Heinz Krug, who was believed to be sending technical information to Egypt from his office at United Arab Airlines in Germany, and who was kidnapped and killed by Israeli agents. Skorzeny's response to this was to take Jewish hostages each time a Nazi was attacked. At that time there were a number of Jewish communities in Egypt, and Skorzeny had his pick of whom to snatch.

By 1965, however, Nasser had begun making overtures to East Germany and the Soviet Union. American support for Egypt—and covert American support for the Nazi presence in Egypt—was dwindling. Skorzeny, however, as an adherent of the "third way," saw no issue with dealing Soviet and East German arms to Egypt if the American and West German sources dried up. Either way he made money and his cause was furthered. During this period he brokered millions of dollars' worth of arms from Communist-bloc sources to clients in the Middle East and elsewhere. Mertins, as well, had no problem in selling weapons to both India and Pakistan. Arms dealers cannot afford to be too choosy. But the true faith was never abandoned; it may have had to adapt its outward form to reflect new environmental factors, but it remained true to its core beliefs, and that is where the problem lies. If we mistake the form for the function, we will be lulled into a false sense of security when the form changes, not realizing the function is the same.

Another key figure in the underworld of the global Nazi network—and close friend of Skorzeny, Rudel, and Schacht—was the Swiss financier and former Abwehr agent François Genoud (1915–1996). Although a Swiss citizen, Genoud was a devoted Nazi to the end of his days, like his colleagues. The difference lay in Genoud's post-war profession as a financier. It has largely been accepted that the funds to which Genoud had access were secret accounts held in Swiss banks by Nazi leaders and fugitives. He managed to parlay what was a considerable fortune into even greater wealth through a series of shrewd investments, as well as what might be called "protection money" from a variety of sources. He was the literary executor of the works of Adolf Hitler, Martin Bormann, and Josef Goebbels, among other claims to fame, and collaborated with the Holocaust denier and historian David Irving (whose name also appears in the Rudel address book, along with Genoud and Skorzeny). As the post-war decades progressed, Genoud would become a key figure in the financing of Arab liberation movements throughout North Africa and the Levant.

There is a British Intelligence document dated 20 Nov 53, entitled "Francois GENOUD" [sic], which contains some background on this mysterious Swiss. It notes that he is the literary executor for both Hitler and Bormann and "possesses many Nazi documents." He is described as being in contact with British fascist Sir Oswald Mosley at the time, as well as with Paul Dickopf (who would eventually become head of West Germany's equivalent of the FBI, the BKA, despite his impeccable Nazi resume; indeed he was even for awhile head of Interpol like his predecessor Ernst Kaltenbrunner). Genoud worked for Dickopf in the Abwehr, and his credentials as an Abwehr agent are referenced in the British document, as well as his connection with the Naumann Circle and with one Frau Lucht of Dusseldorf, which indicates the H.S. Lucht firm of Dusseldorf managed by Werner Naumann.

Prior to the war, Genoud had been a member of the National Front, a pro-Nazi organization in Switzerland. In 1936, he traveled to Palestine and met with the Grand Mufti Hajj Amin al-Husseini himself, and the two developed a life-long friendship. Once war broke out, Genoud moved to Berlin and met al-Husseini again, becoming very involved in the Palestinian independence schemes of the pro-Nazi Mufti.

In 1954, he began financing the Algerian Liberation Front, an organization to which he already had been supplying weapons after meeting members of the Front in Egypt. In 1955, he created AraboAfrika, another "import-export" company, to assist the Algerian cause and to provide a cover for anti-Israel propaganda. In 1958, he went on to create a medium for the transfer and laundering of cash for Algerian, Moroccan, and Tunisian liberation groups—the Arab Commercial Bank—with the indispensable Hjalmar Schacht as a partner. By 1960, he added the Palestinian cause to his resume, and in particular financed the defense of members of the Popular Front for the Liberation of Palestine (PFLP) who blew up an an El Al airliner in Zurich. This involvement in providing expensive defense teams extended to the trials of Klaus Barbie and Adolf Eichmann, with Genoud generously supplying whatever funds were needed to obtain the best possible representation.

In 1969, he put members of the Palestine Liberation Organization (PLO) in contact with Nazi personnel who would provide training in weapons, sabotage, and infiltration techniques. (This was the same period—from about 1967–1969—that the author made contact with the PLO at their offices in New York City, having first dealt with a German woman who was their receptionist.) Genoud was a serious supporter of Palestinian liberation throughout his life and, according to author Peter Wyden, was also a confidant and mentor of Ahmed Huber, the Swiss supporter of Nazi and Islamist causes. Huber also created his own bank in order to finance these missions. He is mentioned in the Introduction to this book.

If Hjalmar Schacht was "Hitler's Banker," Genoud was the banker of the Nazi and Arab resistance movements in Europe and the Middle East. He was a friend of the notorious assassin "Carlos the Jackal"—Ilich Ramirez Sanchez—and assisted the terrorist in several of his missions. He also helped financially support the Ayatollah Khomeini during the latter's exile in France during the regime of the Shah of Iran. Genoud and Schacht were partners in many of these ventures, and Genoud represented Schacht's financial interests where feasible—occasionally helping the older man make sound investments, or in brokering deals between Arab nations and the European firms that were in Schacht's comfort zone. That both men were instrumental in providing financial and logistical support to ODESSA is not in question; but they extended that assistance to ODESSA's natural allies, the Islamist resistance groups that were founded to remove all traces of their former colonial masters in North Africa and the Levant, and to wage an ideological war—a global jihad—against Israel and the West, under the guise of religious fervor.

In the aftermath of the attacks of September 11, 2001 many forget that a wave of terror had been building since the end of World War II. Assassinations and bombings had been taking place throughout Europe, North Africa, the Middle East, and Latin America. These were directed at Communists and suspected Communist sympathizers. At the same time, groups like the PLO and the PFLP were running terror operations against Israel. Gradually, it has been revealed that much of the financing for these operations came from money under the control of François Genoud: money that had been deposited in Swiss banks since the early 1940s. The source of Genoud's funds were never in doubt to those who worked with him; it was only after increasing scrutiny by the Swiss, American, and other authorities in the 1990s that the extent of Genoud's control over Nazi gold was becoming known. Not all of ODESSA's financing came from these accounts, of course. Skorzeny had access to mysterious sources of funds as well, with rumors linking him to Juan and Evita Peron of Argentina and the gold that was shipped to Buenos Aires to help pave the way for a wave of Nazi fugitives after the war. Rumors of the wealth allegedly secreted by Martin Bormann also surface from time to time, and Skorzeny was even suspected of having been involved with the Great Train Robbery of 1963.[59]

As more of these "rumors" become substantiated in the ongoing declassification of intelligence files, the full scope of the problem will become known. The explosion of oil revenues in the Middle East was one possible source of funding for terrorist operations and groups, but by no means the only source. Arab governments had their own agendas, and often they did not include whole-hearted support for the liberation movements—as the very idea of a national liberation movement challenged their own hegemony. The Palestinian issue was allowed to simmer on indefinitely. The Western governments were wooing the Arab governments, keeping them out of the reach of the Soviets. The Shah of Iran was installed as the ruler

---

59 See Piers Paul Read, *The Train Robbers*, Philadelphia: J.B. Lippincott, 1978, pp. 233-250.

of that ancient kingdom, and the Ayatollahs bided their time. Saddam Hussein was America's ally against the Ayatollahs when the Shah was deposed. The Soviets were ousted from Afghanistan with the assistance of the CIA and the *mujahideen*. It seemed like politics as usual in the Middle East. And then the Soviet Union fell, and everything changed.

In 1996, Swiss authorities were becoming more aware that Genoud and his colleagues had been financing terror groups worldwide for decades, and that the Swiss banker and former Abwehr agent knew where the Nazi gold had been stashed. Genoud also knew how it had been used to create the largest terror organization in the world—known by its various names as ODESSA, Die Spinne, the Bruderschaft, Condor, etc. Increasingly aware of the danger he faced, Genoud decided to take his own life.

And this he did, on May 30, 1996.

The Skorzeny Hunting Society had been decimated by that time. Rudel died in 1982. Skorzeny himself had died in Spain much earlier, in 1975. Schacht, five years before that. It seemed as if the old networks were being rolled up. The songs unsung. The flags unflown. The old dreams dying off with their dreamers.

Not a chance.

CHAPTER EIGHT

AMERICAN JIHAD

I assure you that I never fail in any communication with Arab leaders, oral or written, to stress the importance of the spiritual factor in our relationships. I have argued that belief in God should create between them and us the common purpose of opposing atheistic communism.

>—President Dwight D. Eisenhower, in a letter written to Edward Elson of the Presbyterian Church, July 31, 1958.

The President said he thought we should do everything possible to stress the 'holy war' aspect ... Mr. Dulles commented that if the Arabs have a 'holy war' they would want it to be against Israel. The President recalled, however, that Saud, after his visit here, had called on all Arabs to oppose Communism.

>—General A.J. Goodpaster, Staff Secretary and Defense Liaison Officer to President Eisenhower, "Memorandum of Conference with the President" dated September 7, 1957.

Max Oppenheim invented the concept of global jihad in order to convince the Ottoman Turks to side with Germany against Great Britain, France, and Russia in the First World War. Nazi Germany renewed that idea during the Second World War, with the assistance of Hajj Amin al-Husseini, the Grand Mufti of Jerusalem. It didn't work either time.

Now the American president, who more than any other represented the Allied forces in their defeat of Nazi Germany when he was Supreme Allied Commander, had revisited the old idea once again. Ironically, the only common denominator between the First World War, the Second World War, and the Cold War was the singular presence of Russia as the adversary in all three conflicts. Godless Communism would be opposed by fanatical Muslims intent on a jihad ... or that was the idea, anyway.

In the 1950s a number of Muslims of various ethnic backgrounds were living scattered throughout Europe. Some of them had fought with the Nazis against the Soviets; others had been refugees or displaced persons, victims of the shifting borders that take place during armed conflicts. There were a number of ostensibly Christian organizations that had been organized around ethnic lines to oppose Soviet Communism, and the Russian Orthodox Church was perhaps the most famous. Composed of White Russians clustered around memories of the Czarist aristocracy, the Russian Orthodox Church had been largely pro-Nazi during the war, as had been the Ukrainian Orthodox Church and to some extent the Romanian Orthodox Church. All of these churches had been penetrated to greater or lesser degree by American, and other Western, intelligence services. In addition, the Roman Catholic Church had provided escape routes and false identity papers to Nazi fugitives to enable them to escape to other parts of the world and carry on the fight against Communism. Some of the Protestant denominations were also involved. As the Cold War developed through the 1950s, many other religious groups found themselves acting as fronts for intelligence operations, or at the very least cooperating with CIA and FBI in their anti-Communist activities. The author himself has personal and direct knowledge of some of these, dating to his involvement with questionable Orthodox churches in the 1960s and 1970s.

It would seem to reason, then, that other religious organizations would be approached with an eye to using them as tools against the Soviet adversary. As we will see in the following chapter, Buddhism was not immune from this manipulation; but for now our attention should be directed towards Islam.

One can sense the frustration that must have been felt by American military and intelligence chiefs that greater use could not be made of Muslims in the effort to isolate and undermine the Soviet Union. After all, there was a large and growing Muslim population in the territories claimed by Russia, such as Turkmenistan, Azerbaijan, Uzbekistan, Tajikistan, etc. If the Muslim populations in these

Central Asian lands were to rise up against their Soviet overlords, then the Cold War would be over quickly, or so it was believed.

What we have called the cynical manipulation of religion by the German intelligence and military organs was a strategy inherited by the Americans after the defeat of Germany. Sincere spiritual sentiments were to be ruthlessly exploited once again, but this time with devastating consequences: what is known in espionage jargon as "blowback."

Pulitzer Prize-winning journalist Ian Johnson reveals the depth of the insanity in his book *A Mosque in Munich: Nazis, the CIA, and the Rise of the Muslim Brotherhood in the West.* The subtitle says it all. The CIA inherited a raft of pro-Nazi Muslims who were stranded in Europe in the decade after the end of the Second World War and decided to use them to fight Russia. In order to do so, CIA found itself financing Muslim Brotherhood activities in Europe, including a mosque in Munich that would become the center of intrigues against the West. Ironically, of course, it was Munich where the Nazi Party was born. (And it was in the Hamburg, Germany, apartment of Mohamed Atta that the final details and main participants of the September 11, 2001 attacks would be determined.)

In 1953, President Eisenhower's support was solicited for an important meeting that would take place in September of that year at Princeton University. The meeting was to be an Islamic Colloquium. Leading Islamic scholars from around the world would be attending, including one Said Ramadan, "Delegate of the Muslim Brotherhood."

The history of the Muslim Brotherhood is too long to cover in any detail here. There have been numerous studies of the Brotherhood ranging from the purely academic to fringe conspiracy theories, but a synopsis is in order.

The Muslim Brotherhood—or The Society of the Muslim Brothers or *al-Ikhwan al-Muslimun*—was founded in 1928, in Egypt, by reformer and Islamic scholar Hassan al-Banna. The original idea behind the Brotherhood was to promote a pan-Islamic message in the face of what was perceived to be European oppression. Egypt in 1928 was still a British protectorate, had been since 1882, and would remain so until 1953 when General Naguib was

elected the first President of the Republic. He would be replaced by
Nasser a year later. Thus, at the time of the formation of the Muslim
Brotherhood in the town of Ismailia, the country was still occupied
by British troops. Close by, in Palestine, there were riots against the
British presence in that territory and against the perceived invasion
by European Jews as promised by the Balfour Declaration. Hence,
as the Grand Mufti of Jerusalem was agitating against both the
British and the Jews in Palestine, Hassan al-Banna was urging a
return to Islamic values in Egypt in order to counteract the effects
of Western decadence.

The Brotherhood managed to attract thousands of followers
very early on. It built schools and hospitals and ran support systems for the poor and the dispossessed. It spoke out openly against
colonialism and chided Muslims for having abandoned the faith.
Eventually, al-Banna and al-Husseini would join forces, each with
his own agenda but seeing in the other a potential ally in the fight
against the European powers.

To be sure this was a movement based on narrow interpretations
of Islamic teachings and laws. Al-Banna's desire was to reinstate
the Islamic caliphate from the Middle East to Indonesia, creating
an Islamic empire based on religion, rather than the German or
British or Dutch colonial empires based on materialism and profit.
Gradually, the slogan of the Muslim Brotherhood changed from
the relatively benign, "Believers are Brothers" to the more insistent,
"Allah is our objective; the Qur'an is our Constitution; the Prophet
is our leader; jihad is our way; death for the sake of Allah is our
wish." The reference to jihad and death is instructive and has been
interpreted to mean that the Muslim Brotherhood advocates violence. Brotherhood leaders deny this, and have come out against
violence from time to time; the problem is that Brotherhood members also have taken it upon themselves to get involved in violent
struggles in Egypt, Palestine, and elsewhere. The Palestinian political party in Gaza that has been listed as a terror organization—
Hamas—is staffed by members of the Brotherhood, and of course
there are Brotherhood members in the PLO, and other groups that
are engaged in violent confrontation with those whom they deem
the enemies of Islam, most notably the Jews. Ironically, Osama
bin Laden criticized the Muslim Brotherhood. He said he did not

believe they were true to the intentions of its founder; i.e., they were not violent or radical enough. This apparent rupture between al-Qaeda and the Muslim Brotherhood led several experts in intelligence matters relating to Middle Eastern affairs to decide that it might be advisable to side with the Brotherhood against al-Qaeda; and this has led to many misunderstandings and subsequent controversy in the United States.

Before the Brotherhood became synonymous (in some circles) with terrorism, they were considered politically important enough for the United States Government to take them seriously and woo their support against the godless Communists. Hence the Islamic Colloqium at Princeton University in 1953, and the meeting between President Eisenhower and Said Ramadan.

As noted above, Eisenhower was convinced that the idea of holy war or jihad could be used to mutual benefit by the Arabs and the American administration as a way of containing Soviet intentions in Eastern Europe and Central Asia, as well as the Middle East. He believed he had an understanding with King ibn Saud of Saudi Arabia in this regard, not realizing that the Saudi royal house was not that influential among the Arabs of North Africa and the Levant, who had their hands full with Israel on the one side, the Russians on the other, and the Americans on still another. Saud's relationship to the West was largely that of a mutual admiration society: the Americans admired Arabia's oil reserves and the Saudis admired America's money. It was—and remains—a "special relationship," out of all proportion to what is actually taking place on the ground.

In the 1950s, however, the Cold War was the determining factor in America's foreign policy. Everything was predicated on the balance of power between America and the Soviet Union, and nothing was left to chance, each side jockeying for position, trying to get the best of the other without actually going to war. Resistance movements in Central Asia against Soviet authority were one way to distract the Russians and divert resources away from strengthening their hold over Eastern Europe. The Brotherhood had its own problems, however, for it was banned in Egypt in 1948 for having participated in a series of bombings and assassination attempts against government leaders. Hassan al-Banna himself was assassinated in what was believed to be retaliation for the assassination of the Egyptian prime minister. However, within the Brotherhood there existed a secret cell of army officers who were plotting against the government. In 1952, the leader of this secret cell—Gamal Abdel Nasser—participated in the coup that overthrew the Egyptian government and put Naguib on the throne as Egypt's first President. Ironically, it would be Nasser who would ban the Muslim Brotherhood yet again, ostensibly for having attempted to assassinate *him*. Thousands of Brotherhood members were rounded up at that time, and many were tortured and killed. Others fled to Saudi Arabia, where they were welcomed as a kind of Islamic intelligentsia in a land that was in dire need of teachers and educators. This circumstance would backfire on the Kingdom in later years, when it was realized that the Brotherhood had a stranglehold on the entire educational system in the country. By 2014, the Saudi government declared the Muslim Brotherhood a terrorist organization.

However, in 1953, the Muslim Brotherhood had branches in most Islamic countries outside of Egypt, including even in Shi'ite Iran. They were a force to be reckoned with, easily the only pan-Islamic (if not pan-Arab) organization in the world, including a presence in Europe. If the Eisenhower administration could get the support of the Brotherhood, then between the two of them they could easily upset Soviet designs wherever the Brotherhood had chapters. As a religious as well as a political organization, the Brotherhood had connections within the Soviet territories that could be exploited for intelligence purposes, including espionage and sabotage. The wide variety of languages and ethnicities meant another level of complexity, but this was one that CIA intended to exploit through their European operations—specifically using Muslim Brotherhood members to create print and broadcast media directed against the Soviet Union, and emphasizing the atheistic and immoral nature of Communism.

This was essentially what CIA was already doing with their Christian networks and their infiltration of the World Council of Churches, the World Anti-Communist League, the League of Captive Nations, and so many others. It didn't require much imagination to port the Christian strategy onto a Muslim-based agenda. Some of this was done through Radio Liberty, a CIA asset in Europe that beamed pro-Islamic and anti-Communist programming into the Soviet Union. The CIA operation utilizing Muslims—and specifically members of the Muslim Brotherhood—was run by an agent named Bob Dreher. The US government felt that helping to build an Islamic Center in Munich would attract the "right kind" of Muslims to their cause, and to that end, a mosque was built that later became the foothold in Europe (and the West) that the Brotherhood needed. They used the mosque to disseminate Brotherhood-oriented propaganda and to act as a kind of safe house for Brotherhood members. The Muslim Brotherhood official Said Ramadan became central to that strategy, and in 1953 he had his photo oppportunity with the President of the United States.

None of this was happening in a vacuum, of course. Anti-Communist hysteria was at an all-time high. The McCarthy Hearings had begun and the 1950s was an era of Red-baiting and emotional accusations and counter-accusations. Communists were believed to have infiltrated every level of the US Government, as well as the military and even the CIA. The effect on the entertainment industry was no less dramatic, as screenwriters and actors were blacklisted. The only safe position to hold was that of a right-wing zealot, a passionate anti-Communist who could suspect even President Eisenhower of being a Communist, and there were plenty of these.

An entire generation of high-ranking US military officers became embroiled in anti-Communist organizations and intrigues throughout the 1950s and 1960s. Men like Major General Charles A. Willoughby, Major General Edwin Walker, Lieutenant General Pedro del Valle, and Major General George Van Horn Moseley were in the forefront of the anti-Communist crusade in the United States.

Willloughby (1892–1972), to whom General Douglas MacArthur referred as his "pet fascist," had been born Adolf Karl Tscheppe-Weidenbach in Heidelberg, the son of a German baron and an American mother from Baltimore. He became MacArthur's Chief of Military Intelligence during World War II and the Korean War, and then became involved in a series of pro-Nationalist intrigues in

Japan. He was an ardent supporter of Franco in Spain and traveled to Madrid a number of times in the early 1950s as an adviser to the Spanish dictator. He was also involved in a number of anti-Communist, Christian crusades, including the International Committee for the Defense of Christian Culture, a front organization founded by oil magnate H.L. Hunt.

Edwin Walker (1909–1993) was so right-wing he accused President Harry Truman of being a Communist, and tried to tell the men serving under him for whom to vote (in violation of American law). In 1962, he was instrumental in leading the riots protesting the admission of African-American student James Meredith to the University of Mississippi, leading then-Attorney General Robert F. Kennedy to have him committed to an insane asylum for observation. Walker would later become well-known as the first target of alleged John F. Kennedy assassin, Lee Harvey Oswald, in 1963.

Pedro del Valle (1893–1978) was a highly-decorated veteran of World War II and the Pacific theater of operations, the first Latino general of the Marines. He commanded the 1st Marine Division at Okinawa, for which he received the Navy's Distinguished Service Medal. Yet in 1948, he wound up in Cairo as a representative of ITT. That year, the Muslim Brotherhood was implicated in acts of terrorism directed against the Egyptian government after the humiliating defeat of Egypt and its allies by the newly-recognized State of Israel. The atmosphere was poisonous in Cairo, so Del Valle left Egypt and began working for ITT as president of the company's South American division, this time in Buenos Aires, Argentina during the Peron regime. A dedicated anti-Communist and member of a number of crusade-like committees, he once quoted from the *Protocols of the Learned Elders of Zion* at a political rally in order to demonstrate the links between World Jewry and Bolshevism. His involvement with ITT at this time and in those locations is suspicious, as that firm had long-standing ties to the Third Reich before, during, and after the war. As an anti-Semite and anti-Communist, his postings to Cairo and Buenos Aires during periods of great political upheaval in those countries are suggestive—if not indicative—of an intelligence function.

George Van Horn Moseley (1874–1960) retired from military service in 1938 but not before suggesting that European refugees fleeing persecution in Nazi Germany be sterilized before they were allowed to enter the United States so as not to pollute the gene pool. Once out of uniform, he became if anything more vociferous, attacking the New Deal as a form of dictatorship, and praising both fascism and Nazism as the means to innoculate the United States against the Jewish and Communist virus coming from Europe. He believed that the Second World War was a device created by the worldwide Jewish conspiracy, and said the persecution of the Jews in Nazi Germany was payback for their crucifixion of Jesus.

Thus the atmosphere that was being prepared in the post-war period was reminiscent of that which obtained in the immediate pre-war period: attacks on the US Government and whatever administration—the Democrat administrations of Franklin D. Roosevelt and Harry S. Truman, or the Republican administration of war hero and five star general Dwight D. Eisenhower—as being Communist, or Jewish, or both. The US State Department in the middle of all of this political and cultural angst tred carefully. They sponsored reports and briefing materials that extolled the value of religion in the fight against Communism. They actively sought a partnership with former pro-Nazi and current anti-Semitic individuals and groups, like the Muslim Brotherhood, in the struggle against what was perceived to be Soviet hegemonic intentions. The spooks in the State Department and CIA intrigued with various Islamic factions in an effort to build a consensus for a strategy directed at encouraging the Muslim ethnicities behind the Iron Curtain to resist, revolt, and to collaborate with their American case officers. In this, the official position and operations of the US Government were not so far removed from those of the pro-Nazi American generals who were causing such controversy in the media. Covert US support for such infamous Nazis as Klaus Barbie and Otto von Bolschwing has already been officially demonstrated in declassified intelligence files. Their utility to the US government was to be found specifically in their anti-Communist credentials. If CIA was covering for Nazi military leaders, then they could tolerate the home-grown American versions.

Some of these generals were involved in bizarre little conspiracies and secret societies of their own. Willoughby, for instance, was prominent in something called the Shickshinny Knights of Malta

(SKOM), a fraudulent Order of Malta, founded in the small town of Shickshinny, Pennsylvania. The SKOM became a kind of fascist think tank, with former or retired members of the US military and intelligence establishments meeting to decide what to do about the dangers posed by creeping Communism in the American heartland.

By the time the 1960s had rolled around, however, the focus had shifted to Vietnam. There the generals actually had a theater of operations for their ground war against Communism. They had been stalled at the 39th parallel in Korea. The attempted invasion of Cuba to oust Fidel Castro had failed miserably. There had been CIA operations in Guatemala, Iran, the Dominican Republic, Laos, and elsewhere. But these were brush fires compared to the conflagrations desired by what outgoing President Dwight Eisenhower had called the "military industrial complex" in his Farewell Address to the nation in 1960. The United States was finally at war with Communism, albeit in a proxy war being fought in a small Southeast Asian country on the other side of the world.

The thinkers and plotters in Washington D.C. had always been aware that Communism was not merely a Russian threat. Communism could also come from China, from North Korea, from North Vietnam. The Communist threat was two-fold, and the United States decided it had to fight on two fronts. In Europe, it was a Cold War; but in Asia, it was a hot war brought to the boiling point by religion once again.

Eisenhower knew back in 1952 that the "holy war" he envisioned against Communism would not be restricted to the European theater of operations. The American jihad would be extended to include Muslims all over the world. This was, after all, the global jihad that Oppenheim and al-Husseini had always desired. And when the dust had cleared the American jihad would include not only Muslims—but Buddhists, too.

To the plotters and planners of the anti-Communist (read "anti-Russian, anti-Chinese") holy war, God indeed was great.

PART THREE:

THE SHAMBHALA FACTOR

CHAPTER NINE

THE NAZI ARCHIPELAGO

General Willoughby: Fiscal responsibility is one of the prime requisites of orderly Government. Nationalist aspirations can hardly be made an excuse for practices that are unacceptable under the norms of the free economy. ... The very recent outbreaks against the Dutch, the seizure of legitimate business by Communist controlled labor unions, and so forth, confirm the fiscal and economic irresponsibility of the Sukarno "Republic."

Mr. Arens. Are there any counterbalancing influences in this situation?

General Willoughby. They are found within the Mohammedan party, initially called Serika, later "Masjumi," in the immediate entourage of former Vice President Mohammed Hatta ...

> —From a report entitled *International Communism (Communist Designs on Indonesia and the Pacific Frontier: Staff Consultation with General Charles A. Willoughby, Former Chief of Intelligence, Far Eastern Command, Under General Douglas MacArthur* by the Committee on Un-American Activities, House of Representatives, Eighty-Fifth Congress, First Session, December 16, 1957.

As can be seen from the above citation, our General Willoughby had insinuated himself into the foreign policy situation with regard to Indonesia. This 38-page document is replete with references to Communists in the US Government, and how the US foreign policy reflected that lamentable condition. The only possible way to counteract the influence of Communism in Indonesia was, to use Willoughby's words, the "Mohammedan party." As we have seen, this is very much in line with US foreign policy generally under the Eisenhower administration at that time.

What is remarkable is the fact that this testimony was given before the House Committee on Un-American Activities (HUAC) and not before Congress as a whole, or before an appropriate foreign policy or military committee. Willoughby was sounding the alarm that at any moment Indonesia could fall to the Communists. What he called the "Malay Barrier"—roughly a line that went from Malaya to the outer islands of the Indonesian archipelago—was the only thing standing between Australia and the dreaded People's Republic of China.

Someone must have listened, for the less than six months later the CIA mounted an operation to support anti-Sukarno rebel forces in Sumatra and Sulawesi, losing a B-26 aircraft at Ambon in the process. The entire story of this operation is still classified; CIA Director George Tenet refused to declassify the relevant documents as late as 1998 due to the sensitive nature of the information contained within them. Fletcher Prouty, however, was not so reticent and revealed that upwards of 42,000 American troops were stationed at various bases in the Philippines, ready to provide ground, sea, and air support to the rebel forces in Indonesia. One of the men who was ordered to the Philippines to take part in this clandestine operation—according to Prouty—was Lee Harvey Oswald.

Another was a man personally known to the author, who met him in New York City in 1984. At the time he had a position with a European electronics manufacturer and my company was sourcing materials from him for a project in China. One day, he mentioned that he had been given an award by President Kennedy himself for a secret mission undertaken in Indonesia in 1958. The man in question was a submarine commander.

How had things turned out this way in Indonesia? How did Indonesia become a flashpoint for anti-Communist intrigues and violent rebellions? What was America's interest in this former Dutch colony, with its chains of volcanoes and ancient architecture?

It goes back to a meeting that was held in the Indonesian town of Bandung in April of 1955, a meeting that caused a sensation of fear throughout the Western world—and especially in the United States. It was a conference that had thrown a figurative gauntlet

Adolf Hitler. More than a political figure, Hitler was the leader of a nationalist cult that has inspired millions since he first came onto the scene in the years after World War One. The defeat of the Third Reich in World War Two was not the defeat of Nazism: a philosophy that combines politics with religion, race, and violence and which has survived to this day in the support of global terror. This is the Hitler Legacy.

Max Von Oppenheim was an amateur archaeologist and confidant of Kaiser Wilhelm during World War One. He convinced the Kaiser—and later the Ottoman Sultan—that what was required was something the world had never seen: a global jihad of Muslims worldwide against the "enemies of Islam."

Sultan Mehmet V of the Ottoman Empire. German agent Max von Oppenheim convinced the Sultan to declare the first ever global jihad.

Lord Balfour, author of the Balfour Declaration which guaranteed a Jewish homeland in Palestine in return for Zionist assistance against Germany and the Ottoman Empire during World War One.

F. Georges Picot, one of the framers of the Sykes-Picot Treaty that divided the Middle East between France and England after World War One and which contributed to the situation we face today.

The British half of the treaty, Mark Sykes was a lower-level bureaucrat whose tragic error in dividing up the former Ottoman Empire between England and France has led the world to its current debacle.

T.E. Lawrence, "Lawrence of Arabia," British intelligence agent and archaeologist, assisted the Arab Revolt against the Ottoman Empire while suspecting the British would not honor their commitments to the Arabs under Prince Faisal. He helped draw the map of the post–World War One Middle East.

Gertrude Bell, the famous archaeologist and founder of the Baghdad Museum, worked with Lawrence in creating the current Middle Eastern landscape including: Iraq, Saudi Arabia, Jordan, Syria, Lebanon, etc.

Hajj Amin al-Husseini, the Grand Mufti of Jerusalem, collaborated with the Nazis before, during and after World War II as spiritual leader of Palestinian Muslims. He was the bridge between the global jihad of World War One, the Holocaust of World War Two, and the current situation in Palestine and Israel.

Nemesis of the Extreme Right in 1930s America, President Franklin D. Roosevelt was characterized as a Jew and a Communist, a dictator whose New Deal was described as the "Jew Deal."

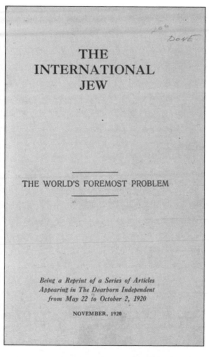

THE
INTERNATIONAL
JEW

THE WORLD'S FOREMOST PROBLEM

Being a Reprint of a Series of Articles
Appearing in The Dearborn Independent
from May 22 to October 2, 1920

NOVEMBER, 1920

Henry Ford, one of the American industrialists who openly supported Hitler and the Nazi Party from their earliest days, and was awarded Nazi Germany's highest honor for a foreigner for his efforts.

This is a copy of The International Jew, *by Henry Ford. The book has been translated into dozens of languages worldwide, including Spanish, Arabic, Urdu, and Indonesian, and can be found in bookstores worldwide*

William Dudley Pelley, American-born Nazi, esotericist, and leader of the pro-German Silver Shirts in the 1930s. He predicted the world would change in September, 2001.

AMERICAN FASCISM 1920–1940

Father Charles Coughlin, the Roman Catholic "Radio Priest" of the 1930s in America. He openly promoted anti–Semitism and supported Nazi policies in his broadcasts and print media. He was involved with the pre-war Nazi underground in the United States.

Anastase Vonsiatsky, White Russian emigre and self-proclaimed fascist who conspired with the Nazi Underground in America to overthrow the US government.

Hjalmar Schacht, Hitler's Banker, during the Nuremberg Trials. Schacht would
become an important player in the post-war
Nazi Underground in Europe, the Middle
East, and Asia.

Wilhelm Keppler at Nuremberg.
Keppler was the founder of the
Freundeskreis Keppler which became
the Freundeskreis Himmler. He
organized a cabal of German
industrialists and financiers to
support the Nazi Party and to
pressure Hindenburg to proclaim
Hitler Chancellor of Germany.

Baron Kurt von Schroeder in a photo
taken at Nuremberg. Schroeder was
one of the original financiers of the
Nazi Party, along with Emil Helfferich. He was also a member of the
Freundeskreis Himmler.

An early photo of General Charles A. Willoughby, MacArthur's head of military intelligence in the Pacific theater during World War II and later member of various extreme-right and pro-fascist groups in the United States. He was also implicated in the acquisition of "Black Eagle" (i.e. Nazi) gold used to finance right-wing politicians in Asia.

General Edwin Walker, who was the target of an assassination attempt allegedly by Lee Harvey Oswald. Walker was one of a number of American generals who were sympathetic towards Nazism.

Lt. General Pedro del Valle, anti-semite who believed in the Protocols of the Learned Elders of Zion, and who charged that an "Invisible Government" composed of Jews and Communists had overthrown the Russian Czar and was then plotting to do the same to the United States.

General Van Horn Moseley, an energetic pro-fascist and anti-semite, and member of the cabal of American military men who believed the US government was being run by Jews and Communists.

Otto "Scarface" Skorzeny, Hitler's favorite commando and one of the leaders of
ODESSA and Die Spinne.

SS Major General Otto Remer, another
leader of the Nazi Underground.

Hans-Ulrich Rudel, ace fighter pilot, and
one of the leaders of ODESSA

Nazi Propagandist Johann von Leers
who converted to Islam and moved to
Egypt to work for the Nasser regime after
a brief sojourn in Argentina.

Aribert Heim, one of the many Nazis who converted to Islam and escaped to the Middle East after the war. A medical doctor who experimented on prisoners in the camps, he was one of the most wanted war criminals in the world.

Klaus Barbie, the "Butcher of Lyon," was known as Klaus Altmann in Bolivia. He became head of the Bolivian secret police and was a linchpin in the South American branch of ODESSA.

Gerhard Mertins, Nazi and post-War Arms Dealer to the Middle East

President Juan Peron of Argentina, a major supporter of the Nazi Underground in Latin America.

President Alfredo Stroessner of Paraguay. Stroessner appears prominently in the Rudel address book as a supporter of the Nazi Underground in Latin America.

Meeting of President Augusto Pinochet of Chile with Henry Kissinger. The Nixon-Kissinger Doctrine in Latin America mandated the removal by force of Pinochet's predecessor, Salvador Allende. Pinochet became a central figure in the Nazi Underground and in Operation Condor which was run largely by former Nazis in Bolivia, Argentina, Paraguay, and Chile to assassinate leftist personalities in Latin America and abroad. "Courtesy of Archivo General Historico del Ministerio de Relaciones Exteriores de Chile.

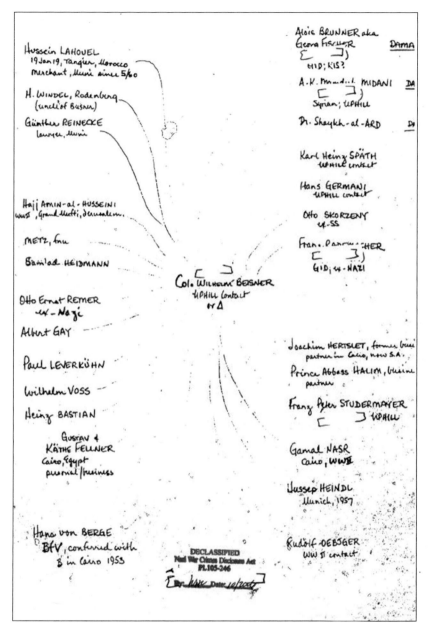

This is a page from a declassified American intelligence file concerning SS Sturmbann-fuehrer Wilhelm Beisner, who worked in Cairo as an arms dealer after the war often in concert with SS General Otto Remer. Described as Skorzeny's representative in Egypt, this document shows Beisner's connections to a wide network of Nazis who lived and thrived in the Middle East in the 1950s and beyond. (see Martin A. Lee, The Beast Reawakens, *p. 142.)*

Yasser Arafat and President Gamal Abdel Nasser of Egypt. Nasser employed hundreds of former Nazis in positions ranging from security services to propaganda to the design of WMDs. Arafat himself had trained under Nazi security experts in Egypt.

Photo showing Yasser Arafat (left) and Dr. George Habash (right). Arafat was head of the Palestine Liberation Organization and Habash (a Christian) was head of the Popular Front for the Liberation of Palestine. Habash was heavily funded by the Swiss Nazi financier Francois Genoud. Arafat had been a student of Amin al-Husseini.

POST WAR ISLAM

President Sukarno of Indonesia. In 1955 Sukarno attempted to create an international bank that would rival the World Bank and the IMF, but designed to be used by the Non-Aligned Nations. He was the target of a CIA plot to overthrow him in 1958. By 1965, Sukarno had been removed from real power by the anti-communist General Soeharto who remained President of Indonesia until 1998.

This is the Gedung Merdeka in Bandung, Indonesia in 1955: site of the Bandung Conference, that was attended by al-Husseini and members of the Muslim Brotherhood, as well as leaders of the Non-Aligned Nations.

Abu Bakr Ba'asyir—mastermind of the Bali Bombings of 2002—at his pesantren in Solo, Indonesia in 2007. During our meeting he spoke of the global Jewish conspiracy to control the world in the words of the Protocols of the Learned Elders of Zion. *Indonesia is a country that has fewer than 100 Jews among its more than 220,000,000 people, most of whom are Muslims. Ba'asyir was the co-founder of Jemaah Islamiyyah, the terror group that is considered the Southeast Asian affiliate of Al-Qaeda. (photo by the author)*

Heinrich Harrer, before his famous journey to Tibet, shown on the right of Hitler after Harrer's climb up the north face of the Eiger. Harrer is now believed to have been an espionage agent, first for the Nazis and then for a Western intelligence service. Although a member of both the SS and the SA, he remained a close friend of the Dalai Lama for the rest of his life, like Bruno Beger and Miguel Serrano.

Bruno Beger, Nazi anthropologist, during the SS Expedition to Tibet. Beger remained friendly with the Dalai Lama, even though he had more than 80 prisoners of the Natzweiler concentration camp murdered so he would have specimens for his proposed museum of anthropology.

Chilean Nazi Party member and former Chilean ambassador Miguel Serrano, meeting Nehru of India in 1957. Serrano believed that Hitler was the avatar of a Hindu god. A friend of the Dalai Lama, Serrano also presided over the funeral of SS officer Walter Rauff in Santiago. Rauff had been the inventor of the mobile gas van for the execution of Jewish prisoners. Serrano was also deeply involved with Colonia Dignidad, the Chilean node of Operation Condor, where WMDs were being developed until the overthrow of Pinochet in 1990.

D.T. Suzuki, the world-famous expert on Zen Buddhism, wrote glowingly of Japanese fascist and racist policies in Korea, Manchuria and China. An admirer of Nazism and apologist for the Reich's policies against the Jews, he was a close friend of Gestapo officer Karlfried Graf von Durckheim.

Karlfried Graf von Durkheim, the noted expounder of Japanese Zen philosophy in the West, was a committed Nazi and had been a Gestapo officer in Tokyo during the war. He was a friend of D.T. Suzuki and helped introduce Zen Buddhism to the western world. Durckheim was arrested by the Allies during their occupation of Japan and served more than a year in prison as a member of the Gestapo.

THE MONEY

This mine represents one of the stashes of Nazi gold and other valuables, in this case discovered in Merkers Mine in Thuringia, entered by the US Army on April 7. 1945. "The inventory indicated that there were 8,198 bars of gold bullion; 55 boxes of crated gold bullion; hundreds of bags of gold items; over 1,300 bags of gold Reichsmarks, British gold pounds, and French gold francs; 711 bags of American twenty-dollar gold pieces; hundreds of bags of gold and silver coins; hundreds of bags of foreign currency; 9 bags of valuable coins; 2,380 bags and 1,300 boxes of Reichsmarks (2.76 billion Reichsmarks); 20 silver bars; 40 bags containing silver bars; 63 boxes and 55 bags of silver plate; 1 bag containing six platinum bars; and 110 bags from various countries." (Source: Greg Bradsher, "Nazi Gold: The Merkers Mine Treasure" in Prologue: Quarterly of the National Archives and Records Administration, Spring 1999, vol. 31, no. 1.)

Treasury Secretary Henry Morgenthau at the Bretton Woods conference during his attempt to close down the Bank of International Settlements.

Krunoslav Draganovic, the Croatian Catholic priest who created the first Ratline in order to help members of the Nazi Croatian Ustase government escape to Argentina. He later became influential in helping many war criminals flee to South America, and was briefly on the payroll of the CIA.

This is evidence that the Pochs had escaped Salzberg and were wanted fugitives. What is not known from the wanted poster is why they were wanted, and who wanted them.

Artur Seyss-Inquart, Military Governor of the Netherlands and patron of the Pöchs, later executed at Nuremberg

The Penninsula Plaza Hotel in Singapore, Arms Dealer PT Novanindro's Legal Address. The Novanindro office is that of a local law firm. (photo by the author)

Prince Soeryo Goeritno, Indonesia's pre-eminent arms dealer. Fight promoter, former taxi driver, rock musician, who speaks fluent Russian and has a Russian wife and two children, works with Moscow, searches for buried gold on Sumbawa, and sells guns to the Taliban. He was also the first to publish a book on the mysterious Dr. Georg Anton Poch and did everything he could to get his hands on the remaining documents. (photo credit: www.boxing-indonesia.com)

Oswald in the Back Yard. This is the famous photo of alleged Kennedy assassin Lee Harvey Oswald showing him holding a Mannlicher Carcano rifle and a copy of a Communist periodical. This helped to condemn Oswald as a Communist sympathizer, when the opposite may have been the case.

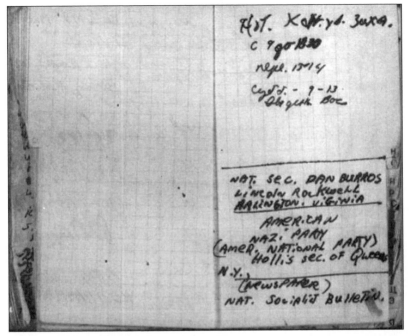

Page 55 of Lee Harvey Oswald's address book makes references to the American Nazi Party and Dan Burros. Dan Burros was a Jewish member of the American Nazi Party. When his ethnicity was revealed, Burros committed suicide in the home of Klansman Roy Frankhouser.

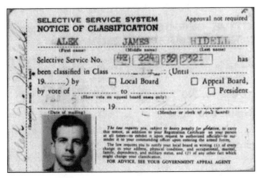

Oswald Draft Card

Oswald USMC. This is Oswald as a Marine. He would serve at Atsugi Naval Air Station in Japan and later, according to Fletcher Prouty, took part in the CIA sponsored coup against President Sukarno in Indonesia, an attempt that failed.

Page Thirteen — Oswald
William K. Stuckey
Nov. 24, 1963

He said it was when he was stationed in Japan with the Marine Corps — "and saw the terrible conditions of life there, how the people lived" — that he made up his mind to go to Russia. Marxism, he concluded then, was the best means evolved to date to solve such human problems.

His comments were on life in Russia, again, were candid and disarming.

"I was disappointed with Russia," he said. "It wasn't what I expected. In many ways, it's just as bad as it is here. In the factory where I worked, I saw a lot of selfishness and pettiness. It seems like they are trying to copy many of our ideas about the economy and about production, many capitalist ideas. They are a long way from true Communism."

I then got the idea that Oswald was possibly a young man who was shopping for the perfect revolution. This tendency, his conversation indicated, led him to espouse the "purer" revolution of Fidel Castro.

At home, he said, he was also reading books on Indonesian Communism and on Sukarno. He added that he felt Sukarno was only an opportunist who was using the Communists, not a Communist himself.

He was having trouble drinking his beer, and declined a second. He didn't appear to have much money.

In trying to explain some of his views to me, he sometimes adopted the attitude that he was wasting his time because "you couldn't of course understand this." This also strenghthened my impression that Oswald regarded himself — but without really offensive arrogance — as a man living among intellectual inferiors.

"You know, most of you think that Russia and the Iron Curtain countries are all alike," he remarked. "That's not true. Each country — Poland, Hungary, China, Cuba — have their own separate national identities."

more

Here is a single page extract from a memoir by William Stuckey of his meeting with Oswald in New Orleans, at the time of the Fair Play for Cuba Committee episode. It is relevant to our story because it mentions Oswald's interest in Indonesia and his assessment of Sukarno as an opportunist.

down on the table between the two superpowers—the United States and the Soviet Union—and which threatened to upset the delicate balance of money and influence that had been carefully crafted since the end of the Second World War. This was the Asian-African Conference, sometimes referred to as the Bandung Conference. One of the attendees was the Grand Mufti of Jerusalem himself, Hajj Amin al-Husseini.

The purpose of the meeting was to consolidate what Sukarno had called the "Newly Emerging Forces," or the Non-Aligned Forces, of what was then called the "Third World," and which we now call the Developing Nations. These were countries that formerly had been colonized by the West, and which were now reluctant to side with either the Soviet Union or the United States; in other words, they represented not only the Third World but also the Third Way. Indonesia was the host of this meeting, and as the most populous Muslim nation in the world, the implications were serious. Attendees included not only the Grand Mufti, but Muslim leaders from the Middle East and Africa as well as the Muslim Brotherhood. Sukarno had decided to put into play an idea that had germinated within his revolutionary brain ever since a series of meetings with a famous financier in Jakarta in 1951: none other than Hjalmar Schacht, "Hitler's Banker."

Had this story only been about Dr. Georg Anton Pöch and his mysterious journey to Indonesia, it would have been a good story but not enough for two books. What kept me coming back to the subject was the realization that there was an aspect to Asian history that has been largely ignored. This is the fact that there was a Nazi presence in Asia long before the war began, replete with Nazi Party meetings, U-boats, and escape routes. It has not attracted much attention—and this is probably due to the Japanese aspect of the War in the Pacific that overwhelms all other narratives. Yet, when put against the volume of available literature on the Nazis and the war in Europe, not much is really understood about the Japanese war and the series of invasions that characterize their terrorizing of an entire continent. Most Japanese war criminals escaped justice; very few were arrested, tried, convicted and sentenced; yet their record of atrocities equals—and at times exceeds—anything that took place in Europe.

Nazi Germany's role in the region has long been obscured by history's focus on Japan. To be sure, the Pacific was not a theater of operations for the Nazis in any coherent fashion. But there were vital trade deals with the Japanese, and even before the war had begun, the Nazis were very involved in the region in political and military matters. It is true they had left the management of the area to the Japanese—at least until Germany would conquer the Middle East and India, and be able to turn her eyes to Southeast Asia and the abundant natural resources that region could offer.

Thus there is a shadow presence in the Indonesian archipelago, the longest archipelago in the world. It represents a Nazi Archipelago. To understand the context for Pöch's flight to the region, and the reasons why even Hitler would have seriously considered it as a sanctuary, we will examine the weird and unexpected world of the Asian Nazis.

Southeast Asia, at the turn of the century, was largely a collection of European colonies. Malaya (including Singapore) was a British colony. Indochina (later Vietnam) was a French colony. What is today Indonesia was a Dutch colony. The Philippines had belonged to Spain but was ceded to the United States after the Spanish-American War of 1898. Taiwan had become a Japanese colony in 1895, after having been fought over by the Spanish, the Dutch, and the Chinese.

With the Japanese invasion of much of Southeast Asia beginning at the end of 1941—the year that also saw the attack on Pearl Harbor in the Hawaiian islands, a US territory—the colonial hegemony over these territories was interrupted. Japan had come in the guise of a liberator, promising the Indonesians (for instance) that they would gain their independence from the Dutch, and the Malayans from the British. This struck a responsive chord with some nationalist leaders who believed they could work with the Japanese, if it meant that centuries of colonial rule would end. What they did not expect was that the Japanese would see themselves as the new colonial power in the Pacific, raping the land; seizing gold, property and other valuables; and enslaving large segments of the populations as a labor force, including women as sex workers for the Japanese troops. But they were between a rock and a hard place.

In Indonesia, the nationalists were happy that the Dutch had lost control over their most valuable colony; leaders such as Sukarno made speeches in Tokyo, praising the Japanese and calling for war against the Americans and the British as well as the Dutch; and announcing that the Third Reich would put Germany at the very apex of world nations. But the situation was problematic, for not all the Dutch were on the side of the Allies, and not all Indonesian nationalists were pro-fascist or pro-Nazi.

There had been pro-fascist and pro-Nazi supporters in the Netherlands before the Germans finally invaded that country in 1940. While there was determined resistance by Dutch troops against the Nazis, the Dutch forces finally capitulated to keep their country from being completely devastated by bombing runs over their main cities. Once the Nazis were in power, the nascent Dutch Nazis wanted to form their own, pro-Nazi, government. The legitimate government and the Royal family had fled to Great Britain ahead of the Nazi invasion, and while they claimed to be the legitimate government of the Netherlands, in practice the Dutch Nazi Party was fighting to control its own destiny and to keep the Netherlands Dutch. The German Nazis had a different idea, however, and they eventually installed native Austrian Artur Seyss-Inquart as the Governor-General of the Netherlands.

What is usually not remembered by World War Two historians is that much of the wealth of the Netherlands had come from its colony in Southeast Asia. Known as the Dutch East Indies and controlled by the Dutch East India Company (or VOC to give it its Dutch initials), the colony extended to the entire archipelago east of Singapore and Malaya, and included the huge islands of Sumatra and Java as well as Bali, Lombok, Sumbawa, etc. It was a rich source of rice, rubber, coffee, tea, and other raw materials and natural resources. Thus one could not talk of the Netherlands without including a discussion of its most important colony and the source of much of its economic power. When the Nazi invasion of the Netherlands finally took place on May 10, 1940, it was with the understanding that control of the Netherlands eventually would bring with it control of the Indies. When their ally the Japanese invaded Southeast Asia in 1941, and proceeded to remove the by-now autonomous Dutch government in the Indies in early 1942, it looked as if the prize possession was coming under the control of the Axis powers. But the foundation had already been laid as early as 1925.

During the 1920s, the Governor-General of the Dutch East Indies put down a threat to Dutch control in the region represented by an Indonesian communist party. It was the failure of this revolt that inspired Indonesian nationalist leaders to contemplate the successes of Mussolini in Italy and, eventually, Hitler in Germany, and to consider a fascist—rather than a communist—response to their Dutch colonial masters.

At the same time, there was a German Nazi presence in the Dutch East Indies, one that has been largely missed by historians. This was the Nazi Party apparatus that had been put into place by Walter Hewel, the man who would become a German ambassador without portfolio under the inept (and possibly insane) Nazi Foreign Minister Joachim von Ribbentrop. Hewel had been one of Hitler's closest friends, allies, and confidants going back to the time when Hewel had marched with Hitler and Himmler under the swastika banner during the failed Beer Hall Putsch of 1923. Hewel had only been a teenager at the time, but was imprisoned along with Hitler and his other co-conspirators in Landsberg Prison. He was released after a year, and went to England for one year to study business, after which he was sent to the Dutch East Indies to work as a trader. While in England—and on the advice of Rudolf Hess, Hitler's closest supporter and fellow inmate at Landsberg Prison—Hewel made contact with British fascists there and, thus inspired by fascist ideology from both England and Germany, he went to Indonesia to put his beliefs into practice.

He remained in what is now Indonesia for *ten years* before returning to Germany when Hitler had become Chancellor and had installed Ribbentrop as Foreign Minister. For a brief period, Hewel was stationed in Spain before permanently returning to the side of his old comrade-in-arms, Adolf Hitler.

But his time in Indonesia was not spent in the tea trade alone, although that was his ostensible reason for being there. Hewel was a dedicated Nazi, a true believer. He set up Nazi Party cells in all of Indonesia's major cities among the expatriate German populations there. Based for awhile in the coastal city of Surabaya—where Georg Anton Pöch would die in 1970—he became known back in Germany as "Surabaya Wally."

He remained at Hitler's side for the rest of the war. Hewel was a great raconteur, and Hitler loved to hear the stories Surabaya Wally would tell of his experiences in Indonesia. Hewel was one of the last to leave the Berlin bunker in May, 1945, and was never seen again, although it was reported that he died—or committed suicide—while trapped in a basement in Berlin during the Russian advance. But, like Hitler, his body was never found.

He was more than just a teller of tall tales and an entertaining figure to have around. When SS Obergruppenführer Ernst Kaltenbrunner was being questioned by the Allies in 1945, he told them how important Hewel was:

HEWEL belonged to HITLER's closest circle and was one of his main advisers on questions of foreign policy. K. always tried to give important reports to HEWEL since he was certain that they would reach HITLER. He also used HEWEL to obtain information about what was going on in the German Foreign Office.[60]

Ernst Kaltenbrunner (1903–1946) was an Austrian who rose to the highest rank in the SS next to Himmler, and who was also head of Interpol during the war. He was arrested in Austria near the alleged site of the National Redoubt: the area around Salzburg where the Nazis would hide in the complex series of salt mines and caves and stage their "Werewolf" guerrilla campaign against the Allies. While most historians today scoff at the existence of the National Redoubt,

60   Vol. XCVII 38.02. Kaltenbrunner. HQ 12th Army Group. Interrogation Center. Prisoner: O/Gruf KALTENBRUNNER, Ernst. SECRET 28 June 1945.

the Allies had good intelligence that it existed. There were aerial photographs of bunkers being built, and large transport caravans making their way to the Salzburg area. It was in one area of the purported National Redoubt—the Alt Aussee—that a large cache of stolen art was recovered, believed to be some of Goering's personal treasure, as well as that of Hitler's personal art collection destined for the Adolf Hitler Art Museum in his hometown of Linz, Austria ... a project that was, of course, never realized. Kaltenbrunner was discovered hiding in this region, using the documents and identity papers of a medical doctor to disguise his own identity, and even carrying a medical bag as an ordinary doctor would. As Kaltenbrunner would later demonstrate, they were the real identity papers of a real military doctor[61] and not forged papers.[62]

This last fact is important for it shows how it was not only possible but likely that some Nazis escaped justice by using the papers of other Germans who were not wanted by the Allies and, in this particular case, the papers of a medical doctor. In other words, like Kaltenbrunner's fellow Austrian, Georg Anton Pöch. Heinrich Himmler, Kaltenbrunner's boss, also used the genuine identity papers of a member of the German police in his attempt to escape, not realizing that the German police were also on the proscribed list. Himmler committed suicide when he realized that the Allies had recognized him once he was captured, but Kaltenbrunner was hanged at Nuremberg for war crimes in 1946.

Kaltenbrunner is referenced here because of his knowledge of Hewel and of Hewel's importance to Hitler. Kaltenbrunner himself wanted more access to the Foreign Office and was using Hewel to bypass Ribbentrop and go directly to Hitler. (Ribbentrop was

---

61 Identified by Guy Walters as Dr. Josef Unterwogen in *Hunting Evil: The Nazi War Criminals Who Escaped and the Quest to Bring Them to Justice*, New York, Broadway Books, 2009, p. 14. In the same text, Walters identifies the CIC agent as Captain Robert E. Matteson.

62 This comes from a declassified CIA report entitled "The Last Days of Ernst Kaltenbrunner" approved for release on 22 September 1993 by the CIA Historical Review Program and published on the CIA website *https:// www.cia.gov/library/center-for-the-study-of-intelligence/kent-csi/vol4no2/html/ v04i2a07p_0001.htm* last accessed on June 20, 2013.

also hanged at Nuremberg.) Kaltenbrunner is interesting as well for his role in setting up a clandestine underground network of Nazis—including the SS, but also former Nazi diplomats and Gauleiters—as a "stay-behind" organization to fight the Allies and, in particular, the Russians. One of Kaltenbrunner's inner circle was Otto Skorzeny who, as we have seen, would go on to become one of the more visible leaders of the Nazi underground after the war. Kaltenbrunner and Skorzeny had been having meetings right up to the very end, as late as May, 1945, in the Salzburg area after Hitler's death had been announced. Thus in Kaltenbrunner we have a nexus of connections to Hitler, Hewel, Skorzeny, and the Nazi underground, as well as to the National Redoubt and the buried gold and art treasures later discovered in the Salzburg area.

A CIA report insists that the National Redoubt existed:

After the Siegfried Line was breached and Nazi Germany began to fall apart, it was said that the hard core of Party leaders and their Waffen SS would hole up in a National Redoubt which they had made ready in the Austrian Alps and from there descend to prey like werewolves on the Allied occupation forces. This bad dream, of course, never came true, and later there was a good deal of scoffing at the "myth." But at the beginning of May in 1945 there was nothing mythical about either the Werewolves or the National Redoubt. General Walter Bedell Smith said, "We had every reason to believe the Nazis intended to make their last stand among the crags." All of our intelligence pointed to the Alpine area east and south of Salzburg as the final fortress for the Goetterdaemmerung of the remaining Nazi fanatics. Reconnaissance photographs showed that they were installing bunkers and ammunition and supply depots in this mountain region. Interrogations of military and political prisoners indicated that government officers, ranking Party leaders, and the SS troops were moving to the Redoubt, leaving it to the Wehrmacht to stem the allied advance.[63]

---

63 CIA report on Ernst Kaltenbrunner, op.cit. General Walter Bedell "Beetle"

In other words, all available intelligence showed that there was, indeed, such a plan in place and pilot Hannah Reitsch confirmed that it was a topic of conversation in the Berlin bunker as late as the last week of April, 1945. This is something of which Hitler and Hewel were, of course, intimately aware. Kaltenbrunner was in the area of the National Redoubt because Himmler had put him in charge of whatever forces remained in southern Europe; he left Berlin in April of 1945, shortly before the fall of that city to the Russian Army, and wound up in the Salzburg area, which is where he was eventually captured.

In fact, it was SS officer Friedrich Rauch who was in charge of the transport of the gold reserves of the Berlin Reichsbank to the Salzburg area in 1945. This gold was earmarked for the use of a "Fourth Reich" after the war, and we know it was never recovered in full ... by the Allies.[64]

Kaltenbrunner had been cooperative with the American interrogators, but when he was transferred to London for interrogation by the British everything changed. According to the CIA report quoted above, Kaltenbrunner was tortured while in British custody. From that point he refused to cooperate in any way with anyone, became withdrawn, and suffered a cerebral hemorrhage which interfered with his ability to stand trial at Nuremberg. It did not stop the proceedings, however, and Kaltenbrunner eventually was tried, convicted and executed. The secrets of the National Redoubt and the possible escape of important war criminals—as well as the stay-behind agent network he had been setting up throughout Europe—died with him.

Kaltenbrunner was deeply interested in the foreign affairs of the Reich, which is why he cultivated Hewel. He would have been one of those familiar with Hewel's Indonesian past and whatever current connections Surabaya Wally had back in the Indies. But that was not his—or the Reich's—only connection to Indonesia.

Smith (1895–1961), of course, became DCI of the CIA soon after its formation in 1947, from 1950 to 1953.

64   See Uki Goñi, *The Real Odessa*, p. 248. Rauch benefited from the services of Father Draganovic and the Ratline, and he arrived in Buenos Aires on February 12, 1948.

One enduring rumor that circulated among the Nazi elite was the idea that Josef Goebbels—the short, club-footed chief of the Nazi Propaganda Ministry and the man who forced his six children, his wife, and himself to die in the Berlin bunker—was actually part Javanese. His mother had been Dutch and her ancestors had been born in Indonesia. The rumors stated that there was Javanese blood in her background, and that Goebbels's odd physical appearance was a result of this breeding with an "inferior" Asiatic race.[65]

With two of Hitler's closest friends—two of the men who were with him to the bitter end in the bunker—having ties to Indonesia, and in Hewel's case with actual experience in that country, it is no wonder that another rumor could be started that Hitler had actually fled to Indonesia after the war. Add to that the growing body of evidence showing a close link between Indonesia and the fascist and Nazi parties of the Netherlands—with extensive branches in Indonesia—and one could come away with an excellent argument that Hitler did, indeed, plan an escape to that tropical country on the other side of the world from bombed-out Berlin.

As early as 1931, there had been both fascist and Nazi parties in the Netherlands. The NSB or *Nationaal-Socialistische Beweging in Nederland* (National Socialist Movement in the Netherlands) was founded in Utrecht in 1931. One of its founders was Anton Mussert (1894–1946), who envisioned a fascist party along the lines of Mussolini's Black Shirts in Italy. At this early stage of its existence the NSB did not have a policy of anti-Semitism but that would change with the influence of another party member, Meinoud Rost van Tonningen (1894–1945). Van Tonningen was born in Surabaya, Indonesia (another Surabaya connection), the son of a Dutch general responsible for putting down an armed revolt of Indonesians against Dutch rule in Bali and Lombok, as well as in Aceh. He studied at the University of Leiden and and lived for a time in Austria, before returning to the Netherlands and joining the NSB in 1936. It was van Tonningen who tried to move the NSB towards a more openly pro-German and pro-Nazi ideology, including anti-

---

65   Robert Payne, *The Life and Death of Adolf Hitler*, London, Corgi Books, 1973, p. 284.

Semitism. There was a power struggle between Mussert and van Tonningen, but Mussert remained head of the party with van Tonningen[66] a strong second.

In 1935, Anton Mussert traveled to the Dutch East Indies where he received a warm welcome from the Dutch Governor-General, both in Batavia (now Jakarta) at the governor's official residence, and also at the governor's home in Bogor. Film footage of the visit shows a smiling Mussert being greeted by members of the Dutch community and giving the fascist salute. The NSB had been active in Indonesia since 1933, to the point that five percent of the total NSB membership was to be found there, with almost thirty percent of all revenues collected by the NSB coming from Indonesia.[67] The NSB had roughly five thousand members in Indonesia by the time of Mussert's visit, although that number would start to drop off by 1940.

One can compare that number to those of the Nazi Party in Indonesia as a whole, which constituted roughly 29,000 at the time the war broke out, most of whom were Germans. Thus, anywhere from ten to fifteen percent of the total number of Nazi Party members in Indonesia at any given time were Dutch.

In Indonesia, the NSB had its first meetings in Bandung, the town where we will find the Asian-African Conference in 1955. Hewel's Nazi Party apparatus, however, extended from Batavia (Jakarta), to Makassar, Surabaya, Medan, Padang, Semarang, and Bandung.[68]

NSB leader Van Tonningen, although he was more completely pro-Nazi and pro-German than his rival Anton Mussert, was not

---

66   Van Tonningen's widow would become an important player in the post-war Nazi underground and was closely associated with Miguel Serrano, Leon DeGrelle, and other Nazi stalwarts who were in the process of planning a Fourth Reich.

67   See Konrad Kwiet, "Zur Geschichte der Mussert Bewegung" in *Vierteljahreshefte für Zeitgeschichte*, 18. (1970), 164–95 and cited in Walter Laqueur, ed. *Fascism: A Reader's Guide*, Berkeley, University of California Press, 1976, p. 112.

68   Jeffrey Hadler, "Translations of Anti-Semitism: Jews, the Chinese, and Violence in Colonial and Post-Colonial Indonesia," in *Indonesia and the Malay World*, Vol. 32, No. 94, November 2004.

allowed membership in the SS because he had been born in Indonesia, and could not prove his racial purity back to the year 1800 (for regular SS men) or 1750 (for officers). This restriction was lifted in 1944 when the SS was taking virtually anyone, but it had to have bothered van Tonningen considerably. He had salve for his wounds, however, as he was put in charge of the Dutch banking system during the war. It has been alleged that it was due to his intimate knowledge of how illegal funds had been transferred and moved around—including the gold that had been seized from Jewish and other accounts. It is believed that when he fell to his death in Allied custody in 1945, he was deliberately pushed. His widow insisted that he was killed to keep him quiet about these financial transactions, and she may very well have been right. The story of Nazi gold has not yet been told in its entirety. We will examine more of the story in the chapter entitled "Sukarno's Gold."

Mussert himself seems to have benefited financially from his position as "Dutch Führer" during the war, for it has recently been discovered that Mussert died a multi-millionaire. Historian Dr. Tessel Pollmann has revealed that Mussert—far from being the "honest politician" he was made out to be—became the owner of "five houses, a major printing company and director of a thriving publishing house. He also owned various precious antiques and a villa, all unrightfully taken from Jewish owners."[69]

Then there was Willem Sassen (1918–2001) a Dutch Nazi and SS officer who volunteered for the Dutch Legion (under command of Dutch officers in the Waffen-SS), and was a war correspondent for the "Voice of the SS" in the Netherlands. After the war he obtained fake ID—via the "Catholic Circle" in Amsterdam (a group of fanatically Nazi priests), and left the Netherlands in September of 1948 to go to Argentina via Dublin, Ireland. He served as a public relations assistant to fascist dictators Gen. Pinochet of Chile and President Stroessner of Paraguay, and famously inter-

---

69 Interview with Dr. Tessel Pollmann by Cnaan Lipshiz, published in *Haaretz*, April 8, 2009.

viewed Adolf Eichmann at length. Sassen eventually died quietly in
Chile, forgotten by everyone.[70]

It becomes necessary at some point to view the Third Reich a
bit differently—as a gang of bank robbers and highwaymen. The
SS and other elements of the Third Reich moved through Europe
like a chainsaw, not only killing and raping on a scale heretofore
unimaginable, but also stealing anything that wasn't nailed down,
and much that was. While the thieving had begun in the very earliest days of Hitler's rule as Chancellor with the Nuremberg Laws—
that made all Jews in Germany non-citizens with the right of the
State to confiscate their property—by the time the war was ending,
any Nazi leader with access to treasure—gold, art, antiquities, rare
books, jewelry, anything—had improvised ways to get it out of the
reach of the Allies.

One of the ways that was available to the highest-placed criminals was the U-boat. This German version of the submarine had a
long and legendary service during the war. Admiral Doenitz—who
briefly became head of the Reich after the "death" of Adolf Hitler—
had begun his career in U-boats in the First World War. It was he
who famously declared that there was a "Paradise" awaiting Hitler
if he should decide to flee, transport courtesy of his U-boats.[71] It
was General Wilhelm von Faupel who organized a shipment of
Nazi gold from Spain to Argentina by U-boat with the help of one
Captain Dietrich Niebuhr (d. 1964) and one Gottfried Sandstede
(who ran the Gestapo in Argentina during the war). Clearly, then,
the U-boats had other uses than purely military ones.

One of the facets of the Second World War that has fascinated
me since I first learned of it was the extent of Nazi U-boat traffic
to Asian ports. We tend to think of the Germans as fighting in the
European theater and nowhere else, except for the brief and doomed
mission of Erwin Rommel—the "Desert Fox"—in North Africa.
The idea that there was regular traffic to and from Asia using Nazi
U-boats is rather startling, for it opens up new vistas of possibilities.

---

70 Well, maybe not everyone. As the Rudel address book demonstrates, Sassen was deeply involved with everyone from Adolf Eichmann to Josef Mengele,
Klaus Barbie and Walter Rauff in Latin America after the war.
71 As referenced in my *Ratline*.

While some U-boat missions to Asia may have been purely military in nature—the sinking of Allied shipping, for instance—as the war progressed, and as Japan consolidated its hold over the former European and American colonies in the Pacific, the Nazis exploited this situation for their own benefit. They desperately needed raw materials to help support their war machine, and this included—among many other natural resources—rubber.

The rubber plant most used in rubber production was not indigenous to Southeast Asia; in fact it was brought to Malaya and the Indies in the 1860s by Dutch entrepreneurs who saw in the tropical environment an excellent place to plant rubber trees. Although there were wild rubber trees in Java and Sumatra before the Dutch arrived, it was found that imported trees were better suited for the type of rubber production the Industrial Age would require. The local Dutch government encouraged the practice and found foreign investors who would help create the rubber plantations to help service the growing need for rubber products, such as tires for motor vehicles. Germany had to import rubber from Asia in order to fill its growing demand for all the rubber products used on cars, trucks, jeeps, tanks, and planes. Japan, on the other hand, needed products that it could only source from German factories. Eventually, German blueprints and designs for advanced weapons systems were included as the Third Reich began to realize it was losing the war. They decided to help the Japanese cause further destruction among the Allies in the Pacific, perhaps hoping that a sudden reversal in the Asian theater would take the pressure off of Berlin which was now fighting on two fronts: Russia to the east, and the Allied advance to the west.

To that end, Nazi U-boat depots were created in Penang, Malaya; in Singapore; and in Batavia: all in Japanese-occupied Southeast Asia. As the Allies became victorious in the region and began bombing Penang from air bases in India, the U-boat station was moved to Singapore, and then to Batavia. The U-boats that were sent to Asia were not designed as Wolfpack-type submarines for search and destroy missions. They had been redesigned for cargo. They would refuel in the Indian Ocean before making the final leg to Malaya and then, when Malaya became too dangerous, to Indonesia.

When the war in Europe was over, the Nazi submariners who were in Indonesia were caught between a rock and a hard place. They could not go home—the travel would have been impossible. Their submarines would have been attacked and destroyed; fuel was a precious commodity; and there would be no useful purpose (in Japanese eyes) for sending these very valuable warships back to Europe to fall into Allied hands. So the German crews were set ashore and the U-boats rechristened as Japanese submarines.

Some of the U-boat crewmembers never made it back to Germany. In some cases they were arrested and thrown into prisoner-of-war camps. Some tried to help the Indonesian nationalists fight against the Dutch; in some cases they were mistaken for Dutch themselves and killed.

Some of the crewmembers died in Indonesia. They were buried in a cemetery near the city of Bogor—where the Dutch Governor-General had a vacation home—on land that had been owned by a close friend of Heinrich Himmler, one Emil Helfferich (1878–1972), one of the members of the so-called *Freundeskreis Himmler* that included Hjalmar Schacht and the infamous Oswald Pohl, Otto Ohlendorf, and even Ernst Schäfer of the SS-Tibet Expedition. Helfferich was a German tea plantation owner, and had ties to Walter "Surabaya Wally" Hewel as well as to the Reichsführer-SS: another indication as to the extent (and the depth) of Nazi connections in Indonesia.[72]

With the end of the Second World War a new conflict came to Indonesia. Much to US President Roosevelt's dismay, an agreement had been reached at Yalta that ensured the colonial powers—principally England, France, and the Netherlands—would get their colonies back once the war was over and Germany and Japan defeated. It was this agreement that launched another series of brutal military conflicts all over the region—from revolts in India and Malaya against British rule, to the anti-French guerrilla war being carried out by Ho Chi Minh in Vietnam, to the liberation movement against the Dutch in Indonesia. While Yalta had guaranteed the

---

72 This story is told in more detail in my *Ratline*, especially chapter four, pages 85–96.

Dutch would retain their valuable colony, the Indonesians themselves had not been asked their opinion.

At the same time, just as the Japanese were leaving Southeast Asia they made good on their promise to grant independence to Indonesia. It was a futile gesture, for it was nothing they legally could give; and there was no way for the Indonesians to enjoy their brief moment of freedom before the Dutch returned in earnest to retake the archipelago by force.

Thus, there followed another five years of armed conflict between the Dutch colonizers and the Indonesian nationalists. Sukarno was the more charismatic of the revolutionary leaders and had identified himself and his cause with Nazi Germany and Imperial Japan during the war. Many Indonesian nationalists were ambivalent about fascism and Nazism; while they could sympathize with nationalism in general, their longing was more towards re-creating the indigenous empires of old: Srivijaya or Majapahit. There had been flirtations with fascism in the development of new Indonesian political movements, such as the *Partai Fasis Indonesia* (PFI) the "Indonesian Fascist Party," and within the Indonesian National Party (PNI). The Indonesian nationalists did not see any benefit in helping their colonial masters—the Dutch—fight against the Nazis who had invaded Dutch territory in Europe. Why would they side with their oppressors to fight a man—Hitler—who clearly had all the colonial powers on the ropes?

Sukarno was probably less of a true fascist than an opportunist and a nationalist. It is hard to understand nationalism in the post-World War Two era as anything other than fascism and Nazism on one side, or as Communism (admittedly more an international than a national movement) on the other. Both movements fought rampant capitalist hegemony and supported anti-colonial movements everywhere. In Europe, Nazi Germany declared as its enemies the very colonizers with whom Asia had the most problems: the English, the French, and the Dutch and, later, the Americans in the Philippines. The Communists were fighting the French in Indochina, as well as establishing a liberated China. Sukarno, himself, was in serious flirtation with China and with the Indonesian Communist Party, the PKI, when he was deposed in 1965–67. Per-

haps Sukarno's case, more than any other, illustrates the ideological and philosophical conundrum resulting from a nationalism that
puts nationhood and national identity and freedom above all other
human values. In the case of Nazi Germany, Hitler's brand of fascism—the Nazism represented in his major work, *Mein Kampf*—is
a kind of "revenge politics": revenge against the Bolsheviks, against
the businessmen, landowners and landlords, against the academics and scientists, and against the Jews and all other non-German
peoples, for what had happened to Germany at the end of World
War One (and also for what had happened to Hitler in his personal
life, which was a catalogue of rejection). Revenge politics results in
a kind of euphoria over vanquishing one's oppressors, but it will be
short-lived. The anti-climactic period is one where the true character of a nation will be tested. At a certain point, there has to be more
depth to a political program than a single idea, even the single idea
of anti-colonialism and liberation from colonial powers.

Unfortunately, this phase of national growth does not happen
in a vacuum. There is usually not enough time to contemplate the
creation of a model state when there are other forces in the world
that threaten a new nation's survival. As Sukarno tilted against the
superpowers in his famous Bandung Conference of 1955, to which
the leaders of the non-aligned nations were invited, it was a thrown
gauntlet. The United States began looking for ways to thwart Sukarno's popularity with the Non-Aligned Nations, nations that seemed
to include an inordinate number of socialist-leaning governments.
There was also the idea in the back of Sukarno's mind of creating an international bank that would be the Non-Aligned Nations's
equivalent of the World Bank or the IMF—both of which Sukarno
viewed as puppets of the superpowers and especially of the United
States. The creation of such a financial institution—independent
of the World Bank and hence independent of Western control—
would be viewed by the West with considerable alarm.

Who suggested this course of action to Sukarno? Who would
have a vested interest in seeing Indonesia financially strong—it was
already the strongest of the undeveloped nations in Asia—and taking on the Western powers at their own game?

If there were a financial mastermind behind this bold idea of

Sukarno, one need look no further than the same financial master-mind who helped create the banking structure and economic power of the Third Reich and who allowed Germany to re-arm in spite of the strictures of the Versailles Treaty: Hjalmar Schacht.

As we have seen, Schacht had been President of the Reichsbank and Minister of Economics for the Third Reich until his ouster in 1937 over policy differences with Hitler—although he remained on salary as a Minister Without Portfolio until 1943. He helped to finance the German industrial giant, I.G. Farben —the exploiter of slave labor during the war and the manufacturer of Zyklon-B, the gas that was used in the gas chambers in the death camps. Schacht was one of the group of industrialists that petitioned Hindenburg to appoint Adolf Hitler as Chancellor of Germany, a goal that was attained on January 30, 1933. He also tried to form an alliance with China—rather than Japan—which was favored by many Nazi leaders who saw in the Chinese Nationalist movement an impulse similar to their own. However, Schacht and his clique of pro-Chinese Nazis lost to the pro-Japan bloc (championed by Ribbentrop), and the rest is history.

Schacht was arrested on suspicion of having been involved in the July 20, 1944 assassination plot against Hitler and wound up in Dachau. As the war came to an end, he was transferred to a prison camp in the South Tyrol, which is where he was found and arrested by the Allies. He stood trial at Nuremberg but was acquitted, and went on to become a consultant to international banking institutions. He even formed his own bank in 1953.

Prior to that, however, he would be found in Jakarta, Indonesia in 1951.

That year Hjalmar Schacht was interviewed by author William Stevenson at the Hotel Capitol in Jakarta. Schacht had been nervous about the interview, but it had been arranged by a family friend. The fact that Schacht's friend was Otto Skorzeny, Hitler's commando, the rescuer of Mussolini, and a leader of the worldwide Nazi underground, meant that Schacht would take the call.

The conversation in Jakarta revolved around the danger that Indonesia was in of going communist, and of how men like Schacht—with experience in piloting the ship of state through perilous economic and political times—could help. Schacht had been instrumental in helping re-arm Germany at a time when doing so was in violation of international treaties set in place at Versailles after World War One. Schacht had engineered complicated financial transactions that ensured Germany could still buy much-needed resources from abroad, even though she owed huge amounts in foreign debt. Schacht knew how to deal with Communist threats to a new country, as he had done with tremendous success in Germany and now hoped to do for Indonesia. Schacht's only problem came when Martin Bormann decided that he was a rival, and did what he could to manipulate circumstances in such a way that Schacht was forced out of government. That Schacht was a committed Nazi and anti-Semite is beyond doubt. The fact that he did not directly participate in war crimes is what got him off the hook in Nuremberg, even though the Russians had every intention of seeing him hang.

Now, in Jakarta in 1951, Schacht was plotting another major coup. Indonesia's status as an independent nation had just been achieved the previous year with the end of the National Revolution. There were separatist movements in Maluku, Sumatra, and Sulawesi during this time that threatened the newborn regime. Groups like Darul Islam favored an Islamist state, while others represented varieties of socialist, communist, and democratic ideals. Schacht was trying to convince Sukarno that he should create a kind of financial and political Maginot Line out of his archipelago that would provide a buffer against the spread of Communism from China and Indochina—one that would then extend "in a vast Islamic crescent from Australasia to the Arab nations of the Mideast."[73] This is a preview of what later would appear as the *khalifa* or caliphate dreams of the Islamic fundamentalists of the 1970s, 1980s, and down to the present day: Islamists who want to create just such an "Islamic crescent" from Southern Thailand, through Malaysia, Indonesia, and the Philippines. To start. To think that this might have been suggested—or at least supported in its very early stages—by former Nazi Economics Minister Hjalmar Schacht is almost surreal.

---

73 William Stevenson, *The Bormann Brotherhood*, New York, Bantam, 1974, p. 164.

It also prefigures exactly what General Willoughby would tell the HUAC members in 1957: that the "Malay Barrier" would be an effective blockade against Communist influence from China. Schacht in 1951 and Willoughby in 1957—the minds of these two devoted anti-Communists and fascists worked remarkably alike. The difference was that Willoughby thought like a general, and Schacht thought like a banker.

The idea that had come to Sukarno (possibly from Schacht) at about this time was nothing short of revolutionary: to create an international bank that would compete head-on with the World Bank and the International Monetary Fund. Both of these institutions had come out of the Bretton Woods meetings that tried to decide the disposition of Nazi funds being held in Switzerland by the Bank of International Settlements. Ironically, Sukarno would "prime the pump" of his newly-imagined bank with gold that had recently arrived in Jakarta, courtesy of the Bank of Portugal, where it had been held for the account of ODESSA.

But Sukarno proved to be too intransigent, too immune to overtures from the Nazi underground. They saw him going over to the Communist side. They could not afford their investments to disappear into a Communist-designed fiscal black hole. Thus Sukarno was removed and a more flexible regime—that of General Soeharto—put in his place. Once that was accomplished and the dust settled, in 1968 the West German government sent Dr. Hilmar Bassler as its ambassador to Jakarta. Bassler—an exceedingly dictatorial and unpopular ambassador whose introduction to the Indonesians had been his official car running over and killing a small child—had been a member of the Gestapo and the SD (*Sicherheitsdienst*, the Nazi secret service) during the war. Bassler had been in charge of East Asian propaganda for Ribbentrop's Foreign Office. (In that capacity he knew Hewel personally, since Hewel had excellent first-hand knowledge of the region. Bassler reported directly to Ribbentrop.)[74]

---

74 Buried deep within a US military file on the Vietnam War, we find Hilmar Bassler referenced in the context of military operations involving the "strategic hamlet program" and US-FRG (Federal Republic of Germany, i.e., West Germany) relations. It would seem from this spare listing that Bassler—at that time

Of course, the CIA wanted Sukarno removed as well, and tried several different approaches to have him taken out of commission prior to 1965, including the famous attempted coup—at least partially organized by CIA—in 1958. Sukarno's move to the Left worried the Americans as much as it did the Nazis with whom they had made common cause. One such alliance between American intelligence and Nazi survivors was the Gehlen Organization (the Nazi spy group that served as the CIA's Eastern European and anti-Soviet operation for a number of years, until it was determined that working with your former dedicated enemies was not necessarily an efficient way to go about spying on another set of enemies). Operation Paperclip was another. And there were other alliances with "former" Nazis in Latin America, Europe, and the Middle East: alliances that remained in place at least through the 1980s and possibly even later.

It was into this pressure-cooker atmosphere replete with espionage and intrigue, Nazis and Communists, that two Europeans, two dedicated servants of the Reich—a man and a woman, a husband and a wife—disembarked in Jakarta from their ocean liner after a two week journey from Rotterdam, and an eight-year life on the run.

And just in time for the 1955 Asian-African Conference in Bandung.

---

not yet German ambassador to Indonesia—was either briefing, or being briefed, on relations with the US in the context of the Vietnam War. See Frame 0602, File POL 27 S Viet, Subject: Military Operations, April 1–8, 1964 in the *Guide to the Microfilm Edition of Confidential US State Department Central Files, Vietnam 1963–1966, Part 1: Political, Governmental, and National Defense Affairs*, Lexis-Nexis 2005.

Chapter Ten

Doctor X

In *Ratline*, I discuss the mysterious case of two Austrians—a husband and wife—who escaped the Allies at the end of World War Two and made their way to Indonesia, where rumors began to spread that the husband and wife were, in fact, Adolf Hitler and Eva Braun. They had been discovered by an Indonesian doctor and Army officer, Dr. Sosro Husodo, who wrote about it in a privately-printed document he circulated among a few people in the Indonesian government. Sosro Husodo had been traveling with the American hospital ship, USS HOPE, in 1960 and had disembarked at Sumbawa, where he encountered the strange "German" doctor with the Charlie Chaplan moustache.

Years later, when news of the identification and extradition of Klaus Barbie made world headlines, and the Hitler's Diaries hoax was exposed at the same time, Sosro Husodo read the accounts in the local newspapers and magazines. He put two and two together: the "German" doctor—whom he referred to as "Doctor X"—and his wife were not what they appeared to be. They were, in actuality, Adolf Hitler and his wife, Eva.

The wife eventually left Pöch alone on the island and returned to Europe. Pöch himself remarried. Sulaesih was a local woman, and Pöch—like so many other Nazis—converted to Islam in order to marry her and took a Muslim name. Sulaesih became a source for much of what we know about her husband, and documents she had in her possession wound up in the hands of Dr. Sosro Husodo. From there, after Sosro's death, they were passed to a Chinese man in Singapore who will not let them out of his sight, not even to permit authentication of the documents or clarification of their contents. It took me six months in Singapore before I could manage to see important portions of those documents, but even then key elements were withheld.

Instead, I read everything I could find on this case—which was not much, and moreover was in Bahasa Indonesia, the language of that beautiful and captivating country—and made my way to the cemetery where Doctor X was buried, in the exotic port city of Surabaya in East Java. I noted several anomalies in the tombstone itself, most especially the lack of dates for birth and death, as if (like a bad joke) no one was really sure who was buried in Pöch's tomb.

The only comprehensive account of the affair was in a local language pamphlet written and published by an Indonesian arms dealer who spoke fluent Russian. There were odds and ends of interviews in the Indonesian press and some of these accounts made it online. Basically, however, I was on my own.

I know considerably more about the Pöch couple today than I did when I wrote *Ratline*. The reason for this is several people have come forward with additional information, including the person in Singapore who has possession of what is left of the original documentation. I have seen Georg Anton Pöch's passport, as well as what I call the "Testament" of Georg Anton Pöch that was found scribbled in Gabelsberger shorthand in his address book.

That the two people who alighted from an ocean liner in January of 1954 were actually Georg Anton and Hella Pöch and not two other people—Adolf Hitler, say, and Eva Braun Hitler—cannot be proven definitively at this time. What *is* certain is that the documents left behind by the man calling himself Pöch are documents that belonged to the real Georg Anton Pöch no later than 1954. In other words, what I had at my disposal that were original documents—the passport and parts of the address book—were dated to *before* the Indonesian period. The passport was issued shortly before the trip to Indonesia, and the address book had been kept from the late 1940s to perhaps no later than the early 1950s ... at least, the entries that I saw all dated from that period.

The upshot of this is that all I know for certain is that these are genuine Pöch documents. They could have been in the possession of other parties since then—they certainly belonged to Sulaesih, and then Dr. Sosro, and then the current Singaporean owner in a chain of custody from 1970 to the present day—and there is no guarantee that the real Georg Anton Pöch had them in Indonesia. Like Kaltenbrunner's fake doctor papers, they could have been used by other criminals to escape justice. To be fair, I am leaving that door open for it would be dishonest of me to claim with any degree of certitude that it was Georg Anton Pöch who died in Surabaya that January of 1970, or that it was definitely Georg Anton Pöch who lived on Sumbawa in 1960. All we know for certai is that the man who lived there called himself Pöch.

Whether or not this was the real Pöch or an impostor is almost immaterial at this point since the story is compelling enough as it is. The Pöch documents open a window onto the world of the Ratline, showing us the extent to which Nazi war criminals worked with each other on the run. They kept in contact, communicated, stayed current with names and addresses all over the world, and—at least in the case of Pöch—were bitter at their fate and maintained a steadily-burning hatred for their enemies, even decades after the end of the war. The Pöch documents are unique. They tell that story better than any historian can hope to equal. It is the story of highly-educated, accomplished people, professional people, with enormous credibility among their peers, who participated in—and in some cases instigated—the worst crimes against humanity the modern world has ever seen. The Pöch address book is the 1940s equivalent of today's Facebook page, replete with a self-description and friends list, along with the occasional wry comment and the odd exclamation point, but minus the smiley faces.

For now it is important to know just who the Pöch couple was. Did they survive the war and wind up in Indonesia? Or were they some other couple, using the papers of Georg Anton and Hella Pöch in order to escape as far away as possible from their fellow Germans, their fellow Austrians, their fellow Nazis?

While not much is known about Georg Anton Pöch, considerably more is known about his more famous wife, Hella Pöch. Hella was born Hella Schürer von Waldheim in 1893 in Austria. She had been a student of Rudolf Pöch (1870–1921), one of the fathers of modern anthropology and ethnography, and one of the first to use modern technology—video and audio equipment—in the field. Although she was twenty-three years his junior, they were married a few years before he died prematurely at the age of 51.

Rudolf Pöch had been involved in what would later turn out to be a very controversial practice of buying corpses in Africa and shipping them back to Austria for study and display. In some cases, he was accused of stealing the corpses from their graves. Then, during the First World War, Pöch saw the prisoner of war camps as excellent places to gather data on ethnicity, due to the various ethnic groups that comprised the prisoner population.

It was this cavalier attitude towards human beings—seeing them as specimens to be studied, with no actual humanity of their own—that set the stage for the kind of hideous experimentation that would take place later in the death camps of the Third Reich. Robbing graves in Africa, measuring the skulls of prisoners … treating human beings (non-German, non-Caucasian human beings) as objects to be examined—dispassionately and with no regard for any kind of social context—seemed like the height of the scientific method. The lack of emotional identification, of empathy, is a prerequisite for this type of approach. The bodies of dead Africans had no value beyond that of specimens for the laboratory and museum. The value of Slavic prisoners was limited to what their bone structure could tell of how the races had intermingled and evolved. That these same prisoners would suffer terrible deprivations in the camps, some of them being killed or tortured, was of no interest to the calm objectivity of the race scientist. It was irrelevant.

It could be argued that the father of modern ethnography made a sinister contribution that has not been recognized. While he broke new ground in using motion picture cameras and phonograph recording devices in the field to capture the speech of Bushmen in Africa (for instance), he also established a kind of legitimacy for the "scientific" approach to race that allowed the scientist to treat his subjects like butterflies stuck with a pin to a board. Germans (and Austrians) were at the forefront of all the sciences in the early twentieth century, and were major contributors in the fields of philosophy, psychology and theology. They were giants in their respective disciplines who commanded the respect and even the awe of their colleagues from other countries, and Rudolf Pöch was at the forefront. There is today a Rudolf Pöch Institute at the University of Vienna where his massive collection of studies of non-German peoples is still studied and evaluated.

Rudolf Pöch began with a mission to Bombay (now Mumbai) India at the end of the nineteenth century to study the plague. He had been educated as a medical doctor, and it was through the study of disease in India, and his work in combating malaria in Africa, that he became interested in physical anthropology. In 1901–1906, Pöch was conducting field research in Australia and in Papua, New Guinea (in the areas once claimed by Germany and Great Britain on the eastern side of the island; the western side is claimed by Indonesia today but was Dutch territory until the 1960s). He is credited with the first scientific evidence for the existence of pygmies. He made over seventy recordings of Papuan speech, songs, and music which are still studied today.

Gradually, his attention began to turn to race science and race hygiene and he became one of the founders of the movement to study races with a view towards determining which races were more "evolved" and which were "mongrelized" to greater and lesser extents. This led to the classification of European races, as well as of non-European races in Africa and Asia. Some Europeans were declared to be "eastern," which became a pejorative for non-Aryan. These included Slavs and other Eastern European ethnic groups. The determinations were made on various observations of the shape of noses, cheekbones, other skull details, hands, feet, hair and eye color, etc. It was this type of research that eventually evolved into the "science" of determining paternity based on racial characteristics, with their associated "positive" and "negative" associations. This was the kind of research that would later inspire monsters like Josef Mengele, the "Angel of Death" at Auschwitz, who experimented on the eyes of prisoners in an effort to turn them blue and thereby more "Aryan."

There is no space to go into detail on the research and methodology of Rudolf Pöch and his peers in the German and Austrian anthropological circles of his day. It is important to remember that his research assistant became his wife, Hella Pöch, and that she worked with him in the Austrian prisoner of war camps and learned his anthropometric and ethnographic techniques. When Rudolf Pöch died in 1921—shortly after the end of World War One—much of his research material was inherited by his former assistant, University of Vienna Professor Josef Wenninger (1886–1959). Wenninger was a committed National Socialist in Austria at a time when the Party was banned in that country. His research assistants were all Nazi Party members.[75]

Hella Pöch continued with her growing interest in paternity studies, which would prove to be so valuable to the Reich in identifying who had Jewish ancestry. This obsession with identifying "Jewish" characteristics led Hella Pöch to one of her more controversial research proposals.

It was understood that most studies of European Jews were of the Ashkenazic, or Western, Jews. These were Jews who had come from Eastern Europe and who—according to Hella—could be differentiated from the Sephardic (or "Eastern") Jews who were largely found in Spain and Portugal as well as in the Middle East. It was therefore important—in order to be thorough when it came to identifying Jews for the Reich—that both types of Jews had their racial characteristics studied, evaluated, and made available for ready identification by the proper authorities. When the war broke out and the Third Reich was in full swing, the "proper authorities" meant the Race and Settlement Main Office of the SS which would make the final determinations when it came to protecting the Aryan race from Semitic pollution.

But there were not many Sephardic communities in Europe, and virtually none in Germany or Austria with enough "material" for comprehensive research. So Hella looked eastward, to the Netherlands.

As an Austrian anthropologist who had worked with Rudolf Pöch, Josef Wenninger, Martin Hesch, and many others, she also knew Artur Seyss-Inquart. Seyss-Inquart was a fellow Austrian

---

75 Wenninger was another Nazi academic who did not suffer imprisonment or discomfort after the war but who was allowed to regain his position at the University of Vienna as early as 1945.

who had belonged to the outlawed Nazi Party in Austria since its earliest days. In that capacity, he knew Wenninger and the circle of academics around him who were, for the most part, all Nazi Party members as well. After Anschluss, Seyss-Inquart rose in prominence in the Nazi hierarchy. After the invasion of the Netherlands in 1940, he was made Governor-General of that country, overseeing the complete eradication of its Jewish community. Before he could complete the "cleansing" of the Netherlands of all Jews, however, he was approached by his old friend Hella Pöch who wanted to conduct some anthropometric studies on the Sephardic Jews in the Dutch camps.

The Netherlands was practically alone in western Europe when it came to having a large Sephardic community. Based mostly in Amsterdam, they had come to the Netherlands at the end of the fifteenth century from Spain and Portugal—when King Ferdinand launched his Inquisition against the Jews at the same time that he was ridding his country of the last Islamic caliphate in Grenada. The Dutch had no laws restricting Jews and had become independent from Spanish rule, so many Jews and crypto-Jews (Jews who had converted to Catholicism to save their lives but who practiced their Jewish faith in secret) made their way from the now-hostile Iberian penninsula to safety behind Dutch borders.

That meant that the Sephardic community in the Netherlands enjoyed a kind of four hundred-year-old unbroken line of genetic "purity" that Hella Pöch could study with benefit. She could study whole families of Sephardic Jews and derive much-needed data from these prisoners in the concentration camps, all of whom were scheduled to be deported to the death camps for "final processing." This data would help the Reich uncover further evidence of Jewish blood in subjects previously thought to be free of Semitic origins.

She put the proposal to Seyss-Inquart, who approved it immediately. She and her new husband—Georg Anton Pöch, a medical doctor like her first husband and chief medical officer of the Salzburg Gau—would accompany her on the research trip. Between his medical knowledge and her anthropological training they would be able to conduct a thoroughly professional—if equally hideous—program of study on helpless prisoners about to be sent away for execution. Hella could imagine the ghost of her first husband smiling down at her, congratulating her for having learned so much during her first research work in the prisoner of war camps in Austria during World War One. Now, a second World War would provide her with even greater data, and she could see her name lauded in the peer-reviewed journals of her profession as she made discovery after discovery.

Publish, or perish. Especially in Nazi Germany.

But, alas, the project was not to be. Seyss-Inquart was in a tearing hurry to rid the Netherlands of all Jews. Before Hella and Georg could pack their syringes and calipers most of her potential research subjects were being shoved onto transports for the trip to Auschwitz.

When the smoke had cleared, it was learned that the Netherlands had lost nearly all of its over 100,000 Jews. Of the 140,000 "known" Jews in that country, only 30,000 had survived the war. One who did not survive was Anne Frank, who was on the last train out of the Netherlands headed for the death camp.

At the end of the war, Seyss-Inquart was hauled before the Nuremberg court and summarily hanged.

We do not know much about the other activities of Hella and Georg Anton Pöch in the period of 1940–1945. Prior to the war, however, Hella Pöch was doing a lot of traveling herself, to South Africa and the Middle East. She had made friends with a number of adventurers and explorers, following in her first husband's footsteps, retracing some of his travels, and expanding upon his research. She also became the chairperson of the Vienna Anthropological Association, maintaining her relations with the foremost Nazi academics of the day.

When it comes to her second husband, Georg, however, we are left pretty much in the dark. While the life and career of Hella—and of her first husband Rudolf—is well-documented, at least through the decades of the 1920s, 1930s and early 1940s, what we know of Georg Anton Pöch is rather limited. There are references to his role as chief medical officer in Salzburg during the Nazi regime, and the assumption that he was involved in euthanasia programs, as well as whatever else Nazi doctors did to amuse themselves. It seemed that, when put next to Rudolf Pöch, Georg Anton was a bit of a stick in the mud. We don't see extensive foreign travel by Georg, or a slew of important papers under his name. There are a few, here and there, dealing with the etiology of disease, but it's tame stuff compared to the far-reaching race studies of his wife. We have some evidence that he went to the United States in the 1920s, for his name shows up on a ship's manifest heading for New York. We also have a statement he made to an American tourist visiting Indonesia in the late 1950s that he had a medical degree from Johns Hopkins in the States.[76] However, a search through the records of that venerable medical school does not reveal the name of Georg Anton Pöch at any time, although the ship's manifest does suggest he traveled to the States about the same year he claimed he graduated.

We know that his medical acumen was recognized by at least one American colleague, for they co-authored a paper. Charles N. Leach of the Rockefeller Foundation co-authored, with Georg Anton Pöch, "A Diptheria Immunization Campaign in Austria" for *The American Journal of Public Health* (February, 1935). Dr. Leach (1885–1971) was a major figure in the Rockefeller Foundation's medical research program and served as the Foundation's director in the Philippines in the 1920s, with particular emphasis on the etiology and treatment of hookworm in the islands. Thus, the interests of Leach and Pöch intersected in the area of public health issues; but Leach could not have known that in 1935 his Austrian colleague was already involved with the illegal Nazi Party in Austria along with his famous spouse. When Pöch got a chance to really shine in the area of "public health," it was only a few years later as the Nazi official in charge of "public health" in the Salzburg Gau. This is probably not the path Leach anticipated his co-author would follow. This is especially poignant when we discover that Dr. Leach was in Manila when that Philippine city fell to the Japanese in 1941, and was interned, returning to the United States in

---

76 I am indebted to Katarina Matiasek for this information and for the copy of the notebook in question, "Komodos, Beyond Bali," as well as for other background information on Hella Pöch.

December of 1943 as part of a prisoner exchange program.[77] Other medical research personnel that had been caught in Manila at the time of the Japanese invasion were still in Japanese custody at the time, and all the records of the Rockefeller Foundation in Manila were destroyed by the invaders. Leach had lost thirty pounds while in Japanese captivity, but that did not stop him. He would later put on a British uniform and try to help prisoners of war at the notorious Bergen-Belsen concentration camp after its liberation in 1945.

Charles N. Leach first served in World War One as an ambulance driver and at a MASH-type field medical unit. He was sent by the Rockefeller Foundation to Johns Hopkins to get a degree in public health, and went on from there to become deeply involved with the International Health operation of the Rockefeller Foundation, serving with the Foundation in China and Japan as well as the Philippines before the war broke out in 1941. Parenthetically, he served in Vienna immediately after the end of World War One, and it is possible that this is where he met Pöch for the first time. He would return to Austria in 1956 to work at a Hungarian refugee camp.

It is tempting to look at the two careers—Charles Leach and Georg Pöch—side by side and come to some obvious conclusions. Leach was a genuine medical hero, working tirelessly in very dangerous circumstances to bring health care and education to countries around the world. His co-author, on the other hand, was a dedicated anti-Semite and Nazi whose idea of health care was contained within the euthanasia programs of the Third Reich. It is true (at least, on paper) that Pöch eventually found himself in Indonesia, in a very remote area, handling health care for the poor and disadvantaged on Sumbawa. If this is true, it might have been a search for redemption—an unconscious (?) emulation of his former colleague, a man, who had suffered from the Axis Powers as a prisoner while Pöch thrived as a Nazi officer. How ironic, then, that Leach would eventually find himself walking among the desperate prisoners of one of the Reich's own concentration camps ... concentration

---

77 Rockefeller Foundation *Annual Report*, 1941, p.6. and *Science*, March 31, 1944, vol. 99, no. 2570, p. 260.

camps whose *raison d'etre* was put into place and legitimized by Hella Pöch, Georg Anton Pöch, and their academic peers.

Again and again we find Pöch rubbing shoulders with actual medical men and women, with doctors whose primary concern is the healing of the sick. First Charles Leach, and then Sosro Husodo, and who knows how many others?

For a few years the Pöch couple lived in the city of Eisenstadt, the capital of the district of Burgenland in northeastern Austria. It is not certain at which point they moved—if, indeed, they did move—to Salzburg, where Georg Pöch had his official posting. The Russian Army occupied Eisenstadt in 1945, whereas the Americans occupied Salzburg at the same time. This may be relevant when it comes to a statement that Pöch made to his second wife Sulaesih, that the Russians had come to his house and that he had to hide behind a door to escape them.

However, as the Testament reveals, both Georg and Hella Pöch were living in Salzburg when they were questioned by the American CIC. Possibly the Pöchs fled Eisenstadt and made for Salzburg; but this is doubtful, as it would have been extremely difficult to break through the Russian lines when the troops were indiscriminately killing, looting and raping their way through the areas of Austria—including Vienna—that they controlled.

At this point, it will be beneficial to quote as much of the Testament as possible. It is contained on two pages of the address book, written in Gabelsberger shorthand. One of the questions that hovers around analysis of the address book is the purpose behind the use of Gabelsberger. Was it only because it was easier and faster for Pöch to write in shorthand, or was it an attempt to write some of the information in code? As Gabelsberger was in common use among educated Austrians and Germans at the time, its use as a coding system would have been limited. Thus, it is my opinion that Pöch used shorthand simply as a faster way to record his thoughts, and possibly also as a means of saving space in the very small address book.

What Georg Anton Pöch has done is write down the circumstances of his flight from Salzburg to Italy. Parts of this Testament

were reproduced in a book entitled *Hitler Mati di Indonesia* by the
Solonese prince (and arms dealer) Soeryo Goeritno, and also appear
in my previous work, *Ratline*. It was translated for Doctor Sosro by
the German expert Hans Gebhardt into the German language. It
was then translated—presumably by Sosro—into the Indonesian
language. I have used the German original as provided in Goeritno's book and translated the text into English directly. Thus, any
errors are my own.

The Testament
    Short chronological representation of personal prosecu-
tion by the Allies and local "authorities" in Salzburg 1946.
    While the two of us, my wife and I, had been affected rel-
atively little in Salzburg in 1945 (except for an altercation with
a Jew who insulted my wife and came to the apartment with
the remark that we should not remain here any longer) the
united persecuted group, which consisted of blacks and Jews,
about April 1946 began—by way of a newspaper article in the
communist newspaper in Salzburg—to call the attention of
the occupying power, the CIC, to ourselves. We were attacked
because of the paternity tests and me, especially, because of
my justification towards dismissal from the civil service. There
now followed interrogations by the State Police, the Metro-
politan Police, twice with the reason that I had made false
statements concerning my membership in the party and for
collaboration with Nazi organizations. Personal freedom of
movement was completely restricted within the barrier zone
until mid-September 1946.
    Beginning in October 1946 there were visits from a CIC
minion named "Topic" (of course, a code name for a Jewish
subject, as what these crooks turned out to be). There were the
basic charges, which were obtained both from the Jew Adrow
and also the Jew Kohr, which were composed by a Jewish lawyer. Five times we got together with the minion of the CIC,
sometimes at home and at other times at the CIC itself. His
interrogation method began in an ingratiating and seemingly
benevolent manner, but once he let the copy of his own draft

indictment fall open, it was revealed that because of the forgery of my questionnaire and of war crimes—probably because of alleged persecution of Jews—I was to be taken to Camp Macorr.

Certainly, personal documents incriminated me which had been dug up from the office of the state government, or likely put at his disposal, by Mr v. Kurz, a very inferior subject who eked out his existence by ignominious denunications, doing everything he could to take revenge on me personally. He was certainly very much used even by the Judo-Americans because he was the typical, morally inferior being that was not hard to find, especially since all such tactics are always built on such foundations.

What is interesting is that, until April of 1946, the CIC had no knowledge of the Pöchs or of their involvement in the Holocaust until they were informed upon. Thus, my earlier insistence—in *Ratline*—that the Pöchs were not wanted and did not appear on any known list of war criminals is justified.

Then, on my own, I was able to identify Camp Macorr, something that had been bothering me since I first saw the name mentioned in the Goeritno book. Camp "Macorr" as referenced in the Pöch Testament is Camp Marcus W. Orr, a POW camp set up by the Americans in Salzburg which served as the headquarters of the CIC (the Counter Intelligence Corps), in charge of denazification (at least until about 1947). Pöch's remarks in this early part of the Testament is riddled with allusions to "Jews" and he certainly seems to have been a rabid anti-Semite.[78] How he would have managed to avoid arrest and possible conviction seems difficult to say once the CIC had his complete dossier at their disposal. The reference to a

---

78 There actually was Jewish translator working for CIC in Austria at the time (1946-1948). His name was Meir Ben-Horin, a well-known academic who was born in Germany in 1918 and who attended the Hebrew University of Palestine in 1937–1939 and the Jewish Theological Seminary (1941), getting his PhD at Columbia in 1952. He was a Special Agent and Special Agent in Charge of the CIC responsible for investigating suspected war criminals, which puts him in close proximity to Pöch at the time in question. He died in 1988.

Mr. v. Kurz is still mysterious, but it seems to have been someone in the Health Office of the Salzburg Gau who had an axe to grind with Pöch.

Then, just before the indictment against Pöch comes down, he decides he has to escape. He can no longer stay in the American zone, which means he has left the relative safety of Austria for a place known only as "J."[79] He first goes with his wife to "G," a city in Austria, where they stay with her relatives while they find a way to get out of the country. This information comes from the pamphlet published by Soeryo Goeritno and is based on the complete text of the Testament to which he had access.

"G" is Graz, and indeed, is where Hella Pöch has her relatives. An exhaustive search through archives has revealed that the family Schürer von Waldheim still has members in Graz, and did for decades after the war. It seems from his statement that while both are in danger, Pöch feels he is the more obvious target and must get away first. The indictment he refers to does not seem to mention his wife, but is only focused on his own role as a Nazi medical officer.

Again, according to Goeritno's account of the Testament, he then goes to an area "geographically and strategically difficult." By analyzing the possible escape routes from Graz (as opposed to Salzburg, from where originally I believed they had escaped), it is clear that Pöch traveled across the border from Graz to Yugoslavia. A look at the map will show that this was the most obvious—although quite dangerous—route to take if one wanted to avoid the American Zone. I find myself agreeing with Sosro that the "J" in this sentence refers to "Jugoslawien" which is the way Yugoslavia is written in German.

It seems that his wife was not able to make the initial crossing into Yugoslavia with her husband but only met him later. Pöch makes his way to "B." "B" is probably Bolzano (Bozen), which was the headquarters for a major element of the Ratline, and where he would have stayed for quite some time.

---

79 This string of letters appears in Goeritno's book with associated speculation as to their meaning.

In December of 1946 he states that they have to go to "R" to get identity documents. It can be assumed that "R" means Rome. In any event, he obtains a German passport from the German embassy in Rome, but not until 1951. Prior to that he might have had papers issued by the Vatican, via Draganovic. This is where the mystery deepens, for why would he have a passport made out in his own name if he was wanted by the authorities?

There is still a great deal we don't know about Pöch.

So the question remains: can this still be Hitler?

It is not a Hitler memoir by any means. It is a Pöch memoir. But who was the last person to own it before Sulaesih? Was the Pöch memoir only one of a set of documents and artifacts (such as the passport), that another escaping Nazi used once the Pöchs were carefully disposed of? We can't discount this possibility yet. Until more information comes in, we are left with the possibility that Pöch might have been Hitler. But the evidence in the Pöch memoir clearly describes Georg Anton and Hella Pöch, thus suggesting that they escaped justice in 1946 and wound up safely in Italy at the end of that year.

Between 1946 and 1953, when someone using the Pöch passport sets sail to Indonesia, anything could have happened. As we have seen, Ernst Kaltenbrunner himself was using a real doctor's identity papers—even carrying a medical bag—in his attempt to escape the Allies from the Salzburg region—the same region from which Pöch has to flee. While the suggestion seems incredible, it is still within the realm of possibility that whoever left the Netherlands for Indonesia in 1953, they were not Georg Anton and Hella Pöch.

Why this single-minded goal of reaching Indonesia, with the result that once he landed there he would never leave? We have no evidence that Pöch had ever set foot in Indonesia before. However, the Pöchs did have friends among high-ranking Nazis in the Netherlands (the colonial power ruling Indonesia until about 1950). It is possible that he would have heard a great deal about Indonesia at that time. That is still not enough motivation to decide to leave Europe forever. Was this more Hella Pöch's idea than his?

He also spent an inordinate amount of time in the Italian border town of Bolzano, a town full of Nazis on the run, and one of Draganovic's major centers of operation. What was he doing there from 1946 to 1953, a full seven years? Did he, at that point, become involved in an intrigue the nature of which we do not know as yet?

Once Pöch landed in Jakarta on January 9, 1954 he would never set foot in his native land again. In fact, he would never leave Indonesia for the rest of his life.

Before we proceed further, it is useful to look at another document—this one not by Pöch but by an anonymous author of a small notebook. An American traveler in the region of Sumbawa, Bali, and Flores recorded his meeting with Pöch in the spring of 1956 while on his way to see the Komodo dragons. At this time, Pöch was living in the town of Dompu on Sumbawa (before his move to Sumbawa Besar). The note-taker states:

> "150 German doctors brought to Indonesia 3 years ago, mostly in small communities."

It would seem that this was told to the writer by Pöch himself. However, there is no evidence that what Pöch said is true. If it were true, it would be quite interesting. Where would Indonesia get 150 German doctors?[80]

The writer then goes on to describe his travel across the island of Sumbawa, and notes the prevalence of snakes everywhere—including a fifteen foot python—and monkeys, and "rolling hills—wind-

---

80 After the war, many Latin American and Middle Eastern nations were scouring the refugee camps in Europe for people with useful skills to supplement their own domestic economies. A number of Nazis were able to enter Argentina, for instance, as skilled laborers or engineers even if they did not actually possess those skills but had the forged identity papers necessary to match the quota requirements. But Argentina and the other interested countries had the finances and the means at their disposal to support these skilled laborers and engineers. There is no evidence at this time to prove that Indonesia was in the same category and, in any event, medical practitioners would have been in the highest category of desirable workers.

ing road. Rough as hell! … Fat goats. Velvet hats. … Snakes slither across road. … Jungle noises heard over jeep motor."

Then he talks about his meeting with Pöch in Dompu.

Pöch tells him that he has been in Indonesia (or specifically on Sumbawa, it's not clear) for nineteen months. He also says he attended Johns Hopkins from 1922–1923. He then goes on to state:

> "Dr. Poch says no doctor for Sumbawa's ½ million people until 2 or 3 years ago when he, Dr Erfenstein [sp?] and an Indian doctor in Bima brought out by govt on three year contracts.
>
> "Endemic malaria and yaws here.
>
> "Complained no one teaches natives to grow fruit and vegetables to supplement vitamin deficiencies.
>
> "Result people undernourished.
>
> "Said only one or two Europeans a year come through here. Last ones from ICA in Jakarta."[81]

There is no mention of Hella Pöch in the notebook, and the writer continues on with observations about Sumbawa in general, no longer referencing Pöch.

There are a few problems with the notes. The first is identifying the other German doctor, which I have so far been unable to do. This may be a problem with the writer using a phonetic version of the name. Also, as I have pointed out, I have been unable to find any record of Pöch having attended Johns Hopkins in the years listed.

ICA in Jakarta refers to an American economic aid program that was in place by that time in Jakarta and which was developing financial assistance programs for specific projects based in the countryside. This is in itself suggestive of a much larger circumstance, as the ICA—or the International Cooperation Administration, as it was known—was a US State Department program, a forerunner of the US Agency for International Development, USAID, that was used as a vehicle for CIA operations overseas. Created by John Foster Dulles ICA only lasted a few years (1955–1961) but managed

---

81 This is all from the notebook "Komodos Beyond Bali" kindly provided by Katarina Matiasek.

to employ one of the more notorious personalities of American history—Georges de Mohrenschildt—the White Russian benefactor of accused Kennedy assassin Lee Harvey Oswald.

De Mohrenschildt was working for ICA in Yugoslavia in 1957, ostensibly as part of a geological survey but was accused by the Yugoslav government of spying on military fortifications. He was debriefed on his return to the United States by the CIA. This may mean nothing, but it is worth noting since the ICA comes up, a propos of nothing, in the notebook composed by this American tourist who went out of his way to see Pöch. The Doctor tells him that the last "Europeans" who came through were working for ICA in Jakarta.

ICA did indeed have an Indonesian "desk" (the Administration was run along the same lines as the State Department), and funds were allocated for various purposes ranging from agricultural to medical; but the ICA was an American program, run by the State Department, and somehow employed "Europeans" including, of course, George de Mohrenschildt in its operations. There may be more to this story, but files pertaining to US-Indonesian relations during the period in question are still mostly classified. We are forced to rely on scattered eyewitness testimony and those documents that have managed to escape the classification process.

It still begs the question: who was Dr. Georg Anton Pöch, really? Was he another of these mysterious "Europeans" working for ICA in the 1950s? Pöch was a Nazi; de Mohrenschildt was refused direct employment by the US intelligence agencies because of suspicions he had been a Nazi during the war. As a White Russian, it is possible that he was, indeed, a Nazi or at least pro-Nazi. His involvement with Lee Harvey Oswald—as many authors have noted—had all the elements of an intelligence operation: an anti-Communist intelligence operation on behalf of a cabal of right-wing fanatics, perhaps.

Sadly, De Mohrenschildt committed suicide on March 29, 1977 on the same day he received a request for questioning concerning his relationship with Lee Harvey Oswald by an investigator for the House Select Committee on Assassinations.

One implication of the notebook is that Pöch at this time spoke English well enough to have communicated all this to the American traveler passing through. Indeed, Pöch was willing to talk to him. He may have felt safe enough by this time.

But the timeline is a bit problematic. Pöch states that he was there for nineteen months. This was in March of 1956. We know he landed in Jakarta in January of 1954, which represents a period in-country of twenty-six months. Possibly he was in Jakarta for a long period of time—six or seven months, perhaps for some orientation or other training—before being sent to Sumbawa, but we have no evidence of this as yet.

Just as this book was being finished, however, one of those strange coincidences took place that sometimes happens to researchers. A friend of mine, who is a TV producer in Hollywood, met a woman—a photographer for national magazines—whose mother knew Hella Pöch. In fact, she had in her possession a valuable additional document: a "Wanted" notice that appeared in Salzburg on September 23, 1946, offering a reward for information concerning the whereabouts of "Dr. Georg Pöch and his wife Hella" last known at Karolinenplaz 2, in Salzburg. That document appears in the photographic section of this book. The person or agency who placed the notice is not identified, giving only an address at the local ticket office in the Old Market in Salzburg. Thus, we have further confirmation that the Pöch Testament is correct in every respect, for it substantiates Pöch's claim that he was on the run in September of 1946.

Another document from the same collection indicates that Hella was working for none other than SS-Captain Kurt Mayer (1903–1945), Director of the Reich Genealogical Authority, who committed suicide at the end of the war. Mayer's office was concerned with determining racial purity: an important requirement since the implementation of the Nuremberg Laws of 1935. The law denied Jews, and other undesirables, positions of influence within the German government, educational institutions, and other areas where they could conceivably pollute the racially-pure. The document in question is a decision signed by Mayer that—based on Hella Pöch's findings (she is referenced twice in the two page

letter)—a certain individual has been determined to be Jewish. The
letter is dated January 12, 1943, Berlin.

Finally, there was the strange meeting in Surabaya.

Dr. Pöch—who hated to leave Sumbawa for any reason—
would go to Surabaya on January 14, 1970, ostensibly to accompany
a patient to a hospital in that city.[82] He had his heart attack on that
date, and died the following day.

Why did he go to Surabaya? The report that he was accompanying a patient does not make much sense. There is no further
evidence that this was the case, and why would the Doctor abandon
his clinic for the long and exhausting trip to the port city of Surabaya instead of assigning someone else to go? Was he summoned by
someone with a claim on his attendance that was too important, too
dangerous to ignore? After all, he died the following day.

This is, of course, pure speculation: but if someone wanted Pöch
dead—retribution for war crimes, perhaps—it would have been
quite difficult to kill him on Sumbawa, where a foreigner (or any
stranger) would be visible for miles and the subject of endless gos-
sip. On the other hand, Surabaya is a large, bustling, and very busy
seaport. Anonymity would have been guaranteed there to a degree
unobtainable on Sumbawa.

In fact, is there more to the story of Georg Anton and Hella
Pöch than meets the eye? The relevance of this story to the larger
issue of the Hitler Legacy is to be found in one of two possibilities: in the first instance, it reveals in somewhat anecdotal form, the
flight of a Nazi war criminal to the most populous Muslim nation in
the world, a flight consistent with those of other Nazis who wound
up in the Middle East, and the conversion of that Nazi to Islam,
which is also consistent. As described in *Ratline*, Pöch also made a
very intriguing visit to the island of Bali during the Year of Living
Dangerously, when there was an enormous crackdown on suspected
Communists by the army. Bali, itself, suffered the massacre of thousands of civilians at the time the enigmatic Austrian doctor went to
visit. He claimed to his new wife, Sulaesih, that he had gone to see

---

82   According to Goeritno, *Hitler Mati di Indonesia*, 2010.

Konrad Adenauer there (an impossibility since Adenauer had never been to Bali in his life and was no longer Chancellor of West Germany at the time). The reference to Adenauer is interesting since the former Chancellor was known to hire many former Nazis and place them in positions of prominence in his government. But if Pöch did not go to see Adenauer, as seems obvious, whom did he see, and why? What role did Nazi agents have in the overthrow of the seemingly pro-Communist Sukarno regime? Was Pöch, for whatever reason, a part of this operation?

The second possibility is, of course, the most outrageous: the relevance of the Pöch material to the larger question of the Hitler Legacy is the idea that Pöch was, indeed, what Dr. Sosro Husodo claimed he was. Adolf Hitler himself.

As described at length in *Ratline*, there is no physical evidence to prove that Hitler died in the Berlin bunker on April 30, 1945. In fact, there is so much badly planted evidence as to suggest that the suicide story was a complete fabrication. Add to that the strange actions of Russian military intelligence personnel who transported what were supposed to be the bodies of Hitler and Eva Braun through several East German towns, burying them and then digging them up again, over and over, and we have what appears to be a cover-up effort of enormous implications. And then, only a few months after the death of Pöch in Surabaya, Indonesia in 1970, the KGB decides to dig up the "Hitler" body one last time (after twenty-five years in the ground) and cremate it in a secret operation, scattering the ashes into a nearby river.

Like the cremation, perhaps, of a Hindu ascetic whose ashes are scattered into the Ganges.

Chapter Eleven

Tibetan Reich

I stumble into town just like a sacred cow
Visions of swastikas in my head
Plans for everyone
It's in the white of my eyes

...

I'll give you eyes of blue
I'll give you men who want to rule the world
    —David Bowie, "China Girl"

In his book on Pöch, Soeryo Goeritno mentions that the address book contained entries for South Africa and Tibet. I did not see the South African entry for it pointlessly was withheld from me, but I did manage to see the Tibetan entry. Thus, I can attest that Dr. Pöch did indeed have the address of someone who was living in Tibet at the time the address book was compiled.

That an Austrian Nazi would have a friend or friends in Tibet is not as unusual as it may seem. There had Nazi expeditions to Tibet—I wrote about the most famous of these in *Unholy Alliance*: the SS-Tibet Expedition of 1938—and there had been a romantic fascination with Tibet on behalf of northern Europeans for at least a century. The Swedish explorer Sven Hedin had traveled in western China close to the Tibetan border, and as we will see he was a Nazi sympathizer who signed his letters "Heil Hitler!". In fact, there was a Sven Hedin Institute set up by Heinrich Himmler in admiration for the remarkable travels and adventures of this indefatigable explorer.

Other travelers such as Madame Helene Blavatsky and Alexandra David-Neel wrote obsessively about Tibet and the traditions of Tibetan Buddhism, captivating a generation with tales of mystic powers and the extreme isolation of the Hidden Kingdom.

But perhaps the most famous traveler to Tibet in the last half of the twentieth century was the Austrian mountain climber and SS man, Heinrich Harrer, author of the famous memoir *Seven Years in Tibet*. Escaped from a British prison camp in northern India, Harrer (1912–2006) would trek across the Himalayas with his friend Peter Aufschnaiter (1899–1973). The event would become immortalized in the film starring Brad Pitt in the role of Harrer.

Harrer became a tutor to the young Dalai Lama, teaching him English as well as various lessons concerning the way of life in the outside world. Harrer was with the Dalai Lama up until the Chinese invasion, and left soon before the Dalai Lama himself was forced to flee to India.

The English-language edition of *Seven Years in Tibet* bears a foreword by Peter Fleming. This in itself is rather interesting, for Fleming was James Bond creator Ian Fleming's older brother, and the man who got Ian Fleming into the British Secret Service. Peter Fleming was a member of the Special Operations Executive (SOE) during World War Two, based in Asia, and had met many OSS personnel during his sojourn in India at that time. Thus Peter Fleming was a traveler and adventurer who had written his own books, and was experienced in intelligence work, as well as in the culture and history of the Indian sub-continent. He seemed like an excellent choice to introduce Harrer's work on Tibet, but was there another agenda?

In 1950, China invaded Tibet although its hold over the kingdom was not yet complete. There was the Korean War to the east that had just begun, with the United States throwing its support behind the South Koreans and conducting what it called a "police action" rather than a war, a euphemism that fooled no one. China had gained its liberation in 1948 with the ascendance of Mao Zedong and the Chinese Communist Party. Indonesia had just proclaimed its own independence; the government of President Sukarno would fall fifteen years later due to suspicions of a Chinese Communist presence influencing his administration.

In June of 1951—according to declassified State Department memos—the elder brother of the Dalai Lama, Thubten Jigme Norbu, known as Taktse Rinpoche, met with the U.S. Consul General Evan M. Wilson, his attaché Robert H. Linn, two vice consuls, as well as George Patterson (referred to as a "missionary," which was hardly the reason for the presence of this famous explorer at this meeting). The subject of the meeting was, "organizing of resistance in Tibet [and] the provision of military and financial assistance …" to the young, sixteen-year-old, king. It should be noted that Heinrich Harrer was still in Tibet, at Lhasa, at this time and would have known about the meeting with US officials from the Dalai Lama himself, since he had become such a close personal friend of the monarch, if his books are to be believed. (It should also be noted that the United States was in talks with the government of the Dalai Lama as early as 1943, via OSS Captain Brooke Dolan, who had impetuously offered the Dalai Lama the recognition and support of the US Government, something he was not empowered to do and, indeed, this support never actually materialized. By recognizing the Peoples Republic of China, the United States is unable to recognize the Dalai Lama's government-in-exile in India, just as it is unable to recognize the Republic of China, based in Taiwan.)

Thus we have the strange tableau of an SS man and committed Nazi in Lhasa, at the same time that his friend, the Dalai Lama, is officially in contact with the US government concerning the Chinese situation. What did Heinrich Harrer know of these negotiations? How much did the Dalai Lama himself know at this time? Even more to the point, was American intelligence—in the form of the CIA and the State Department—aware of Harrer's presence in Lhasa and the influence he had over the king?

Harrer would remain a close friend and ally of the Dalai Lama for the rest of his life. As a Nazi and a member of the SS as well as of the SA (the *Sturm Abteilung* or Storm Troopers), Harrer would have been a devoted anti-communist, and would have seen in the struggles of the Tibetan people against Chinese Communism an echo of his own country's fight against the Soviet Union. Harrer, as someone with a demonstrated and intimate knowledge of the landscape, culture, languages, and environment of northern India and Tibet would have been an excellent choice for American intelligence as an asset to run operations against the Chinese. After all, the CIA had hired the Gehlen Organization at the end of World War Two to run ops against the Russians from eastern Europe.

Reinhard Gehlen was a Nazi intelligence officer who bartered his way to freedom from prosecution by offering his services (and those of hundreds of his close personal friends in the SS, Gestapo, and SD) as an anti-communist fighter against the Soviets. It would have made perfect sense to hire Nazis who had experience of Asia in the fight against Chinese-style Communism.

In fact, as Thomas Laird reveals:

> Only during the past ten years, State Department documents have been declassified that show Harrer may have been involved with several covert operations for the Americans after he left Tibet.[83]

Tibetans were seen as one of those peoples of Inner Asia—along with Mongols and the Khazaks—who could be useful in the fight against Communism in that part of the world. It would require the weaponization of Buddhism, just as the Cold War in Central Asia and the Middle East required the weaponization of Islam, but it could be done. Harrer had the right connections, and as a Nazi, former SS and SA member as well, he had the anti-Communist credentials. In fact, he had already begun supplying CIA with maps of Tibet, knowing full well that if he was caught by the Chinese he would be executed as a spy.[84] Once this relationship with CIA was established, it is likely that he would have been used in future projects—such as the time he spent in Indonesia in 1962, ostensibly as an explorer, as recounted in his book *I Come From the Stone Age*, first published in German in 1963. The story as told by Harrer in this volume was so patently false that some academic reviewers were of the opinion that Harrer had gone to New Guinea for reasons totally unrelated to exploring or ethnography. One such reviewer, Denise A. O'Brien, went so far as to claim in a review of the book for *American Anthropologist* that it was "wildly inaccurate,"[85] saying,

---

83 Thomas Laird, *Into Tibet: The CIA's First Atomic Spy and His Secret Expedition to Lhasa*, Grove Press, NY, 2002, p. 228.

84 Laird, pp. 233–234, p. 327 fn.

85 O'Brien, D.A. (1966). Review of H. Harrer, *I Come from the Stone Age*,

"Harrer was either misinformed or has misrepresented certain government and mission activities," and "Ethnographically it's useless." It is the misrepresentation of government and mission activities in this book that begs the question of whether or not he was guilty of similar misrepresentations in *Seven Years in Tibet*.

Then we have Peter Fleming. With his intelligence credentials and his experience with espionage operations in India and Southeast Asia, Fleming's friendship with Harrer might inadvertently reveal another aspect of the Harrer story. Was Harrer then not working only for American intelligence but for the British spy agency, MI6, as well? Great Britain had hired former Nazis for their own purposes, though perhaps not to quite the extent that the Americans and the Russians did. Harrer might have seemed like a safe choice for he had excellent cover. Due to his fame as an author, and his travels as an adventurer, he was suitably placed to use his profession as a cover for intelligence work.

Harrer, of course, was not the first Nazi to visit Tibet. He was not the last Nazi to befriend the Dalai Lama. This story perhaps is upsetting to those who see in the Tibetan king and priest an icon of peace and of deep spiritual illumination. Nevertheless, it is well-documented. The reader may be excused if the implications of this research seem to undermine everything about the Dalai Lama and Tibet that he or she has been told or has read over the past fifty years or so.

Welcome to the club.

When the author was first researching the book that would become *Unholy Alliance*, he was confronted with a mass of documents—stored at the National Archives in Washington, DC—of Heinrich Himmler's pet project, the SS-Ahnenerbe or "Ancestral Heritage Research Foundation." This organization was a boondoggle for crank academics of all sorts, from anthropologists and archaeologists to meteorologists and astronomers. Their brief was to research pre-Christian and non-Abrahamic religions and cultures,

London: Rupert Hart-Davis, 1964. American Anthropologist, 68: 297–298 and to prove the existence of the "Aryan" race. In some cases, like that of SS officer Otto Rahn, they were expected to find hidden relics such as the Holy Grail (among others).

One expedition mounted by the SS-Ahnenerbe, and with the specific blessing of Heinrich Himmler, was the 1938 SS-Tibet Expedition led by Ernst Schäfer and including the anthropologist Bruno Beger among the expedition members. While the Dalai Lama was only three years old at the time of this expedition, the Panchen Lama was available to greet the Nazis to the Himalayan kingdom and to provide them with texts (including the 108-volume Tibetan scripture, the *Kangjur*), animal and plant specimens, and photographic footage to take back with them. In addition, Beger conducted ethnographic and anthropometric research among the Tibetans, measuring their skulls with calipers, for instance. Photographs of this expedition are still extent and examples of it are found in the photographic section of this book, including a famous photo of Beger measuring the skull of a smiling Tibetan maiden.

It is possible that one of Ernst Schäfer's missions in the expedition was to form an alliance with the Tibetans against the British in India. Hitler had intentions of bringing his armies across the Suez, meeting up with Arab armies to take Central Asia and to invade British-controlled India. Hitler had formed an alliance with Subhas Chandra Bose, the Indian nationalist leader who viewed Hitler as an avatar of Kalki: the god who would come out of the North to wreak vengeance on the immoral and unclean world. Had Hitler been successful in his ill-advised Russian campaign, he would have been able to do support Rommel in North Africa and to seize the Suez Canal, thus crippling the world's economy and gaining control over the flow of oil. The Arab nationalists would have welcomed Hitler as their liberator from the colonial powers of England and France, and would have rallied around the Nazis as they made for India. Whether they would have been successful that far is anyone's guess and, indeed, the logistics of crossing from the Middle East through to Afghanistan and what is now Pakistan, might have given even a German-Arab alliance pause. Nevertheless, that was the plan, and Tibet could have played a role in keeping some of the

British forces in north India occupied and unable to come to the defense of the country in the south.

To the extent that the Nazi Party was not a political party in any normative sense of the word but a cult, it's members would have found common ground with Tibet. Tibet, after all, was a theocracy. The Dalai Lama was the secular ruler as well as the sacred ruler of Tibet. In this, he was not so different from the Führer of the Third Reich, who was the spiritual as well as the political leader of Germany and the Germans. They both relied on the heavy use of symbols and rituals to maintain power over their populations and—as each of these kingdoms fell to the onslaught of their enemies—it was revealed that this power was largely illusory.

Be that as it may, by the time the SS-Tibet Expedition arrived back in Germany, the Second World War was just beginning. Bruno Beger—the anthropologist with the calipers—found himself gainfully employed in building an ethnographic museum of the human race, moreover one which would demonstrate the superiority of the Aryan over the Semitic peoples. In order to do this, he needed a representative sampling of human skulls for his collection.

Eighty persons were murdered at Natzweiler-Struthof concentration camp to satisfy this requirement.

After the war, Beger was denazified. While he was convicted of the murder of more than eighty individuals for the express purpose of building his skull collection, he never served a day in prison. In fact, he remained a close friend of the Dalai Lama all his life, just as his old SS colleague Heinrich Harrer.

And then there was Miguel Serrano.

Readers of my *Unholy Alliance* will be familiar with the name of Serrano. A former Chilean ambassador to Austria and India, among other postings, Serrano was one of the earliest members of the Nazi Party in Chile. In the 1930s and 1940s he edited a magazine called *La Nueva Edad* or "The New Age," which was filled with articles on spiritual and political subjects—a kind of South American version of Order of the New Templars founder Lanz von Liebenfels's *Ostara* magazine that so captivated a young Adolf Hitler in Vienna.

Serrano developed close friendships with such leading lights as Carl G. Jung, the famous Swiss psychiatrist who has been characterized as pro-Nazi by some of his critics, and the German author Hermann Hesse (*Siddharta, Steppenwolf, Journey to the East*), and wrote a book about these relationships. What many admirers in the United States and Europe did not realize, however, was that Serrano was an unrepentant Nazi to the end of his days. His other works—many of which are so far untranslated from Spanish into English, and thus unavailable to the wider audience that would be horrified to learn of his allegiances—include *Hitler: el ultimo avatar* and *El Cordon Dorado*: works that combine Indian spiritual concepts and occultism with emphatically Nazi race science—*Rassenkunde*—and Nazi political ideology. To Serrano and to many of his followers Hitler was *el ultimo avatar* or "the last avatar": a demigod appearing on earth to pave the way for Serrano's "New Age." This combination of Asian spiritual and esoteric concepts with patent Nazism was not unique to Serrano, as authors such as Nicholas Goodrick-Clarke have pointed out. Indeed, early copies of the Asian-inspired works of Mme. Helena Blavatsky—founder of the Theosophical Society—bore the swastika on their covers, not as a nod to Nazism (which did not exist when her books were written) but to the ancient Asian use of the symbol which nevertheless was adopted by the Nazis as emblematic of the Aryan race Blavatsky describes.

Serrano was fired from his post as ambassador when the Socialist Salvador Allende Gossens was elected President of Chile in 1970. Declassified documents from the Nixon White House reveal the extent to which Nixon and Kissinger had plotted the overthrow of the democratically-elected Allende even before the inauguration, and with their financial, moral, and military support they were able to do so on September 11, 1973. What may come as a surprise is the fact that Allende was more than a doctrinaire Socialist. During World War II, he had been an outspoken opponent of Nazism and of his countrymen's allegiance to Nazi ideals, countrymen like Miguel Serrano.

Photographs of Serrano with the Dalai Lama are as numerous as those of Bruno Beger or Heinrich Harrer with the Dalai Lama. Serrano had met the Tibetan leader during his tenure as ambassador to India, and later adopted many Tibetan concepts in his own works. There is an almost childish fascination of Nazi ideologues with Tibet, as if the romantic stories of Alexandra David-Neel and other famous travelers to the Himalayas had summoned dreams of an ancient and mystical race, dwelling high in the snowy mountains, aloof from the trials and tribulations of the world, concentrating on meditation and the development of paranormal powers. Some of the responsibility for this romanticism concerning Tibet is due to popular writers such as Blavatsky and David-Neel, of course, but also to the Swedish explorer and adventurer Sven Hedin (1865–1952).

The author in *Unholy Alliance* has written briefly about Hedin and his connection to the Third Reich. Hedin had traveled extensively in Asia and wrote even more extensively about it. He was one of those early twentieth-century explorers in company with some of the other individuals mentioned in the Pöch address book. Hedin ventured deep into the deserts of China and Mongolia, and crawled all through Central Asia and across the Himalayas into Tibet. He was a hero to many a European schoolchild, and his exploits were the stuff of legend. An expert on Tibet and on the unmapped places of Central Asia, he was in demand as much for his intelligence value to the Great Game as he was for his spectacular reports on ancient cities lost in the sands of the Gobi, the Taklamakan Desert, and Mongolia. Today, his detailed geographical studies and maps of Central Asia are still in use, most recently by US forces in Afghanistan. Yet only a small portion of his extensive documentation, books, field notes, photographs, and other resource materials have been studied—so voluminous was his output and so wide-ranging his explorations. Hedin spoke many Asian and European languages and dialects, and this makes a competent and thorough analysis of his work a gargantuan task.

But Hedin also had a dark side, and this is referenced in *Unholy Alliance*. Documents have surfaced from the Sven Hedin Institute for Inner Asian Research—an organization formed by the Nazis— with Hedin's signature and "Heil Hitler!" prominently above it. This Institute became part of Heinrich Himmler's *Deutsche Ahnenerbe*, the Ancestral Heritage Research Division of the SS. Sweden officially was neutral during the war, but supplied the Reich with much-needed machine parts and steel. Sweden was considered almost as Aryan as Germany, so there was no particular advantage in alienating the country's sympathies with an invasion. By acknowledging Hedin as a hero and worthy of his own institute, the Nazis were incorporating the Hedin body of work into their own repertoire. Although there is evidence that Hedin interceded on behalf of Jewish prisoners in the concentration camps—particularly those who were friends of his—his willingness to write articles and books praising the Third Reich and its ideals (admittedly under pressure from the Nazis as a kind of extortion in order to save his Jewish colleagues from execution) cast a long shadow over his otherwise illustrious career.

To be sure, Hedin was sympathetic towards the Nazis and met with Adolf Hitler several times, even receiving awards and decorations from the Führer. Hedin shared Hitler's aversion to Russia and believed that the peoples of Sweden and Germany should stand shoulder-to-shoulder against the threat from the East. Like others we have discussed, his pro-Nazi stance was largely fueled by a fear of Communism that was tainted with a racist viewpoint of the presumed barbarism of the Slavs. Hedin was an enemy of democracy, preferring instead the dubious benefits of a strong monarchy. In this, he would have found a friend in the Dalai Lama.

> I'm always against violence. But the Tibetan guerrillas were very dedicated people. They were willing to sacrifice their own lives for the Tibetan nation. And they found a way to receive help from the CIA.
> —The Dalai Lama, *New York Times* interview, 11/28/1993

Analysis of recently-declassified documents on the flight of the Dalai Lama from Tibet to freedom in India reveals the extent to which the Tibetan leader was used by American intelligence as a propaganda tool against Chinese Communism. In return, the Tibetan leader asked for military assistance to support an armed resistance movement against the Chinese ... one that would use Tibetan monasteries and temples as "safe houses" and part of an underground intelligence and support network. In other words, the Tibetan equivalent of the Roman Catholic "monastery route." The parallels between post-war Europe and post-invasion Tibet are striking.

Both Hitler and the Dalai Lama were secular rulers of their respective countries. Both had been the spiritual rulers of their peoples as well. Both revered the swastika as a symbol of their identity. And both were fighting Communism: Hitler against Russia, and the Dalai Lama against China. And just as Nazi officers were incorporated into the US and British intelligence operations against Russia, so were Tibetan political and military leaders incorporated into American intelligence and paramilitary operations against China. The followers of both Hitler and the Dalai Lama were (and are) moved by ecstatic worship of their leaders and dreams of a paradisiacal future.

While the position of the Dalai Lama appears to have mellowed somewhat in recent years, in the 1950s and 1960s he was a prominent anti-Communist who lent his support to American efforts to resist Chinese hegemony in Asia. The CIA trained Tibetan troops in the state of Colorado during this period, sending them back to wage a doomed guerrilla war against the Chinese; but the Tibetan troops became seconded to the Indian Army for direct military action against Bangladesh as well.

This might have been consonant with an esoteric tradition in Tibet, enshrined in the seminal work of Tibetan Buddhism, the *Kalachakra Tantra*. In this work, mention is made of the Kalki: a kind of God-King that will storm out of Shambhala (the secret, hidden kingdom in the Himalayas made famous by the film *Shangri-La*) and put to waste all non-Buddhists, in a jihad worthy of the most insane fantasies of frustrated terrrorists everywhere. The Dalai Lama is known to be fascinated with the machinery of war, as he himself mentioned during the *New York Times* interview above-referenced.

It would be a stretch to accuse the Tibetans of the same type of war crimes of which the Nazis have been charged. There is no indication of genocide or "ethnic cleansing" as a result of Tibetan policies, for instance. However, if we subtract genocide from the political inclinations of both the Nazis and the Tibetans as represented by the Dalai Lama, we are left with the uneasy feeling that there was much they had in common. Both the Nazis and the Tibetan Buddhists represent religions that are non-Abrahamic in nature. The Nazis embraced a kind of neo-paganism as their spiritual resource, and with it a rejection of the ethical and moral ideals of Judaism, Christianity and Islam.

It should be noted, however, that the *Kalachakra Tantra*—which forms the backbone of the type of Buddhism promulgated by the Dalai Lama—includes similar ideas. There is a patent rejection of non-Buddhist religions and the promise of the appearance of the Kalki: an avatar of Vishnu and the last ruler of the Kali Yuga (the dark age in which we presently live). Kalki was associated with Hitler by Miguel Serrano, and by the Indian nationalist leader Subhas Chandra Bose, among others. The Kalki would come out of his mystical kingdom of Shambhala at some point in the future and cleanse the world of non-Buddhists in a major, apocalyptic-style conflagration. This seems a trifle inconsistent with the concept of "mercy." The Dalai Lama is considered to be an incarnation of Avalokitesvara, the Indian God of Mercy and Compassion; perhaps something is lost in the translation.

We do not see the Dalai Lama sitting down and smiling benignly with Communist leaders, of course. We do see him embracing Nazis. One can assume that the Sea of Compassion that is the Dalai Lama has managed to bestow mercy on even these unrepentant war criminals and fear-mongers, and perhaps that is the lesson he wishes to teach us; but it is not a lesson he has the moral right to teach.

Just as it wasn't the moral right of the Catholic Church to extend mercy to Adolf Eichmann, Klaus Barbie, Franz Stangl, Josef Mengele ... the list goes on and on. Mercy and forgiveness are the prerogative of the victim, not a bystander or a co-conspirator. But in each case the "Church"—whether the Catholic Church in Europe, or the Tibetan "Church" in Asia—extended the hand of friendship to some of the worst criminals and violators of human rights the modern world has ever known.

The declassified Tibet memos show a pattern of collaboration between the Tibetan leadership and the CIA spanning decades.

In 1952, the Dalai Lama was warned specifically:

> "We believe that if you should return to China your life will be in jeopardy. ... they will murder you the moment your usefulness to them is over. ... If you leave Tibet and if you organize resistance to the Chinese Communists, we are prepared to send you light arms through India."

A little later that same year:

> "Gyalo and Shakabpa with DL's knowledge seriously considering forming secret organization infiltrate Tib from Ind and possibly Nepal using Tib monasteries as centers anti-Commie resistance, propaganda first, weapons later."

In 1955, the year of the Bandung Conference, the US Department of State reported that they would use something called the Tibet Flood Relief Committee, "for propaganda coup against Chinese Communists, and buttress position Tibetan resistance groups." It should be noted that the Dalai Lama was in China during the Bandung Conference, and had what appeared to be a cordial relationship with Premier Zhou En Lai—who, it is said, was the target of CIA assassination attempts at the time. In other words, the Dalai Lama was playing a double game himself. Of course, this is understandable and forgiveable, as China had invaded his country and, to all practical intents and purposes, had deposed him as a national leader. But it does indicate that the Tibetan leader was a pragmatic politician who was not above shaking hands with Premier Zhou one moment and fomenting an armed resistance against him the other.

By 1958, the Tibetan Resistance Army was formally established, with aid and training from the CIA.

And by March 1959 the Dalai Lama left Tibet on his celebrated journey out of the country to India, which granted him and his government-in-exile asylum. A note from an aide to the Dalai Lama reads, in part:

> "The Dalai Lama and his officials arrived safely at the India border March 31. They will arrive at Tawang on April 3. ... You must help us soon as possible and send us weapons for 30,000 men by airplane."

That level of support did not materialize, however, although there was an airdrop in January of 1961 that served to arm 800 men instead of the requested 30,000.

This is mentioned in a State Department memorandum for "Special Group/1/" dated January 9, 1964, with the subject line "Review of Tibetan Operations" where it is revealed that:

> "The CIA Tibetan Activity consists of political action, propaganda, and paramilitary activity. The purpose of the program at this stage is to keep the political concept of an autonomous Tibet alive within Tibet and among foreign nations, principally India, and to build a capability for resistance against possible political developments inside Communist China."

In addition, it is revealed in this important memo that the CIA

> "... is supporting the establishment of Tibet Houses in [*less than one line of source text not declassified*] Geneva, and New York City. The Tibet Houses are intended to serve as unofficial representation for the Dalai Lama and to maintain the concept of a separate political identity. The Tibet House in New York City will work closely with Tibetan supporters in the United Nations, particularly the Malayan, Irish, and Thai delegations."

The Tibet House in New York City is well-known to the author, as he availed himself of their resources when researching *Unholy Alliance*. It is closely connected to Hollywood celebrities such as

Richard Gere, and to such illustrious Tibetan scholars as Robert Thurman (father of actress Uma Thurman). The fact that it is a CIA front may have been common knowledge among its supporters, but at the time he was there researching the SS Tibet Expedition in the early 1990s, it wasn't known to your demonstrably naïve correspondent.

A memo from the US Embassy in New Delhi, India dated February 11, 2010 gives us the following statistics:

> "… approximately 6,000 Tibetans now serve, and over 30,000 Tibetans have been trained, in Establishment 22, a joint Tibetan-Nepali border force within the Indian Army that reportedly emerged in 1962 following a failed Tibetan uprising in China. Membership in Establishment 22 was compulsory for Tibetan students graduating from Tibetan Children's Village (TCV) schools until the late 1980s. … They fought in the Indo-Pakistan War of 1971 that created Bangladesh and in Operation Meghdoot during the 1999 Indo-Pakistan fighting in Kargil."

In other words, Tibetan students were drafted into Establishment 22 from 1962 until the late 1980s, and fought in wars that had nothing to do with Tibetan independence. Conditions at the TCV were squalid in the extreme—when visitors from outside the community were allowed to inspect it; and all these children had to look forward to after a rudimentary education was forced military training and assignment to various Indian wars against Pakistan and Bangladesh. And, of course, the Indian Nationalist movement had been sympathetic to Hitler for precisely the same reasons that Palestine had been: they were both colonies of the English and saw in Hitler the Kalki Avatar: a semi-divine being whose coming is foretold in the *Kalachakra Tantra*, a warrior who will rid the world of evil.

None of this is particularly unique to fascist or Nazi regimes, obviously. Communist countries and democratic countries can be accused of the same, or worse. But it is the disconnect between the popular image of Tibet as a spiritually-advanced Buddhist paradise (at least, before the Chinese invasion), and the reality of pointless and ineffective armed struggle, the drafting of children to fight the wars of other countries, and the close collaboration of the Tibetan leadership with the CIA and with Nazi academics and war criminals that makes one pause.

Once we realize that the world is really not what it seems, that a realistic appraisal of international politics and military adventures necessarily leads one to understand that most of what we learn in school and in the media is propaganda and manipulation, we can better come to grips with such seemingly outrageous claims that Hitler escaped to Indonesia, or that there was a shooter on the Grassy Knoll, or that 9/11 was an inside job. This doesn't mean that we have to believe six impossible things before breakfast, but it does require us—if we are to maintain any degree of intellectual integrity—to question everything we hear. This applies not only to government press releases and front-page headlines, but also to the conspiracy theorists and the madmen on both sides of every political aisle.

Heinrich Harrer was just as comfortable in the company of Hitler as he was with the Dalai Lama. He stood at a nexus between what we believe was the most evil man of the twentieth century and the holiest man of the twentieth century. How was this possible? Was Harrer some kind of psychopath in need of intensive therapy, or is the therapy better applied to ourselves—who so naïvely believe in such convenient dualities as "good" and "bad," "right" and "wrong," Nazi and Communist, war criminal and saint? Perhaps Harrer achieved that kind of *advaita* or non-duality that is the goal of Tibetan Buddhism—represented in his balancing act between Hitler and the Lama—bringing them together in his fractured soul as some kind of Unity. Cannot demons become angels, sinners become saints?

Dream on.

CHAPTER TWELVE

THE WAY OF THE (HOLY) WARRIOR

> As we reflect on the recent events [of 11 September 2001] in the U.S. we recognize that in the past our country engaged in hostilities, calling it a "holy war," and inflicting great pain and damage in various countries.
> —Statement of the Myōshinji General Assembly[86]

Holy war is not just a prerogative of Muslims and Christians. As the above quotation demonstrates the Japanese Zen community realizes that they were complicit in the Asian version of the Holocaust. This one was aimed at the Chinese, Koreans, and other nationalities in the Asia Pacific theater of operations during what Westerners call World War Two, and the Chinese call the Great Imperialist War of Aggression.

This is a relatively new branch of religious studies, one that is controversial. It is sure to be upsetting to many people as they realize that one of the most revered authors on Zen Buddhism—D. T. Suzuki (1870–1966)—was, in fact, a devoted fascist who glorified the role of the Japanese warrior in the conquest of China.

What may come as a surprise to many others is the fact—amply supported by documentation—that one of the Western world's most respected interpreters of Zen Buddhism, Karlfried Graf Dürckheim, was a Nazi Party member, SA man since 1933, and the head of Nazi propaganda in Japan, reporting directly to Reich Foreign Minister Ribbentrop. A committed Nazi, Dürckheim was eventually arrested by Allied forces after the fall of Japan and sentenced to sixteen months in prison.

These two men—Suzuki and Dürckheim—became fast friends for the duration of the war. They had a great deal in common, and

---

86   As referenced in Brian Daizen Victoria,"Zen as a Cult of Death in the Wartime Writings of D.T. Suzuki," *The Asia-Pacific Journal*, Vol. 11, Issue 30, No. 4, August 5, 2013. The Myōshinji is a branch of the Rinzai Zen sect.

Zen was the glue that bound them together. Bushido—the "way of the warrior"—had resonance for both the Nazis and the Japanese nationalists. The latter were slaughtering their way across the length and breadth of Asia. Zen Buddhism, like Islam, had become weaponized.

The critical point to take away from this discussion is the fact that religion—religious organizations, influential clergy, even religious sentiments—could become the servant of the state. Spirituality, often considered the highest form of human experience, becomes relegated to being another tool in a government arsenal designed for causing the violent end of another human being and the victory of the state over another nation, ethnic group, or religious entity. This is, after all, what a "holy war" is: men and women united under one religion, sect, or denomination slaughtering men and women united under another. It becomes difficult to differentiate whether religion is the cause or the medium for violent conflict; from the point of view of both the victims and the perpetrators, it probably doesn't matter.

In the case of Buddhism, it seems counter-intuitive that a philosophy whose most exalted practitioners refuse to eat meat or to harm any living thing could be recruited to convince a lay population to take up arms and invade another country, murdering its inhabitants, and claiming that this is consistent with what the Buddha taught. Yet, this weaponization of religion is precisely what took place in the twentieth century under the influence of extreme nationalism in Europe, the Middle East, and Asia. Japanese nationalism was seen as analogous to—if not identical with—the nationalist movement in Germany, and observers and commentators noted this similarity favorably.

Brian Daizen Victoria has been writing about this phenomenon in a number of peer-reviewed journals—notably *The Asia-Pacific Journal*—and has published a number of books on the subject. Speaking Japanese and having access to the previously-unknown war writings of D.T. Suzuki and many other Zen masters, he has revealed—not without controversy—the understanding of Zen initiates that Bushido (the "way of the warrior") and Zen Buddhism are inextricably linked. Further, that mindless devotion to the state and following its orders—no matter what they are—constitute the highest form of Buddhist selflessness. The writings of these Japanese monks and scholars on the subject of suicide, and the willingness to face death and lose one's life in the service of the Empire, can be compared to those of Islamist suicide bombers and terrorists, with little distortion between the two. What difference, after all, is there between a Palestinian in a suicide vest and the Kamikaze pilots of Japan? We may say that the former are non-state actors (in the current parlance of terrorism studies) and therein lies the difference, but the key motivation that makes it possible for a human being to fly a bomb into a ship is the same as that which inspires the suicide bomber to ignite his vest. They are both losing their lives for a higher cause, and causing as much human devastation as possible in the process.

Unfortunately, this higher cause has been defined and codified by other human beings with ulterior motives, cynical men and women who are undestandably reluctant to follow suit. The manipulation of spiritual beliefs and sentiments by state and non-state actors alike is nothing less than what they used to call "mind control" back in the 1950s and 1960s. The weaponization of religion is a means of controlling (and weaponizing) the human psyche on a massive scale, using terminology and symbolism that are widely recognized by the masses and not specific to any individual. Religious feelings are strong, but they are also ambiguous and largely resistant to logic and verbalization, and thus subject to re-interpretation and redirection by a competent leader. It is the religious passion itself that is the food of the political and military commander; it matters little whether the outward manifestation of that passion is devotion to Jesus or Marx, Buddha or the Emperor. It is the closest emotion to love, and love, as we are reliably informed, conquers all.

Karl Friedrich Alfred Heinrich Ferdinand Maria Graf Eckbrecht von Dürckheim-Montmartin (1896–1988), to show him in all his Teutonic glory, was born in Munich to aristocratic but impoverished parents. He served with distinction in World War One, seeing action at Verdun and the Battle of the Somme, and was awarded several honors. Returning to Bavaria after the war, he joined a Freikorps brigade. This in itself is very revealing, for the Freikorps were the militias that fought against Bolshevism in the streets of Munich. Composed of former soldiers of the defeated Kaiser's army, they roamed through the city like heavily armed gangs. Many of the men who would later become prominent in the Third Reich had been members of one Freikorps brigade or another, such as Ernst Röhm and Heinrich Himmler.

It was during the tumultuous period of the Weimar Republic in Germany that Dürckheim got his first taste of Asian religion. He had come across a copy of the *Dao De Jing* that his future wife was reading. A passage in the book caused Dürckheim to experience a sudden and brilliant illumination, a kind of *satori*—setting him on the path he would follow for the rest of his life.

In 1923, Dürckheim received a doctorate in psychology, and by the early 1930s he was on intimate terms with the Reich's foremost geopolitical theoretician (and fellow Bavarian) Karl Haushofer. Haushofer (1869–1946) had been a general in the Kaiser's army during World War One. Depressed by Germany's defeat, he became obsessed with finding a solution to his nation's ills. This led to his development of geopolitics, and the insistence that Germany become more aware of the global political situation and its role within it. Haushofer developed the idea of *lebensraum*—or "living space"—that was used to such great effect by the Nazis to legitimize their conquest of Eastern Europe.

The bond between Dürckheim and Haushofer was most likely their shared appreciation of Asian religion and culture. Haushofer had spent years traveling in Japan as well as through parts of China, Korea, and Southeast Asia in the years before the First World War. He recognized the natural affinity between Japanese nationalism and the growing German nationalism represented by the Nazi Party, and sought to create political bonds between the two countries, in part based on their mutual abhorrence of Communism, and their glorification of the warrior as the best symbol of national identity. His philosophy had tremendous impact on the ideas of Adolf Hitler—who adopted lebensraum and other geopolitical ideas created by Haushofer—as planks in his party's platform.

Haushofer's son Albrecht would later be implicated—rightly

or wrongly—in the July 1944 assassination attempt on Hitler's life
and was executed by the SS. Haushofer himself was captured by
the Allies, interrogated, and then in March of 1946 committed suicide, together with his wife. After his death many rumors flourished about the mysterious philosopher, including that he had been
a member of the Thule Gesellschaft, had created his own secret
society, had been a student of Gurdjieff, etc. none of which has been
proven. He did, however, have a long friendship with Rudolf Hess,
who served as the second-most-powerful man in Germany until
his bizarre flight to Scotland in May of 1940, on what has been
described as an abortive peace mission. Hess had his own esoteric
credentials, of course, having been born in Alexandria, Egypt and
become fascinated with occultism and astrology. It is said that the
date of his flight to Scotland had been determined through the use
of a horoscope—thus leading to the arrest and imprisonment of
astrologers throughout Germany once Hess's flight had become
known. It has been claimed that Haushofer knew in advance of
Hess's intention and this might have been another reason for his
falling out of favor in the last days of the Reich.

Thus in Karl Haushofer, as well as Karl Dürckheim, we have
ardent German nationalists and war veterans with a deep and abid-
ing interest in Asia and specifically Japan. In 1933, Dürckheim
joined the Nazi Party and the SA (*Sturmabteilung*, or Storm Troopers). He was sent briefly to South Africa where there was a large
German colony with the mission to urge the local Germans to support the Reich. During this period he made contact with the Nazi
underground in that country. (There was a South African reference
in the Pöch address book, as mentioned, as well as in the Rudel
address book.)

A problem arose, however, when it was discovered that Dürck-
heim's great-grandmother was Jewish, the daughter of Salomon
Oppenheim. Incredibly, this means that Dürckheim was related to
Max von Oppenheim, the creator of the concept of global jihad.
The services of the German doctor were too valuable to jettison,
however, and in 1938 he was sent instead to Japan as a special envoy
of Ribbentrop rather than lose his status within the Party. As a
Mischlinge, or mixed blood, it is conceivable that under normal cir-

cumstances, he would have been dropped from the Party rolls and would have found it difficult to find work.

Instead, Dürckheim flourished in Japan. He met D.T. Suzuki and the two men developed quite a friendship. He was under orders by Ribbentrop to develop Nazi propaganda in Japan, and he did that by emphasizing the correspondences between the Nazi warrior ideal and that of Japan—which was by now fully engaged in Manchuria. By 1937, Japan had invaded China with devastating results.

Dürckheim's exposure to Suzuki had profound implications for generations of spiritual seekers in the West. After the war, when the psychologist found himself back in Europe developing his own method of analysis, it was he who introduced the concepts of Zen Buddhism—and specifically those of his friend, D.T. Suzuki—to America and Europe. He was a friend of Alan Watts, and this paved the way for the writings of Suzuki to become better known. It is now safe to say that these two men, more than any other, introduced Zen Buddhism to a wide audience in the Western world and made it fashionable and even trendy.

And they were both Nazis. Dürckheim was a card-carrying member of the Party and a Storm Trooper, working for the Reich's Foreign Ministry, and promoting anti-Semitism as well as German nationalism around the world. Suzuki was a fellow-traveler, an admirer of Hitler and the Nazi Party, who agreed that the similarities between Bushido and Zen, on the one hand, and Nazism, on the other, meant that the two countries were on the same page both politically and spiritually.

Suzuki was not the only Zen scholar who felt that way, but to Western eyes he was easily the most important, since he was the author of seminal works on Zen that were widely read in America and Europe. Other Zen masters also chimed in with their appreciation of Nazism, but especially extolling the virtues of the warrior's way and the spiritual beauty of fighting and dying for your country. Partly this was due to a Japanese government proclamation in 1937 calling for "the total spiritual mobilization of the people."[87] Based

---

87 Brian Daizen Victoria, "Zen Masters on the Battlefield (Part 1)" *The Asia-*

on the understanding that "total war" included enlisting not only factories and farms in the war effort but religion as well, this proclamation was a call to arms for Zen Buddhist teachers and monks to instill in the Japanese people an almost supernatural desire to fight and die for the Emperor. This was carried out with alacrity, as more and more Zen scholars chimed in with their support of Japan's invasion of China and the brutal suppression of an entire race.

Suzuki himself had direct experience of Nazi Germany and its programs, for he went to Europe in 1936 to deliver a set of lectures on Zen. While in Germany he listened to many people discuss their admiration for Hitler and their hatred of the Jews. Thoughtfully recording his thoughts on these conversations, he wrote:

> The fact that they have no country is karmic retribution on the Jews. Because they have no attachment to the land and are wanderers, it is their fate to intrude into state structures created by others. ... In the case of today's German people they find it extremely difficult to accept their country being disturbed by a foreign race.[88]

This is essentially the Nazi Party line. In fact, as Brian Daizen Victoria notes in the same article from which the above quotation was extracted, the editor who wrote the foreword to Suzuki's book on Bushido published in 1941, claimed: "Dr. Suzuki's writings are said to have strongly influenced the military spirit of Nazi Germany." It would be astonishing indeed, and not a little demoralizing, to discover that Zen Buddhism had made the Waffen-SS even more courageous, more brutal, more dedicated than they already were. Perhaps it was the relationship between Suzuki and Dürckheim that gave greater impetus to the pollenization of these ideas in both cultures.

A related article,[89] this time by Dr. Karl Baier of the University of Vienna, gives careful attention to those of Dürckheim's writings

88   Quoted in Brian Daizen Victoria, "D.T. Suzuki, Zen, and the Nazis," *The Asia-Pacific Journal*, Vo. 11, Issue 43, No. 4, October 28, 2013.
89   Karl Baier, "The Formation and Principles of Count Dürckheim's Nazi

that are more closely focused on Nazism, texts that are not easily accessible to American readers and which have not yet been translated from German. They are revealing of the way that the German Zen aficionado felt about National Socialism, and its role in tapping into the unconscious wellspring of the German *Völk* in order to achieve spiritual enlightenment. This emphasis on the *Völk*—the German people themselves, considered as a whole racial unit—is exclusionary on its face, and would not include members of other ethnic groups no matter how long they may have lived in the country. In this rendering, the German people are those with the deepest connection to the land itself. Those with no such relationship—such as the urban Jews—could not possibly hope to understand, much less participate in, this type of mystical union. It was synonymous with the "blood and soil" mystique of Nazi philosopher Walther Darré, who was in charge of German agriculture under the Reich, as well as some of its more pagan elements.

As Suzuki says above, the Jews are wanderers without connection to the land. and are therefore a "disturbing" foreign element in Germany. This was, of course, the basis for the complaint against Soviet-style Communism—in that it was a "foreign element" that was not indigenous to either Russia or Germany, but an artificial creation by people who had no bond with the soil, and therefore could agitate for such imaginary constructs as human rights, workers unions, and the seizure of land and property that was not "theirs." This is a point of view that easily can be ported to other political positions, such as the rejection of colonialism that is the hallmark of Islamist activism.

To quote Dürckheim from a work published in Japan in 1942:

The accusation of harshness, which is time and again levelled against National Socialism, is a typical statement of a sort of mankind that cares about individuals and has lost sight of the superior whole.[90]

Worldview and his interpretation of Japanese Spirit and Zen," in *The Asia-Pacific Journal*, Vol. 11, Issue 48, No. 3, December 2, 2013.
90 Dürckheim, *Neues Deutschland, Deutscher Geist—Eine Sammlung von Aufsätzen*, Tokyo, Sansusha, 1942.p. 151; in Baier, op. cit.

This defense of Nazi brutality was echoed by Suzuki, when he defended Germany's treatment of the Jews on the basis that Germany was in a state of crisis and had to take extreme measures to defend itself. The jibe at the "sort of mankind that cares about individuals" is an indictment of the theory of human rights, which even Marx characterized as a "Jewish" invention to guarantee a level of survival for themselves in a hostile world.[91]

It is this acceptance (if not worship) of extremism in any form—political, military, even religious—that is one of the defining characteristics of both Nazism and the kind of Bushido or Zen warrior philosophy represented by Suzuki and Dürckheim. It is part of the warrior principle that sees no value in anything less than supreme effort and extreme conduct, even to the point of death (your own, or others'):

> German soldiership could well be the starting point of a comprehensive realisation of the German mind.[92]

This is consistent with Bushido philosophy, especially in the way it was interpreted at the time by Suzuki and other Zen scholars, who saw in this quintessentially Japanese practice all the best characteristics of what it means to be Japanese. In an era of total war, every human being is a soldier; and therefore every human being is a warrior hero, achieving his or her apotheosis on the battlefield, dying selflessly in an ecstasy of spiritual union with the Divine.

In this concept, the individual achieves completeness through sacrifice for the good of the community, what Dürckheim calls *Gemeinschaft*. The community, in the Dürckheimian sense, can only be composed of individuals who share a common origin, even a common ancestry. There is no voluntary "joining" of such a community; you are a member by virtue of your blood. In spilling that blood, you reaffirm your membership, your social identity; because

---

91 Karl Marx, "Zur Judenfrage," *Deutsch-Französische Jahrbücher*, February 1844.
92 Dürckheim, 1942, op. cit.

your blood is not your own but the product of the race that bore you, which itself comes from the land that nourishes the race:

> As the centre of this faith we find the breakthrough of the great subject Germany within the individual. ... the inspiring force coming from the joyful experience of a higher whole, that resides within you and wants to become reality through you—and this with such a power that one cannot help but to serve this higher will and sacrifice everything that is only personal.[93]

This exclusionary principle rejects the scientific fact that the percentage of genetic difference between a member of the Nordic "race" and a member of the Jewish "race" is negligible, and that all humans are products of the same planet and share the same earth. Yet, how can Dürckheim show respect for the Japanese who are not, after all, German *Völk*?

To him the Japanese represented a different—but just as racially-pure—*Völk*. They are a product of their land, with an ancient history and continuity that demands respect from the only other pure race on the planet, the Aryan. Both Germany and Japan, according to Dürckheim, are higher cultures that have taken foreign influences (Christianity and Buddhism, respectively) as creative challenges, enabling each to discover within themselves their true *Völkisch* identities.[94] What is left is not Christianity or Buddhism in their original forms, for these religions are international in scope (like Communism) and therefore repress the natural racial characteristics of the people they try to convert. (This same argument can be used to describe how Nazism was at once National and Socialist.) Both Germany and Japan valued the soldier, the warrior, the hero above all other cultural archetypes. The brave human being who is so dedicated and spiritually pure that to risk everything, even life, for the sake of the community, the *Gemeinschaft*, the *Völk*, the Emperor, is a joy and a duty. Obviously this has resonance with the

---

93 Ibid.
94 Baier, op. cit.

suicide bomber and the terrorist who die for their religion, too, theoretically out of identification with a different type of *Volk*—the co-
religionist—but which is really a reaffirmation of the same ideals as
the Nazi storm trooper and the Zen martyr. Both Nazism and the
type of militant Zen we are discussing were emotional responses
to the effects of military or cultural defeat by foreign powers (the
humiliation of the German defeat in World War One, the effects
of foreign subjugation of Japan during the Meiji Restoration). Both
countries suffered the agony of what was perceived to be moral and
spiritual decadence and decay, as a result of gross materialism and
abandonment of spiritual values which had weakened each nation
and made them vulnerable to foreign influences.

In order to overcome the effects of this degradation it was necessary to return to the old ideals that had served the empires—and
the caliphates—so well. This is in line with every popular Islamic
reformer from Muhammad ibn Abd al-Wahhab (the eighteenth
century founder of Wahhabism) to Sayyid Qutb of the Muslim
Brotherhood, (whose two years spent in the United States on a
scholarship convinced him of the emptiness of Western values and
of the need to return to a fundamentalist approach to Islam; and
which led him to attempt the assassination of Nasser in 1954 when
he realized the Egyptian president would not turn his country into
a theocracy).

This return to one's roots is echoed in Dürckheim's glow-
ing description of Japan's return to its primal nature, it's "völkisch
power."[95] Baier goes on to state that, according to Dürckheim, "the
primal source of Japan's power was the politicizing of its original
faith."[96]

In 1940, and writing under a pseudonym, Dürckheim would
clarify what he meant even further:

> The righteous man does not revolt out of selfishness. But if his
> honor is concerned, if his nation is in danger or God's concern

---

95 Dürckheim, "Tradition und Gegenwart in Japan," *Das XX Jahrhundert.* Juli
1939, pp. 196–204, in Baier, op.cit.
96 Baier, op. cit.

is violated within himself or within the World, then this calls him to fight and transform him into a sword.[97]

Dürckheim would be released from prison after the war and return to take up his former profession as a psychoanalyst in Germany in 1947. His books and conferences blending Zen Buddhism with depth analysis and what he called "Initiation Therapy"became quite popular, and he began to develop close ties with Western commentators on Asian religions, such as Alan Watts, Albert Stunkard, and Philip Kapleau. At his suggestion, some of them began to make the visit to Japan to seek out Suzuki, his old mentor, and the explosion of Zen literature and practice in the West began.

Dürckheim—Nazi Storm Trooper, psychoanalyst, and popularizer of Zen Buddhism—died in 1988 at the age of 92. D.T. Suzuki had died much earlier, in 1966, but not until he had changed the discourse in the Western world concerning Zen. His fierce nationalism and defense of the Japanese invasions of Korea and China were not well-known at all outside of Japan, and even then to only a small circle of like-minded scholars. The exception would be his student, Dürckheim himself, who held identical views. Both of these men, responsible for the tremendous interest in Zen in the West in the post-war period, kept this secret history to themselves. Like Heinrich Harrer, they lived in a state of denial concerning their Nazi (and Japanese nationalist) past. That is not to say that they disavowed their beliefs for they did not. Whatever their later views or justifications, by 1945 the damage had been done. An entire generation of German and Japanese soldiers represented the politicization of religion by the state, the weaponization of spiritual beliefs by secular governments. This tactic would be taken up again and again in the decades that would follow, by American spies, extremist zealots, and Islamist jihadists.

Dürckheim's psychotherapeutic system, perhaps unconsiously, mimics his political beliefs. His "wheel of metamorphosis" repre-

---

97 Dürckheim, writing as Karl Eckprecht, in *Vom rechten Mann. Ein Trutzwort für die schwere Zeit*. Berlin, Herbert Stubenrauch Verlagsbuchhandlung. 1940, as cited in Baier, op. cit.

sents this perhaps as well as anything else. In this system there are three stages to psychological change. The first stage is described as "All that is contrary to essential being is to be relinquished." The second stage involves "dissolving" that which has been relinquished. The third stage involves the development of a new core of being that is free of those elements that were "contrary to essential being."

Taken as a description of Dürckheim's and Suzuki's views on how the "Jewish question" should be handled in the ongoing purification of the *Völk*, it is remarkably consistent. There is no mention of integrating disparate elements of one's personality, for instance, but only of removing those elements that are not identified as being part of one's essential being, i.e., of purifying the core and ridding it of foreign influences. Thus, even some forms of psychotherapy are not immune from what we have been calling the Hitler Legacy.

Chapter Thirteen

The Lord of War

One of my initial sources for information on the Pöch mystery came from a small book published in 2010 by a company caled Titik Media in Jakarta. It was entitled *Hitler Mati di Indonesia* ("Hitler Died in Indonesia") and was written by Soeryo Goeritno, a man described as a prince of the Solo Sultanate, as well as a fight promoter and a member of a band called Equator.

What the author bio does not state, however, is that Soeryo Goeritno is an arms dealer.

His date of birth is given as January 30, 1943. In 1964 he began studying at the Gubkin Oil and Gas Institute in Moscow. This was during the last years of the Sukarno era, when the Indonesian leader had developed ties to Communist regimes. Sometime during his Moscow period he met and married Lyudmila Alexandrovna, who bore him two sons.

He returned to Indonesia with his wife and sons in 1971, but that was during the early stages of the Soeharto "New Order" era, and his connection to the Soviet Union was not appreciated at the time. He held a variety of odd jobs, including taxi driver, until 1980 when Soeharto resumed relations with the Soviet Union. People with Goeritno's background, training, and fluency in the Russian language were suddenly valuable commodities. He began arranging technology transfers on behalf of the Indonesian government.

We are not certain when his involvement in the arms trade began, but by 1993 he had formed PT Novanindro and the arms deals began in earnest. PT Novanindro was Goeritno's brainchild, and he used it as a facility to buy weapons from Russia but also from other countries and sources. At one point he even claimed that he sold weapons to the Taliban in Afghanistan.

These were not limited to small arms. PT Novanindro was involved in everything from AK-47s to helicopters and rocket launchers, and the sales were not restricted to Indonesian military or political requirements. His company was approached by separatist movements in Indonesia as well, such as the rebels in Aceh (with whom he says he declined to trade).

He has maintained his close links to Russia even after the fall of the Soviet Union, as is obvious from the timeline. His ability to move easily into the world of arms trading reflects contacts he made in Moscow while still a student there, with fellow students who went on to occupy positions in the Russian military and intelligence services. At the same time, due to his influence in the Indonesian government, he also has extensive contacts in that country's military and intelligence services, as well as with its leading political figures. Goeritno is proud to point out that he has been personally acquainted with every president of Indonesia since Soeharto.

Short in stature, bearded, and wearing his trademark cowboy hat, Goeritno became involved in a series of other projects that had nothing to do with arms. He became involved with a rock band, called Equator (about which not much is known) and as a fight promoter, representing Chris John. It is as if his early days scrounging around Jakarta, looking for work after his return from Moscow, has scarred him for life, and he seeks out things to do that are unconnected to each other.

Like pursuing the Pöch story.

It is not known exactly when Goeritno became interested in this affair, or why. What we do know is that he wrote (or, as the author believes, hired someone else to write) the book that became a kind of Indonesian bestseller on the subject. He did this with some limited access to the original Pöch documents now being held in Singapore. It is assumed that he had photocopies of many of these (more than this author had at his disposal) as well as the Sosro memoir, for he quotes from the memoir extensively without attribution. The book has some information on Hitler, Klaus Barbie, and the escape routes—but these are almost completely cribbed from the Sosro memoir, which themselves are taken from popular journalistic accounts of the mid-1980s. Clearly, Goeritno's thesis is that Pöch actually was Hitler, and he refers to him as "Hitler" throughout the text.

Goeritno deviates from the Sosro memoir in two places in particular. In the first he references the discovery—made in 2009 by Dr. Nick Bellantoni—that the skull the Russians claim is Hitler's skull is actually that of an unrelated female. That discovery caused ripples in the international press where it was widely reported. It was this single event that triggered a landslide of speculation as to the lack of forensic evidence that Hitler died in the bunker; and cases were made for the Führer's escape to Spain, Argentina, and—with the Sosro memoir—Indonesia. It became the foundation of a *Mystery Quest* special for the History Channel on "Hitler's Escape," a well-done piece of journalism that followed Dr Bellantoni to Moscow, where he examined the skull in front of the cameras and then managed to bring a small piece of it back with him for forensic testing in Connecticut.

I had had the good fortune to have spoken with Dr Bellantoni by phone in the early 1990s concerning another sensational case with which the State Archaeologist of Connecticut was involved—the famous "vampire cult" discovery that took place in eastern Connecticut near the Rhode Island border. When the news broke of the Moscow skull—and as it dovetailed nicely with my own research on Pöch—I phoned him again and asked for his opinion. He very kindly spoke to me for awhile about the case. It was his opinion that Hitler was too sick to have traveled out of Berlin in the last days, and that he had probably died in Berlin during the Soviet advance on the city.

When I asked him if it would be necessary to dig up the Pöch grave in Surabaya to ascertain if the body was indeed that of Pöch or Hitler, the question of DNA came up. The only Hitler DNA in private possession was obtained unethically, he told me, and the surviving members of Hitler's family do not wish to cooperate in any way with this type of research, so we were at an impasse.

Then he told me that perhaps one of the more important things to look for—in case the body in the Pöch grave was ever exhumed—was the height of the body. If the height was off, he said, there was no way it could be Hitler's.

As it turns out Pöch's height, as shown in the passport, closely matches Hitler's known height.

The second piece of information not contained within the Sosro memoir was Goeritno's own research undertaken (by himself or by an associate) in Sumbawa Besar. He managed to locate some individuals who had known Pöch and his second wife Sulaesih, and interviewed them for the book. There is not much in the interviews that adds to our understanding of the case, but the original research indicates that Goeritno took the project seriously enough that he spent the time and money necessary to follow up every available lead: in Bandung, in Sumbawa, and in Surabaya.

His book ends with photographs of himself standing over the Pöch grave in the Surabaya cemetery.

Hitler Mati di Indonesia was published in 2010, hot on the heels of the Bellantoni revelations concerning the "Hitler" skull. It appeared just as I was doing my own independent research on the case, and the information contained in the volume was helpful and frustrating at the same time. Goeritno—or his ghostwriter—had little understanding of the context of the war in Europe and made a number of incorrect assumptions, which I was at pains to correct. Also, only scraps of the Sosro memoir were provided, including some of the Pöch Testament that only added to the confusion. The German translation in the Goeritno book was replete with typographical errors, and it seemed the Indonesian language translation was similarly degraded. In addition, while photocopies of some of the relevant documents were reproduced in the book, their quality was so poor that it was difficult to make out the texts.

Still, with all of that, it was a useful guide insofar as it went, but I wished I had more.

The question that lingered long after I had finished writing *Ratline* was the character and motivation of Goeritno himself. He was wealthy and was still being interviewed concerning Indonesian policies and military matters long after his book was published. He was a mover and shaker in the world of Indonesian—and international—politics and, of course, the global weapons trade. Why would he identify himself so strongly with the Pöch case?

Was there another agenda?

As he became older in the first and second decade of the twenty-first century, he found himself becoming more cautious. One newspaper interview with Goeritno has him staying away from windows, admitting he was afraid of snipers. It seems melodramatic, but the sense one gets from the news reports is that Goeritno had become paranoid about people wanting to do him harm. He may have been correct in that assumption, for in mid-2012, Soeryo Goeritno had been summoned to Moscow for a last minute meeting.

It was a quick trip, and unusual for Goeritno. There was none of the usual wining and dining that normally takes place under these circumstances. He was called to Moscow, and then was back on a return flight the same or the following day. As he passed through Customs and Immigration at Jakarta's Sukarno-Hatta International Airport, he suddenly fell to the floor in a seizure.

He has been in a wheelchair since that day, unable to speak. The cause of his seizure is unknown.

Was there a hidden agenda to Goeritno's uncommon interest in the Pöch affair?

I learned, during the course of this investigation, that before his stroke or seizure or whatever it was that had silenced him, Soeryo Goeritno had formed a joint venture with Singapore's most prominent corporation—Temasek—for the purpose of mining for gold.

On Sumbawa.

The money aspect of this case is the thread that ties all of these disparate elements together. Our other arms dealers—Skorzeny, Genoud, and Mertins, for example—were dedicated Nazis as well as businessmen involved in trading guns for money all over the world. It is entirely possible that their paths would have crossed with Goeritno's at some point, for the world of the arms dealer is quite small. This becomes especially true when markets overlap, such as in Afghanistan when American, Russian, and Chinese-made arms competed for share.

However, I have not been able to uncover any declassified files on Goeritno. This may be due to the fact that he was primarily a dealer for the Indonesian government and had ties to the Soviets, and, later the Russian Federation. Whatever files may exist on

Goeritno's business dealings or that of his corporation, P.T. Novan-indro, would be deeply buried with bullet-proof classifications.

Yet, the project with Temasek intrigued me. It had been buried in a news report on Goeritno. The off-hand manner in which it was mentioned was enough to make me suspect there was much more to the story.

There were rumors that contained within the Pöch documents is a map. This may be one of the reasons why the current owner of these documents is so reluctant to show them to anyone, fearful of losing access to what might be a fortune in gold whose location may be indicated on this alleged map. It would explain Goeritno's interest in the Pöch affair, a circumstance which is otherwise inex-plicable.

Did the strange Nazi doctor bury gold somewhere on Sum-bawa? Or did he discover gold indigenous to the island? Was there any evidence that Nazi gold made its way to Indonesia during or after the war?

The answer to that last question, at least, is "yes."

CHAPTER FOURTEEN

SUKARNO'S GOLD

As we have seen, the Indonesian military is all over this story. First, with Doctor Sosro Husodo who was a Lt Col in the Indonesian Army. Then with Soeryo Goeritno, an arms dealer. Dr Sosro also worked for Pindar, an Indonesian weapons manufacturer (and in that capacity may have met Goeritno, although Goeritno does not mention this connection at all).

I learned that the Indonesian Ministry of the Interior had quashed a journalist's story on Pöch and Sosro back when the dictator Soeharto was still running the government. Sosro had insisted that there were mysterious agencies of foreign countries that would be after him once his memoir was published.

There thus would seem to have been more to Sosro's tale than even the claim of the former Nazi dictator living peacefully on a remote tropical island.

Much more.

This aspect of the story may prove to be the most unbelievable, and yet it is the only aspect that solves some of the outstanding questions on the obsession of so many people where the Pöch affair is concerned. In order to understand the context and to realize why this may be relevant, we need to look back once again at the very end of World War Two and the scramble of the Axis powers to save their lives and their wealth, in order to finance a rebirth of their movement at some future date.

We have to discuss Sukarno's gold.

In 1997, a rather exotic individual by the name of Dr. Edison Damanik died in the United States after having disappeared months earlier from his home in Jakarta, Indonesia. The circumstances of Damanik's death, as well as of his life, are shrouded in mystery. His role in the affair we are about to describe has been characterized as a sham and a hoax by some, and by others as evidence of one of the darkest secrets of World War Two and its aftermath: a secret that some of the world's most celebrated political leaders want kept hidden.

It is important to understand from the outset that, where possible, this story has been thoroughly documented. Admittedly there are elements of the story that cannot be verified and these are identified in the narrative. We may be discussing fraud on a massive scale, or we may be talking about a series of crimes perpetrated upon some of the world's most populous nations, nations that suffered greatly during the Second World War. In either case, and whatever the reality of the events that follow, one thing seems certain: it was belief in the truth of this story that attracted some of the less savory characters to the Pöch documents.

Here is what we know:

Dr. Edison Damanik was a real person. Born on November 30, 1930 in Pematang in North Sumatra, he was a former Indonesian police officer with the rank of Inspector, and was an adviser to Indonesian President Soeharto and a consultant to his government. The details of his consultancy or how he advised Soeharto have not been revealed. What has been revealed is that he was the chairman of something called the PT Galaxy Trust, on Jalan Rawa Kepa VI, in the Tomang area of Jakarta.

He was married to Etty Purnama-Damanik who survived his death. In the months leading up to his disappearance from his home in Jakarta, two rather strange persons were known to be living near him and keeping his house under some kind of surveillance. These two have been identified as one Frederick Robinson, an oil industry executive whose base was in Bangkok, Thailand. The other was Paul V. Morse, who was staying in the nearby Citraland Hotel for the eight months prior to Damanik's disappearance.

Both men have been described in various places as agents of the CIA, but that of course has never been confirmed.

The story that has been told of Damanik and PT Galaxy Trust is complicated and involves a widespread rumor that there existed—

in the name of President Sukarno—a vast fortune in gold, most or all of which represented the fruits of Japanese and German war crimes: the seizing of art, jewelry, antiques, as well as gold, and its disposition in hidden places around the world for eventual re-use. Much of this gold, and art treasure was buried in caves throughout the Philippine islands—where some of it has actually been found— and the rest in other areas of Southeast Asia, notably in the Indonesian archipelago. What is not certain is whether or not Damanik actually had what he claimed he possessed: genuine gold certificates worth billions of dollars at today's prices, certificates representing accounts in foreign banks in the name of Sukarno himself.

This, then, is the story of Sukarno's gold. Whether one chooses to believe in the story or not is irrelevant; what is relevant is that many people did, and still do, believe in the story and they have taken steps to acquire these certificates and have them honored by the banks in question. What is bizarre is the reaction of the banks (and governments) when confronted with these documents. The certificates are almost never honored, but the owners of the certificates are often arrested and thrown in prison ... only to be let out without explanation. Some of the "owners" have suffered persecution because of their proximity to the certificates; others have simply disappeared, or died under mysterious circumstances.

As the war came to an end, there was a scramble by the Nazis and the Japanese to hide as much of their war loot as possible from the Allies. This had begun as early as 1944 when it was obvious the war was lost; some sources claim an even earlier date. We know that some of the Nazi-looted art and valuables was hidden in the salt mines near Salzburg, where Pöch lived and from where he escaped in September of 1946. Salzburg is also where the CIC headquarters in Austria was based, and it was where many of the top Nazis made their way as the war was winding down and they needed an escape route to the Italian Tyrol.

Some of the Nazi art and gold was loaded onto transports and sent to Spain and Portugal. From there, some of it made its way to South America by ship or U-boat. But it was revealed in the 1990s that forty tons of "Black Eagle" gold had been shipped to the Portuguese colony of Macau, near Hong Kong, in what is now China. And twenty tons of that gold wound up in Indonesia.[98]

As reported in the *New York Times* in 1997 and in the years since then, more than 400 tons of Nazi gold made its way to Portugal during the war as payment for much-needed tungsten, an essential component of steel. While we know of forty tons of that gold that made its way to Asia, the disposition of the rest of the gold is still unknown. It is believed that much of it still lies beneath the streets of Lisbon in the vaults of the Bank of Portugal, but there has been so much traffic between officially "neutral" Portugal and Nazi Germany, as well as between Portugal and Latin America and its colony in Asia, Macau, that an accurate record of the amount of gold and its current whereabouts is impossible to verify.

Black Eagle gold was so called because it was gold that had been derived from everything from gold trinkets and tableware to the gold teeth pulled from victims of the Holocaust, and then smelted down into bars and stamped with the Black Eagle insignia used by the Nazi Reichsbank, and given a registration number.

At today's prices of about one thousand US dollars per ounce, twenty tons of gold would be valued at over 600 million dollars. And this was only one shipment of which we have any information.

In addition to this single Macau lot of Black Eagle gold, there were other shipments—mostly from Spain—to points around the world. At the same time that the Nazis were shipping gold out of Europe, the Japanese were burying gold all over Southeast Asia and shipping the rest to South America. They could not risk taking the gold back to Japan where the Allies would most likely sieze it, so they followed the iconic example of pirates everywhere and resorted to the "buried treasure" model. Using caves and tunnel systems in the Philippines and Indonesia, the gold was buried, and the workers who did the hard labor of digging the holes and transporting the gold were murdered to keep the locations secret. Maps were created,

---

98   As reported by Eduardo Gonçalves, in *The Observer*, 2 April 2000, "Britain allowed Portugal to keep Nazi gold" and by Marlise Simons, "Nazi Gold and Portugal's Murky Role," in the *New York Times*, January 10, 1997.

encoded, and hidden. By the time the war was over and the last bar of gold buried there were fewer than a few dozen individuals (and possibly even fewer than that) who had access to the maps. Fewer still who could decode the maps and locate the gold.

In addition to the Nazi "Black Eagle" gold, there was gold that had been shipped out of Southeast Asia by the colonial powers themselves when they saw the Japanese invasions about to take place. The Dutch government in Indonesia began shipping its gold to America and Australia from Java; the Americans shipped tons of gold and valuables out of the Philippines, some of it reaching San Francisco via Hawaii, and the rest seized by the Japanese at Corregidor and shipped to Japan. The man in charge of the evacuation of the Philippine gold was our old friend Major General Charles Willoughby.

Willoughby, as we have seen, was born Adolf Tscheppe-Weidenbach in Germany. He attended the University of Heidelberg, after which he moved to the United States in 1910, and changed his name to the more American-sounding Charles Willoughby. During and after World War Two, Willoughby was in charge of all intelligence operations in the Far East under General MacArthur. He was a devoted anti-communist who flourished during the McCarthy Era. He consulted with the House Committee on Un-American Activities and was a member of a variety of organizations with pro-fascist and, one might even say, pro-Nazi viewpoints. He supported Franco in Spain and praised Mussolini in Italy. He was a member of the International Committee for the Defense of Christian Culture, and the Young Americans for Freedom, as well as the Shickshinny Knights of Malta: a group founded in the 1950s by one Charles Pichel, who had Old Catholic Church connections and a desire to replace the Sovereign Order of the Knights of Malta with his own group, headquartered in the town of Shickshinny, Pennsylvania. The Shickshinny Knights became a cabal of extreme right-wing military and intelligence men plus a gaggle of Russian nobles who had lost their lands (and possibly their minds) after the Russian Revolution of 1917.

Willoughby had a specific interest in Indonesia, as revealed in the report to Congress we already discussed (see chapter nine).

In this report he characterized the 300 year Dutch occupation of Indonesia as "successful" and "humane," and wrote that the Dutch proposal for returning to Indonesia to rule it as before was "suited to the limitations of the average Indonesian." He disparaged "Merdeka" (Freedom) as a phony propaganda slogan, and claimed that trying to unite the many Indonesian ethnic groups into a single country was doomed to failure, and would open up Indonesia (and by extension the rest of Asia) to Communist rule.

He likened Russian designs on Asia as identical to Japanese intentions during the War, and claimed that people like Indonesian nationalist leaders Sukarno and Hatta were cooperating with the Soviets just as they had formerly cooperated with the Japanese. What does not seem to have occurred to Willoughby is that if a leader can work with the Japanese imperialists one day and the Soviets the next, it should be obvious that this leader is an opportunist and not an ideologue for either fascism or communism.

The more likely explanation, however, is that Willoughby was not as naïve as he appeared. At the end of the war, the Office of Strategic Services (OSS, wartime forerunner of the CIA) was finally allowed into the Pacific theater of operations (MacArthur had forbidden the OSS any access to the theater during the war, restricting OSS activities to China, India, Tibet and Indochina). Their agents reported back that Sukarno and his colleagues were just that: political realists who were not ideologically committed to Communism at all, but who were dedicated nationalists finding their way towards a democractic form of government unaligned with their former colonial masters.[99] This, however, was not what Washington wanted

---

99   One of these OSS agents who reported back on Sukarno was Jane Foster Zlatovski, a friend of television chef (and former OSS agent) Julia Child. Jane Foster was one of the first to interview Sukarno, Hatta, and many other Indonesian nationalists immediately after the end of the war and her impression was that they were ardent nationalists and not Communists, men who wanted to improve their relations with the United States and renew the international trade and exports that had been disrupted by the war. Zlatovski's warning was that if the US did not help in the anti-colonial movement there would be a string of revolutions throughout Asia that would threaten American interests in the region. She was, of course, proven right, but that did not stop the US Congress from indicting her as a Communist agent and a subversive.

to hear, and operations against Sukarno began, with the intention of upsetting his position as president of Indonesia and replacing him with leaders who would be more pro-American and anti-Soviet.

As an aside, one of those sent to Indonesia in the late 1950s as part of the overall plan to disrupt the Indonesian political process was none other than alleged assassin of President John F. Kennedy, Lee Harvey Oswald.

I have no clue if this fact is relevant or not to the overall case of Pöch, Hitler, Sosro, etc., but the connection of not only Oswald but also CIA operations in Indonesia in the 1950s is certainly relevant. Fletcher Prouty is an impeccable source. He worked for years as liaison between the intelligence community and the military, and he was probably the most credible critic of the *Warren Commission Report on the Assassination of President Kennedy*, having known many of the players for decades before the assassination. He was a consultant on the Oliver Stone film of the assassination, *JFK*, and made several appearances with Stone at press conferences to discuss the case. Oswald's service record certainly puts him in both the Philippines and Japan during his career as a Marine, however, and that is where the rest of our story takes place.

There is no space to go into all the ramifications of what has become known as the Black Eagle Trust. The tentacles of the treasure reach into many countries, and have affected the political lives of hundreds of millions—if not billions—of people around the world. There are influences at work in virtually every American presidential administration since Truman, and in covert action in South America, Africa, the Middle East and Asia where the gold was used to finance operations that could not appear on the books of Congress or of the democratically-elected houses of other nations. It would seem that the story of the buried treasure of World War II is the record of a vast slush fund. And a case has even been made that the attacks of September 11, 2001 in the United States were the result of a frantic effort to destroy financial records, and even to murder investigators who were hot on the trail of what would only be a scandal of epic proportions.

This author has his doubts about the 9/11 theory, as may be imagined, since 9/11 was itself a scandal of major proportions. If

the conspiracy theorists are correct when they connect the Black
Eagle Trust (or whatever its more modern designation may be) to
the events of 9/11, then "overkill" would seem to be the operative
term. In fact, this may be an attempt to deflect more sober analysis
of the phenomenon: the complex and bewildering trail of gold, gold
certificates, banks acting badly, and false imprisonment and even
death that surrounds any discussion of this matter.

As fantastic as this story of Black Eagle Gold sounds, it has
been verified and well-documented. The work of Sterling and Peggy
Seagrave is probably seminal in this regard. Interested readers are
advised to read their copiously-sourced *Gold Warriors: America's
Secret Recovery of Yamashita's Gold* for all the sordid details..

All we can do at this point is to summarize some of the material here, supplemented by what I have learned in the course of this
increasingly bizarre investigation.

As one example:

The trial took place in a US Court in Hawaii in 1996. It awarded
the heirs of one Rogelio Roxas—a Filipino locksmith—a judgement
of *US$ 43 billion* against the estate of former Philippine President
Ferdinand Marcos: the largest civil award in US history. The story
of Mr. Roxas is incredible, but it is part of the public record as are
the trial transcripts of the case.

In January of 1971 Rogelio Roxas—an amateur treasure
hunter—discovered a tunnel behind a hospital in the town of Baguio,
a former WW II headquarters of Japanese General Yamashita
Tomoyuki. The tunnel contained a 28-inch tall Burmese statue of
Buddha weighing a ton of solid gold, and thousands of smaller gold
bars. They had found the discovery of the century. ... but not before
dealing with the overwhelming stench of dead bodies that had lain
in the airless tunnel entrance for more than twenty-five years, workers slain to keep the location of the cache secret.

A few months later, in April of that year, armed men with a
search warrant arrived at the Roxas home and at gunpoint removed
the Golden Buddha, the gold bars, and a large amount of diamonds
and precious gems that had been hidden within the Buddha. They
beat Roxas's brother with gun butts when he tried to intervene.

The warrant had been signed by a local judge who had been

asked to do so by his nephew, who just happened to be President Ferdinand Marcos.

When Roxas attempted to raise a hue and cry over the affair, he was arrested by plainclothes officers and beaten, tortured with electric cattle prods, and blinded permanently in his right eye. In the meantime, they found one of the men who had helped Roxas find the hidden tunnel, and tortured him to discover its location by pulling out his teeth. When they finally got the location pinned down, they returned to the tunnel in force and made off with the rest of the buried treasure. The estimate of the booty by one observer is said to be roughly 10,800 gold bars weighing 75 kilos each.[100] That's over 800,000 kilos for a total of roughly US$ 28 billion at today's prices (approx US$ 1,000.00 an ounce). The Golden Buddha alone would be worth US$32 million today.

In the end, Roxas escaped to an undisclosed location where he lived in secrecy until the day Marcos was deposed and democracy came to the Philippines. That is when the machinery was put in motion to sue the Marcos family for the gold that had been stolen from Roxas, which, as it turned out, was a drop in the bucket when compared to the other gold and valuables the Marcos regime had discovered buried by the Japanese in caves in the years since the Roxas find.

The Golden Buddha hoard was only part of what has become known as Yamashita's Gold. This was the name given to virtually all the gold that was hidden by the Japanese as the war was winding down, although Yamashita probably was not involved in all the gold burials in Southeast Asia. It has been claimed that stories about Yamashita and his frantic burials of gold and other treasures all over the Philippine islands was a legend and purely imaginary … until a US Court decided otherwise. The amount of documentation supporting Roxas's claim was staggering, including photographs of the hoard, eyewitness testimony, and more. In fact, the Marcos defense

---

100 For this and most of the Roxas "Golden Buddha" story, see Sterling and Peggy Seagrave, *Gold Warriors: America's Secret Recovery of Yamashita's Gold*, Verso Books, London, 2005, pp. 141–146.

team did not challenge the story as given by the Roxas prosecution and allowed it to stand.

This event is pointed out because it illustrates one very important fact. At the time of the Roxas affair, the official word from the Philippine government was that there was no gold; that the story of Yamashita's gold was a fiction; that there had never been any such gold found in the Philippines, etc., etc. That was the consenus view. That was reality. That was the story that was reported in the press. The "official word" carries a lot of weight, and if it weren't for a very well-documented find, we would have never heard of Rogelio Roxas and he would never have been awarded forty-one billion dollars.[101]

The gold that had been found in Baguio represented the tip of a proverbial iceberg. And not all of that gold was hidden in the Philippines. There is ample evidence to suggest that other caches of gold were hidden in the Indonesian islands before the war was over.

The archipelago stretches for more than three thousand miles and consists of more than seventeen thousand islands of which only about six thousand are inhabited. The Japanese had effectively controlled all of it, even including Irian Jaya (Papua) and Lombok, Bali, Flores ... and Sumbawa. As an example, the Nagara class Japanese cruiser *Isuzu* was sunk off the coast of Sumbawa in April, 1945, after having dropped off troops at the city of Bima, Sumbawa only the day before. The *Isuzu* had participated in the Battle of Leyte Gulf, and had been sent to Surabaya for repairs in December of 1944 before making its way to Sumbawa. We do not know why troops had been brought to Sumbawa this late in the war when it was obvious Japan was losing. An educated guess might be that they were on a mission that had nothing to do with winning the war or consolidating their position in Indonesia.

The Japanese did not leave Indonesia until after the end of the war in the Pacific and, in some cases, were still fighting in Indonesia

---

101 While the court had awarded Roxas US$ 41 billion, the Hawaii Supreme Court reversed the decision in 1998, but only in terms of the amount of gold that allegedly was stolen by Marcos and not the fact that it was stolen: a crime that no one denies took place. There are currently two claims by the Roxas family against Imelda Marcos for a total of about US$ 20 million, a claim that has been upheld by the US courts.

as late as October, 1945 due to the confused state of affairs that existed between Japan, the victorious Allies (American, Dutch and British), and the rise of Indonesian nationalist groups. The Japanese had tried to temper the hideous nature of their brutal occupation by cutting deals with nationalist leaders in some areas, while ceding authority to the British in others. What this means for our narrative is that the Japanese presence in Indonesia was strong enough, even by the end of the war, to permit them to use the islands of the archipelago as hiding places for gold: whether Yamashita's or gold of the Black Eagle variety.

The Indonesian prince, Soeryo Goeritno, had published his book on Pöch in 2010. He began harrassing the family of Doctor Sosro in 2011,[102] and attempted to cut a deal for the Pöch documents in 2011 and 2012. The only explanation for why he would continue to be involved in such an aggressive fashion over the documents—many of which had already appeared (albeit poorly reproduced) in his book—indicates an ulterior motive.

One of the documents to which Goeritno did not have access was the map.

Basically, no one knows what the map reveals. It remains one of the best-kept secrets of the entire Pöch affair. The map—plus the address book—taken together could be the key that Goeritno for which was searching. By 2007, he had announced that he was the local partner of Singapore's largest and most venerable multinational corporation—Temasek—for the purpose of gold mining on Sumbawa.

There are no public records available to measure the success or failure of that enterprise, but if the Sumbawa venture was coming up dry, the existence of a treasure map formerly in the possession of Sumbawa's most famous (and probably only) Nazi might be the break Goeritno needed. After all, Pöch had lived on Sumbawa without visible means of support other than whatever salary the Government of Indonesia was paying him. However much it was,

---

102 Information based on a phone call with Chandriana, Sosro's daughter, in the spring of 2013.

it seems to have enabled Hella Pöch to make multiple trips back to Europe during a ten-year period.

The one aspect of the Pöch affair that no one has addressed is the financial aspect. How did the Pöch couple manage to live—and by all accounts to live well—during their Sumbawa sojourn? Of course, the cost of living on the island would be much less than the same lifestyle in Jakarta, and much less than that in any of the European capitals, but that still doesn't answer the question. From photographic and other evidence it can be construed that the Pöchs were people of some means.

Did Pöch have his own secret slush fund? How was he able to access it while on Sumbawa in the days before Internet banking and ATM machines? How did Hella Pöch manage to pay for all those trips back and forth to Europe?

The Indonesian widow of Georg Anton Pöch—Sulaesih—managed to retire to Bandung, and live in a compound near the university there. It is well-guarded and quite secure. When two local Indonesian reporters tried to visit her, they were prevented from doing so, and instead could only provide an aerial photograph of the compound in their book. This is quite different from a house in the wilds of Sumbawa, replete with snakes on the road and monkeys stealing your lunch.

So what was the story of Pöch's hidden wealth?

In the *Straits Times* of Singapore, on January 24, 1987, the story of Sukarno's gold made headlines.

The story reads, in part:

> "The Indonesian government has announced it will use every means available to track down a secret fund that might contain billions of dollars left over from former President Sukarno's administration. Cabinet Secretary Moerdiono confirmed that the government had been investigating the so-called "revolutionary fund" for the past year to see how much money was left and whether it was recoverable.
>
> Mr. Moerdiono told reporters that former Foreign Minister Subandrio, now serving a life sentence in connection with

a communist coup attempt in 1965, had notified the government of the fund's existence and offered to help recover the money. The fund was officially set up in 1960 by the flamboyant President Sukarno to finance special projects, with money reportedly deposited in Swiss, Dutch and London bank accounts.

The deputy chairman of the ruling Golkar Party, retired Brig-Gen. Suhardiman, said last month the Sukarno government had deposited millions of dollars worth of gold at the Union Bank of Switzerland in Geneva in 1960 as a "revolution fund."

He estimated that with interest accrued over the years, the fund should be worth more than US$ 1 billion (S$ 2.1 billion). ...."[103]

This is another one of those impossible stories that nevertheless, at least in this case, has the stamp of authenticity. A former Sukarno cabinet minister, in prison for life because of the events of 1965, wants to cut a deal by revealing the location of Sukarno's gold; and the Indonesian government takes it seriously, even getting corroboration from a brigadier-general in the Indonesian Army and deputy head of the ruling political party. This is not just another legend whispered between bored expatriates amusing themselves in a Singapore bar. This is a statement verifying that Sukarno had, indeed, set up a "Revolutionary Fund" during his tenure.

The rumors that I heard during my long experience in Asia were, like most rumors, contradictory, and sometimes unbelievable in the extreme. But those concerning Sukarno and his fabled treasure were remarkably consistent. According to the generally-accepted version, President Sukarno was intent on creating a Revolutionary Fund. It would help support Indonesian works projects and other measures to improve the economy of his country in outlying areas that normally did not enjoy great attention from the central government in Jakarta. It would also help to support programs in

103 "Hunt for secret fund," *The Straits Times*, January 24,1987, p.2 and p. 7; "Big hunt on for billions in secret Sukarno fund."

other—non-aligned—nations. At the famous Bandung Conference of Non-Aligned Nations, Sukarno had thrown down the gauntlet to the world and said, essentially, a "plague on both your houses." He experienced first-hand the tremendous pressure brought to bear by Western countries on the developing nations to adhere to Western ideas of capitalism and economic progress, or face the consequences. A truism of the time held that if you were not pro-Western or pro-American, then you must be Communist. There were simply no other paths to follow during that period known as the Cold War.

Sukarno realized that the colonial powers had not given up on their desire to control their former colonies—if not militarily or politically then economically. The corollary to this was the importace of having an independent source of financial support that did not depend on the largesse of the Western nations—neither the World Bank nor the International Monetary Fund, both of which were viewed as puppets of the American government. The Revolutionary Fund would help developing nations stay independent of foreign demands that they follow a strict capitalist system, or that they support the interests of the Western powers.

But it was also important to remain non-aligned where Communist nations were concerned as well. While the Soviet Union paid lip-service to supporting "indigenous" people's revolutions, this also came at a price. The Communists expected that the developing nation would allow Soviet military assistance and advice in the country, making it another Soviet satellite in the global chess game Russia was playing against the United States, Great Britain, and the other Western powers.

Thus Sukarno, perhaps naïvely, thought that the developing nations could and should remain aloof from these power-plays and control their own separate destinies. Sukarno had no interest in exporting an Indonesian concept of political or military philosophy (other than his very general *Pancasila* doctrine[104]). Indeed, Indonesia was still in the process of developing its own organizing prin-

---

104 *Pancasila* means literally "five principles" and is the cornerstone of Indonesian democracy as envisioned by Sukarno. The five principles are a belief in one God, a just and civilized humanity, unity, democracy,and social justice. *Pancasila*

ciples. However, both the United States and the Soviet Union were engaged in a kind of missionary activity towards the developing nations—trying to convert them to their ideological points-of-view and re-arranging their political (and military) systems to reflect their own ideas as to how the world should be run.

Such patronizing attitudes by the technologically more advanced nations toward the developing nations of Latin America, Africa, and Asia were rejected. They were seen as another form of the colonialism the developing nations had fought wars to erase from their borders. The competing major powers refused to acknowledge there could be more than two positions—either Communist or Capitalist. Both were determined to impose their views on as much territory as possible.

The Bandung Conference pulled attendance from the very countries in Africa and Asia that the United States feared would swing towards Communism. The basic premise of the conference was the rejection of colonialism and neo-colonialism in all its forms—which meant that the Soviet Union found itself censured as well as the United States (which did not send an official representative to the conference). Even China's premier Zhou En Lai took part in the conference after narrowly escaping an assassination attempt on his way to Indonesia. With its emphasis on an end to colonialism and the need for self-determination for all nations, it appeared to the West that what Sukarno called the "Newly Emerging Forces" could constitute another front in the Cold War.

As moves were being contemplated and implemented to get rid of Sukarno who, because of his enormous popularity and charisma, was managing to bring together representatives of at least one-quarter of the world's population in a bloc that could prove difficult if not impossible for the West to control, the Indonesian president was formulating the idea of the Revolutionary Fund.

Sukarno knew as well as the other Southeast Asian leaders that the Japanese had hidden large quantities of gold and other valuables throughout the region. The United States had been engaged

---

could not have been adopted by the Soviets or the Chinese due to the requirement for a belief in one God.

in an ongoing covert mission to find and acquire as much of this gold as possible, through operatives such as Willoughby and CIA agents, like the well-known veteran of many Asian intelligence campaigns, Edward Lansdale. Their focus was on the Philippines, whose government had a conveniently pro-American attitude, and on Japan itself whose government was virtually a creature of the United States. Japan had become important during the Cold War as an ally against the Chinese, and as a logistical rear area for Korean operations. Okinawa would remain in American hands for decades after the War, and Atsugi airbase (where Lee Harvey Oswald was stationed) would become a vital link in the U2 spy plane missions flown over the Soviet Union. That enormous infusions of capital were made to support sympathetic Japanese politicians, military officers, and organized crime leaders (sometimes all three in the same person) was no secret to anyone.

But Indonesia was a different case. The United States had very little leverage in the archipelago, and indeed had been running covert operations in Indonesia since the early 1950s with the goal of insuring that Communism would not gain a serious foothold in the nation. As early as 1953, the US State Department's Office of Intelligence Research had prepared a 569 page report entitled *Communism in the Free World*, which was declassified and released by the CIA only in the year 2007. This report included an analysis of the strength of the Communist Party of Indonesia (PKI) and the degree to which it had infiltrated labor unions, youth and women's groups, and government ministries. The United States was obviously concerned about the spread of Communism in Indonesia, and as the developments of the next few years would demonstrate, the CIA would become involved in serious efforts to undermine the Sukarno regime. One wonders if secret knowledge of the extent of the buried gold in the country was one motivating factor, especially as Sukarno was making noise about creating his own international bank.

But the United States did not have the ability to go around digging up buried treasure in the archipelago. Sukarno, however, did. A cache of Nazi and Japanese gold bars could be the jump-start that his economic plan needed. His dream of a Revolutionary Fund that would bring financial independence for Indonesia and for other Newly Emerging Forces in the non-aligned world could become a reality … if the Western powers and the Soviet Union let him live and the gold remain in his possession. But moving tons of gold around and getting cash in return is not as easy as one might think. Revealing the existence of the gold could cause serious repercussions in world financial markets. If enough gold was suddenly dumped on the banks the price of gold would plummet, and the value of the gold reserves of the United States and other countries would be cut dramatically, plunging the world into economic chaos. The gold would have to be handled discretely. It would have to remain hidden, and shares of the gold sold like government bonds. Some of the gold could be taken out of hiding and shipped to banks abroad for safe-keeping and as collateral for the certificates, but there would always be the problem that the banks could not be trusted and would in the end deny that the gold ever existed. As the world has seen in the past ten years, banks are not necessarily as safe as churches. In fact, even churches are not as safe as churches.

One of the ways in which Yamashita's gold was hidden and the money laundered in the post-war period was through the same channels that allowed Nazi war criminals to escape: the Church. The Roman Catholic Church was just as much a bulwark against Communism in Asia as it was in South America and Europe. The same facilities could be used to help Nazis escape to Asia as well as Nazi gold to make it safely through the system from its hiding places in the caves of the Philippines and Indonesia. One of the primary actors in the search for Yamashita's gold and Black Eagle gold was an agent who worked for the Vatican: Severino Garcia Diaz Santa Romana, known as "Santy." As the Seagraves reveal in their book,[105] Santy was a member of the fanatical Catholic military order Opus Dei (made famous in the Dan Brown novel, *The DaVinci Code*) in the Philippines. He was one of those (along with the CIA's Edward Lansdale, mentioned above) who tortured General Yamashita's former chauffeur in an effort to locate the 170 sites in the Philippines where gold was buried. The chauffeur gave up 12 of these.

---

105 Sterling and Peggy Seagrave, *Gold Warriors*, p.245–246.

During the war, Santy ran an underground network of clergy
and Catholic laypeople throughout the Philippines as a resistance
movement against the Japanese, taking note of which churches and
other buildings owned by the Church were being used as places
where gold was being hidden. The Philippines is a predominantly
Catholic country, so churches, convents, and monasteries are abundant and plentiful and make excellent hiding places for buried treasure, riddled as they are with secret passages, catacombs, and other
creative design features. While the story of Santy and the Black
Gold traffic is far beyond the scope of this book, let us take a leaf
from the Seagrave material and apply it to our case in Indonesia.

Both Doctor Sosro Husodo and Soeryo Goeritno were Catholics. Goeritno, in an interview for an Indonesian newspaper, admitted that he was Catholic (which may seem somewhat strange for
the son of a Sultan, but which is not so unusual in practice). During the mass violence that accompanied the overthrow of Sukarno
in 1965, the Catholic Church was a major player. As an opponent
of Communism, the Church took an active role in assisting the
anti-Sukarno forces, and Catholic priests were known to have been
present during some of the bloodletting that took place. Soeharto—
who organized the overthrow of Sukarno—had Catholic support
against the PKI. Thus, he trusted the Catholics as much or more
than the Indonesian Muslims—who could, at times, work against
his "New Order" policies. If this seems familiar, there is a reason
for it. The Catholic Church played an active role in the opposition to Communism in Europe since at least the 1930s through to
the collapse of the Soviet Union, often working side by side with
Nazis to do so. The Church's position remained the same, regardless
of where in the world it was located. The same was true in Latin
America, where the Church sided with the oligarchy against Communism and against any kind of people's revolutionary movement.
Juan Peron of Argentina was as dedicated a Catholic as he was a
fascist and anti-Communist. This is the same paradigm wherever
we find it.

Thus, it should come as no surprise that this cabal of Roman
Catholics, anti-Communists, and Indonesian military officers and
arms dealers would be interested in finding (and securing) Sukar-

no's Revolutionary Fund for themselves, and for their work against the forces that threatened their stability.

After the death of Sukarno, it was widely believed that he left instructions as to the disposition of the Revolutionary Fund with trusted advisers and not, as it turned out, with family. In addition to the instructions there were the actual gold certificates themselves. There have been many efforts by family members (and the Indonesian government) to gain access to the funds, but all to no avail. The line of succession is murky, but occasionally someone surfaces who has documents that seem to be genuine gold certificates: statements on official bank stationery, like stock certificates, giving details as to the ownership of millions of dollars' worth of gold deposits in Sukarno's name. The certificates have been virtually impossible to negotiate, for banks react immediately to their appearance by claiming they are fraudulent. They rarely claim that the certificates are forgeries: to do so would be to admit that such certificates exist in the first place, and that they cannot or will not do.

Instead the bearers of these certificates are routinely harrassed, threatened, arrested, imprisoned … or worse. As an example, according to one informant, a man who had one of these certificates and was attempting to broker it wound up dead in a hotel room in Singapore.

The certificates are quite unusual in design and execution, and seem to argue against being hoaxes by virtue of the fact that there are very clearly typographical errors that seem intentional. For instance, a certificate can be beautifully printed on heavy, embossed paper with a flurry of stamps and signatures—all perfect and verifiable—as well as account numbers and other details concerning the value of the certificate. Then, oddly after all of this work, the name of the beneficiary will be deliberately misspelled. Ironically, this is considered proof that the certificate is genuine. This is because a clever forger would not have made the mistake of misspelling the beneficiary's name. In order to guarantee the authenticity of the certificate, the name would be slightly misspelled as a kind of coding system, verifying that the certificate was genuine. It seems counter-intuitive but then the best cryptography often is.

If this sounds insane, it gets worse. Much worse. The world of international gold transfers and certificates is surreal and frought with danger and complexity. The amounts are simply staggering and the effect of negotiating them on the global money supply (even at ten cents on the dollar) would be enormous. Only those previously entrusted with the certificates are able to negotiate them; they cannot be brokered or sold to third parties, for if they are the banks will simply seize them and call the police. The certificate will vanish and no one will be the wiser, except for the innocent man or woman who naïvely tried to cash it in at their local branch and who now find themselves accused of all sorts of felonies.

That is not to say that fraud in the world of gold certificates is non-existent. The stories that swirl around Yamashita's gold, the Black Eagle Trust, and Sukarno's Gold have made it easy for confidence men to create phoney certificates and then "broker" them to unsuspecting customers for a small percentage (paid in advance, of course). So the actual market in gold certificates has created a fake market in gold certificates, thus allowing the banks to act as if every certificate is fake. It also enables district attorneys and federal prosecutors the leeway they need to arrest and prosecute both the known criminal and the genuine broker alike.

Thus, the safest approach to take is to ignore the gold certificates altogether and literally "go for the gold." According to one source,[106] some of the gold that was used to back Sukarno's Revolutionary Fund is buried on Irian Jaya (today's Papua) in Indonesia. Like the Roxas find in the Philippines, this is a cave system in the jungles with crates of gold and documents giving account numbers and quantities in meticulous lists. Papua is a remote and forbidding island, half of which belongs to Indonesia, and the other half which enjoys a certain degree of independence. It is a land of headhunters and pygmies, and it is an island where the Catholic Church is strong.

It is also the island visited by former SA and SS man Heinrich Harrer in the year 1962, two years after Doctor Sosro's visit to Doctor Pöch. How strange that these two Nazis could be found in the same country, at the same time, on the other side of the world ...

---

106 Mentioned by David Guyatt in his web-based series on *Secret Gold*.

and on an island where it was believed Nazi gold had been buried
… and at a time when Sukarno was arranging for that gold to be
the bedrock of his Revolutionary Fund. As we have seen, the mission of Harrer to Papua in 1962 is controversial, with experienced
anthropologists claiming that Harrer's visit had less to do with ethnography and exploration and more to do with a covert operation.

Was this one of the reasons why Soeryo Goeritno was obsessed
with Pöch, Sumbawa, and gold? Pöch lived on Sumbawa: an island
occupied by Japanese forces at the end of the war. Sumbawa is on
the way to Irian Jaya from Jakarta, as the crow flies, but the Pöchs
could have met Harrer in Surabaya which would have been more
convenient for Harrer. The close proximity of the two men in 1962
is almost too good to ignore, but alas we have no reliable information that they did meet at that time.

So what then of Sukarno, his gold, Sumbawa, and Soeryo
Goeritno? To address that let's go back to the beginning of this
chapter and our mysterious Dr. Damanik.

Dr Damanik claimed that he had been approached by a member or members of Sukarno's family who desired to negotiate the
gold certificates that were in their possession. This is the essential
problem: these are not bearer bonds or bank checks, or even personal checks. These are basically statements that such funds exist,
that they have the requisite account numbers, and that the banks
verify that these funds exist. In essence, the bank acts as a witness
to the existence of the gold or cash—and will act as a kind of intermediary in some future transaction that is covered by an arcane and
complex set of rules that were established at the time the accounts
themselves were established. Similar to the idea of a Swiss bank
account that can be numbered and anonymous, but accessed by a
person with the right codewords or code numbers, these documents
can only be negotiated by the people or agencies—commonly
referred to as "trustees" but sometimes, as in the Sukarno case, as
"gurus"—listed in the documentation attached to the certificates.

These gurus were not necessarily Sukarno family members.
Unless they were listed as trustees or gurus, family members would
not have access to the accounts, not even under laws of inheritance.
Dr. Damanik was not one of the assigned trustees; he was acting as

a middleman on behalf of the genuine trustees or "gurus" who could not negotiate the documents in their own country (Indonesia) for a variety of reasons, not all of them very clear. Dr. Damanik then went to the United States in an attempt to negotiate these instruments in good faith with the US Federal Reserve Bank, but instead wound up arrested and imprisoned for fraud.

There are two versions as to how he died. One version has it that he died in the United States after being released from prison. Another version is that he returned to Indonesia and died there. Whatever the truth of the matter, it seems that he had tried to enlist others in his attempt to have the certificates authenticated and then negotiated. One of these people was an Australian, Peter Johnston, who wound up imprisoned for fraud, even though he had not attempted to defraud anyone. He had merely stored one of the famous gold certificates with a bank for safe-keeping, only to discover that the bank manager had phoned the authorities because of his concern that the document was a forgery. While the bank never affirmed that it was a forgery, and Johnston had never attempted to move the certificate, he was nevertheless charged and convicted. Damanik and Johnston were accused of being accomplices in a massive scheme to defraud investors and banks, but it was never proven. As in the case of Damanik, the charges were inexplicably dropped with no explanation.

Another man who was not so lucky was Tommy Lee Buckley of Arizona, who took it upon himself to try to get the Damanik gold certificates authenticated and negotiated. To help finance his twenty-year mission he published a newsletter documenting his progress and promised his subscribers a percentage of the award if and when he was successful. It is important to know that he presented one of these certificates to the Federal Reserve Bank in Dallas in 1991; in other words, he was not attempting to defraud anyone, but was approaching the Fed to determine whether or not the certificate was genuine. He was arrested by the Secret Service at that time but soon released. He claimed that the certificates in his possession were worth trillions of US dollars, and that some had been made out to such world leaders as Saddam Hussein. The misspellings in the names of the leaders were taken as evidence that

Buckley had forged the documents himself, even though the rest of the certificates were pristine.

For some reason his twenty-year attempt to have the certificates authenticated—and raising money from newsletter subscribers to help him in this project—was considered a federal crime, and he was tried and convicted. He never went to prison, however, because he committed suicide before sentencing. That was in June of 2011, at the same time that Soeryo Goeritno was actively seeking access to the Pöch documents.

One problem with this entire story of gold certificates worth trillions of dollars is that the instruments themselves are unique. They are not normal banking instruments, but instead were created for a special purpose: to control the movement and ownership of large stores of gold and other valuables that would be held outside the standard banking channels and used only by and for a select group of insiders. The treasure had been stolen—by the Nazis, by the Japanese—and would not be returned to their rightful owners. In fact, as the gold had been melted down into solid bars and "biscuits," it would have been virtually impossible to determine provenance. The source for the treasure spanned nations and continents and eras. Paintings and sculptures could be identified and their rightful owners located; the gold and the jewelry were another matter. One can almost see the wheels turning in the brains of American, Indonesian, Filipino, and other military and political leaders as they gazed on the piles of shining wealth—deciding that these were the spoils of war, spoils that could be put to better use to prop up dictatorships, overthrow unfriendly regimes, and enrich a select group of insiders who had been blooded by war and revolution. In fact just such a situation existed in April, 1945 after the discovery of the Merkers Mine treasure in Germany.

According to official US Government reports, this enormous find included, "8,198 bars of gold bullion; 55 boxes of crated gold bullion; hundreds of bags of gold items; over 1,300 bags of gold Reichsmarks, British gold pounds, and French gold francs; 711 bags of American twenty-dollar gold pieces; hundreds of bags of gold and silver coins; hundreds of bags of foreign currency; 9 bags of valuable coins; 2,380 bags and 1,300 boxes of Reichsmarks (2.76

billion Reichsmarks); 20 silver bars; 40 bags containing silver bars; 63 boxes and 55 bags of silver plate; 1 bag containing six platinum bars; and 110 bags from various countries." It was understood at the time that the find confirmed, "previous intelligence reports and censorship intercepts indicating that the Germans were planning to use these foreign exchange assets, including works of art, as a means of perpetuating the Nazism and Nazi influence both in Germany and abroad."

Generals Dwight D. Eisenhower, Omar Bradley and George S. Patton met at the site to determine what to do with the hoard. Patton wanted information about the site kept secret and not communicated to the media. When asked why, Patton responded that they should bury the gold until such time as they needed to buy additional weapons once peacetime broke out and military budgets were reduced. [107]

If the ends justified the means, and it was permissible to assassinate political leaders in order to ensure that the "right" people were running the show, why would the theft of billions of dollars be any less acceptable?

In the early 1950s, before Sukarno conceived the idea of a Revolutionary Fund, he received the advice of former Nazi Reichsbank president Hjalmar Schacht. Schacht's close friend, as we have noted, was Otto Skorzeny, the man responsible for managing the Nazi underground—along with his friend Hans-Ulrich Rudel, another Nazi adventurer—and for running the illicit traffic in stolen treasure. Shortly thereafter, the idea of an "anti-bank" is created, an institution that would rival in power that of the World Bank and the IMF.[108] Sukarno, knowing that his huge extended family

---

107 This comes from the official US Government account of the find by Greg Bradsher, "Nazi Gold: The Merkers Mine Treasure," in *Prologue: Quarterly of the National Archives and Records Administration*, Spring 1999, vol. 31, no. 1. Patton died later that year, from complications due to a traffic accident in Germany that some have claimed had sinister elements implying an assassination.

108 One can see parallels between Sukarno's project and that of Joseph Smith, Jr., the founder of the Church of Jesus Christ of Latter Day Saints, who tried to set up a similar "anti-bank." See the author's *The Angel and the Sorcerer* (2012) for more details on this Mormon banking system.

would be unreliable where managing this vast treasure was concerned, appointed a small group of "gurus" to manage the Fund; but rumors of its existence began to circulate. In 1987, a former member of Sukarno's cabinet—his Foreign Minister—claimed he knew the location of the gold and of the accounts representing the gold. At the same time, a retired Brigadier-General, and deputy head of the country's most powerful political party, admitted that the Revolutionary Fund existed. Ten years later, the Indonesian attorney Edison Damanik—in his attempt to have some of these certificates authenticated and negotiated—was thrown into a US prison for his pains and died soon thereafter.

Recently, the Indonesian press reported an interview with Sukarno's most famous daughter, Rachmawati Sukarnoputri, concerning a news report in the Austrian newspaper *Kronen Zeitung* of December 17 and 19, 2012. The report claimed that efforts were being made by a Gustav Jobstmann to recover US $180 million from the Union Bank of Switzerland (UBS, the bank whose name pops up most regularly in these cases). This was in connection with a putative member of the Sukarno clan, a man named Seno Edy Soekanto, whose name figures prominently in the Sukarno Gold affair. But Ms Rachmawati claimed she had never heard of him, or of the treasure. However, she stipulated that if it did exist it was to be used for the Indonesian people ... a puzzling statement if she had no knowledge of the famous Revolutionary Fund.

In another statement—this time by an irritatingly anonymous source referenced by researcher David Guyatt—we discover the claim that Sukarno's gold was buried in caves in Irian Jaya (Papua today), as well as on "other islands" in the Indonesian archipelago. The "guru" in this case was a Filipino associate of the late President Sukarno who controlled access to the treasure. Damanik himself made the connection between Sukarno's gold and Ferdinand Marcos of the Philippines, as well as to Black Eagle gold from Nazi booty.

More smoke? More mirrors? There is so much documentation available on these cases—from hundreds of pages of signed and sealed bank statements, official-looking documents from government agencies, and the certificates themselves—that it seems the hoax (if such it is) is truly massive in scale, and yet with very little payback. No bank, no government, seems willing to verify the authenticity of these documents. If it is a hoax, then why? Who is being hoaxed and to what extent? And why would someone go to all the trouble of creating beautifully designed and printed bank certificates only to misspell the names of the beneficiaries in childish ways? And why are those in possession of these documents being sentenced to lengthy prison terms, far out of proportion to their "crimes"?

Soeryo Goeritno worked with Temasek to mine the gold on Sumbawa island. A few years later, Goeritno receives a summons from Moscow and is laid low by a stroke the following day. Was he a victim of what Sosro had called the agencies of foreign countries who would be all over him once his memoir was published? Was he another victim of Sukarno's Gold?

CHAPTER FIFTEEN

FOLLOW THE MONEY

(FROM THE TERRORIST ENTREPRENEUR
TO THE MUILTINATIONAL TERROR ORGANIZATION)

In the world of the asymmetric[109] actor perpetrating acts of ter-ror against a more organized enemy there are two distinct mani-festations: the terror cell, composed of several operators getting their instructions and their funding from a central command, and the lone wolf terrorist who has been indoctrinated and perhaps even trained by a central command but who is now operating solo behind enemy lines. Today, security officials in many countries are concerned about the rise of the lone wolf terrorist since they operate without discernible links to a larger, more visible, organization and are thus harder to identify and impossible to predict. As terrorism expert Jeffrey D. Simon reminds us, there have been lone wolf ter-ror attacks by both neo-Nazis and Islamist sympathizers in many countries around the world and the threat continues to grow.[110]

One could say there have been so-called "lone wolf" opera-tors in every country, every age. It is a term that is used with very little attempt at a clear definition. Any person operating alone and committing a political act—of terrorism or assassination—could be said to be a lone wolf. One wonders what difference there may be between a lone wolf and the "crazed lone assassin" of modern con-spiracy lore. What does the term "lone" really mean in this context?

---

109   Discussions on asymmetric warfare include Ekaterina Stepanova, *Terror-ism in Asymmetrical Conflict: Ideological and Structural Aspects*, Oxford University Press, 2008; and Ivan Arreguín-Toft, "How the Weak Win Wars: A Theory of Asymmetric Conflict", in *International Security*, Vol. 26, No. 1 (Summer 2001), pp. 93-128.
110   Jeffrey D. Simon, *Lone Wolf Terrorism: Understanding the Growing Threat*, New York: Prometheus, 2013.

When we write of a "crazed lone assassin" such as Lee Harvey Oswald was said to be, we imply that this is an independent actor with no affiliations, operating under his own steam and fueled by his own desires and motivations. Basically, not part of a group. The Mad Bomber who terrorized New York City in the 1930s was one of these; Ted Kaczynski, the Unabomber, was another.

A lone wolf, however, is a semi-autonomous operative acting under direction if not control by an outside agency. If the lone wolf were completely autonomous, he would not be considered a lone wolf but put into a category like that of the Unabomber. Instead, a lone wolf belongs to a specific ideology and has allegiance to a specific group, and undertakes his actions under what we may call a strategic umbrella: that is to say, the general, overall strategy of the group is known to him and he undertakes his actions in accordance with that general strategy. The tactical decisions are his alone.

That was the idea behind the creation of the Werewolf campaign at the end of World War Two, when the defeated Nazi military apparatus created cells of independent operators who were expected to wage a disorganized guerrilla campaign against the victorious Allies. These "lone wolves" were scattered throughout Austria and Germany and expected to cause as much havoc as possible. Nothing much came of the Werewolf campaign and it may have been designed to distract the Allied forces from what was really taking place: the expatriation of assets and personnel through the ratlines to countries outside of Allied control.

In the present era we now face a resurgence of the Werewolf concept in the phenomenon of the lone wolf terrorist. These are indoctrinated actors with (usually) limited resources, living "off the land" so to speak who carry out terrorist acts on their own initiative. They are usually tied back to a terror cell or training camp somewhere in the world which is where they received their training and their ideology. They are not in constant contact with superiors; there is no discernible chain of command. In this, they are no different from their Nazi ancestors and it is entirely possible that the Nazi Werewolf was the model for the current spate of Islamist "lone wolves."

Although lone wolf terrorism usually does not require access to large sums of cash and the secret means for moving it, the organizations that inspire the lone wolves do. There are logistical concerns to address as well as coordinated propaganda and recruiting efforts that are multi-national in scope. In the case of the Nazi Underground, there was no end of funding for operations ranging from assassinations and bombings in Europe and Latin America to the printing and disseminating of anti-Semitic and other racist literature, foreign travel for important functionaries (such as Skorzeny and Rudel), and the supply of weapons, explosives and other materiel. Most of these operations were well-coordinated attacks, and experts such as Stefano delle Chiaie and "Carlos the Jackal" were supplied with whatever they needed to carry out these attacks. Even the 1976 assassination of former Chilean ambassador Orlando Letelier and his assistant Ronni Moffitt was carried out in Washington, D.C. by an American agent of the Chilean secret police with assistance from anti-Castro Cubans recruited for the purpose: a well-planned and carefully-crafted plot that required access to substantial funds. (In fact, both Michael Vernon Townley—the American assassin—and Stefano delle Chiaie—the Italian terrorist responsible for several bombings in Germany and Italy, as well as attempted assassinations of political leaders—were employed by DINA, the Chilean secret service operating under the aegis of Operation Condor.)

The techniques required for funding terrorist activities are as arcane and byzantine as those for other illegal endeavors such as drug running and arms dealing. In fact, quite often the same methods are employed by drug dealers, Islamist terrorists, and the Nazi Underground and often make use of the same international monetary facilities.

The Initial Investments

The international terrorist phenomenon of the post-World War II era was jump-started by the smuggled gold coming out of Europe that had its origins with the Reichsbank and other financial institutions and organizations based in Nazi Germany—and its occupied territories (such as the Netherlands), and its "neutral" allies (such as Spain). Much of what we know today about the transfer of funds and other assets from the Third Reich to safe havens abroad comes from the research conducted by the "Gold Team" created by the Clinton Administration in the late 1990s. The findings are incredible even as they are frustratingly limited in scope.

For instance, we learn[111] that as late as March 1945 the Reichsbank—through the auspices of the Bank for International Settlements (BIS) under its American president Thomas McKittrick—transferred the incredible amount of 500,813.00 kilograms of fine gold for the account of the Bank of Brazil. Five hundred thousand kilos represents 1,100,000 pounds of gold. Each pound consists of sixteen ounces, making 17,600,000 ounces. Using a conservative value of around US $1,000.00 per ounce that means this single transaction would be worth today US $17,600,000,000.00 or an amount in excess of *seventeen billion US dollars*. Tantalizingly, that data was obtained from a declassified US government file dated May 15, 1945, in a box labeled "Vatican City (Correspondence File)." One can only imagine what the relationship was between this gold transfer to the Bank of Brazil and Vatican City.

That gold and other assets seized or owned by the Nazis made their way abroad where they would be out of reach of the Allies is not in dispute. The actual amounts are often debated and, of course, much of the relevant paperwork was either lost or destroyed or, in some cases, never existed in the first place. Considering for a moment that a substantial fortune did escape—and not only in tangible assets such as gold, jewelry and artworks, but also in the transfer of technology to friendly regimes, as well as the massive distribution of funds and expertise throughout the German industrial empire that extended throughout the world, survived the war, and was therefore considerably protected from any attempt by the Allies to confiscate it or control it—we must speculate on how that fortune was controlled, invested, disguised, and distributed.

---

111   Clinton Library, Working Draft, "Bank of International Settlements 1938–1948, Preliminary Report", May 16, 2000.

We have already seen that Nazi financiers such as Genoud and Schacht had their plans in place, and were active in moving among Nazi sympathizers in various countries and continents after the war. They were experts in setting up foreign banks, and in arranging wire transfers and other instruments, that would move money across international borders. Genoud was openly supporting anti-colonial regimes in North Africa as well as the Palestinian movement: support that was made possible by the Nazi gold he controlled in numbered Swiss accounts.

As the post-war years became the post-war decades, however, did that fortune dry up? How was the money invested? Who was managing it? Who was distributing it?

The Growth of an Industry

We know that Klaus Barbie, from his sanctuary in Bolivia, was involved in gun running and drug smuggling. These were excellent methods for creating vast fortunes in wealth—if you were already a seasoned military officer with no scruples and a strict personal code, who was capable of commanding a small army and enforcing obedience. Barbie—with his bizarre underground cadres of former Nazis known as the "Fiancés of Death"[112]—made a considerable fortune working for Operation Condor, a fortune that was invested in the ODESSA network. US military assistance to countries in Latin America that were fighting Communism, such as Argentina and Chile, took the form of financial support for anti-Communist (or simply anti-leftist) terrorist operations and assassinations. The money was laundered through the armies and intelligence agencies of those countries.

Considerable funds were laundered through Colonia Dignidad in Chile, as one example, and these funds were used to develop chemical and biological weapons, as well as to run the torture and interrogation center at the Colony after the overthrow of Allende. The Colony itself was part of both Operation Condor and

---

112 See the author's *Unholy Alliance*, New York: Continuum, 2002, pp. 303–308.

ODESSA. This is, by now, well documented by Chilean government investigations as well as by eyewitness testimony, and can be viewed on a number of documentary films that have come out in the past few years as Chile comes to grips with this scandal within their own borders.

By far the best source of funding for the post-war German renaissance came, of course, from German industry itself. Companies such as Thyssen had diversified their holdings worldwide in the years before the German defeat and managed to safeguard their assets with considerable American assistance. It is discouraging to learn that some of America's most influential businessmen and politicians were deeply involved with this effort, and in helping protect these assets from Allied attempts at securing reparations—and in divesting German industry of any assets that could be used to develop a war capability in the future. On the contrary, political and economic dynasties such as the Bush-Harriman-Walker nexus saw to it that American companies that were engaged in questionable, if not treasonous activities, during the war were protected and allowed to thrive. In order to do this, they also had to protect the German corporations which owned all, most, or a considerable percentage of the shares of the American companies. Most Americans are not aware that Standard Oil began its life as a German company, and that its most important board member was also a member of the *Freundeskreis Himmler*: Emil Helfferich. Or that the estimable Schroeder Bank was actually the bank owned and controlled by Baron Kurt von Schroeder, of the same *Freundeskreis Himmler*. The Union Banking Corporation (UBC) that was so crucial in moving funds for the Reich, and whose assets were seized by the US Government under the Trading with the Enemy Act, was actually a creation of the American firm Brown Brothers Harriman as a strategy for holding the shares of the Thyssen bank, Bank voor Handel en Scheepvaart, N.V. These were the corporations (along with Henry Ford, ITT, IBM, and so many others) that had backed Hitler from the earliest days. Just as the Nazis did not abandon their ideals with their military defeat, the American supporters did not abandon the Nazis.

As the Soviet Union began to crumble, some of the same personnel we first encountered during the Cold War began to focus their
attentions on a different enemy. Said Ramadan, who was instrumental in the operations of the Muslim Brotherhood in Europe,
became involved with the Al-Taqwa Bank of Switzerland. One of
the founders of Al-Taqwa was none other than the Swiss Nazi and
Islamist Ahmed Huber, who met with Muammar Gaddafi, Saddam
Hussein, the Ayatollah Khomeini, and many other Middle Eastern
despots. It should be remembered that Jörg Haider—the Austrian
politician and fascist we met in the opening of this book—had been
receiving financing from Gaddafi and Hussein as well. Thus, the
Nazi-Islamist networks were running as late as the year 2008, more
than sixty years after the end of World War II, and almost one hundred years since the idea of global jihad first occurred to the amateur
archaeologist Max von Oppenheim.

Some of the methods of earning and laundering money by the
Islamist groups were based on the same methods used by ODESSA.
The opium crops of Afghanistan are being used to finance terror
groups today just as the cocaine fields of Latin America were used
to help finance ODESSA through the Barbie operation. In fact, the
no-man's land that exists in a triangle of geography between Argentina, Paraguay and Brazil is a haven for drug-smugglers, human
traffickers, Nazis and their sympathizers, and Islamist groups.[113]
Thus some of the money that is used to finance Islamist terror organizations comes from the same region notorious as an underground
railroad for ODESSA.

As the Soviet Union fell, one of the banks that was used by
CIA to launder money during the infamous Iran-Contra operation, was the Bank of Credit and Commerce International (BCCI).
Set up by a Pakistani financier in the late 1960s, with considerable
investment by the Bank of America and the Sheikh of Abu Dhabi,
ownership of the bank by the 1980s was held by several prominent
Saudi intelligence officials, among others. Revelations of the bank's
involvement in criminal activities—as well as its acting as a conduit

---

113   See Rachel Ehrenfeld, *Funding Evil: How Terrorism is Financed—and
How to Stop It*, Chicago: Bonus Books, 2011, pp. 56–57.

for intelligence agency financing including the movement of funds during Iran-Contra—led to the bank's collapse in 1991, as several of its overseas offices and branches were raided and closed down, its assets liquidated. At its height, BCCI was the seventh largest bank in the world.

A similar financial institution was Nugan Hand Bank, founded by an Australian lawyer and a former US Green Beret. The bank had considerable intelligence connections, including what appeared to be large loans to CIA Director William Colby, among others. The bank seemed to function as a CIA conduit for much of its existence, like Castle Bank and Trust (registered in the Bahamas), that was used to fund anti-Castro operations from a base on Andros Island. Account holders at Castle Bank and Trust included the National-ist Chinese warlord Chiang Kai-Shek, as well as organized crime figures.

The Shadow Funds Transfer System

By far the most insidious form of international monetary transac-tion is known as *hawala* (Arabic for "transfer").[114] This is an efficient yet invisible system that requires little or no official paperwork and whose transactions are virtually untraceable by outsiders. Hawala "dealers," or *hawaladars,* can be official money-changer establish-ments or even jewelry shops or other neighborhood outlets that are known to the users through word of mouth, in areas where such transactions are illegal. One goes to the hawaladar in the United States (as an example) and passes an amount of cash to the hawala-dar, along with a code number or other identifier. In Pakistan, or

---

114 For an in-depth study of this system see the Interpol study, *The Hawala Alternative Remittance System and its Role in Money Laundering,* undated; and Edwina A. Thompson, "The Nexus of Drug Trafficking and Hawala in Afghani-stan" in United Nations Office on Drugs and Crime (UNODC) publication *Afghanistan's Drug Industry: Structure, Functioning, Dynamics, and Implications for Counter-Narcotics Policy,* Buddenberg and Byrd, editors, undated, pp. 155–188. In a related context, see Jean-Charles Brisard, "Terrorism Financing: Roots and trends of Saudi terrorism financing," Report prepared for the President of the Security Council, United Nations, New York, 2002.

another country where the same system is employed, a notice is given to the local hawaladar and the recipient merely shows up with the code number or other identifier to pick up the cash. This is similar to a common wire transfer except that there is no paper trail outside of the internal bookkeeping of the hawaladars themselves. Since there are often no banks involved, it is a difficult system to monitor and its transactions enjoy a great degree of anonymity. It is an ancient system of sending money around the world that has been in existence since medieval times, It has been used to finance drug, arms, intelligence, and terror operations in the last fifty years or longer. No money is actually transferred between hawaladars for each transaction—but the debt may be settled at the end of each accounting period, using different commodities such as gold, drugs, arms, electronics, or other valuables. It is an honor system, and employs familial, tribal, and other relationships to ensure efficiency. A small percentage is taken from each transaction, and it is usually much cheaper than using more conventional methods of sending money. Further, it operates well in areas—like Afghanistan—where conventional banking networks may be non-existent.

Since the hawala system has been around for centuries it cannot be considered solely in terms of terror financing or money laundering. Most hawala transactions are innocent and involve persons sending money home from abroad, or financing the purchase and sale of consumer goods, etc. across borders. However, the attraction of hawala for criminal and terror groups is undeniable, particularly where the drug trade is concerned. The biggest problem in running drugs is moving and laundering the enormous amounts of cash involved. It is estimated that a large percentage of hawala transactions in Afghanistan involves funds that were derived from the opium trade, which is that country's largest and most valuable export. Drug money is known to have been a major source of financing for the Taliban as well as for the Northern Alliance, and this funding has also made its way into Al-Qaeda's coffers.

In some cases, money that has wound up in regular bank accounts in the United States and elsewhere had its origins in the hawala system, which makes it virtually untraceable even when the money is deposited into a legal institution. Hawaladars can use formal wire transfer systems to send money, but they do so cognizant of local strictures. For instance, in order to avoid scrutiny by the US government, wire transfers may be broken up into several individual transfers, each less than US $10,000, and may be sent to different accounts in different countries before they wind up aggregated at the destination site. Some of the funding used to finance the 9/11 operation passed through accounts in the SunTrust Bank of Florida, for instance, and can be traced back only a step or two before the trail disappears.

While I have no evidence that ODESSA is using the hawala system, it is clear that its colleagues and partners do: from drug-running in the Argentina-Brazil-Paraguay triangle to arms dealing in North Africa and the Levant. It provides another level of security at a time when the movement of money comes under increasing scrutiny by the world's governments. The wire transfer system that relies on an extensive paper trail, incorporating a great deal of personal identification and verification at both ends is thus supplanted by a method where members of a specific community use an honor system to move money without official paper, and often even without actually moving the money itself. In a system such as this, "follow the money" becomes less a tactical process of investigation than a quaint memory of a simpler time. Nevertheless, the much-touted war on drugs (had it actually ever been undertaken in a serious way) would have revealed the extent of this and other financial methodologies. It would have traced such methods back to the initial funding of terrror by ODESSA since the 1950s—using gold that had been smuggled out of Europe—which then made its way around the world, propping up dictators and arming assassination and terror squads, long before "Islamist" and "jihad" became household terms.

As we have seen, Allied intelligence at the close of the Second World War was concerned about the Werewolf organization. There had been everything from vague rumors about its existence to open declarations by Goebbels and others. SS officer Ernst Kaltenbrunner was sent to the Salzburg region of Austria with specific instructions by Himmler to oversee the Werewolf operation. Several Nazis were apprehended by the Allies in the months after the war, and were found to be Werewolves who had been plotting terrorist acts against Allied positions. Their sole motivation and agency was determined by their own oaths of loyalty to the Führer and the commands they were given to continue the fight, even at the risk of their own lives. The deployment of lone wolf operators is cheap and deniable—much more cost-effective than the elaborate plots hatched in Central Asian caves or Southeast Asian apartment buildings—and much more secure. They also perform an important additional function: they tap the resources of Western intelligence agencies, forcing them to chase ghosts, while deeper and more dangerous operations are being planned, involving greater numbers of actors.

Modern terror organizations have learned much from the lessons provided by Nazi leaders, commandos and ideologues. In many cases, the terrorists of the 1980s and 1990s were trained directly by Nazi security personnel and SS officers, with whom they found common cause. As we have seen, not only did the Western intelligence agencies and politicians turn a blind eye to this phenomenon, in many cases they openly supported and encouraged its development. It is because we refused to take the Nazi threat seriously after the war (or because many of our leaders in the military, intelligence agencies, and at the highest levels of our governments welcomed the collaboration for their own agendas) that we now face the greatest threat to global security since the rise of the Third Reich.

CHAPTER SIXTEEN

HITLER'S LEGACY:
THE SKORZENY SYNDROME

Terrorism, the Skorzeny Syndrome, is flourishing in the
modern world, a reminder that Hitler and Nazism are still
taking their toll more than three decades after the Third Reich
collapsed.
  —Glenn B. Infield[115]

The above quotation is from Infield's biography of Otto
Skorzeny, published in 1981, and the facts are as true today
as they were then. Infield writes of the relationship that existed
between Skorzeny and Yassir Arafat, for instance, and reminds us
how Skorzeny advised the PLO and Al-Fatah from his base in
Cairo. Infield knew and interviewed Skorzeny, and his biography of
"Hitler's Commando" is relevant to any contemporary study of the
origins of modern terrorism.

What the world has been experiencing since at least 2001 and
certainly for years earlier than the attack on the World Trade Center and the Pentagon has been what analysts refer to as "asymmetrical warfare" conducted by "non-state actors." This is a technique that
was developed to perfection by Skorzeny and the other leaders of
what we have called ODESSA. The fact that the Western intelligence agencies turned a blind eye to Skorzeny's activities has contributed to our inability to confront and defeat what we have called
Islamist terrorism.

Arms dealing, covert international banking systems, targeted
assassinations, terror bombings, the "strategy of tension" as it
was described and defined by fascist terrorist Stefano della Chi-

---

115   Glenn B. Infield, *Skorzeny: Hitler's Commando*, New York: St. Martin's
Press, 1981, p. 238.

aie, already existed as part of an underground terror network long before al-Qaeda was born.

After World War II, the American people thought that Nazi Germany had been defeated and the "war" was over; this book demonstrates that it never was. Instead, we were told that Communism was the new threat and we had to pull out all the stops to prevent a Communist takeover of the country. And so our military and our intelligence agencies collaborated with surviving Nazis to go after Communists. We refused to pursue worldwide right wing terror groups and assassins. After all, they were killing Communists and leftists; they were doing us a service. Like Hoover and the Mafia, the CIA refused to believe a Nazi Underground existed—even as they collaborated with it (via the Gehlen Organization and the like).

The whole thrust of this book has been that American leaders in business, finance, media, and politics collaborated with Nazis before, during, and after the war. The West's share in the "blame" for Al-Qaeda, et al, goes back a long way—before Eisenhower—to a cabal of extremist US Army generals and émigré Eastern Europeans who didn't have much of a problem with Nazism since they feared Communism more. The Church, the Tibetans, the Japanese, the Germans, the Croatians—and the Americans—all felt that Communism was the greater danger, long before WW II. We enlisted war criminals to fight on our side. We appropriated the idea of global jihad from the Nazis and their WW I predecessors. We amped up their plan to weaponize religion and convinced Muslims, who hated each other, to band together to fight Communism. And when Afghanistan was liberated and the Soviet Union was defeated?

September 11, 2001.

Our cynical exploitation of religion has delivered a hideous stream of blowback that threatens the world still.

With the Nazi diaspora, the leaders of the Third Reich who had survived—who were either living underground, or were "denazified" and living freely above ground—constituted a government-in-exile. They remained in contact, reinforced each other's beliefs, provided logistical support where possible, and kept the faith alive.

They became involved in political and military intrigues around the globe, always with the goal of causing an imbalance in global power structures. Motivated by anti-Semitism, they collaborated with Arab leaders and guerrilla organizations in attacks against Israel, even going so far as to develop weapons systems in Egypt. They wrote propaganda against Israel and against Jews in general, repeating the same libels as before. They formed "neo-Nazi" groups in Europe, Latin America, North America, and elsewhere, cultivating a fawning new generation of followers on every continent. They support Holocaust deniers and right-wing extremists everywhere, even when they do not agree on all points. They found official positions within extremist governments in the Middle East and Latin America.

They also constitute an army-in-exile. They trained troops, instructed security forces in interrogation and torture, ran guns. They conspired to assassinate objectionable leaders in various countries, as well as those who betrayed their own network. They developed weapons of mass destruction long before the identical claim was laid at the door of Saddam Hussein.

They are "non-state actors" like Al-Qaeda, with the difference that they recently had a state. They conduct "asymmetric warfare" because they can no longer field battalions made of tanks and planes and submarines—and no longer really need to do so. Using terror as a weapon has proven to be far more effective.

They move money silently and unseen through the world's financial institutions. People like Schacht and Genoud wrote the book.

And they are loosely organized. Individual units possess a certain degree of deniability, something that newer terror groups have copied.

Al-Qaeda, Hamas, Hizbollah, Fatah, Jemaah Islamiyyah, Lashkar-e-Taiba, etc. are all children of ODESSA. The pact between Nazi anti-Semitism and Arab anti-Semitism was made with Hajj Amin al-Husseini all those years ago—and has been renewed every decade since—with refinements as necessary to reflect emerging political realities in the aftermath of the fall of the Soviet Union. Skorzeny, al-Husseini, Genoud: one big happy family.

Emboldened by the defeat of the Red Army in Afghanistan, aided and abetted by CIA, the militant forces of that remote yet deadly landscape turned their attention on the West. Repudiating Western decadence and liberalism, the Taliban enforced strict and even idiosyncratic interpretations of *syariah* law. Proponents of the Third Way, the Taliban were equally disgusted with Soviet atheism and Communism, and with American materialism and liberalism. Yet, they won the war against the Soviet invasion using asymmetric warfare. They were not able to field armored divisions, but had to wage a long and exhausting guerrilla war against helicopter gunships, tanks, and rockets.

Asymmetric warfare is usually defined as the conflict between two, dramatically unequal, forces. The war of the United States in Vietnam is given as one example, where the vastly superior (in terms of economy, numbers, and military strength) US forces fought the guerrilla forces represented by the Viet Cong, and the regular North Vietnamese forces represented by the Viet Minh. Often the Israeli-Palestinian conflict is given as another example, with the army and air force of the Israeli military opposed to the various guerrilla factions represented by the Palestinian Liberation Organization (PLO), plus those of Hamas and Hizbollah.

In most, if not all cases, of asymmetric warfare of the last hundred years or so, it has often been that of a powerful western country embroiled in a conflict with numerically and economically weaker non-state actors, which the current problem with Al-Qaeda and ISIL seems to represent. In these cases, the non-state actors are fighting for their own territory, language, ethnic identity, etc., often against a colonial or former colonial power, such as England, France, the Netherlands, Spain, etc.

There is one type of asymmetric warfare that is usually not recognized or included in studies of this phenomenon, however: it is when a powerful state loses its power yet continues to fight the forces that defeated it, using the same means as non-state actors— such as terrorism and assassination. There is to my knowledge only one such example in the modern world, and that is Nazi Germany.

As pointed out in studies of terrorism and asymmetric warfare, nationalist and ethno-nationalist groups are those most likely to engage in this type of protracted and violent conflict. That is not to say that leftist, "internationalist" groups do not, and have not, also been involved in asymmetric warfare; of course they have. The number of violent incidents involving leftist groups is actually larger than those perpetrated by nationalist groups; however the number of fatalities is substantially greater in those incidents perpetrated by the nationalists and ethno-nationalist, anti-colonial groups.

Nationalism is a hallmark of the type of terrorism we have come to experience in the post-World War Two period. It was actually given a form and an agenda by the Nazis who created the Werewolf concept: a stay-behind guerrilla force that would use asymmetric tactics to wage war against the Allies. This was an example of a state that refused to cease hostilities even after defeat.

Another type of asymmetric actor is the religious ideologue. As has been pointed out in studies of terrorism—especially since the events of September 11, 2001—this new type of adversary may not be identified with a single ethnicity or geographic territory. Even though the origins of the violent religious terrorist may be found in the post-colonial period, the nature of the conflict has changed considerably since then.

What many fail to realize is that the ideology of the Nazi Party— particularly as refined by the SS—was essentially a spiritual ideology. I have made the point elsewhere that the Nazi Party was a cult. To try to understand it as a purely political entity (in a modern, American context) is to make a grave mistake.

The Nazi network that was formed in the last days of the war and which has existed, in one form or another in the seventy years since then, is comprised of both a nationalist *and* a religious agenda. The Nazi Party has its origins in esoteric Aryanism, such as represented by the writings of Guido von List and Lanz von Liebenfels, as well as occultist groups such as the Armanenschaft, the Germanenorden, and the Thule Gesellschaft. These groups combined racist ideology with spiritual, mystical ideas and practices, some of which were adapted from more mainstream esoteric groups such as the Theosophical Society and the writings of its founder, Helena

Blavatsky. The Social Darwinism that is one of the hallmarks of the Nazi regime is the "outer court" of the spiritual Darwinism that is clearly elucidated in Blavatsky's works. What this means is that Nazism is just as much a spiritual philosophy as it is a political one.

Thus the basic components of the non-state actor in asymmetric warfare are present in the Nazi Underground (what we have been calling ODESSA). The terrorist acts perpetrated by this Underground are precisely those of the modern non-state actors with which we have all become familiar. The motivation for ODESSA runs parallel to that of "Islamist" terror organizations: a spiritual viewpoint that both organizations wish to impose on the world through the medium of terrorism, assassinations, and the like. Both ideologies are exclusive rather than inclusive; both are anti-Semitic; both are anti-American and deplore what they see as Western "decadence." (One could make a very good case that Hitler's objection to modern art, modern music and modern culture in general is virtually identical to the point of view of Islamist critics concerning the same.)

In addition—and this may be more important than it seems at first glance—many members of the SS and the Wehrmacht converted to Islam after the war, and found employment and residence in Muslim countries. In some cases, they actively supported Arab regimes in their opposition to the State of Israel by providing technical expertise, engineers, and training in interrogation, espionage, and related arts of war.

I believe this provides an important perspective into the current terrorist phenomenon, as it shows a continuity of purpose combined with tactical and operational methods that have their origin in the murky world of the first days of the Cold War—when a cynical manipulation of religion using non-state actors took place under the aegis of a decades-long and often poorly thought-out campaign of state-sponsored anti-Communism.

During the course of many years of research (from about 1968– present) into the origins of religious violence I have come into personal contact with both the PLO and Jemaah Islamiyyah (JI), as well as with North American racialist and white supremacist groups such as the National Renaissance Party (NRP) and the Ku Klux Klan (KKK) among others, as well as with the South American

Nazi sanctuary and nexus for Operation Condor, Colonia Dignidad in Chile. I lived in Malaysia for seven years, in an apartment that was only a few blocks from where the 9/11 attacks were originally discussed, and in Indonesia where I met Abu Bakr Ba'asyir, the architect of the Bali Bombings in 2002, and founder of JI.

I have also been on intimate terms with a number of conventional and non-conventional religious organizations spanning various forms of Judaism, Christianity and Islam as well as Buddhism, the religious of India, Afro-Caribbean religions, and modern so-called "New Age" movements such as Wicca, Satanism, and the secret societies of Western Europe and America. I believe it is this unique perspective on both religion and politics that informs my thesis that the choices we made as a country in the immediate post-war period have resulted in the current state of affairs where terrorism, "Islamism," and other forms of asymmetric conflict are concerned.

To quote Infield again:

> It has become evident during recent years that major wars in the nuclear age will be fewer than those in the past but individual and group terrorism will increase steadily. Skorzeny and his commandos during the Third Reich and Skorzeny and his ODESSA members during the postwar years were leaders in modern day terroristic tactics. Skorzeny's followers and students adhere to his teachings today.[116]

It was Skorzeny and his colleagues in ODESSA who, as early as 1950 and the outbreak of the Korean War, proposed forming a bloc of non-aligned nations in Asia, Africa, and Latin America to stand up to America and Russia: exactly the same position taken by Sukarno five years later. The position of the Islamist theoreticians of today is not dissimilar: the difference is that the Soviet Union has already fallen.

While China may develop into a threat, Uzbek and other activists in western China are creating another Muslim front with the intention of destabilizing that regime. Seen as both Communist

---

116 Infield, p. 237.

and Capitalist, China could be an interesting adversary for the Third Way position of contemporary Nazism. China is at least as nationalist as its former enemy, Japan.

As for Japan itself, it has recovered remarkably since the devastation of the Second World War and two atomic bombs. Japan and Germany are economic powerhouses. Even though Japan has been struggling in recent years, it is still one of the most prosperous nations in the world.

As for Germany, it has developed exactly as planned so long ago. It is reunited and the leader of the European Union, easily its most powerful and influential member. It is true that growing numbers of immigrants from Eastern Europe and especially Muslim immigrants from Turkey, the Balkans, and North Africa, are providing an environment where questions concerning German identity and responsibility are being raised. But as German cities have been rebuilt, industrial growth is strong, and memories of the war are fading with each new generation, it is doubtful whether any serious soul-searching will occur. With tensions rising in Europe over the fate of Ukraine and the Russian annexation of Crimea, it may be that the world will look to Germany again to provide the buffer between a newly-aroused Russia and the much more vulnerable nations of Eastern and Southern Europe.

It is doubtful whether the world will once again be confronted with jack-booted storm troopers wearing swastika armbands, singing the Horst Wessel song; but that does not mean that Nazism has disappeared. It has merely changed uniforms and moved to a different theater of operations. I do not wish to deprive the Islamic groups of agency in their present conflict with the West, but it is important to emphasize that they were as manipulated and exploited by the Germans in two World Wars as they had been by the colonial powers. The concept of global jihad was foreign to Islam until created by a German spy—of Jewish ancestry, no less—with a view towards using Muslims as proxy soldiers in Germany's fight with the Allied forces of England, France, and Russia. And when the Cold War began, they were manipulated once again: this time by American intelligence efforts to weaponize Islam against the Soviet Union. To continue the struggle against the Western world that was begun by Westerners themselves for motives that had nothing to do with

Islam or with genuine jihad is to cooperate in Western strategies that only will result in the destruction of more Muslim lives and the desolation of more Arab lands.

This is especially true with regards to Palestine. The Palestinians themselves must realize that no assistance is coming their way from the vastly wealthier and populous Arab world. The devastation of Gaza and the ongoing occupation of the West Bank is the legacy of decades of Arab indecision and manipulation. It is obviously far more beneficial to have the Palestinians live in squalor and die in refugee camps than to have the Arab nations work together to create a more productive solution. The Arab leaders have long since realized that the Nazi and Zen ideals of heroic death on the battlefield are dated notions, suicidal and non-productive, that can only end in annihilation. Yet they tolerate and even encourage the raging anti-Semitism of Hitler, Goebbels, and von Leers because it directs Palestinian anger towards Israel (and the United States), and away from the Arab leaders themselves who have found themselves in an increasingly vulnerable situation since the revolts of the Arab Spring.

Palestinian suicide bombers, however, have looked towards Hitler and Hajj Amin al-Husseini as avatars of the New Islam, of the desire to create a caliphate that will stretch from Jerusalem and Mecca all the way to Southeast Asia. To Kuala Lumpur, and Jakarta.

And, yes, even to Sumbawa.

We are still fighting World War One, and we will continue to fight it. We are redrawing the world map once again in lines of blood and steel. America should be at the forefront of the fight to end these conflicts, but our moral leadership has been called into question again and again. We made mistakes at the end of World War Two: we sided with the colonial powers when we should have made common cause with the indigenous peoples of the Middle East, Africa, and Asia who looked to us as their natural allies. We enlisted the aid of Nazis and Nazi war criminals to accelerate our space program and to field espionage agents against the Soviet Union. We allowed dedicated and committed anti-Semites with a history of violence and bloodshed against civilian populations to run freely in the developing nations, training torturers and assassins.

We acted out of fear; we co-opted our values, trading them for greater security.

This, too, is the Hitler Legacy. We thought we could control the Devil that was the Nazi Party and the SS, using them to protect ourselves against Russia. We used the strategies developed by the Germans in two world wars to coerce and cajole Muslim believers to declare a holy war—a holy war that would one day be aimed at *us*.

We lived up to the charges made against us by the Islamists— that we were without faith, bereft of spirituality, obsessed with materialism, cold enough to the summons of the soul that we could contemplate weaponizing religion: seeing it as just one more tool, one more element in our ever growing arsenal of destruction. We could urge Muslims and Buddhists to risk their lives in attacks against our enemies, willing to fight to the last drop of *their* blood, using their faith—and clumsy, awkward protestations of our own— as the motivation for deadly, violent action when we had no moral, no legitimate right at all, to demand this of them.

Is it any wonder, then, that the blowback was so severe, the hatred so concentrated?

The networks still exist, transforming softly from time to time, changing with every new political development on the world stage. There are names in the address book of ODESSA chief Hans-Ulrich Rudel of people who are still alive as this is being written: people scattered all over the world, devotees, true believers, carrying the torch in a virtual Nuremberg Rally, feeling more and more comfortable by the day.

New groups are being formed, new leaders chosen from among the faithful. Xenophobia is at an all-time high in Europe and increasingly in America. The Internet has provided new and improved means of communication. Arab systems of money transfer such as *hawala* are used to defeat the strictures of the international banking system, made more severe after the events of 2001. The hysteria we used to feel about secret Communists has been replaced by hysteria over terrorism. We lost our way, briefly, in the 1950s over Communism; and innocent people were ruined, reputations destroyed. Now again we are equally paranoid to the extent that TSA agents pat down the elderly and infants in strollers. We are increasingly made to disrobe before we can board a plane, and we are thankful because this means we will be safer.

But, if we want to, we can walk across the border into Canada or Mexico.

As the political life of every country becomes more and more polarized between "right" and "left," the men of ODESSA can only laugh at our discomfort. When the Berlin Wall came down many thought that the world had become a safer place. They did not realize that this was only phase one of the overall plan, the one that might have been hatched in Strasbourg in 1944 at the Maison Rouge Hotel. Or not. But it was the plan.

And when the Soviet Union fell, many patted themselves on the back thinking that history was at an end, that all serious conflict was over, except maybe for a little clean-up here and there. Nothing to worry about. Our side won.

Dream on.

On the sixth of June, 1948 Savitri Devi—the woman historian Nicholas Goodrick-Clarke called "Hitler's Priestess"—met the venerable old Swedish explorer Sven Hedin. Distraught over the destruction of the Reich and the executions at Nuremberg, she asked him:

"And I'd like to know, can we have any hope?"
He said, "Why do you say, 'Can we have any hope?' Do you have no hope?"
She then replied, "Those of Nuremberg, they have killed them."
Sven Hedin said, "Don't fear. Germany has more such men."
"Yes, but when will they appear?"
"They'll appear in time."
"What about the Führer? Is he dead or alive?"
"Whether he's dead or alive, he's eternal."[117]

---

117   Abridged from Savitri Devi, *And Time Rolls On: The Savitri Devi Interviews*, R.G. Fowler, editor. Counter-Currents Publishing, 2013, p. 54.

Appendices

Nazi Converts to Islam in Egypt

This is by no means a complete listing. Some of the names are quite well-known; most may be unfamiliar. Where possible a description of the individual is given to place him in context. This list originally was compiled by an Italian journalist, added to by various researchers, and widely disseminated in several languages.

Given Name	Islamic Name	Other Information
Hans Apeler	Salah Ghaffar	Egypt Ministry of Information
Gestapo Franz Bartel	el-Hussein	"
SS nfn Baumann		Instructor of PFLP
Erich Altern	Ali Bella	Gestapo; trained PLO
Walter Balmann	Ali ben Khader	
Fritz Bayerlein		former aide of Gen. Rommel
Gestapo Hans Becher		instructor of Egyptian police
Wilhelm Beissner		Gestapo
SS Bernhard Bender	Bashir ben Salah	advisor to Egyptian political police
SS Wilhelm Boerner	Ali Ben Kasher	Instructor of PFLP
SS Werner Birgel	el-Gamin	Ministry of Information
SS Wilhelm Boeckler	Abd el-Karim	
SS Alois Brunner	Ali Mohammed	Damascus, Syria
SS Friedrich Buble	Ben Amman	Public Relations Dept.
Franz Bünsch		Eichmann collaborator
SA Erich Bunzel		
Gestapo Joachim Daemling	Ibrahim Mustafa	Radio Cairo
SS Oskar Dirlewanger		Cairo since 1950
SS Dr. Hans Eisele		Buchenwald, died Cairo 1965
SS Wilhelm Farmbacher		Military advisor to Nasser

SS Eugen Fichberger		
SS Leopold Gleim	al-Nasher	Egypt State Security
Gruber nfn	Aradji	Advisor to Arab League
Baron von Harder		Former Goebbels assistant
Ludwig Heiden	al-Haj	Translator of Mein Kampf in Arabic
SS Heribert Heim		Doctor at Mauthausen, then Doctor of Egyptian police
Gestapo Franz Hithofer		
Ulrik Klaus	Muhammad Akbar	
SS Johann von Leers	Omar Amin	Anti-Israel Propaganda
Hitler Youth Karl Luder		War Ministry, Cairo
SS Rudolf Mildner		In Egypt since 1963
SS Alois Moser		Instructor of the Green Shirts, paramilitary youth group in Cairo
SS Oskar Münzel		Military advisor, Cairo
Gerd von Nimzek	Ben Alì	
Georges Oltramare		French collaborator, - broadcaster for the Voice of Cairo
Achim Dieter Pelschnik	el-Said	
SS Schmalstich		
SS Seipel	Imad Zuher	Security Service, Interior Ministry
Gestapo Heinrich Sellmann	Hasan Suleyman	Ministry of Information, Cairo
SS Albert Thiemann	Amman Qader	"
SS Erich Weinmann		advisor to police, Alexandria
SS Heinrich Willermann	Naim Fahum	
Ludwig Zind	Muhammad Saleh	

In addition to the above there were hundreds more who went to Egypt for various lengths of time and who did not convert.

LEE HARVEY OSWALD AND THE NAZIS

One of the curious aspects of the entire JFK assassination controversy is the presence in Lee Harvey Oswald's address book of several references to American Nazis as well as some rudimentary vocabulary in German.

We have already noted Oswald's possible presence in Indonesia during the attempted CIA-backed coup against Sukarno in 1958. We find from other sources that Oswald was still interested in Indonesia even after his return to the United States from the Soviet Union. So, Indonesia is somehow on Oswald's radar for whatever reason.

The German aspect, though, is equally inscrutable and perhaps it does not begin with the address book but considerably earlier.

As is well-known, after Oswald got out of the Marines he defected to Russia soon thereafter. What is not so well-known is the fact that he applied to a bizarre little college in Switzerland first. This was the Albert Schweitzer College located in the tiny village of Churwalden, in the Alps. At the time he applied, the village itself had only about 500 inhabitants and the local people had not even heard of the college.

Surprisingly, Oswald's application to the college and correspondence he received from the college on their stationery including the envelope recently went to auction and earned more than ten thousand dollars. (What these documents were doing in private hands and being auctioned off is anyone's guess, but it is borderline criminal considering the ongoing controversy in this case.)

In any event, it seems that the college was the dreamchild of a few Unitarians in the United States who were working for the US government in various capacities. This included Perceval Brundage, who was chief of the Bureau of the Budget under President Eisenhower. Incredibly, he was also on the board of Project HOPE, the program that sent the hospital ship of the same name to Indonesia in 1960 and from which Doctor Sosro Husodo disembarked to find our Doctor Pöch.

The college did not advertise and indeed only ever had as many as fifty students per semester, mostly by word-of-mouth. Yet, Oswald knew of the school and was so enthusiastic over this unknown college that he sent the sum of twenty-five dollars (a lot of money in 1959) to reserve his place for the April 1960 semester. Even more surprisingly, he was accepted without demur. Anyone having any experience in applying for college understands how strange this is, particularly considering Oswald had no academic record to speak of.

However he never made it to the school, instead winding up in Moscow when he was supposed to be in Switzerland studying German, among other things, and the rest is history.

Later, after the assassination, his address book was discovered to contain the contact information for a German teacher in Russia as well as some rudimentary German vocabulary. This indicates that as late as his defection to Moscow he was still interested in learning German. Why?

On another page is the entry that has conspiracy enthusiasts most interested. It is the address of the American Nazi Party in Hollis, Queens, New York and the name of Dan Burros (1937-1965) who was the aide to Party founder George Lincoln Rockwell.

Burros was secretly Jewish, and when news of his Jewish ancestry was made public he committed suicide, on Halloween, 1965 at the home of Roy Frankhouser in Reading, Pennsylvania.

Readers of my *Unholy Alliance* may remember that I knew Frankhouser personally and went to his Klan office and home in Reading where I was confronted by "Riot Roy" who placed a Luger on the table between us after unceremoniously kicking his mother down the stairs outside. I was met there by James Madole and his entourage, of the National Renaissance Party: the quasi-mystical Nazi organization that Madole headed and which had formed an alliance with the Ku Klux Klan.

Seeing the address of the American Nazi Party as well as the name of Dan Burros in Oswald's address book was something of a shock. How much more so to learn that Oswald's mother was being represented by none other than H. Keith Thompson.

Thompson (b. 1922) is a well-connected and well-placed figure in Nazi circles. Born in New Jersey he nevertheless became a member of the SD (*Sicherheitsdienst*) in 1941 due to his support of the German-American Bund and America First. The list of his contacts in the American, Latin American and European Right is extensive, from fascist theoretician Francis Parker Yockey to George Sylvester Viereck (a colleague of Aleister Crowley during the First World War when Crowley was involved in spying on the Germans) to Otto Skorzeny,

Hans-Ulrich Rudel, SS General Otto Remer, Cuba's President Batista, Nazi Germany's "Last President" Admiral Dönitz, and even James Madole of the National Renaissance Party whom Thompson investigated on behalf of ODESSA to determine whether or not the organization was reliable.

Thompson was registered as an agent of Otto Remer's Socialist Reich Party, and was also an agent for Johann von Leers's *Der Weg* at the time the periodical was being published by Leers in Argentina. He was also involved in providing weapons to Batista, and arranging funding for various extreme-right causes. His contacts in ODESSA were so extensive that there exists a substantial FBI file on him.

Therefore to find him representing Marguerite Oswald—the accused assassin's mother—was a little startling, to say the least. When asked by a researcher what he knew of the Kennedy assassination, Thompson actually pleaded the 5th amendment and would not comment.

Did Oswald have some connection, however tenuous, with Nazism either as a sympathizer or as a spy for some other agency, American or Soviet? What was his involvement in the proposed Indonesian coup of 1958? We know now that both President Eisenhower and John Foster Dulles—who created the ICA in 1955—were determined to oust Sukarno. We know that U2 overflights above Indonesia were gathering intelligence to facilitate an invasion, and that these flights would have been known to Oswald since most likely the flights would have originated from Atsugi Air Base in Japan where he was stationed. We also know that the dedicated anti-Communist and White Russian Georges de Mohrenschildt was working for ICA, possibly spying on Yugoslavia for the US government. Further, as a statement by Oswald acquaintance William K. Stuckey, dated November 24, 1963 reveals, Oswald was reading books about Indonesia and believed that "Sukarno was only an opportunist who was using the Communists, not a Communist himself." A remarkably prescient observation and one that matched exactly what an OSS agent had written years before.

Additionally, we have the testimony of Delphine Roberts who worked in the office of former FBI agent Guy Banister in New Orleans (the office associated with Oswald and his phony Fair Play for Cuba operation). A white supremacist and anti-Semite herself she knew Banister well, and claimed that he was a member of the American Nazi Party and got their material through the mail. In fact, according to a sworn statement dated February 20, 1968 before the New Orleans

District Attorney's office by former Banister investigator Jack S. Martin, Banister even arranged bail money for George Lincoln Rockwell when the latter was arrested for picketing the movie *Exodus*. Thus he was closer to Rockwell than we might have imagined. Did Oswald simply pick up this information around the office?

Even more suggestive is another name found in the Oswald address book, this time of Henry Warner Kloepfer. Kloepfer (1913–1982) was an important eugenicist and member of various societies devoted to genetics and a regular contributor to their publications. His wife Ruth admitted she knew the Oswalds and that she also knew Clay Shaw. In fact, in 1963 the Kloepfers were living in an apartment building in New Orleans owned by Clay Shaw. In the 1950s Kloepfer made several trips to Cuba and later to Mexico City, and his daughter visited Moscow in 1963.

The data on Thompson, Oswald, Burros, and Banister plus the mystery surrounding the Albert Schweitzer College in Churwarden, Switzerland (which never really recovered from being linked to the assassination and closed down a few years later) as well as the strange entries in the Oswald address book as usual raise more questions than answers, but the questions all seem to come from the same basic source: the presence of a racist, pro-Nazi element in the shadows of the Kennedy assassination. We know of the extensive right-wing opposition to Kennedy and the accusations that he was soft on Communism, had ruined the Bay of Pigs invasion against Cuba, and had cut too many deals with Russia. He and his brother, Robert F. Kennedy, had come down hard against extreme right-wing General Walker when he tried to start a riot over the forced integration of the University of Mississippi. Ads in Dallas that fateful day in November by other right wing extremists had called for Kennedy to be arrested for treason.

Could this possibly be another inheritance of the Hitler Legacy?

THE HANS-ULRICH RUDEL ADDRESS BOOK

Section One

Page One

(This is what appears to be a breakdown of payments to individuals and organizations.)

	60%	20%	20%	
Rodaz-Ortis[1]	360,000	120	120	= 600,000 $
(illegible)	-----	---	---	= ------
Sassen[2]	6,000,000	200	200	= 10 mill
(illegible)	180,000	60	60	= 300,000
Stroessner[3]	150,000			= 150,000 DM
(illegible)	120,000 40	40	= 200,000	
(illegible) Sosa	120,000	40	40	= 200,000
Dr Acosta	60,000	20	20	= 100,000 US
Roberto	-----	--	--	= ------
(illegible) Colorado[4]	-----	--	--	= ------
Gustavo[5]	2,100,000	700,000	700,000	= 3.5 M US
(illegible)	200,000	80	80	= 400,000[6]

---

1 A private school in Paraguay.
2 Willem Sassen, an ardent Dutch Nazi, SS member, and interviewer of Adolf Eichmann, among other claims to fame.
3 Either the Paraguayan President himself, or a member of his family.
4 Possibly refers to the Colorado Party of Paraguay, of which Alfredo Stroessner was its chief member.
5 Possibly Gustavo Stroessner, who was worth an estimated $100,000,000 at the time of his death.
6 This is obviously a calculation error for the sum adds up to 360,000 not 400,000.

This is followed by a paragraph in German which is illegible, and then four more entries, as follows:

Fabrico				5,000,000 DM (illegible)
Obregon	---
(illegible)	600,000	200,000	200,000	= 1,000,000 US
(illegible)	240,000	80,000	80,000	= 400,000 DM

The bottom of this page has a notation "Rudel"

Page Two

(Thus begins a straightforward address book. The handwriting is completely different from that to be found in the second section, implying that they were the property of two different people. The numbers to the far right are phone numbers, in some cases they are antiquated and reflect earlier exchanges for their respective cities.)

Gen. Bassfeld[7]	Ahernallee 10	4400 Munich	0251-316315
Brixmer (?) Kurt	5-6971 Gersheim	Wurzburg	
(illegible)		1 Berlin	8264330-06030
F. Brindner	5020 Salzburg	06153-2724 / 06222-21643	
(illegible)		8120 Bad Tolz	08041-25
Blumenhoff (?)	(illegible)		
(illegible)		Asuncion	
Bischof	-------		22869 60184
G. Behling (?)	4571 Wiernn	Odenburg	05431-669
H.E. Bob Richard	(illegible)	7800 Freiburg	0761-52999
Dr. Brodnick		Wien	315442 / 523581
Flughpt. H. Baur[8]	Neuw Widdersberg	38–8036 Hersching	

---

7 The maiden name of Ulrica Rudel (the wife of Hans-Ulrich Rudel) was Bassfeld. This is presumably a relation.
8 This is Hans Baur (1897–1993), best known as Hitler's pilot. He was an SS Gruppenführer and *Generalleutnant* of the Police, among his other titles. He was one of the last to leave the Berlin bunker in 1945, and was later captured by the Soviets and held in detention for ten years before being released, only to be

Annersee			08152-1279
Dr. Y. Block	Villa Ballester (Argentina ?)		768-5414
Dr. Norber (?) Burger			02641-354
Butz [9]	2214 Central St. Evanston, Illinois		312-869-9664
			Office 492-3269
(illegible) Sarmiento		Buenos Aires	464036-39
Bank (illegible)	(illegible)	Zurich	0501 2341111

Botschaft USA (USA Embassy) Boltzmanngasse 18-190 Wien (illegible)

PL 20222-315511

Botschaft Amman (? Asuncion) 26480-61801

Page Three

(Illegible) Peter		address in Graz	
Dr Ellertz Christian		8220 Traunstein[10]	0861-625627
(illegible)	address in Bonn, Germany		08022-8870
Dr Eicholz Herbert		address in Tegernsee[11]	
Leon Degrelle[12]	de Ramirez	address in Spain	4460273
(illegible)		address in Asuncion, Paraguay	
Dyckhoff (illegible)		address in Mexico DF	
(illegible)		address in Hamburg	040-3771
(illegible)	address in Sponheim, Germany		06758-64
Dinger, Friedel – Vzoni (?)		address illegible	
(illegible)		address in Innsbruck, Austria	
Dilger[13]	address in Xenia, Ohio 45385		513-372-1013

---

arrested by the French and imprisoned for two more years. He had a plan to fly Hitler out of Berlin and had a plane standing by, ready to evacuate him, but Hitler suggested he save himself and Martin Bormann that way. Hitler was the best man at Baur's wedding in 1935.

9 This is Arthur R. Butz, a professor of electrical engineering at Northwestern University who also wrote *The Hoax of the Twentieth Century*, a book denying the Holocaust took place.

10 A town in Bavaria

11 A town in Bavaria

12 This is the famous Belgian Nazi, Leon Degrelle, who was part of the Nazi underground with Rudel and Skorzeny.

13 This is Col. Robert Dilger, USAF (ret'd), a combat ace from Vietnam and colleague of Pierre Sprey, q.v.

Dangl Pozos 360   Buenos Aires   243-3579

Helmut Diwald[14]   Mittl Neuberweg 16a 8200 Wurzburg 0931-73695

Distribuidora Recin (?)   Av Erasmo (illegible) 2558 Rio Machado (Brazil)

Dharre[15]   Asuncion   46673

Dreckmann Willi[16]   an address in 4358 Haltern   02364-4105

Dyckerhoff-Widmann[17]   Posfach 810280 Munich   089-9255
                                                          priv 7931439

Dainz Max   Untere Heide 51-8721 Schwebheim[18] 09723-1561

Hanns Rudel[19]   Irminweg 5   852 Erlangen   09131-33435

Gen. Harlinghausen[20]   address in Gutersloh, Germany   05741-(illegible)

Hamann Ernesto[21]   20 de Junio   Bariloche, Argentina   540-22503

Dr Heft   address in Munich   4304368-670145

Hugo Hermann   Friedrichstrasse 77 Dusseldorf   0211-381334
                                                       Priv. 523650

Holzer (fnu)[22]   8205 Kiefersfelden   08033-8565

Hacker (?Hecker) Gabriele   an address in Munich   648051-3460

Helmsdel (?)   a phone number in Tokyo   045-62-6611-0456808?

---

14 This is the Wehrmacht veteran and WW II historian (1924–1993) who died in Wurzburg.

15 Possibly a reference to a family member of Richard Walther Darré, the Minister of Food under Hitler and advocate of the Blood and Soil philosophy of the Third Reich. Darré was born in Argentina.

16 This is a member of the Christian Democratic Union (CDU) in Germany, in this case in Haltern am See. The CDU was the party of Konrad Adenauer as well as Angela Merkel, and developed after the end of World War II. While considered a "center right" conservative party, it also attracted a number of Nazis and neo-Nazis to its ranks in the 1960s and 1970s. As late as 2013, Dreckmann was a harbor master at Haltern and member of the Sailing Club of Haltern-am-See.

17 Dyckerhoff and Widmann is a construction company in Germany that used concentration camp labor during the war.

18 This is a town in Bavaria whose famous castle was heavily bombed by the Allies during the war.

19 This is the only Rudel in this section of the book. The name Hanns argues against it being Hans-Ulrich Rudel, as "Hanns" is a familiar given name that would not be confused with Hans.

20 This is General Martin Harlinghausen (1902–1986), a highly-decorated Luftwaffe commander during the war who also served in the West German Luftwaffe from 1957–1961.

21 Ernesto Hamann (1914–2008), an employee in some capacity for the National Atomic Energy Commission (CNEA), Atomic Center of Bariloche, Argentina.

22 The only Holzers I have been able to find in this region—Oberaudorf, a suburb of Kiefersfelden—are tax consultants, Anton and Stephan Holzer.

Ilse Hess[23]	Gailenberg 22 Hindelang, Allgau	08324428
Kurt Huhn	a phone number in Wiesbaden	0611-672318
Heinz Hoffmann[24]	San Martin 1033 5000 Cordoba (Argentina)	33-7864
		Priv. 814864
Peter Hill	Waldseestrasse 42 403 Ratingen (Germany)	02102-17245
Lilian Holler (?)	Mayor Bullo 957 Asuncion (Paraguay)	21449
Dr. H. Hatzel	Kiefersfelden (Germany)	08033-8594
Walter Huss[25]	Spitzsteinweg 8201 Aising/Rosenheim	08031-67777
Krones[26]	Bad Wiessee (Germany)	08022-8761
Dr. (illegible)	an address in Vienna	524121/02252-7852
Kurt Kaschke	(illegible address)	
Kernbach[27]	Rochelle Park, NJ	201-845-6674
Frank Krause	Kornblumweg 44 Konstanz (Germany)	
Dimitri Kakabadse[28]	Box 2207 Quito, Ecuador	239079

---

23 This is Ilse Hess (1990–1995), widow of the infamous Hitler aide Rudolf Hess, at her home in Hindelang, Bavaria. Mrs Hess was a committed Nazi her entire life, and wrote for right-wing publications in Europe and corresponded regularly with a coterie of Nazi admirers.

24 This might be Major Karl Heinz Hoffmann (1912–1975), the former head of the Gestapo in Denmark who was expelled from that country after serving only a few years in prison, and settled in Koblenz, Germany, and who was also a witness in the trial of Adolf Eichmann. There is no indication, however, that Heinz Hoffmann ever lived in South America, so this is a mystery still. He is not to be confused with the East German general of the same name who built the Berlin Wall.

25 Possibly Walter Albert Huss who was a specialist in animal nutrition, and who had gone on an expedition to Southwest Africa with the anthropologist Dr. H. Walter in the late 1930s. Huss's war record is murky, but he did receive his doctorate at the University of Stuttgart in 1944 which indicates that even though he is considered a "war veteran" he was able to continue his research during the war.

26 This is the town and phone number for a Paul Krones and Elisabeth Krones. No further information is available.

27 This is Wilfried Kernbach, a White Supremacist and associate of Ben Klassen (author of many supremacist books and the originator of the term RaHoWa or "Racial Holy War") as well as of Dr. William L. Pierce of the National Alliance. It was Kernbach's "Friends of Germany" organization, based in Rochelle Park, New Jersey, that raised funds to sponsor a visit to the United States by Hans-Ulrich Rudel and Otto Skorzeny in 1972, and engaged in a campaign to free Rudolf Hess from Spandau Prison.

28 Most likely this is the same Dimitri Kakabadse who was an Ecuadorian government official as well as Rotary Club president of Ecuador (1964–1965). Members of the Kakabadse family had attended German schools in Ecuador in the twentieth century, and there was at least one Dimitri Kakabadse who was involved

Kenneth (?)			888759 885485
Alois Kohl	Roostr. 15	8 Munich (Germany)	653427
Lechner Kohl Gabriel (illegible)		8 Munich (Germany)	648051
Jurgen Krug[29]	Asuncion (Paraguay)		60386
Kurverwaltung[30] DTZ[31] Walch (?)	Salzburg (Austria)		0622
Wilfried Kulak		Asuncion	47152
Krankenhaus[32] Rosenheim		Rosenheim	08031-3451
Kanéque			priv 782-8619
			Office 46-8407
Kahler Hotel[33]	20 Second Ave SW Rochester, Minnesota		55901
			507-282581

This is the end of the first section of the address book. The second section begins alphabetically with "A" and is written in a different hand, as noted previously. The discrepancies include a totally different way of writing the numerals 1 and 4. The longhand script is much neater and clearer, and considerably tighter. This leads me to believe that these two sections are by two different authors. As the names in the second book include Hans-Ulrich Rudel and Otto Skorzeny, as well as a misspelled Sedlmaier, it is my contention that this second section does not belong to any of these individuals but may very well be Mengele's own address book or of someone close to all of these individuals. To clarify the listings, I have made parenthetical notations mostly to identify the countries where they are not so identified in the original text. Question marks are mine, and indicate places where the handwriting is illegible and where I have made a best guess. Not all entries have been identified, and these are generally left un-footnoted.

---

with a pro-German political party in Ecuador during World War II (but possibly as an infiltrator,and further identified only as of Byelorussian descent).
29 Possibly related to Alban Krug.
30 Kurverwaltung means "Spa Authorities."
31 DTZ is the acronym for *Deutsche Zentrale fuer Tourismus*, the German Tourism board.
32 *Krankenhaus* is German for "hospital."
33 Formerly the Kahler Grand Hotel, this is the nearest hotel to the famous Mayo Clinic in Rochester, Minnesota where it is known Hans-Ulrich Rudel went for treatment.

Section Two • Page One

Dr Acosta Romeo[34]	Asuncion (Paraguay)	41678, 44391
Altmann, K.[35]	Casilla 591, Cochabamba	
	Stawd. (?) Industrial 1993 La Paz (Bolivia)	
Azevedo, R.	Quintana 30 con 505, Rio de Janeiro (Brazil	24-0734
Anzorena	BA (Buenos Aires, Argentina)	841088, 466080, 453879
Sporthotel Achental[36]	Grassau, Mietenkamerstr.	08641-2014

Page Two

Clostermann, P.[37]	an address in Montesquieu	16 (68) 89614
	St Genie-des-Fontaines, France	
Curry[38]	PO Box 588, Columbus, Nebraska	2582 68601
	Office 402-564-7837, 564-1821	
Continental[39]	(Calle) Benjamin Constant	49176, 44132/43
	772 Asuncion Casilla Correo 934 (Paraguay)	
Caseres, Almada[40]	Asuncion (Paraguay)	41542

---

34 A Dr Romeo Acosta was Paraguay's UN Ambassador in 1947 who voted in favor of the State of Israel. It is not certain that this is the same man, of course.

35 This is Klaus Barbie, using his false identification as Klaus Altmann. The address is the same as that for Barbie. Barbie was extradited from Bolivia in 1983, thus this listing must predate 1983.

36 This is a "golf resort hotel" not far from Rosenheim, which seems to be a center for many of the names and addresses in the book, close as it is to the Tyrol.

37 This is Pierre Clostermann (1921–2006), a famous and highly-decorated WW II pilot for the French Air Force and during the Algerian war of the 1950s. He was also a Member of the French Parliament, and expressed admiration for the pilots of the Argentine Air Force who fought against the British in the Falkland Islands campaign of the 1970s. The address is in a small town on the French/Spanish border in the Pyrenees. He was born in Curitiba, Brazil.

38 This is William A. Curry (1947–2013), a Vietnam war veteran, Green Beret, paratrooper and member of the Special Operations Association. He moved to Asuncion, Paraguay in 2008 but returned to Columbus, Nebraska in 2013 and died shortly thereafter. Presumably, Curry came into contact with whoever owned this address book before his move to Paraguay in 2008 since the address book is considerably older than that. Thus, it could be speculated that whoever owned the book was in contact with Curry for decades before Curry's move to Asuncion, and that his move was due in part to this contact.

39 This is Banco Continental, in Asuncion, Paraguay.

40 This is Gladys Almada Caceres, a professor law in Asuncion.

Carrettoni, J.G.[41]	Calle Malabria 2966 Piso 13 Buenos Aires 2167 (Argentina)	49-2766, 45-5047/30
Cramer, H.[42]	5205 Lohmar (Germany)	02246-5283
Carvalho, Pais de[43]	(Rua) Paulo Cesar de Andrade 200-202 26-01 Laranjeiras, Rio de Janeiro (Brazil)	
Calvet[44] LAP	Asuncion (Paraguay)	91047
Dr. (illegible) Trey	8 München 60 (Germany) Paosastr. 2a	priv. 853698 8347003, 885264
Dr. Fratta[45]	Asuncion (Paraguay)	029117 Priv. 202724
Friseur[46]	Buenos Aires (Argentina) Esmeralda 923	328351 320790
Friseur Rienacker	82 Rosenheim (Germany)	33533/12424
Fritsch, Tom (?)	Salzburg (Austria)	419207
Fischer, Dr. Josef (?)	6365 Kirchberg/Tirol Bahnhofstr. I/270	05357-2277
Felder, Dr.	8255 Oberthufkirchen	1345
Fend, Ernst	(a telephone number in Munich)	089-2171-2150
G(illegible), Wilhelm	6338 Huttenberg	
Gartnerei Borg[47]	Steuffenberg	06406-3482
Gabler (Siemens)[48]	Erlangen (Germany)	71-74321
Giesbrecht, Helmut[49]	Cas. Correo 541 Filadelfia – Fernheim Chaco Paraguay	202308 201576, 200561

---

41 This is Jorge Carlos Carrettoni, Argentine politician who sits on numerous corporate boards.

42 This is H. Cramer Verlag, publisher of books on World War II.

43 This is possibly Gabriel Paes de Carvalho on Rua Paulo Cesar de Andrade, a Brazilian businessman with many German clients, especially in the 1960s and 1970s.

44 This is Raul Calvet, a famous Paraguayan Air Force pilot and later head of the Paraguayan national airline, Linea Area Paraguaya (LAP). He was a friend of Alfredo Stroessner, and rescued Nicaraguan dictator Somoza in 1979, flying him to Paraguay. Later, in 1987, his airline was discovered to have shipped 253 lbs of cocaine to Belgium leading to a general scandal and revealing the extent to which the drug trade had penetrated Paraguayan society.

45 Associated with the Hospital Centre del IPS, Asuncion, Paraguay.

46 This word means "hairdresser."

47 A *Gartnerei* is a nursery or garden market.

48 Siemens, of course, is the giant German electronics firm. Gabler is presumably the patronymic of a Siemens employee. No more is known about this person.

49 This is a prominent member of a Mennonite community in the Chaco area

Grolitsch, L.[50]	Strauchergasse 23	
	8020 Graz (Austria)	85128
Gollub, Gordon[51]	8 München (Germany)	089-295166
	Burkleinstr. 16	
Gross, Dr.	2 Hamburg 52 (Germany)	
	Liebermannstrasse 33	
Giesler, Prof.[52]	4 Dusseldorf (Germany)	624209
Gotz, Hannes	852 Erlangen	09131-23886
	(illegible address)	
Gisela	78 Freiburg (Germany)	71735
Giss, Dr. G.[53]	78 " St. Georgen	
	Brunnstubenstr. 46	
Gorring, Dr. H.J[54].	8213 Aschau	2288
	Engerndorferstr. 34	
Genoud[55]	Lausanne (Switzerland)	21-288043
		314659

---

of Paraguay. It is known that Stroessner, Mengele and Rudel traveled frequently in the region.

50 This is Lisbeth Grolitsch, born in 1922, a fanatic neo-Nazi and former Gau sub-leader of the League of German Girls, with a base at this address in Graz, Austria with her partner Herbert Schweiger, a former Untersturmfuhrer SS with the Liebstandarte Adolf Hitler, arrested several times in the 1990s for pro-Nazi activities. They were both close associates of dedicated Nazi and Wehrmacht Major General Otto Remer, himself arrrested for treason because of his outspoken Nazi views after the war.

51 Gordon Gollob (1912–1987) was a famous Luftwaffe ace during the war, born in Vienna. He was a committed Nazi and remained so until he died.

52 Hermann Giesler (1898–1987), a Nazi architect and with Albert Speer one of the two most famous and influential in the Third Reich. He supervised slave labor from the Muhldorf concentration camp, building weapons in underground factories as director of the OT-Einsatzgruppe for the Gaue of Bavaria and the Danube. He was sentenced to life imprisonment for war crimes, but in 1952 he was released and began writing his memoirs and pro-Nazi commentaries.

53 There is a Dr. Gerhard Giss at this address in Freiburg.

54 This is Hans-Joachim Göhring, an attorney who has defended Nazi clients in war crimes trials (such as former SS officer Kurt Franz, a deputy commander at Treblinka, in 1965).

55 This is Francois Genoud (1915–1996), a Swiss financier of the Nazi underground who was also involved in the arms trade and financed the legal defense of Klaus Barbie, Adolf Eichmann and others. He was also accused of being involved in the illegal shipments of Nazi "Black Eagle" gold and other assets out of Germany at the end of the war, and was a major contributor to Arab nationalist causes beginning with that of Emir Al-Husseini and continuing through to the PFLP

Gut, Jegros Edificio[56]	14 de Mayo 5, Py Soldado de Independencia Asuncion (Paraguay)	priv. 60568 bur. 45483 60129 / 64501
Hotel Palm Beach[57]	Las Palmas, Gran Canaria (Canary Islands)	9034-28-7629
Hentschel, Paula	4780 Lippstadt 6 (Germany) (street address illegible)	02941-6295
Major Hantel[58]		03452-2411
Hochtief[59]	(no address)	0201-20121
Humbert, Domingos[60]	Miami (Florida, USA)	6676674
Guttierres, Dr. Bestard	167C Gral. Genes (Asuncion?)	60568

(Popular Front for the Liberation of Palestine) and to Carlos, the assassin known as "the Jackal."

56 This enigmatic reference is to an office building in downtown Asuncion, the Edificio Yegros, about a block from the intersecion of Calle 14 de Mayo and Independencia. I have not been able to identify "Gut" either as a name or as an acronym.

57 Otto Skorzeny and Hans-Ulrich Rudel were known to frequent the Canary Islands during the post-war period.

58 This may be Otto Hantel, former Gestapo officer indicted for war crimes in Luxembourg and who was stationed for several years in Austria, at Innsbruck, where his wife's family lived during the war. The CIA had considered—as late as 1963—using him in some capacity, but according to declassified CIA files it was decided not to do so due to his war crimes indictment (it is not certain whether he was ever convicted) and his membership in the SS and the Gestapo. For several years he served in the "anti-Catholic" and "anti-Jewish" department. It is perhaps coincidental that as the war ended he was given false papers in the name of HENTSCHEL, which happens to be the name preceding his in the address book, and for which we have no further information. He was not a major, however, but the highest rank he attained was equivalent to that of second lieutenant; yet, his whereabouts after 1950 or so are unknown and he may have obtained employment with a military or police organization since his career until that time had been as criminal inspector.

59 The phone number for Hochtief is in Essen and is the number for a Dr. Hermann in the Haus Hochtief. Hochtief is Germany's largest construction company, and was responsible for building the Führerbunker in Berlin, as well as the Wolf's Lair and other Nazi construction projetcs, using slave labor from the camps. It was also responsible for moving the temples of Abu Simbel in Egypt, a massive and controversial undertaking designed to rescue the site from the flooding due to the Aswan Dam.

60 This may indicate President Stroessner's son-in-law, Humberto Dominguez Dibbs, living in one of Stroessner's apartment buildings in Miami. The phone number today is for a cell-phone provider's retail office on Bird Road in Miami and thus may be assumed not to be that of Humberto Dominguez Dibbs.

Gigena obligado	1260 Buenos Aires	783-2688
Geyer	Itzehoe (Germany) (illegible)	04821-3101[61] 74853
Guanes[62]	24002 priv. dienst. 43490 Supervisora: 461	
Gustavo[63]	200320/201 190 Asuncion (Paraguay)	
Kassier, Victor[64]	PO Box 272 Vyrheid 3100 Natal RSA (South Africa)	0381-3822 Bur. 0381-4588 priv.
Rudel, Inge[65]	8731 Aschach bei Bad Kissingen Burgweg (?) 142	09708-386
Just, G.	Postfach 1307 5912 Hilchenbach (Germany)	
Irving, David[66]	London(UK) 81 Duke Str.	00441-449409
Jurgens[67]	Chaco Borreal 247 Asuncion (Paraguay)	60386
Jung, Siemens[68]	München (Germany)	724-22093
Lammeyer[69]	Frankf(urt) Lyonerstr. 22 (Germany)	66770

---

61 Today this phone number belongs to a dentist in Itzehoe; however, there is an Egon Geyer in Itzehoe who is also a dentist.

62 Guanes is a common Paraguayan patronymic. Without further information no identification is possible at this time.

63 This is possibly Gustavo Stroessner, the President's son.

64 This is a South African of German descent who lived his whole life (1932–2009) in South Africa. He can be discovered on the My Heritage genealogical website where one learns that his idol was Hans-Ulrich Rudel. *http://www.myheritage.com/site-family-tree-141398351/otto-und-hanna-kassier.* (last accessed November 5, 2013) One wonders if that is the only reason Victor Kassier appears in this address book. Did Rudel—or whoever owned the book—consider anyone who liked them a suitable candidate for inclusion?

65 This is the first of many Rudels listed in the address book.

66 This, of course, is historian and indicted Holocaust denier David Irving, who has many contacts among the Nazi underground, including the widow of Walter Hewel, Francois Genoud, and many others.

67 There is not enough information to identify this listing. There is a Chaco Boreal street near Calle Dr Telmo Aquino in Asuncion, and this may be an office building.

68 This may be another reference to someone who works at Siemens, the German electronics giant.

69 There is no further information on this name. The address is now an auto parts

(illegible) Krauss, Naurus, Goepel[70]		08123797 8212261
Liebherr, Hans[71]	Biberach (Germany)	67351-411
Liesenfeld & Rhode[72]	Hamburg (Germany) Alsterstr. 21	priv. 803303 30121
Lang, Jochen[73]	(illegible address)	040-302645 priv. 4188
Luftwaffe Buenos Aires[74] Dr Cipka	Commando de Cefe Freiburg (Germany) Brunnstubenstr. 44	329170/32174
Leesemann, Siegfried[75]	Kassel (Germany)	0561-3122789
Lange, Horst[76]	5840 Schwerte 3 Westhofen (Germany)	02304-61423
Lutz[77]	Schliersee (Bavaria, Germany)	08026-4955/56
LAP[78]	(Frankfurt?)	0611-233751
Mario		41940, 41542, 62935
Morath, Dr. Werner[79]	4005 Meerbusch Steinacher 300	priv. 02159-7

---

and service shop in Frankfurt, Germany. There was a Ferdinand Lammeyer who was an artist in Germany during the war, but not much more is known about him.

70 This could be a law firm, but so far unidentified.

71 This is the founder of the Liebherr Group, a Swiss construction equipment consortium with global business based in Bulle, Switzerland and with their crane manufacturing operation based in Biberach, Germany.

72 This is Rohde and Liesenfeld, a shipping, transport and logistics company that was founded in Germany in 1933 and which now has operations worldwide.

73 This is probably Jochen von Lang (1925–2003), a well-known journalist and author who specialized in World War Two history and in biographical studies of Eichmann, Bormann and Baldur von Schirach.

74 Probably the Commander in Chief of the Argentine Air Force, not otherwise identified.

75 This is still the address of Siegfried (1917–2001) and Edith Leesemann, in Kassel on Elbeweg 6. No more is known about this couple.

76 There are many Horst Langes in Germany and at least forty in the Schwerte region, so without more information we cannot identify this gentleman further.

77 Without a first name we cannot be sure of this identification. Schliersee is a hotbed of neo-Nazi activity due to its long Freikorps history. The phone number today is that of a kite-flying club.

78 This is Linea Aerea Paraguayana, the Paraguayan national airline.

79 This is the father of Inge Morath (1923–2002), the famous Austrian-born photographer and wife of American playwright Arthur Miller. Her father, Werner, was a scientist who worked in Berlin specializing in wood chemistry.

Moritz, Vic. Lop.[80]	25 de Mayo 1/25 (Buenos Aires, Argentina)	797-4683
Maitecs (?)	Bailen 8, Barcelona (Spain)	
Muller, Alfred[81]	Engelschalkingerstr. 20 (Munich,Germany) 931885	
Machado[82]	priv. 246-7127, 452-4128, 222-1181	
Morgenstern[83]	Schrammstr. 3 (Schweinfurt, Germany?) 298065	
Marting, Heinz[84]	9100 Windhoek SWA (Namibia) 0026461-24769	
Muckner, Rudolf	Lüneburg (?) (Germany) (illegible)kamp 3	51426
Mattern[85]	Casilla 13294 El Mirador Vitacura (Santiago de Chile)	282815

---

80 Vicente Lopez is a district in Buenos Aires, and the address is that of the Secretaria de Inteligencia (SI), the intelligence service of the Argentine government. It is not known who Moritz may be, but the address is in the Federal District near the Casa Rosada (the presidential palace). The phone number is an older version; today phone numbers in Buenos Aires typically have eight digits.

81 This is the phone number for Alfred and Doris Muller, at Englschalkingerstr 203 (not 20) in Munich, with the later version of the number as 089931885. It is not known what the relationship is between the Mullers and the owner of the address book. It is possibly Alfred Muller (1915–1997), a general of the Wehrmacht who also served with the West German army in the 1950s. It is tempting to think it is Alfred Muller who had been the head of the Nazi Party in Argentina and who was a member of the German Embassy staff in Buenos Aires (who was briefly arrested by the Argentine government in 1940 when it was claimed that the Nazis had written a position paper on seizing Patagonia, among other Argentine assets). Unfortunately, not enough is known at this time of either of these persons to identify Alfred Muller in Munich as it is a very common name.

82 Impossible to know who this is, or where this person is located (country, city, etc).

83 It is not known who this is, but if the address is in Schweinfurt it is the headquarters of the government's Tax Office.

84 This is an address in what is today Namibia in Africa. "SWA" referred to its older designation as "South West Africa" also known then as "German South West Africa." The exchange 0026461 is correct for Windhoek. Heinz Marting had bought the house in Windhoek in 1950. Not more is known about him, save that he is of German descent and lived in the German colony there. He is possibly another admirer of Hans-Ulrich Rudel, like Victor Kassier (above).

85 This is Willibald Mattern, and the location is Santiago, Chile. Mattern went to Chile from Germany in the 1920s and in 1974 wrote a book about Nazi secret weapons and UFOs for the underground publisher Samisdat, run by Ernst Zundel (who also appears in this address book). Zundel would go on to publish works by Savitri Devi (the Greek woman who became a staunch pro-Nazi and supporter of Aryan mysticism, as well as a friend of Hans-Ulrich Rudel and other prominent Nazis).

Mayrhofer[86]	Kiefersfelden (Germany	08033-7484
Muller, H.	6305 Buseck (Germany) Welfenstr. 3	06408-7521
Mezger, Hans[87]	7071 Leinzell (Germany) Gmunder str. 2	priv. 07175-497 apothek: 07175-40
Morandin, Adolf[88]	7125 Neckarwestheim (Germany) (illegible street address)	07133-811
Medari, Hermann[89]	6650 Homburg-Saar (Germany) Kaiser str. 26	3564
Moll, Erna[90]	5270 Gummersbach 1 (Germany)	02261-220
E. Niermann[91]	C.C. 398 Buenos Aires (Argentina)	743-5861
Naumann[92]	588 Lüdenscheid (Germany) Brunscheiderstr 107, Erlenhof	02359-41216

---

86 This is Irmingard Mairhofer, at Kaiser Franz Josef Allee 15, 83088 Kiefersfelden, Germany.

87 This may be the same Hans Mezger who is a famous German automobile engineer and responsible for much of the Porsche technology. Porsche is based in Stuttgart, and Leinzell is a suburb of that city. However, the phone number marked "apotheks" would seem to indicate a drug store or apothecary, and I do not know how this would be related to anything having to do with Porsche's Hans Mezger.

88 There is a landscaper with this name in Neckarwestheim.

89 This is the address for a home for the mentally disabled. I do not know who Hermann Medari is.

90 Erna Moll wrote articles for the neo-Nazi publication *Recht und Wahrheit*, a magazine connected to Otto Ernst Remer and other post-war Nazi propagandists. It is the official publication of the Deutsche Freiheitsbewegung (DDF): the German Freedom Movement Association, whose honorary chairman is Otto Remer. The magazine is a compendium of anti-Semitism, Holocaust denial, and anti-American motifs and sentiments.

91 This is Capt. Ernst August Niermann, a fellow pilot of Hans-Ulrich Rudel, and one who used the Ratlines to escape to Argentina, first using documentation provided by Mgr. Krunoslav Draganovic and by the ICRC. He hid in Bozen (Bolsano) since 1946 and eventually applied for the exit papers in 1948 along with fellow pilot Werner Baumbach. Their applications were filed with the Argentine Commission in Genoa, the same Commission whose address appears in the Pöch address book. It should be noted that Pöch himself was hiding in Bozen from 1946, but mysteriously stayed in Italy until the end of 1953 (long after most others had already left, including Klaus Barbie).

92 This is Werner Naumann (1909–1982), a prominent Nazi in Goebbels's Ministry of Public Enlightenment and Propaganda, a member of the *Freundeskreis Himmler* (along with Schacht, Ernst Schäfer, Emil Helfferich, etc.) and one of the last to leave the Führerbunker in April of 1945. Naumann fled to Argentina after the war where he edited a neo-Nazi magazine, *Der Weg*. He was later

Nikolussi K.[93]	Sigmundskron Frangart (South Tyrol, Italy)	0471-31164
Nauroth, Holger[94]	54 Koblenz-Kesselheim (Germany) Kaiser Otto Str. 51A	0261-81103 / 87887
Ortner	Gunzenhausen (Germany)	09177-1098
Oie, Allikivi[95]	26 Deepdene Ave Bellevue, Adelaide 5050 Heights (Australia)	08276-5066
Oernest, Dr. H.[96]	Central Postoffice Pyramids Gizek (sic) poste restante (Egypt)	
Pereira Gral. Intendente[97]		90228
Priller, Dr, Friedrich[98]	München (Munich, Germany) Versailles Str. 17	
Polizer Präsident Gral. Britez[99]	Asuncion (Paraguay)	46795
Patscht[100]	Asu. Gust. (Asuncion?)	61701
Prasidencia Chile[101]	Com. Mabuc (Chile)	82320/8414

---

arrested (1953) for his involvement with a group of Nazi sympathizers (known as the "Naumann Circle") who were intent on infiltrating or overthrowing the West German government and replacing it with a Nazi regime. Naumann was an intimate of Skorzeny, Rudel, Degrelle, and British fascist and pro-Nazi Oswald Mosley.

93 This is Karl Nicolussi-Leck (1917–2008), a highly-decorated captain in the Waffen-SS who fled to South America but who returned to his native Tyrol in the early 1950s. (Sigmundskron is in the Bolzano area, a region favored by Nazi refugees during the war.) He became heavily involved in Tyrolean arts and culture and was responsible for founding several museums and institutes devoted to South Tyrol arts.

94 Holger Nauroth was the co-author of the monograph *The Defence of the Reich: Hitler's Night Fighter Planes and Pilots* and thus it can be presumed that he was a friend of Hans-Ulrich Rudel.

95 This is Oie and Boris Allikivi and the address of the Estonian Cultural Centre in Adelaide, Australia.

96 This is an intriguing listing for someone in Egypt, but it has not been possible to identify Dr Oernest.

97 This is General Pereira Porfirio Ruiz Diaz (1926–2012), a Paraguayan military commander and head of the Army Corps of Engineers who served as the Mayor (Intendente) of Asuncion, Paraguay from 1976–1989 under Stroessner. He was also, of course, a member of Stroessner's Colorado Party.

98 Priller was an officer of the Association of Reservists of the German Armed Forces.

99 This is General Alcibiades Britez, head of the national police under Stroessner.

100 No clue.

101 This is, of course, the office of the President of Chile who, at the time the

Platzer, Gretel[102]	Klagenfurt (Austria) Karawankenzeile 15	
Rudel, Oni[103]	Puiss (?)	0211-6211379
Rasmussen[104]	Asuncion (Paraguay) Nuestra Senora 766a	90617
Ratleg L.	6791 Steinwenden 2 (Germany) Feurstr. 10	06371-5753
Richberg[105]	3579 Schwarzenborn (Germany)	05686-535
Poltz, Hubert[106]	Salzburg (Austria) (illegible street address)	
Podlesnik	G. Marciceva 9 Maribor (Slovenia)	03062-25022
Prasidencia Baires[107]	(Buenos Aires, Argentina)	30-30-50
Potito, Dr.[108]	Box 412 Ocala, Florida (USA)	904-685-2173
Polysius[109]	Diehl priv. 3638	02525-711
Pertussi Aspersi[110]	Bue. Aires (Argentinaa) Condarco 765 Oficina 611-3628 / 611-762?	785-0415

---

address book was presumably written, was General Augusto Pinochet who took control of the country during the overthrow of Salvador Allende in 1973.

102 This is Margarethe ("Gretl") Platzer, the "first female master locksmith of Styria", employed by Anton Paar Co. with headquarters in Graz, Austria.

103 Another in the list of Rudels in the address book, this one with a phone number in Dusseldorf. The address and even the given name are illegible.

104 This is an interesting listing, for the address is that of the Danish and Greenland consulates in Asuncion, Paraguay and Rasmussen is Caruto Rasmussen Niedergesas, the Consul-General of Denmark and an important businessman in Paraguay with fingers in many pies.

105 This is Haus Richberg and for a time was the home address of West German neo-Nazi terrorist Manfred Roeder.

106 This is Hubert Pölz, a famous Luftwaffe Stuka pilot (like Rudel) who went missing in Spain in 1994.

107 Of course, this is a phone number for the office of the President of Argentina in Buenos Aires (Baires).

108 A Christian Identity minister who is referred to as "Doctor Potito" by his admirers, Oren F. Potito (1931–1995) published the white supremacist *National Christian News*.

109 This is a cement manufacturing company located in Beckum, Germany and which is now part of Thyssen-Krupp. "Diehl" however is a munitions manufacturing company.

110 A company called Aspersion Api (a manufacturer of irrigation equipment) is located at this address in Buenos Aires. It is a small, two-story building with

Rodaz-Ortiz[111]	(Paraguay)	43387
		priv. 290246
R. Queredo	San Isidro (Buenos Aires)	743-894
	Intendente Becco 209	
Ritter[112]	Rom (Rome, Italy)	
	Via Appia Nuova 572/0	
Rammner	Montevideo (Uruguay)	565069
	Camino Carrasco 4336	
Rummel[113]	Grabenstedt (Grabenstätt, Germany)	08661-240
Rauff[114]	Los Pozos 7243	264857
	Santiago (Chile)	
Reyter, Erich[115]	6638 Dillingen/Saar (Germany)	
	Am Voldeck 3	
Rudel, Christoph[116]	8204 Brannenburg (Germany)	08034-7655
	(illegible street address)	
Rudel, Paul	7744 Königsfeld 5 (Germany)	07720-33055
	Holzwiese 20	07725-3452
Rudel, Ursula[117]	4 Düsseldorf-Urdenbach	0211-717181
	Tübingerstr. 25 (Germany)	
Rudel, Martin	8671 Trosen b. Hof	09281-43370
	Kirchstr. 10 (Germany)	
Rudel, Wolfram[118]	2852 Bad Bederkesa (Germany)	
	Im Mühlenfeld 20	

---

a shop on the ground floor and an apartment upstairs. "Pertussi" is Ing. Alberto Pertusi, a Peronist and fanatic right-wing Argentine patriot.

111 This is the school Zoilo Rodaz-Ortiz in Paraguay. Nothing else is known about the school.

112 This is the address of the Italian-Slovak Chamber of Commerce.

113 This is the phone number and town for one Apollonia Rummel. Her significance at this time is unknown.

114 This, of course, is Walter Rauff (1906–1984), SS Standartenführer (Colonel) and inventor of the mobile gas van for extermination of prisoners by carbon monoxide fumes, the forerunner of the gas chambers used in the death camps. He lived out his days in Chile and was given a Nazi funeral by his friend Miguel Serrano (q.v.). A rabid anti-Semite, he followed Rommel's Afrika Korps to North Africa, rounding up Jews in the captured territories as he went. He later became another cog in the wheel of the Nazi underground and one of its most prominent leaders, protected by the Pinochet regime and acting as a consultant to Pinochet's government. Rauff—and Rudel—were frequent visitors to Colonia Dignidad.

115 There is an Erich Reiter in Dillingen/Saar who is a construction consultant.

116 Hans-Ulrich Rudel's son, Johann-Christoph Rudel.

117 This is Hans-Ulrich Rudel's wife.

118 While a Rudel, Wolfram (b. 1918) seems to have been involved with

Dr. Rischbieter G.	8972 Sonthofen Peter Dürfer Str. 7a	08321-2622
Riedl, Varig[119]	8 Munchen (Munich, Germany)	priv. 75381756 554901
Reichert, Hans[120]	Chicago, Ill 60646 (USA) North Caldwell Ave 6465	792-1816 792-1793
Rudel, Hans-Ulrich[121]	4 Düsseldorf-Urdenbach Gippinger Str. 12 (Germany)	0211-717527
Rudel, Siegfried[122]	5883 Kierspe (Germany) Waldheimstr. Tennispark 5277 Marienheide-Börlinghausen Dammen(?) Str. 21	02359-7373 02354-12290
Sage[123]	Cincinnati Ohio (USA)	4719989
Soll	ober: 05332-5382 unter: 5260	
Sims, E.H.[124]	Sarasota, Florida (USA) buro: 803 534 1110	8133662169
Siemens Baires	300411, 300421, 332122	

Jewish survivor issues and was in contact with the Association of Jewish Refugees. I believe this to be Hans-Ulrich's younger brother.

119 May be an associate working for Varig, the Brazilian national airline.

120 Hans Reichert (1920–2007) was born in Austria and seems to have come to the United States in 1955, spending 6 years in Rhode Island and then the last 46 years in Chicago. He owned a string of German-themed restaurants – the Linzer Hof and the Frankfort Hoffbrau Haus—as well as the Belmont Lounge. He was also a musician, and president of the North Side Chess Club. His friends, Jeannie and Vinnie DiFalco, own a jewelry manufacturer in Rhode Island and shared a vacation home with Reichert in Florida. His connection to the Nazi underground (if any) is unknown at this time. The DiFalcos have not answered my attempts to contact them.

121 Of course, this is Hans-Ulrich Rudel himself. His listing in this address book mitigates against it being his, for who writes his own name and address in his own address book, and alphabetically at that? Yet, there are so many Luftwaffe pilots and aviation specialists in this address book that there is a good chance it is, indeed, Rudel's.

122 This is Hans-Ulrich Rudel's partner in "Multisports Kierspe GmbH": a gym and sports sanctuary in this small German town. Siegfried Rudel is also the author of a number of books on sports (skiing), self-improvement and education including works on Rudolf Steiner's Anthroposophy and the Waldorf School.

123 I have not been able to identify this Cincinnati, Ohio listing.

124 I have not been able to identify this listing so far.

Straka[125]	Frankfurt (Germany)	76487
	Stephan Heise Str. 37	
Sedelmaeier[126]	(Germany)	08221-5419
Saum, U.	6831 Neulussheim (Germany)	06205-3536
	(illegible street address)	
Stahl, H.	236 Bad Segeberg (Germany)	
	Eutiner Str. 37a	
Spiess, Dr.		06171-72464
Steubel	München (Germany)	1413167
	Deggendorfer Str. 30 III	
Stroessner, Heinz[127]	Hof/Saale (Germany)	09281-91234
	Robert Koch 86.10	
Sturm, Wolfgang	6050 Offenbach-am-Main	0611-838818
	Taunusweg 38 (Germany)	
Sander, Ernst[128]	6660 Zweibrücken	
	Sundahlstr. 23	
Stroessner, Gustavo[129]	Asuncion (Paraguay)	

---

125 This is Ernst Straka, who now has a different address in Frankfurt but the same phone number (in updated form). It is not known what Straka's connection is to the owner of the address book.

126 This is an interesting listing, for it is that of Hans Sedlmaier, Josef Mengele's go-between. Sedlmaier worked for the Mengele family business all his life, and went frequently to South America to visit Josef Mengele, bringing letters, hard-to-get German delicacies, etc. His home was raided by the West German police on several occasions; on the last one, the police discovered a trove of Mengele *disjecta membra*: diaries, an address book, letters. The phone number here has a Gunzburg exchange, which is where the Mengele operation was located and where Sedlmaier lived. The problem with this listing is that the name Sedlmaier is misspelled. This implies (a) that it is not Sedlmaier's own address book and (b) most likely not Mengele's address book, for it could be assumed that Mengele would known how to spell the name of this most important person in his underground existence.

127 Evidently a relation of President Stroessner, for Stroessner's father was born in this town.

128 Possibly SS Mitglied Ernst Sander.

129 President Stroessner's eldest son (1945–2011), implicated in the financing of Operation Condor: the secret collaboration between South America's military dictatorships in the assassination of political enemies. Gustavo Stroessner was an air force colonel and also heavily involved in the cocaine trade between Paraguay and Europe, along with the Paraguayan national airline which was used to transport hundreds of kilos of cocaine to Belgium in one particular incident. However, the address given here is Asuncion, and the Stroessners fled Paraguay for Brazil in 1989, another indication that the address book cannot date much later than the mid-1980s (or about the time Barbie was extradited to France, and the time

Stimmersee Hotel[130]	Kufstein (Austria)	2756
Serrano, Miguel[131]	Santiago (Chile)	398871
Siemens Meier[132]	846573	722-25984/722-471
Stroessner (President)[133]	Asuncion (Paraguay) Telex no. 111 Py 6568	
Sassen, Wim[134]	Las Lomas 563 (Argentina) Buenos Aires Lomas de San Isidro	747-0994
Skorzeny[135]	Zurich (Switzerland) Madrid (Spain)	0501 211 8113 0034-1-261-3853
Strassenverkehrsamt[136]	Herr Lehnen v. Fassbänder Viersen (Germany)	02162-7241
Dr. Sachs		06173-1314
Saurer[137]	Rua Manapa 145 (Brazil?)	620932/370447
Slabbers W.[138]	4060 Viersen 12 (Germany)	02162-6355
Slabbers, W.	6380 St Johann Weitamweg 54 (Tirol, Austria)	05352-32472

Mengele's death in Brazil was reported and confirmed and Sedlmaier's home in Gunzburg raided).

130 Hans-Ulrich Rudel lived in this hotel for awhile ca. 1975.

131 Miguel Serrano was Chile's most famous Nazi. A former ambassador of Chile to Austria, Yugoslavia and India he was also friendly with C.G. Jung as well as Hermann Hesse. He believed Hitler to have been an Avatar of the Indian god Kalki who had come to cleanse the earth and usher in a New Age. It was Serrano who emceed the funeral for Nazi murderer Walter Rauff in Chile, and who praised Colonia Dignidad as a kind of Shambhala of the Andes. He was also one of the nodes in the Nazi underground and communicated regularly with fugitives such as Mengele, Barbie, Skorzeny and Rudel.

132 This is a phone number in Baden-Baden, Germany and may simply be that of another Siemens employee.

133 The private telex number for President Alfredo Stroessner in Asuncion.

134 The famous Dutch Nazi and member of the underground, Willem Sassen, who came to prominence due to his exclusive interview with Adolf Eichmann.

135 Of course, Otto Skorzeny, one of the leaders – with Rudel – of the Nazi underground, with his phone numbers in Madrid and Zurich.

136 The Motor Vehicle Bureau of the German town of Viersen.

137 Not certain what this indicates. The Saurer company of Switzerland – with branches in Germany and Austria—is a manufacturer of trucks and busses and most famously built the vans that were used—under Walter Rauff's direction—for the extermination of prisoners.

138 Undetermined. There is a car repair company in Viersen with this name. Viersen is also the location of the Motor Vehicle Department mentioned above.

Fr. Slabbers[139]	Viersen (Germany)` Toenisvorsterstr 75	02162-6391
Sitjar[140]	Casilla 1156 (Spain)	81340
Spray, Pierre[141]	Box 264 Rd 26 Glenndale, Maryland (USA)	20769
Schutz, Valdemar[142]	8201 Raubling Innstr. 40	08035-3016 08031-51643
Schulze-Kossens R.[143]	4 Düsseldorf (Germany) Karl-Müllerstr. 13A	
Schwedes	1 Berlin 19 (Germany) Eichkatzweg 19B	302-5409
Schüler	7 Stuttgart (Germany) Postfach 1370	0711-642031
Schneider, Hartwig M[144].	5180 Eschweiler Grobenstr. 48	02403-6940
Schirger, Alexander[145]	Mayo Clinic Rochester, Minnesota USA	507-288-2820 priv.
Schwarz, Dr. Andreas[146]	858 Bayreuth (Germany) Richthofenhöhe 11	0921-43279

---

139 These Slabbers are a bit of a mystery. They are concentrated in and around Viersen (except for the address in St Johann in the Tirol) and they all seem to be involved with cars. This address is for Wolfgang Viersen and his website is *www. autopartk-viersen.de*. Viersen is a town on the Netherlands border.

140 This is Rodrigo Diaz Sitjar, a right-wing author, who wrote that Jewish bankers "have made a pact with the devil" in a 1993 article entitled "The Invisible Government of the World" in the magazine *Más allá de la ciencia* ("Further than Science") which mixes Nazism and anti-Semitism with New Age topics such as UFOs and Egyptology, ancient aliens, etc.

141 This is Pierre Sprey, aircraft designer and defense analyst (and jazz record producer) who was one of the small team that created the F-16 and the A-10. Fluent in German, he interviewed Hans-Ulrich Rudel as part of his research concerning optimum design criteria for jet fighters.

142 A member of the Naumann Circle and a co-conspirator in the planned infiltration and eventual overthrow of the West German government, Schütz (1913–1999) was a member of the Waffen-SS and a number of Nazi support groups after the war. A journalist and publisher, he specialized in extreme-right publications.

143 This is an SS Obersturmbannführer, formerly an adjutant to Foreign Minister Joachim von Ribbentrop.

144 This is Margot Hartwig Schneider, an apothecary in Eschweiler.

145 Alexander Schirger (1925–2013) wrote for a review of metaphysics. The Mayo Clinic, however, is where Hans-Ulrich Rudel would go due to ongoing and chronic problems with his health.

146 Dr Andreas Schwarz organized SS reunions and was chairman of a veterans

Schrott, Rosa	Kufstein (Austria) Langkampfen Str.	44253
Tauffkirchen	8 München (Germany)	981525
Trenz, Friedrich[147]	1020 Wien (Austria) Ibbstr. 30/17	priv. 09131-4112 büro, 645511 priv. 2618154
Troger		priv. 09131-4112
Toliver, R.F.[148]	5286 Lindley Encino, Cal. (USA) 91316	(213) 343-4267
Tiefenthäler, Jakob[149]	8857 Wertingen Gottmannshofer, Eichenweg 12	0821-414903
Weinsheimer, H.[150]	5902 Netphen (illegible street address)	0471-2545?
Weise Martin	Pretoria (South Africa) Box 3219	012-762752
Walther & Co.[151]	Dellbrück	0221-67851
Wirz, Mench	Zürich (Switzerland)	0501-2341111 4721/234411
Weissteiner Tony[152]	39100 Bolen Oswaldstr. 55	040-471-24232
Weidmann	Rosenheim	12084
Winkelmann	Hotel Tyrol	0243-52-1211
Dr Weidenmann[153]	Prinz-Georg Str 102	0211 489 989
Wenzez H.	7410 Reutlingen Berliner Ring 104	
Wolf, Walter		03473-221

---

association for infantrymen.

147 Runs a Luftwaffe photo archive.

148 This is Raymond F. Toliver, World War II historian who has interviewed several Nazis.

149 A member of HIAG, this former SS officer was friendly with Generals Baur, Mohnke, Wolff and others and was involved in the Hitler Diaries hoax through his friend Gerd Heidermann of *Stern*.

150 This is Hans Weinsheimer, a printer.

151 A manufacturer of industrial plant equipment. Employer of Plano Zschernack, q.v.

152 Tony Weissteiner (1921–2012) was a member of the South Tyrol Veterans Association.

153 Possibly Klaus Weidenmann, involved with the Evangelical-Lutheran Church, based in Haan (a suburb of Düsseldorf where this address is found).

Wagner[154]	Rua Antonieta Reverado 462	
	Jardin Hipico St Amaro	
	Sa. P. 04725-2476883 (Sao Paulo, Brazil)	
Widmann Dietrich[155]	7821 Bd Krotlingen	07633-1447
	München (Germany)	08902-3867
Wölfel Wilhelm[156]	Asuncion (Paraguay)	61735
	Colegio de Goethe Espana 443	
	priv. A. Barrios 1245	
Winkler, Fred[157]		04242-26377
Wawke Joel	586 Iserlohn, Dortmunderstr 218	
	4502 Bad Rothenfelde	
Wenke[158]		
Ute Messner[159]	Kufstein-Eichelwang (Austria)	52965
Votter, Hermann & Erma	6365 Kirchberg (Tirol)	
	Sportplatzweg I/279	
Vasseur, Jacques & Johanna[160]	6900 Heidelberg (Germany)	
	Quinckestr. 46a	
Lisa de la Vega	3454 N. Lincoln Ave	472-1577
	Chicago (USA	
Vallemi Dr Nuñez[161]	(Paraguay?)	31912
		priv. 80620
Vasquez, Dr. Finanz		91756
Verdier Federico	Capital Federal 2P 1431	51-3630
	Treveris 2311	
Varic[162]		555206/554-901

---

154 This is the address of Helga (sometimes Hulda) and Georg Wilhelm Wagner (1890–1970?), in Sao Paulo, Brazil. Georg Wagner was a member of the Club Hipico since January 18, 1967 but seems to have died circa 1970. Thus, this would be the contact information for his widow.

155 An IT engineer for the firm Dyckerhoff-Widman (q.v.).

156 This is the Goethe School in Asuncion, a German-Paraguayan institution with which Wölfel is affiliated.

157 This address is at Bahnhofpl. 2A, 9500 Villach-Innere Stadt, and Winkler works with a group supporting war victims and the disabled.

158 Probably Walther Wenke (1900–1982), the youngest general in the Wehrmacht during World War II.

159 This is the daughter of Klaus Barbie. Her husband is Heinrich Messner.

160 Jacques Vasseur was a Nazi collaborator during the war.

161 Slightly confusing, as Vallemi is a town in Paraguay. It is likely that Dr Nuñez can be found there.

162 Possibly meant for Varig, the Brazilian national airline.

Versehrtensport	Karnten	04222-418373
	Tirol (Standingen)	05224-24162
Fendt		08254-3928
Claridge Hotel[163]	Tucuman 535	32-4001
	Bue Aires (Argentina)	
Clinique Le Prairie[164]	Clarens bei Montreux (Switzerland)	
Dr Ynsfran[165]	(Paraguay?)	20892/20895
Zschernak, Plano[166]	5068 Odenthal (Germany)	02202-7818
	In der Follmühle 11	
Zappenfeld, Edelvand(?)[167]	St Marys	623-1127
geb. Muckner	NSW 82 Marsden Rd, Australia	
Zauss Ernie[168]	180 Clare Ave	
	Boston Ma (USA)	
Zundel[169]	PO Box 111	32-0132
	Buffalo NY 14211 (USA)	
Pfeiffer	Habersalt (?)	0501-2231111
(illegible)		

---

163 A five star hotel in Buenos Aires.

164 An institution that specializes in cell therapy, it was created by Paul Niehans, a man with "pronounced Nazi sympathies" who treated – among other celebrities – Pope Pius XII (who died soon thereafter).

165 This is Paraguayan Minister of the Interior Edgar Ensfran, a friend of both Hans-Ulrich Rudel and Josef Mengele.

166 An inventor of safety equipment for industrial environments, he worked for Walther & Cie. (q.v.)

167 The full address includes 40 Loftus Crescent in this small Australian town. Zappenfeld was "geb. Muckner", meaning that Muckner is her maiden name. There is a Rudolf Muckner in the address book (q.v.) who lived in Germany,

168 Most likely Ernest Zaugg is intended: a Boston journalist who covered Vietnam, Algeria and other and who moved to Munich for awhile to run his own news agency, the Hometown Feature Agency. He was hardly a pro-Nazi, however, and was critical of Holocaust revisionists.

169 This is Ernst Zundel, the owner of Samisdat (a neo-Nazi publishing house), and intimate of Willibald Mattern (q.v.) as well as of members of the Nazi underground including Savitri Devi, Hans-Ulrich Rudel, and others. Zundel was based in Canada but used a Buffalo mail drop in the United States as well. He ran afoul of the Canadian authorities as a Holocaust denier.

TERROR TOURISM

This is an account I wrote shortly after my visit to the *pesantren* or religious boarding school in Solo, Indonesia where I met Abu Bakr Ba'asyir, the man who more than any other represents terrorism in Indonesia through his creation of Jemaah Islamiyyah, considered an Al-Qaeda affiliate by US intelligence. Shortly after this meeting he was arrested again and at the time of this writing is in prison.

For the most part, names of attendees have been redacted for their protection. Instead, I have identified their country of origin.

June 19, 2007
2:30 pm

Visit to Al-Mukmin Pesantren

The pesantren is about 20 minutes from our hotel by tour bus, and is close to the Hotel Indah Palace in Solo. We leave the hotel about 1:45 pm or so. The women are told to wear hijabs. We had been waiting for permission to visit the pesantren since we arrived in Solo two days ago. The arrangements were all through Yayah Khisbayah, who kept us abreast of the developing story ("Maybe this afternoon; maybe tomorrow"). She told us that we were going to meet **Abu Bakr Ba'asyir**. Most of those present (from the United States) had no idea who he was. As the writer had lived in Malaysia at the time of the Bali Bombings of October, 2002, he knew very well who he was and was intrigued by the possibility of actually meeting the man many insist was the architect of those bombings. A co-founder of terrorist group Jemaah Islamiyah, Abu Bakr Ba'asyir (or ABB as he was referred to by Yayah) is a notorious figure in terrorism studies. A staunch supporter of the concept of *hilafat* – revival of the Islamic Caliphate that extended from

Thailand through the Malay and Indonesian archipelago to the Philippines – he is an unapologetic anti-Semite and anti-westerner.

The Australians among our group refused to attend this meeting, due to their understandable reluctance to be in the same room as the man who inspired the murder of more than a hundred of their countrymen.

Our bus stops at the side of the road. We have to walk about 300 meters down a narrow, winding street to the pesantren, and arrive about 2:15 pm. We make a bizarre sight: mostly white men and women (the women in some form of headscarf) jauntily parading down the street to the religious boarding school whose most famous faculty member is ABB. As we turn a corner to face the entrance to the pesantren we are met by a horde of photographers (mostly still, but a few video cameras are also in evidence). They are furiously taking photos of everyone in our party.

We number perhaps thirty, or less. We are held up outside the school until someone appears to allow us in but only after informing us that the women must come in last and sit in the back of the room. Yayah is doing the translating and the negotiating. This is causing some heated reaction from the women in our group who see this as a form of discrimination. Odd, that these international peace-keepers were unfamiliar with traditional Muslim practice in a holy place.

Many are objecting to the presence of the photographers. Yayah is doing her best to get rid of them, but has only managed to get rid of the greater part of the crowd. Some photographers will stay behind as long as they can until they, too, are told to leave by the pesantren officials but not before we are all captured on film.

We are led into a classroom—women in the back, men in the front—where we wait for ABB to show up. We take photos ourselves of everything in sight, including each other. Time on our hands. A person sitting next to me is obviously dazzled by this event, and asks me, "Bashir is a simple man.

What do you think?" I respond that this is what I came to find out.

A kind of emcee shows up, dressed like a priest in a black tunic and sporting a wispy beard. He's maybe 5'5" and roughly 30 years old. He carries a microphone. Everyone stands as ABB arrives, at about 2:40 pm.

One of the students opens with *Assalaam aleikhoum* and a brief prayer. We are welcomed to the pesantren. (Yayah translates everything from here on to the end of the visit.)

The head of the school—**Usta Whahayuddin**—is introduced and describes ABB as the "supervisor" of the school. He then goes on to say that the pesantren is the oldest form of educational system in Indonesia. The three aspects of a pesantren are: teacher—compound—students.

There are three types of pesantren: traditional—modern—combination. This particular pesantren was established in 1972. Students at *al-Mukmin* come from different parts of Indonesia and include junior high school, high school, teachers' school, and higher education students as well as *madrassah*. The mission of the pesantren is to educate the next ulama "cadre".

We are briefly interrupted by the azzan, whose call to prayer comes over the loudspeaker.

Whahayuddin goes on to say "We educate them to be ulamat in their communities. The ideal is to establish a Muslim community ready to implement all the teachings of Islam, viz:

Pure monotheism
Ibadah (ultimate submission to God)
Sound morals
Physical soundness and health
Growth of knowledge
Independence (entrepreneurship)
Fighters in the way of Allah
Useful to the community and to themselves

We break for prayers. During the break, we wander around relatively unsupervised. The writer takes a few pictures of the classrooms, the compound itself, a jihadist poster, a cartoon mocking the US military, etc.

After prayers, we return to the classroom and ABB entertains questions from the audience.

The first question is from **Ms. ...** (from Malaysia):

"Why is Bashir accused as a terrorist? And why is this school so feared and accused if the purpose is to create a better person?"

A: (Bashir) "It was not the government of Indonesia who accused me of terrorism, but the USA and the Jews, and Singapore and Australia and the Indonesian government [sic]. I give the true teaching of Islam according to the Qur'an and the Sunnah to my students, and this teaching is feared by the Jews. I demand the implementation of Islamic law, but I can't be arrested for that. So they accused me of terrorism. The true teaching of Qur'an should be implemented by individuals and groups but also at the national level, but *hilafat* on the international level is feared by the Jews, Bush and Lee Kuan Yew. I was not proven to be involved in terrorist activity."

This sounded like a canned speech, something created by a lawyer. It was the only time ABB sounded as if he was reciting something from a script.

Q. (from **Ms. ...** Indonesia) "What is your opinion about implementation of *hilafat* if Indonesia is not an Islamic state?"

A. (Bashir) "All Muslims are required to live under *hilafat*. If it does not exist, Muslims should strive to accomplish it. It is forbidden to live in a country that is *kaffir*. So Muslims should leave the *kaffir* state. There are two duties for Muslims: *dawat* and *jihad*." (NB: *dawat* is an Arabic term meaning "proselytizing".)

Q. (**Ms. ...** American) "We are here as peacemakers. What

do you have to say regarding terror? What does religion have to offer for peacemakers?"

A. (Bashir) "Islam never forces non-believers to embrace Islam, only through preaching. If they accept peaceful coexistence then Islam will accept with one exception: that the kaffir allow Muslims to practice their religion. In Islam to live is not to become rich or reach higher position, but to live in accordance with religion.

"Terrorism is forbidden in Islam. The issue of terrorism was created by Bush to defeat Islam. Armed struggle—such as in Afghanistan, Iraq—and trying to destroy Islam from within—these are the two methods used to destroy Islam. The bombs in Indonesia are counter-terrorism, not terrorism. There is no terrorism in Indonesia. The youth who explode bombs in Indonesia were misled but they had good motivation. They should not have used bombs in Indonesia which is not a conflict area."

Q. (**Ms. ...** Philippines) "Do you believe in the future that people of different religions can live peacefully on earth, even Jews, Muslims, Hindus, etc.?"

A. (Bashir) "People from different religions can live peacefully so long as Muslims are given the right to implement their religion fully. So peaceful coexistence is possible only under the rule of Islam. Muslims cannot live fully under non-Muslim rule."

Q. (**Mr. ...** Indonesia) "What is the ideal Muslim government which can serve as a model? We have Islamic countries such as Saudi Arabia, Iran, etc. but their performance may not be Islamic. How do you mean to destroy Islam from within?"

A. (Bashir) "The ideal Islam is during the era of the Prophet. This is what we want to emulate, especially in justice, peace, moral dimensions. In terms of teaching, we must learn from others. There is no Islamic state; they are all secular, including Saudi Arabia, Malaysia, etc. Crime is higher in Indonesia than Malaysia due to the degree of Islamic teachings in those countries. In Indonesia, the teaching of Islam is not implemented. In the USA, crime is higher than in Saudi Arabia. We do not use economic indicators to determine if a country is successful or failed, but moral standards. Muslims should not use other indicators to decide what is a good state. Indonesia has failed because it uses outside standards and not Islam. Western countries will collapse because their morals declined.

"Regarding destruction of Islam from within, I think our judgment is the Qur'an and Sunnah, which teaches us about the Islamic state and about the life of Muhammed. If we exchange opinions in an honest way we can reach an agreement."

Then it was ABB's turn to ask some questions.

Q. (Bashir) "What do your governments tell you about Islam, since the USA and others are controlled by Jews?"

A. (**Ms. ...** US) "My government is secular and has nothing to say about Islam, only government issues and not religious issues. I hope you hear our point of view. I want us to live peacefully together, for a more just world."

Q. (Bashir) "Have you heard that your government asked the Indonesian government (during the Megawati administration) to send me to Guantanamo? What do you think about that?"

A. (**Mr. W. ...** US) "I am personally very upset with my government regarding the detainees at Guantanamo and the actions of our government in ignoring the Geneva Convention. We say Bush does not have a war on terror, but a war of terror."

(**Ms. ...** US) "Many Americans do not support the actions of our government. Peace through dialogue is more about listening than talking."

(**Mr. ...** US) "We have multiple voices in the USA, extreme voices for violence, for peace, moderate voices in between. We hope you can bring moderate voices from Islam to talk with us for social justice."

(Bashir) "Thank you very much for coming. I pray God

gives you strength to achieve peace in the world. For non-Muslims I ask you to learn about Islam and to embrace Islam so you will be saved. That is what the Prophet taught us. I hope and pray God gives you a nice and safe trip home. For Americans and Australians, please convince Bush and Howard to embrace Islam."

The last sentiment was greeted with laughter, as one might imagine. ABB then stood up and seemed to be waiting for a photo op but no one took him up on it. We made our way out of the pesantren and back up the road to the tour bus, after which we were taken to a batik factory! Terror tourism.

There was consternation at the batik factory as many of the conference attendees were noticeably upset—bordering on hysteria—as to the visit to the pesantren and began blaming Yayah for having put them in that position. Some members were afraid that they would incur problems in returning to their own countries, or that they would wind up on a watch list, or worse. They were frightened of photographs of the meeting appearing in Indonesian newspapers and television (which did, in fact, take place)[170] or, worse, in media in their own countries. The writer found this startling. These were people who made it their career and mission in life to go to conflict areas and try to arrange peaceful resolution, yet they were clearly disoriented by the visit to ABB's headquarters. The Australians who did not attend the meeting with ABB asked me if I thought it was safe to remain in Solo; I assured them that it was, that they were invited guests and that it was Islamic etiquette not to endanger guests. Nonetheless, the Australians contacted their embassy in Jakarta for advice, and were told that they had nothing to worry about from the Australian government, at least.

---

170 The visit was covered by at least five newspapers: *Berita Koran, Radar Solo, Kompas, Solopos,* and *Jawa Pos* (this includes two local Solo papers and three national papers, but not the English-language Indonesian press) and by three local television stations, including Metro TV.

The next morning was a virtual riot as several of the conference attendees openly confronted Yayah for having brought them to the pesantren. Of course, they had been told repeatedly in advance where they were going and whom they were going to see; Yayah assumed they understood the situation when, in fact, they did not. These were psychologists, so they spent the morning "processing" the visit and their emotional reactions to it. (Yayah later confessed to the writer her misery at the way the conference attendees attacked her over this issue. We spoke about it at length on the last day of the conference, at a dinner held at the Prambanan temple outside Yogya.)

The writer left Solo for Yogyakarta that day in order to attend to other business (he was still taking courses at CRCS) and missed the sessions of June 20, 2007.

A Real Odessa File

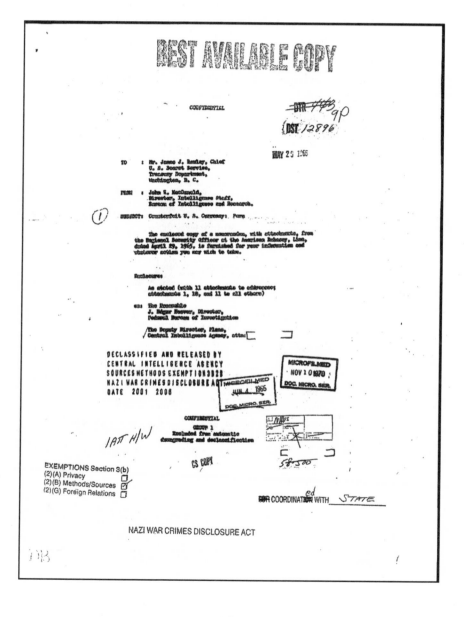

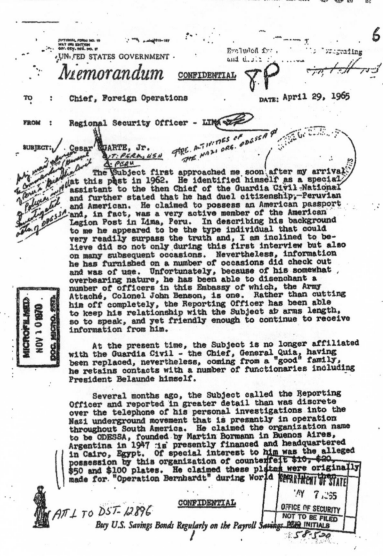

BEST AVAILABLE COPY

6

OPTIONAL FORM NO. 10
MAY 1962 EDITION
GSA. GEN. REG. NO. 27

UNITED STATES GOVERNMENT

Excluded from
and do...   ...grading

Memorandum   CONFIDENTIAL 8P

TO   : Chief, Foreign Operations   DATE: April 29, 1965

FROM : Regional Security Officer - LIMA

SUBJECT: Cesar UGARTE, Jr.   ARE ACTIVITIES OF
            CIT: PERU, USA   THE NAZI ORG. ODESSA
            & PERU

        The Subject first approached me soon after my arrival
at this post in 1962. He identified himself as a special
assistant to the then Chief of the Guardia Civil-National
and further stated that he had duel citizenship;-Peruvian
and American. He claimed to possess an American passport
and, in fact, was a very active member of the American
Legion Post in Lima, Peru. In describing his background
to me he appeared to be the type individual that could
very readily surpass the truth and, I am inclined to believe did so not only during this first interview but also
on many subsequent occasions. Nevertheless, information
he has furnished on a number of occasions did check out
and was of use. Unfortunately, because of his somewhat
overbearing nature, he has been able to disenchant a
number of officers in this Embassy of which, the Army
Attaché, Colonel John Benson, is one. Rather than cutting
him off completely, the Reporting Officer has been able
to keep his relationship with the Subject at arms length,
so to speak, and yet friendly enough to continue to receive
information from him.

        At the present time, the Subject is no longer affiliated
with the Guardia Civil - the Chief, General Quia, having
been replaced, nevertheless, coming from a "good" family,
he retains contacts with a number of functionaries including
President Belaunde himself.

        Several months ago, the Subject called the Reporting
Officer and reported in greater detail than was discrete
over the telephone of his personal investigations into the
Nazi underground movement that is presently in operation
throughout South America. He claimed the organization name
to be ODESSA, founded by Martin Bormann in Buenos Aires,
Argentina in 1947 is presently financed and headquartered
in Cairo, Egypt. Of special interest to him was the alleged
possession by this organization of counterfeit $10, $20,
$50 and $100 plates. He claimed these plates were originally
made for "Operation Bernhardt" during World War II by the

CONFIDENTIAL

ATTL TO DST- 12896

BEST AVAILABLE COPY

CONFIDENTIAL

headed by Federico Schwend who presently resides in Peru. Furthermore, he insists that Schwend is still an active NAZI as are several others which he named.

Attached is a statement he dictated to the RSO secretary and attachments. These documents, a copy of which has been forwarded to CAS-Lima, are forwarded to you for appropriate follow-up action if you deem it necessary. Treasury may be interested.

Incidentally, the Subject claimed to have been on the Los Angeles Police Force for a short period of time as well as having acted in Hollywood in one (or several) movies.

Attachments:

1. Statement of Cesar Ugarte, Jr.
2. Clipping "El Comercio" - Lima, Peru - April 12, 1965
3. Teletype news releases
4. Lima 13 (ANSA) News release
5. Aide Memoire - Press Conference
6. Letter from Dr. Teodoro Binder to Señor Dn. Marcelo Onganía, dated January 12, 1965
7. Letter from Mr. Roland Steinmetz to Senor Don José Antonio Encinas P., Director of "Expreso", undated.
8. Newspaper article "Correo" - Lima, Peru - January 16, 1965
9. Newspaper article "Correo" - Lima, Peru - January 17, 1965
10. Typewriten copy of random notes
11. Typewritten copy of random notes

LRColombo:rvc

2

STATEMENT OF CESAR UGARTE, JR.

From the time of my appointment as technical advisor
for Public Relations to the Commanding General of the
Guardia Civil y Policia of Peru in October 1961 - having
been appointed by the then President of Peru, Manuel Prado -
until my resignation on September 1, 1964, I received secret
telephone calls from a confidential source with whom, to
this writing, I have never had physical contact. My contact would get in touch with me by telephone whenever he
would have any information of importance either for the
Peruvian Government or the United States Government.

To the best of my knowledge, my source has never given
me any false information, thus, I have no reason to doubt
the information contained in this statement. I believe
that he is either Venezuelan, Cuban or Panamanian because
of his Spanish accent. By different tricks on my part I
have come to know that he speaks fluent German, English
and Italian. I strongly suspect that he is a member of
the German Secret Organization called ODESSA which was
established in 1947 in Buenos Aires by Hitler's former
secretary Martin Bormann.

Since the Fall of Peron's Regime ODESSA has found
refuge in Nasser's Government in Egypt and is reported to
have a total of 3,087 NAZI members in this organization
under the payroll of the Egyptian Government.

The first information I received that the ODESSA
Organization was backing up the Communists with money was
given to me at 7:03 PM on July 23, 1964. The information
was the following: Counterfeit plates made for Operation
Bernhardt during World War II which was headed by Federico
Schwend were at present in Sao Paulo, Brazil. These plates
are in the denomination of $10, $20, $50 and $100. My informant's information was that some high former NAZI war
criminal now under the payroll of the Egyptian Government
was due in Peru some time near the end of the year 1964.
This information proved correct when Johann von LEERS arrived in Peru on December 3, 1964 with an Egyptian passport
using the name of Omar Amin von LEERS under the pretext of
buying $100,000 of queer bills. Von Leers had an interview
with Federico Schwend at the United Arab Republic Embassy
in Miraflores, Lima, Peru at 8 PM December 4, 1964. On

3

BEST AVAILABLE COPY

- 4 -

December 9 von Leers left for Sao Paulo, Brazil and from there back to Cairo, Egypt. On January 28, 1965 my informant, during a pre-arranged telephone call, informed this writer that Lima was going to be flooded with queer US dollar bills sometime before July. This information was passed on to US Embassy officials on the same day it was received. Counterfeit bills did, in fact, appear in Lima. On April 6, at 7:22 PM I received a hurried telephone call from my informant quoting the following sentence: "Next port of entry Republic of France". I gathered from this that the Communists, with the help of the former German, von Leers, will introduce over a million dollars queer dollar bills in France. (NOTE: It is interesting to note that if this statement is true, it could play a part in the present French Government's policy of selling dollars for gold.)

The present head of ODESSA Organization in South America is Federico Schwend who entered Peru in 1947 with an Italian passport. At the present time this passport is in an Italian Embassy safe in Lima. Once Schwend was given a German passport by the German Embassy in Lima in 1948 he paid out the sum of S/4 million soles to certain Peruvian officials in power at the time.

(Lt. Colonel) Ben Salam, who in reality is (Sturmbann Fuehrer) Bernard Bender, former head of Special Service Commando in the Ukraine, is now head of Nassar's Political Department. The above named Subject is to make the necessary connections in France with the Communist Party to release US counterfeit monies. At present he is staying at the UAR Embassy.

Special courier, Otto Steft, Jr. of Austrian nationality, was formerly leader of the Hitler Youth Group and until 1961 was a purser for Canadian Pacific Airlines.

Richard Kohlweg is co-owner of Versailles, a combination dining and counter service located at Plaza San Martin, telephone number 82449, Lima, Peru. He is married to a Peruvian citizen who was formerly employed by the First National City Bank of New York, Lima, Peru. Her name is unknown to me at the present time. Kohlweg is suspected as being the Number 4 man in the ODESSA Organization in Peru whose duties are to help distribute counterfeit US bills.

The case of (Dr. Teodoro Binder who is also a member
of the ODESSA Organization and suspected as being its main
contact in the Peruvian jungle) was brought to light on
Thursday, January 1, 1965 at a conference whereby Dr.
Zuzunago Flórez defended Dr. Binder. To my knowledge,
Marcelo Ongania, at present Manager of ANSA, Italian
news agency in Peru, is the only newspaper man who has made
a full inquiry into the background of Dr. Binder. Attached herewith are teletype news releases from the above
named news agency and also a copy of the speech made by
Dr. Zuzunaga at the press conference. It is proven that
Dr. Binder entered Peru with a false passport along with
his wife. The following are the translated questions which
Ongania asked at the press conference:

1. Where is the letter of presentation written
   by a Miss Meyer addressed to a Miss Maria
   Luisa Giademeister?

2. Where does this Miss Meyer live now - what
   part of Germany?

3. Binder gave a talk on Vitbzche at the German
   Club and ended by giving a summary on German
   War criminals. At the press conference Binder
   claimed to have helped the United States Government capture three war criminals.

4. Which passport did he use when he came to Peru?

5. With which passport did his wife enter Peru?

6. Did he serve in the German Army?

7. Where did he stay in Brazil?

8. Why did he not medically operate?

9. Are you a friend of Hans Schaeffer? (Schaeffer
   at present lives behind the home of Federico
   Schwend at Kilometer 17 Central Highway in
   Santa Clara. Schaeffer's former address was
   Rue Roch, Paris, Gestapo Headquarters.)

10. Are you also a friend of Federico Schwend?

5

BEST AVAILABLE COPY

- 4 -

11. Who is Becker? (Becker for 9 months was Dr. Binder's personal guest at the former's hospital in Pucallpa, Peru.)

12. With what kind of documents did you live in Brazil?

13. What were your relationships with a Miss Colitim in a hospital in Hamburg. This woman claims that she knows you under the name of Ollendorfer.

According to Ongania's newspaper investigation, Dr. Binder was a member of the Hitler Youth Group, never studied to be a doctor and served in the German Army from 1941 to 1945 when said Subject escaped to Zurich, Switzerland,

Upon being given information that the next port of entry for the counterfeit US dollar bills will be the Republic of France, Lt. Col, Henry Dufour, French Military Attache, French Embassy, Lima, Peru left for the Island of Martinque to hold a conference with a high official of the French Military Intelligence. He left Lima, Peru on April 2, scheduled to arrive in Bogota, Colombia on April 9 and returning to Lima on April 13. Further information supplied by the undersign to Mr. Rode, Assistant to the French Attache in Lima is to be forwarded to Bogota, Colombia in time to be given to Colonel Dufour. This information will include: Approximate date of arrival in France of Lt. Colonel Ben Salam with Egyptian diplomatic passport. Salam is to make contact with the French Communist Party. It is reported that as yet, not confirmed, that he is to distribute with the help of the French Communist Party the sum of $2 million counterfeit US dollar bills, denomination of $10, $20, $50 and $100 which includes US travelers checks.

6

ATTACHMENT #10   RANDOM NOTES

ODESSA's latest planned escape was for HANS WALTER ZECH-NENNTWHICH, Ex-Capt. SS. This man was up for trail for the mass murder of 5,200 Polish Jews at PINSK. His escape to Egypt from BRUNSWICK PRISON.

ODESSA - its initials are for Organization DER ENEMALIGEN S. S. ANGEHORIGEN (organization of former members of the SS.

This Organization is also known as the "Spider's Web".

Head of ODESSA in Spain is former SS Colonel Otto "Scarface" SKORZENY of resc (?) Mussoline fame.

Of the 2,000 odd ex-members of Hitler's SS Gestapo & SD members list some of the most important on the wanted list and also active members of ODESSA: at present in Lima is OMAR AMIN VON LEERS who is Johann (or Jahannes) von Leers - has made contact with Federico Schwend for the buying of queer dollar bills. The amount to be bought will be that of the equivalent of $100,000 read monies. The price set is at 47 on the dollar - the plates made for "Operation Berhardt" of $10, $20, $50 and $100 are now in Sao Paulo, Brazil.

This queer monies are said to be sent to Cuba and then to find its way to the US. The $100,000 in this writing is being given by the Egyptian Government.

One of ODESSA's main contact here is Baron Von Sothen at present second to the German Ambassador in Peru. At present he is now in Rio de Janeiro apparently on a month's vacation with wife and children - it is known the Baron von Sothen is still an ardent NAZI.

My informant has told this writer that the one man who can give any clue of who has the plates now is Federico Schwend. Schwend has been seen coming out of the United Arab Embassy in Miraflores four times in the past six months - after von Leers left ODESSA's office in Buenos Aires; (after the Fall of Peron) Schwend has taken over as #1 as ODESSA's man in South America. I have not been able to find out under what name von leers is traveling under. He is due to return to Europe and the Far East via Brazil day after tomorrow. I have no reason what so ever to doubt my source of information for it has been proven XXX true in the past. I know not who he is for he gets in touch by phone at no given date only when he has vital information. I have been promised, if at all possible a queer bill.

BEST AVAILABLE COPY

DIR ~~443~~

DST *12896*

~~ATTACHMENT #11~~   RANDOM NOTES

Real names of seven top ODESSA members: 1) Louis El Haj is Louis Heiden known German newspaperman. Former head of the Reich German News Agency. Has recently translated Hitler's MEIN KAMPF into Arabic - has sold over 1,000,000 copies; 2) Lt. Col. Ben Salam is sturmbann Fuehrer Bernard Bender. Former head of Special Service Commando in the Ukraine. Wanted for war crimes. Is now head of Nassar's Political Department; 3) Omar Amin von Leers is Johann von Leers - is head of Nassar's Propaganda Department - is head of ODESSA in Cairo; 4) Lt. Col. Hamid Suleiman is S. S. (Gruppenleiter) Heinrich Sellman - former Chief of Gestapo in Ulm, Germany. Is now head of Egypt's Secret State Police Department. This Department is Nassar's equivalent of the NAZI S. S.; 5) Lt. Col. Naim Iahim is S. S. Hauptstabsarzt Heinrich Willerman - is wanted for sterlization experiments on Jewish Woman. He is now in charge of Samara Concentration camp in the Western Desert, 120 miles South of Cairo; 6) Col. Na'am El Nachar is S. S. (Standarten Fuehrer) Leopold Gleim. Was head of Gestapo in Poland. Is now head of the entire Secret Police in Egypt. Helped Nassar on his coup d'etat when he seized power; 7) Prof. Ben AMMAN is rocket scientist Wolfgang Pilz - is head of Nassar's secret Project 333 which makes atomic weapons.

Otto Semila is former officer of the German Army now working for Scimbet (Israel's Secret Service). Has given vital information of ODESSA's movements in South America.

ODESSA is responsible for the dealth of Eward Peters, Chancellor Ludwig Erhard's personal bodyguard. It is supposed that he hung himself instead of facing charges for war crimes.

Otto Steft Senior, was one of the officers that along with Fritz Knochlein murdered British soldiers of the Norfolk Regiment who surrended at hamlet of de Paradis. This crime is known as the "Paradis Massacre". Knochlein was tried by British Military Court in 1948, was sentenced to death. But Steft escaped. He is now messenger for ODESSA in South America. Has plates for American dollars. At present is in Brazil due to leave for Paraguay on December 8, 1964. Is rumored he killed Shimbet agent few months ago on the Peruvian-Brazilian border. Has been seen with Dr. Josef Mengele. Last time officially seen was at Rio de la Plata on April 18, 1962 in the company of Federico Schwend and Josef Mengele.

8

ACKNOWLEDGEMENTS

The list of people whose contribution—actual or virtual—to this endeavor is a long one, indeed. It is always possible that someone will be left out—inadvertently, to be sure—if only because this project took so many forms in so many different countries and under so many often trying circumstances that the process of creating the Acknowledgements section becomes an act of nostalgia for absent friends, lost time, alien spaces.

That said, pride of place must go to Yvonne Paglia, who financed the first trip to Singapore in expectation of obtaining an author contract and publishing a sequel to *Ratline*. How were any of us to know that this would turn into a struggle lasting six months? For her faith in the project, and in me, she must be acknowledged here.

To Jim Wasserman, for all the usual reasons and perhaps more so for this book!

To Prof. Sita Hidayah, whose understanding of Indonesian life and politics was so useful in providing a context for this endeavor. Indeed, it was Prof. Hidayah who first brought the Pöch story to my attention.

I'd also like to include my friend the filmmaker J. Lyle Skosey, whose serendipitous meeting with a woman who actually recognized the name of Hella Pöch and who had documents to that effect was a bizarre and startling development that took place as the book was nearing completion but which wound up corroborating the Testament and much else besides.

Katarina Matiasek was a great help in providing some additional background material on Georg Anton and Hella Pöch, for which I am truly grateful.

Claudia Kunin, for graciously allowing me to reproduce the "Wanted" poster in this book.

I want to thank Pierre Sprey, now in the music business, for his reminiscences about Hans-Ulrich Rudel and the conversations he had with the ace fighter pilot.

Ian Punnett of Coast-to-Coast AM: he has been unfailingly polite and supportive in giving me a broadcast forum from time to time to update listeners on my various projects. He has a knack for interviewing and asking intelligent, probing questions and he actually reads the books whose authors he interviews! A rare and wonderful contributor to a medium often hijacked by hysterical monomaniacs.

I want to thank Chandriana, the daughter of Dr. Sosro Husodo, for a brief phone conversation in the spring of 2013 in which she confirmed the high strangeness around her father, government officials, and mysterious persons from Germany who wanted to pay millions of dollars for the Pöch documents back in the 1980s.

Thanks also go to my friends at a hotel lounge bar in Singapore that is not to be named, to protect the guilty as well as the innocent, but I must mention the indefatigable Irene Marie Lin—the "godmother"—who kept her sense of humor during long hours and days and weeks of investigation. She and all the regulars were a welcome antidote to what was at times a poisonous miasma surrounding the material in this book.

I also wish to show gratitude to all those Muslims I have met in the course of the past decades, in Asia and Europe and elsewhere. They are shining examples of how Islam is lived in beauty and in peace. اقح نتمم انأ

One also wants to thank—last but certainly not least—one's family, and one's friends, for their patience and understanding during this overly-long and arduous undertaking. I was away from home for many months at a time, during which no one knew if I was dead or alive. Even now, they are not entirely convinced of either condition!

Sources and Bibliography

The primary source material supporting the contentions made in this book come from declassified American (and some British) intelligence files as well as US Government publications where noted in the text. In addition, the address book of Hans-Ulrich Rudel proved to be invaluable as a guide to the Nazi Underground as it existed up to the time of his death in 1982. I was also fortunate to have access to the "wanted poster" for the Pöch couple and was able to view some of the Pöch documents including the address book and passports during my research trip to Singapore in 2012 and 2013.

Recourse was also had to a burgeoning secondary source literature on terrorism, asymmetric warfare, terror financing, and related issues. There is also a developing academic literature around the Nazi-Islamist nexus, as well as the Nazi-Zen relationship.

My own direct experience of white supremacist hate groups in the United States, as well as Nazi front organizations such as the National Renaissance Party, aided me in the selection process of what source materials could be considered reliable as well as valuable. It seems incredible to me now but looking back over the course of several decades of research I realize I have come into direct and personal contact with Colonia Dignidad in Chile, James Madole of the National Renaissance Party (on several occasions), Roy Frankhouser of the Ku Klux Klan, Abu Bakr Ba'asyir of Jemaah Islamiyyah (the Southeast Asian Al-Qaeda affiliate), Dr. Izzat Tannous and Saadat Hassan of the PLO, several religious organizations that served as fronts for American intelligence operations, and many other groups and individuals that have become part of the Nazi Underground we sometimes call ODESSA.

Further, my long career in international trade has brought me into the sphere of corporate leaders and CEOs in America as well as in many countries abroad, including those in Europe, Latin America and of course Asia. This ongoing contact has demonstrated to me that racism, anti-Semitism, and elitism as well as a grudging respect for the principles of the Third Reich, thrive just below the surface smiles, starched shirts and hearty handshakes of many of our most esteemed captains of industry.

This indicates that the Nazi Underground is much closer to all of us than we might imagine.

Archival Sources

Bundesarchiv Berlin

Library of Congress, Washington DC

National Archives and Records Administration, College Park, Maryland

Secondary Sources

Andrew, Christopher & Mitrokhin, Vasili, *The Mitrokhin Archive: the KGB in Europe and the West*, London: Penguin, 2000

Arreguín-Toft, Ivan, "How the Weak Win Wars: A Theory of Asymmetric Conflict," in *International Security*, Vol. 26, No. 1 (Summer 2001), pp. 93-128

Artucio, Hugo Fernandez, *The Nazi Underground in South America*, New York: Farrar & Rinehart, 1942

Baier, Karl, "The Formation and Principles of Count Dürckheim's Nazi Worldview and his interpretation of Japanese Spirit and Zen" in *The Asia-Pacific Journal*, Vol. 11, Issue 48, No. 3, December 2, 2013

Basso, Carlos, *El ultimo secreto de Colonia Dignidad*, Santiago (Chile): Editorial Mare Nostrum, 2002

Bellant, Russ, *Old Nazis, The New Right, and the Republican Party*, Boston: South End Press, 1991

Bennett, Geoffrey, *The Pepper Trader: True Tales of the German EastAsia Squadron and the Man who Cast them in Stone*, Jakarta: Equinox Publishing, 2006

Black, Edwin, *IBM and the Holocaust: The Strategic Alliance between Nazi Germany and America's Most Powerful Corporation*, London: Little, Brown 2001

Blum, Howard, *Wanted! The Search for Nazis in America*, New York: Quadrangle, 1977

Bower, Tom, *Blind Eye to Murder: Britain, America and the Purging of Nazi Germany - A Pledge Betrayed*, London: Warner Books, 1995

Bower, Tom,, *The Paperclip Conspiracy: The Battle for the Spoils and Secrets of Nazi Germany*, London: Michael Joseph, 1987

Breitman, Richard, *Official Secrets: What the Nazis Planned, What the British and Americans Knew*, London: Penguin, 1998

Breitman, Richard & Goda, Norman J.W., *Hitler's Shadow: Nazi War Criminals, US Intelligence, and the Cold War*, Washington (DC): National Archives, n.d.

Brisard, Jean-Charles, "Terrorism Financing: Roots and trends of Saudi terrorism financing", Report prepared for the President of the Security Council, United Nations, Dec. 19, 2000.

Coogan, Kevin, *Dreamer of the Day: Francis Parker Yockey and the Postwar Fascist International*, Brooklyn: Autonomedia, 1999

Copeland, Miles, *The Game of Nations*, New York: Simon and Schuster, 1969.

Cornwell, John, *Hitler's Pope: The Secret History of Pius XII*, New York: Viking, 1999

Dabringhaus, Erhard, *Klaus Barbie: The Shocking Story of How the US Used This Nazi War Criminal as an Intelligence Agent*, Washington (DC): Acropolis Books, 1984, 2009

Dulles, Allen W., *The Secret Surrender: The Classic Insider's Account of the Secret Plot to Surrender Northern Italy During WW II*, Guilford (CT): The Lyons Press, 1996, 2006

Dürckheim, Karlfried, *Neues Deutschland, Deutscher Geist -- Eine Sammlung von Aufsätzen*, Tokyo: Sansusha, 1942

Ehrenfeld, Rachel, *Funding Evil: How Terrorism is Financed -- and How to Stop It*, Chicago: Bonus Books, 2003

Evica, George Michael, *A Certain Arrogance: The Sacrificing of Lee Harvey Oswald and the Cold War Manipulation of Religious Groups by US Intelligence*, Walterville: Trine Day, 2011.

Farago, Ladislas, *Aftermath: Martin Bormann and the Fourth Reich*, New York: Simon and Schuster, 1974

Farías, Victor, *Los nazis en Chile*, Barcelona: Editorial Seix Barral, 2000

Feigin, Judy, *The Office of Special Investigations: Striving for Accountability in the Aftermath of the Holocaust*, Washington (DC): Department of Justice, December 2006

Feinstein, Andrew, *The Shadow World: Inside the Global Arms Trade*, New York: Farrar, Straus and Giroux, 2011

Ford, Henry, *The International Jew*, Johannesburg: Global Publishers, undated.

Fromkin, David, *A Peace To End All Peace: The Fall of the Ottoman Empire and the Creation of the Modern Middle East*, New York: Henry Holt and Company, 2001.

Gallagher, Charles R., S.J., *Vatican Secret Diplomacy: Joseph P. Hurley and Pope Pius XII*, New Haven: Yale University Press, 2008

Galvis, Silvia and Donadio, Alberto, *Colombia Nazi 1939-1945*, Medellin (Colombia): Hombre Nuevo Editores, 2002

Geerken, Horst H., *A Gecko for Luck: 18 Years in Indonesia*, Bonn: BukitCinta, 2010

Goda, Norman J.W., "CIA Files Relating to Heinz Felfe, SS Officer and KGB Spy", Washington (DC): National Archives, n.d.

Goeritno, Ir. KGPH, Soeryo, *Hitler Mati di Indonesia: Rahasia Yang Terkuak*, Indonesia: Titik Media, 2010

Goldhagen, Daniel Jonah, *A Moral Reckoning: The Role of the Catholic Church in the Holocaust and its Unfulfilled Duty of Repair*, New York: Alfred A. Knopf, 2002

Gonçalves, Eduardo, "Britain allowed Portugal to keep Nazi gold," in *The Observer*, 2 April 2000

Goñi, Uki, *The Real Odessa: How Perón Brought the Nazi War Criminals to Argentina*, London: Granta Books, 2002

Goodrick-Clarke, Nicholas, *Hitler's Priestess: Savitri Devi, the Hindu-Aryan Myth, and Neo-Nazism*, New York: New York University Press, 1998

Hadler, Jeffrey, "Translations of Anti-Semitism: Jews, the Chinese, and Violence in Colonial and Post-Colonial Indonesia," in *Indonesia and the Malay World*, Vol. 32, No. 94, November 2004

Harrer, Heinrich, *Seven Years in Tibet*, New York: E.P. Dutton, 1954

Harrer, Heinrich, *I Come From the Stone Age*, London: Companion Book Club, 1964

Harrer, Heinrich, *Return to Tibet: Tibet after the Chinese Occupation*, London: Phoenix, 1984

Higham, Charles, *American Swastika*, New York: Doubleday, 1985

Infield, Glenn B., *Secrets of the SS*, New York: Jove Books, 1990

Infield, Glenn B., *Skorzeny: Hitler's Commando*, New York: St Martin's Press, 1981

Interpol, *The Hawala Alternative Remittance System and its Role in Money Laundering*, undated

Jenkins, Philip, *Hoods and Shirts: The Extreme Right in Pennsylvania, 1925-1950*, Chapel Hill (NC): University of North Carolina Press, 1997

Johnson, Ian, *A Mosque in Munich: Nazis, the CIA, and the Rise of the Muslim Brotherhood in the West*, New York: Houghton Mifflin Harcourt, 2010

Kaplan, Jeffrey and Weinberg, Leonard, *The Emergence of a Euro-American Radical Right*, New Brunswick (NJ): Rutgers University Press, 1998

Kersten, Felix, *Totenkopf und Treue: Heinrich Himmler ohne Uniform*, Hamburg: Robertv Mölich Verlag, 1952

Kirkpatrick, Sidney D., *Hitler's Holy Relics: A True Story of Nazi Plunder and the Race to Recover the Crown Jewels of the Holy Roman Empire*, New York: Simon and Schuster, 2010

Kisatsky, Deborah, *The United States and the European Right, 1945-1955*, Columbus (OH): Ohio State University Press, 2005

Kovel, Joel, *White Racism: A Psychohistory*, New York: Columbia University Press, 1984

Kramer, Dale, *Coughlin, Lemke and the Union Party*, Minneapolis: Farmers Book Store, 1936

Küntzel, Matthias, "European Roots of Antisemitism in Current Islamic Thinking," last accessed July 15, 2014 from http://www.matthiaskuentzel.de/contents/european-roots-of-antisemitism-in-current-islamic-thinking

Küntzel, Matthias, "National Socialism and Anti-Semitism in the Arab World", in *Jewish Political Studies Review*, 17:1-2 (Spring 2005)

Küntzel, Matthias, *Jihad and Jew-Hatred: Islamism, Nazism and the Roots of 9/11*, New York: Telos Press, 2007

Kwiet, Konrad, "Zur Geschichte der Mussert Bewegung" in *Vierteljahresreshefte für Zeitgeschichte*, 18, (1970) pp. 164-195

Laird, Thomas, *Into Tibet: The CIA's First Atomic Spy and His Secret Expedition to Lhasa*, New York: Grove Press, 2002

Lebor, Adam, *The Tower of Basel: The Shadowy History of the Secret Bank that Runs the World*, New York: Public Affairs, 2013

Lee, Martin A., *The Beast Reawakens*, New York: Routledge, 2000

Lepre, George, *Himmler's Bosnian Division: The Waffen-SS Handschar Division 1943-1945*, Atglen (PA): Schiffer Military History, 1997

Levenda, Peter, *Ratline: Soviet Spies, Nazi Priests and the Disappearance of Adolf Hitler*, Lake Worth (FL): Ibis Press, 2012

Levenda, Peter, *Unholy Alliance: A History of Nazi Involvement with the Occult*, New York: Continuum, 2002

Levy, Jonathan, *The Intermarium: Wilson, Madison, and East Central European Federalism*, Boca Raton (FL): Dissertation.com, 2006

Linklater, Magnus and Hilton, Isabel and Ascherson, Neal, *The Nazi Legacy: Klaus Barbie and the International Fascist Connection*, New York: Holt, Rinehart, Winston, 1984

Manning, Paul, *Martin Bormann: Nazi in Exile*, Secaucus (NJ): Lyle Stuart, 1981

Marx. Karl, "Zur Judenfrage" in *Deutsch-Französische Jahrbücher*, February 1844

McGaha, Richard L., "The Politics of Espionage: Nazi Diplomats and Spies in Argentina, 1933-1945", Ohio University, 2009

McMeekin, Sean, *The Berlin-Baghdad Express: The Ottoman Empire and Germany's Bid for World Power*, Cambridge: Harvard University Press, 2010

Melchior, Ib and Brandenburg, Frank, *Quest: Searching for the Truth of Germany's Nazi Past*, Novato (CA): Presidio Press, 1994

Michael, George, *Theology of Hate: A History of The World Church of the Creator*, Gainesville: University Press of Florida, 2009

Mount, Graeme S., *Chile and the Nazis: From Hitler to Pinochet*, Montreal: Black Rose Books, 2002

Noakes, Jeremy and Pridham, Geoffrey, eds. *Nazism 1919-1945, Vol. 1, The Rise to Power 1919-1934*, Exeter: University of Exeter Press, 1998

O'Brien, D.A., "Review of H. Harrer, I Come fro the Stone Age", in *American Anthropologist*, 68: 297-298

Payne, Robert, *The Life and Death of Adolf Hitler*, London: Corgi Books, 1973

Payne, Stanley G., *Franco and Hitler: Spain, Germany, and World War II*, New Haven: Yale University Press, 2008

Pelley, William Dudley, *Star Guests: Design for Mortality*, Noblesville (IN): Soulcraft Press, 1950

Phayer, Michael, *The Catholic Church and the Holocaust, 1930-1965*, Bloomington (IN): Indiana University Press, 2000

Posner, Gerald L. and Ware, John, *Mengele: The Complete Story*, New York: Dell, 1986

Pringle, Heather, *The Master Plan: Himmler's Scholars and the Holocaust*, New York: Hyperion, 2006

Read, Piers Paul, *The Train Robbers*, Philadelphia: J.P. Lippincott Co., 1978

Rollins, Richard, *I Find Treason: The Story of an American Anti-Nazi Agent*, New York: William Morrow & Co., 1941

Rosenberg, Alfred, *Memoirs*, last accessed June 6, 2014 from https://archive.org/details/NoneRosenbergMemoirs

Sandford, Robinson Rojas, *The Murder of Allende and the End of the Chilean Way to Socialism*, New York: Harper & Row, 1976

Schwanitz, Wolfgang G., "Germany's Middle East Policy," in *The Middle East Review of International Affairs*, 11(9-2007)3

Scott, Peter Dale, *The Road to 9/11: Wealth, Empire, and the Future of America*, Berkeley: University of California Press, 2007

Schneppen, Heinz, *Odessa und das Vierte Reich: Mythen der Zeitgeschichte*, Berlin: Metropol-Verlag, 2007.

Seagrave, Sterling & Peggy, *Gold Warriors: America's Secret Recovery of Yamashita's Gold*, London: Verso, 2005

Serrano, Miguel, *El cordon dorado: Hitlerismo esoterico*, Bogotá (Colombia): Editorial Solar, 1992

Serrano, Miguel, *NOS: Book of the Resurrection*, London: Routledge & Kegan Paul, 1984

Serrano, Miguel, *La resurección del heroe*, Bogotá (Colombia): Editorial Solar, 1987

Serrano, Miguel, *Jung & Hesse: A record of two friendships*, New York: Schocken Books, 1968

Simon, Jeffrey D., *Lone Wolf Terrorism: Understanding the Growing Threat*, Amherst (NY): Prometheus Books, 2013

Simons, Marlise, "Nazi Gold and Portugal's Murky Role," in *The New York Times*, January 10, 1997

Simpson, Christopher, *The Splendid Blond Beast: Money, Law, and Genocide in the Twentieth Century*, New York: Grove Press, 1993

Simpson, Christopher, *Blowback: The first full account of America's recruitment of Nazis, and its disastrous effect on our domestic and foreign policy*, New York: Weidenfeld & Nicolson, 1988

Sims, Patsy, *The Klan*, New York: Stein and Day, 1982

Spivak, John L., *Secret Armies: The new technique of Nazi warfare*, New York: Modern Age Books, 1939

Steinacher, Gerald, *Nazis on the Run: How Hitler's Henchmen Fled Justice*, New York: Oxford University Press, 2011

Stepanova, Ekaterina, *Terrorism in Asymmetrical Conflict: Ideological and Structural Aspects*, New York: Oxford University Press, 2008

Steury, Donald P., "The OSS and Project Safehaven", last accessed August 1, 2014 from https://www.cia.gov/library/center-for-the-study-of-intelligence/kent-csi/vol44no3/pdf/v44i3a04p.pdf

Stevenson, William, *The Bormann Brotherhood*, New York: Bantam, 1974

Suciu, Eva Mirela, "Signs of Anti-Semitism in Indonesia," Sydney: University of Sydney, Department of Asian Studies, 2008

Thomas, Gordon and Morgan-Witts, Max, *Voyage of the Damned*, New York: Stein and Day, 1974

Thomas, Norman, "What's Behind the Christian Front?", New York: Workers Defense League, 1939

Thompson, Edwina A., "The Nexus of Drug Trafficking and Hawala in Afghanistan" in United Nations Office on Drugs and Crime (UNODC) publication *Afghanistan's Drug Industry: Structure, Functioning, Dynamics, and Implications for Counter-Narcotics Policy*, Buddenberg and Byrd, editors, undated

Tim Investigasi Solomongrup, *Melacak Garis Keturunan Hitler di Indonesia*, Yogyakarta: Pustaka Solomon, 2011

US Government, *Elimination of German Resources for War*, Washington DC: US Government Printing House, June 22, 1945.

US Government, *Preliminary Report on Neo-Fascist and Hate Groups*, Washington DC: Committee on Un-American Activities, US House of Representatives, 1954

US Government, *International Communism (Communist Designs on Indonesia and the Pacific Frontier: Staff Consultation with General Charles A. Willoughby, Former Chief of Intelligence, Far Eastern Command, Under General Douglas MacArthur)* WashingtonDC: Committee on Un-American Activities, US House of Representatives, 1957

Varas, Florencia and Orrego, Claudio, *El caso Letelier*, Santiago (Chile): Editorial Aconcagua, 1990

Victoria, Brian Daizen, "Zen as a Cult of Death in the Wartime Writings of D.T. Suzuki" in *The Asia-Pacific Journal*, Vol. 11, Issue 30, No. 4, August 5, 2013

Victoria, Brian Daizen, "D.T. Suzuki, Zen, and the Nazis," in *The Asia-Pacific Journal*, Vol. 11, Issue 43, No. 4, October 28, 2013

Victoria, Brian Daizen, "Zen Masters on the Battlefield (Part 1)", in *The Asia-Pacific Journal*, Vol. 11, Issue 24, No. 3, June 16, 2014

Wallace, Max, *The American Axis: Henry Ford, Charles Lindbergh, and the rise of the Third Reich*, New York: St Martin's Griffin, 2003

Walters, Guy, *Hunting Evil: The Nazi War Criminals who Escaped and the Quest to bring them to Justice*, New York: Broadway Books, 2009

Warren, Donald, *Radio Priest: Father Coughlin, The Father of Hate Radio*, New York: Free Press, 1996

Weitz, John, *Hitler's Banker: Hjalmar Horace Greeley Schacht*, Boston: Little, Brown, 1997

Wilson, *Orang dan Partai Nazi di Indonesia: Kaum Pergerakan Menyambut Fasisme*, Jakarta: Komunitas Bambu, 2008

Von Lang, Jochen (editor), *Eichmann Interrogated: transcripts from the archives of the Israeli Police*, New York: Vintage Books, 1983

Zeiger, Henry A. (editor), *The Case Against Adolf Eichmann*, New York: Signet, 1960

Interviews and Conversations

James Madole, National Renaissance Party, 1977
Roy Frankhouser, Ku Klux Klan, 1977
Dr IzzatTannous, Palestine Liberation Organization, 1968
Saadat Hassan, Palestine Liberation Organization, 1970
Abu Bakr Ba'asyir, Jemaah Islamiyyah, 2007
Paul Schäfer, Colonia Dignidad, 1979
Walter M. Propheta, American Orthodox Catholic Church, 1968
Chandriana, 2013

Index

Ratline

Soviet Spies, Nazi Priests, and the Disappearance of Adolph Hitler

PETER LEVENDA

• An exposé of Church and State involvement in the escape of Nazi war criminals around the world.
• A step-by-step refutation of the evidence that Hitler died in the bunker in April, 1945.

While searching through the jungles of Java in 2008, gathering material for his book *Tantric Temples: Eros and Magic in Java*, author Peter Levenda came upon evidence of a Nazi escape route that led from Europe to Argentina, Tibet, and eventually Indonesia. The rumors were persistent; the evidence suggestive.

Was it possible that the world's greatest symbol of evil had actually escaped Berlin in 1945? As the author began his research, more information came to light. In December of 2009, it was revealed that the skull the Russians claimed was Hitler's—salvaged from the bunker in 1945—was not that of Hitler at all. The news made headlines around the world. Then in 2010, files from the Office of Special Investigations of the Justice Department were declassified, revealing a history of American intelligence providing cover for Nazi war criminals.

How did the Soviet KGB, the Catholic Church, and governments around the world collaborate in the escape of this mysterious and most-wanted fugitive? *Ratline* is the documented history of this escape, and the mechanisms by which thousands of war criminals fled to the remotest parts of the globe. It is the story of how the Soviets lied about Hitler's death and continued to lie and change their story for decades to come. It's the story of a man who died quietly in Indonesia in January of 1970 ... and how a body was dug up from a German military base four months later and cremated. *Ratline* raises questions ... but more than anything else—in a time of citizen distrust of its own institutions in Europe, America, and Asia—it demands answers.

$26.95 • Hardcover • ISBN: 978-0-89254-170-6 • 256 pp. • 6 x 9 • includes 8 pages of glossy photographs